Happy Fathers Day Papa! 2019

1955

1956

1959

The many gifts and passions you share with us all will never be forgotten. Thank you for being the best dad a girl could ask for!

Love you to the top of the mountain and back! ♡ Mia

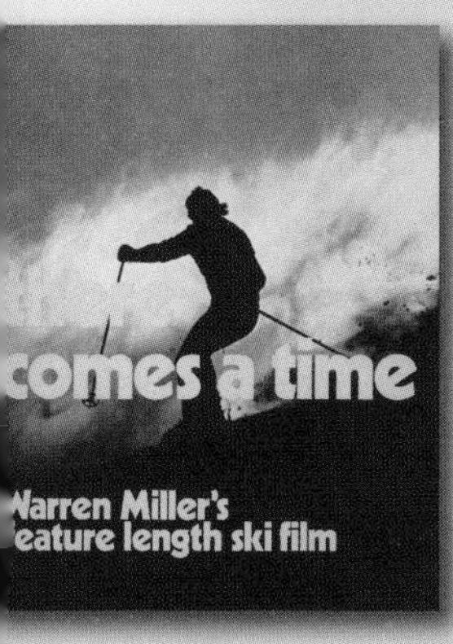

1975

1976

1977

Live to Ski
Ski to Die
– Papa

In gratitude for your support,

WARREN MILLER

proudly presents you

with this second printing of

FREEDOM FOUND

MY LIFE STORY

"I won't ruin a good story

with the absolute truth."

PRAISE FOR
Freedom Found

"Miller's life well-lived is laid bare here, with the sort of winking approach that only a master storyteller could bring to the project. It's a book that should come packaged with down slippers and schnapps."

SEATTLE TIMES

"You get all the sides of Warren Miller, not just the canned narrator."

OUTSIDE

"Warren Miller was—and is—the St. Peter of skiing; the disciple sent into the world to share the glories and character-building adventures found on snow."

DENVER POST

"Warren Miller has weathered near-death experiences, winters living out of his trailer, family embezzlers, and many more misadventures. In exchange, as he often says, he found the freedom of constant thrills. *Freedom Found: My Life Story* takes readers from Miller's broken California childhood to the Matterhorn and beyond, always with his trusty Arriflex in hand."

MEN'S JOURNAL

"A big, beautiful, and touching autobiography of one of America's premier filmmakers."

ASPEN DAILY NEWS

Warren with his Bell & Howell in 1951, when he still had a little hair left.

FREEDOM FOUND

MY LIFE STORY

WARREN MILLER

WITH ANDY BIGFORD

WARREN MILLER COMPANY

ORCAS ISLAND | BIG SKY

Published by Warren Miller Company
P.O. Box 350, Deer Harbor, WA 98243

Book design and publishing services by
Boulder Bookworks, Boulder, Colorado

Proofreading by Kellee Katagi

Cover Photo: Erwin Lenkeit, Rolling Hills, California
Back Cover Photo: Laurie Miller, Orcas Island, Washington
Endpapers (film posters): Warren Miller Entertainment

First Edition
second printing

ISBN 978-0-9636144-6-9

Library of Congress Control Number: 2015918663

Printed in Canada

21 20 19 18 17 02 03 04 05 06 07

For all the skiers

who came to my films:

Thank you for supporting me

from 1950 until today.

Let's see what

the next 90 years hold.

CONTENTS

PART TWO
GROWING OUT

PART THREE
LIFTING OFF

PART FOUR
LURCHING FORWARD

ACKNOWLEDGMENTS

FOR THE GAZILLIONTH TIME, I WAS TELLING A STORY DURING A DINNER party at our winter home in Montana—this one involving a two-week weather delay, a pie-in-the-sky budget, an active volcano, an overloaded helicopter, and an Olympic triple-gold medalist. My wife of many years, Laurie, piped up and said, "Warren, why don't you write your life story, with all the good and bad, and all the interesting people and places you've documented with your camera?" Her comment reminded me that her son, Colin Kaufmann, urged me to put my story down on paper years before. At the time, I was struggling with writing a book on aging when Colin wisely said, "That's an OK topic for later, Warren, but much better if you'd write your autobiography first and then write a book on aging when you get old..."

Our good friend, Kemper Freeman, who was also at dinner that night, had been constantly bugging me to do the same thing. He set me up with a veteran ski journalist, Mort Lund, who helped get me started by recording the narrative of my first few decades before I started writing on my own. I eventually called my friend Andy Bigford, who I had worked with at my film company and *SKI* magazine, to come in and smooth out all the rough spots. I tend to start my stories in one direction and then go off in several other directions, totally mixing up whoever is listening to me in the process. Andy somehow made sense of it all.

I refuse to be old, but I'm definitely getting older. At age 92, I want to make my "thank-you's" here: first to my wife, Laurie, for being by my side supporting and helping me everyday for nearly seven years to write my entire life down; and to my three children, Scott, Chris, and Kurt.

To the late Don Brolin and the rest of my extraordinary, creative filmmaking team for believing in our annual film's efforts and supporting me so loyally for so many years; to Kemper Freeman, Wini Jones, Barbara Bedell, Summer Clark, and Andy Bigford for believing my story should be told and for helping me along the way; and to Colin Kaufmann for seeding the idea and helping me start.

To the positive influences in my life: Josephine Abercrombie, Rich Alaniz, Émile Allais, Craig Altschul, Hobie Alter, Ray Atkeson, Ward Baker, Bruce Barr, Terry Bassett, Richard Brigante, Mike Brunetto, Sam Byrne, Charlie Callander, Bob Craig, Stein Eriksen, John Fry, Paul Garwood, Hal Geneen, Pat Gould, David Graebel, Donna Griggs, Harry Hathaway, Edith and Walter Humphrey, Bill Janss, John Jay, Herbert Jochum, Jack and Joanne Kemp, Everett Kircher, Otto Lang, Art Lawson, Austin Lightfoot, Bob and Nancy Maynard, Dave and Roma McCoy, Jean Horton Miller, Ted Nicholson, Chuck Percy, Jon Reveal, Pappy Rogers, Hoyle Schweitzer, Brian Sisselman, Ray Laurent, Kim Schneider, and Mike Wiegele. And to the unknown Hawaiian, who lived in Topanga Canyon in 1930 and taught me, at age 6, a lifelong love of the ocean.

Please be aware that all errors in the book are mine—I can't blame them on anyone else. Though I've never let the truth get in the way of a good story, the sad truth is that few of those involved in my stories are still alive to call me out.

It's been a great life, and thanks for reading my story. I'll always be grateful to you, my audience, for being a part of it.

WARREN MILLER, June 2017
Orcas Island, Washington, and
Big Sky, Montana

PROLOGUE

1968

The Journey of 7,000 Miles from Hermosa Beach to New Zealand Began with a Credit Card

My camera crew and I watched the Narahoe volcano blow up four days in a row between 3:30 and 4 P.M., emitting a spectacular cloud of smoke, spewing rocks and ash, and leaving a black slash in the snow from the summit to the bottom of the mountain. We were pinned down at nearby Ruapehu Ski Resort on the North Island of New Zealand in non-stop rain for 13 days, unable to start production on a 13-episode TV series that would feature Jean-Claude Killy, who had just won three gold medals in the 1968 Olympics, and his French teammate Leo Lacroix. The daily volcanic eruptions blew rocks and ashes 15 miles downwind and, all the while, the job was running way over budget.

On day 14, we decided that if we reached the volcano summit early in the morning, we could film ski action until sometime between 3 and 3:30 P.M. and have the helicopter fly us back to the hotel before the volcano blew once again.

It had been a 20-year uphill climb in my career with my skis and camera, and a 10-minute helicopter ride to the summit. As we flew close to the crater, the roar of the volcano building up pressure drowned out the sound of the rotors. Don Brolin, my best cameraman, and I climbed out on the rim of the volcano and waited for the chopper to come back with Killy and Lacroix. They liked the idea of being the first skiers ever filmed skiing the rim of a volcano about to erupt, two adrenaline freaks who had put in a lot of time running icy downhill courses at 75 miles an hour with only their ability to hold an edge between them and disaster. Of course, if Narahoe erupted ahead of schedule, we would find ourselves skiing in a cloud of sulfur gas, burning cinders, and flying red-hot rocks, and the footage would be shown posthumously.

There was plenty of time to shoot before the eruption. We filmed Jean-Claude and Leo leaning on their poles, peering into the noxious, smoky crater where the crust of the earth was melting into a fiery liquid layer, roaring like half a dozen four-engine jet planes taking off at the same time. We shot them skiing along the rim against dramatic smoke and steam, and then turning to dive down the snow-covered mountain. There the helicopter picked us up, and we did it again and again. We were getting comfortable by this natural show of skiing, high on the idea of being the first ever to shoot skiers flirting with extinction on the rim of a live volcano. The periods of vibrations underfoot were ominously increasing. By 3, we voted for a seventh helicopter ride up to the rim. We thought we had half an hour until Narahoe blew, but then a Godzilla-like roar filled the air, like a giant hidden in his cave working up to an angry explosion.

The smoke poured out in bigger clouds. The four of us must have gone into brain destabilization. As we stepped off the helicopter at the rim, the noise drowned out our voices, so we used sign language. If skiing is dancing with a mountain, this was dancing with death.

The tremors were now so fierce we couldn't use our tripods as the two French champions sailed through the snow, framed against the darkening cloud over the rim. That was when our helicopter pilot gave us a definitive message. He zoomed in for a landing farther down the mountain, disappearing into a fog bank. He was saying, "This is it! Get down here!"

Killy and Lacroix got the message and they accelerated past us, hunkered down in a low tuck. We chased our French friends on a mile-long schuss into the fog bank and through the pucker-brush. Then we heard and saw the helicopter, its rotors making distinctive, accelerating whop-whop sounds. Killy and Lacroix were already aboard and strapped in, flying to safety. Don and I hoped the pilot would be back in 20 minutes.

That meant 3:45, 15 minutes after the arrival of the daily eruption. We looked at each other with an unspoken question: If the volcano blows, how many rocks are we going to see flying down on us? The Narahoe blow had a range of about 15 miles. For the next 15 minutes, the sweep hands of our watches crawled. Finally, the helicopter came down out of the fog at exactly 3:45.

We strapped in while the pilot revved the engine. Up we went, smothering sighs of relief as our pilot made the V for Victory sign. Our copter climbed rapidly through the fog and popped out into the sunshine. Ahead was the hotel, sitting under its private rain cloud. From the left side of the helicopter, we heard the horrendous roar as Narahoe let go, and we turned to see the biggest eruption of the week, a huge cloud of ash that burst out of the crater rim where we had been filming less than 30 minutes ago—huge, slowly rotating rocks shot high into the sky, falling almost everywhere.

We'd felt safe all along because of a theory about volcanoes and skiing that I learned in my college geology class: If we skied on the windward side of the volcano when it blew, the rocks and ashes would fall on the other side of the mountain. But the wind did not blow on the day we were filming. We did have a big reward for all the risk: hundreds of feet of footage that had never been filmed before (or since) of skiers on a very active volcano.

This was enough for the first episode in "Jean-Claude Killy Skis New Zealand," which we dutifully edited and presented to the network for approval. The committee refused to approve it without a re-edit; they could not believe that anyone would be dumb enough to do what we had done.

But we had the film to prove it.

AFTER WE HAD SHIPPED THE NARAHOE VOLCANO FOOTAGE TO OUR production crew at our studio in Hermosa Beach, California, Jean-Claude, Leo, Don, and the other eight people in the crew, including my son Scott, packed up for the Tasman Glacier on New Zealand's South Island. The Tasman is arguably the world's greatest backdrop for filming skiing—12 beautiful miles in the middle of Mt. Cook National Park, a place of cathedral quiet, usually covered in featherlight powder snow.

We had already fallen two weeks behind schedule, so we spent the extra money to charter a DC-3 to fly directly to Mt. Cook National Park

Airport. We planned to shoot the high points of the Tasman in a single day and needed to find a helicopter pilot who could get permission to land inside the park, generally off limits. Our production manager, Bob Schneider, located a highly regarded New Zealand pilot, Mel Cain, who had the necessary contacts. Cain had agreed to meet us at the Mt. Cook International Air Terminal, such as it was.

Mt. Cook International Air Terminal sits in one of the more remote parts of the South Island and consisted then of a small hangar, a grass runway, and a wooden box with a first-aid kit nailed to a 4-by-4 post. Once we landed, the pilot climbed out of the DC-3 and trotted over to a set of stairs mounted on what looked like wheelbarrow tires. He wheeled the stairs to the passenger door.

After everyone helped carry our mountain of photo gear over the wet mud and piled it inside the hangar, we stood around waiting for the Mt. Cook Hotel bus. It was then that our helicopter pilot flew right through the open hangar door in his three-place Bell, with just a few feet to spare on each side of its blades, and settled it down neatly inside the hangar.

Mel Cain had made his point. He was the best. His machine was the piston engine–type, similar to those made famous in the old "M*A*S*H" TV series, but he had an additional turbocharger for flying at high altitude. He made his living as a bounty hunter. At the time, an out-of-control deer population in New Zealand was devouring all the natural grasses, creating serious erosion. Government officials were offering a bounty of $3 a tail, and Mel had bagged 900 in the past month alone.

Mel managed to get permission from park officials to land anywhere in Mt. Cook National Park by pointing out the possible increase of ski tourists on the Tasman after coast-to-coast exposure on American national television. Once we got going, Cain did things with a helicopter I had never seen before or since.

After five days of seeing sleet every morning through the brocade curtains of my room at the Mt. Cook Hotel, we were three weeks behind in the 20-week production schedule. It had been 18 years since I'd borrowed $100 each from four surfer friends to start the film business, and the company I'd built was now at risk. We were still small, and we were looking at a job usually taken on by big national production outfits with hundreds or even thousands of employees. The film company had overreached in underbidding such a complicated schedule, and, as on the North Island, we again needed a break in the weather.

On day six, while I was in the middle of a long after-dinner walk through the sleet, hunched over in my raincoat, figuring out how much money I was losing each day, a star appeared way up in the night sky. Then another star. Then the hole in the gloom began to get bigger. The sky started to clear, and the Southern Cross appeared. If we could film Killy and Lacroix on the Tasman in a day, we still had a fighting chance.

Before going to bed, I laid out my camera gear, leaving both 10-pound battery belts plugged into the 110-converters on the wall sockets to fully charge them, and ensured all of the gear was properly working. My Arriflex went into my rucksack with its 12-to-120 zoom lens and 20 100-foot rolls of Kodachrome. It was going to be a long day on the glacier. With all this gear, including the heavy wooden tripod, my rucksack weighed at least 40 pounds.

We had a big problem when our two official Mt. Cook park guides arrived. We had assumed we would be sent strong guides who could keep up, but these guides were older gentlemen, and their ski equipment was badly out-of-date. We didn't have time to stand around waiting for them to connect their slow traverses with telemark turns. Also, everyone had told us that it had been very cold on the Tasman this winter, and the glacier's creep down the mountain was only a few inches, probably not enough to open any new, dangerously wide crevasses. With decades of experience among us, we decided to guide ourselves. We still knew to take it carefully wherever the glacial terrain dropped steeply enough to put the glacier under the kind of stress that would open crevasses. We knew that as winter progresses, most of the crevasses are covered. Snow bridges strong enough to hold a skier's weight form when the wind creates an overhang or cornice on one side and then switches directions and forms another one on the opposing side. Interlocking snowflakes in two opposing overhangs create a snow bridge that gets stronger as more snow falls on top, fusing with the lower snow until the bridge becomes strong enough to hold a skier. With luck, that is.

In the middle of a turn, I sat back on the snow with my left leg curled under, like a base runner sliding into second base. My heavy rucksack acted as a drag-brake, and I stopped just at the point where a 3-foot-wide snow bridge gave way, leaving my right leg and ski hanging in space. Moving slowly, I grabbed one ski pole just above the basket, punched the handle into the snow, and used it to pull myself back from the frighteningly deep crevasse. I remembered the old Swiss guide story of a man who fell into a crevasse upright. After a millennium, a frozen body inched its way out to join the world, defrosting at the bottom of the glacier and standing upright, like a figure in a wax museum. If that had been me, my backpack would have preserved 2,000 feet of film that, when projected, would reveal the ancient technique of the two greatest skiers of 10 centuries earlier, Jean-Claude Killy and Leo Lacroix.

We went right back to work. The incredible beauty of the 3-mile-wide expanse of snow, with only four people skiing over it, banished almost all thoughts of danger. Killy and Lacroix made endless turns in a foot or more of light, deep, untracked powder. The two fabulous Frenchmen left their best tracks over the glacier's ups and downs in perfect linked turns, like nothing else we'd ever seen or filmed before.

We asked Mel Cain if he could find us steeper and deeper powder snow. He flew us to a very steep powder slope. Cain had to keep the helicopter hovering in order to let us off. It was ticklish work, lowering ourselves gently into hip-deep powder. After each of us got off, the helicopter rolled a bit as it was freed from our weight. Cain corrected instantly to bring the helicopter back to horizontal. If the rotor blades hit the snow, it would, of course, crash.

Then Killy suggested a quicker way of filming. He grabbed ahold of the helicopter landing gear as the helicopter rose, and he hung dangling a couple hundred feet in the air like a man on the flying trapeze. The copter flew past us at midslope, and near the top, Cain turned it around. Down near the slope, Killy let go and dropped 20 feet into the snow, sending up a cloud of powder that completely engulfed him. Then his head came back into view going down the fall line while his skis threw up more back-lit clouds, like a high-speed water-skier in a sharp turn. By taking shots from a low angle, we made each drop from the helicopter look like a 100-foot-high jump. Nothing like that had ever been filmed before.

Suddenly the sky got dark. We had stayed high on the glacier too long. The helicopter was designed to carry only three people, including the pilot. Mel said, "I can take two of you back now and come back for the other two, but I might not be able to find you in the dark, and you would be dead by morning. Or, I can take all of us on one trip: Two of you ride inside; two of you ride outside, tied to the landing gear." This meant flying a three-seater with five people, plus four pairs of skis and camera equipment, maybe 500 pounds beyond the rated weight. That's a heavy load for taking off from the side of a mountain at 10,000 feet.

Mel suggested flipping a coin to determine who would ride inside and who had to ride outside, but I reminded the group that I owned the film company. "The three of you can flip to see who rides outside." Don won and hopped in while Killy and Lacroix bravely faced their fate. We fixed the skis upside down to the landing gear to create two platforms, and then loaded Killy and Lacroix like a couple of tagged deer tied to the fenders of a car. The Frenchmen had a choice of riding face down or face up: If they got sick riding face up, they would ruin their ski clothes. They decided to ride face down.

Now it was up to Mel to somehow get the overweight Bell off the ground. He revved the engine until the tachometer screamed against the red line. The machine struggled and shook until it finally got a few feet off the snow, where it hovered for a moment before slamming back down with a thud.

It was getting darker by the minute as Mel fine-tuned the controls and gave the engine a slightly different mixture of fuel and air. This time the helicopter rose 5 feet, slipped sideways, and fell back to the snow. After five or six of these 4-foot-high flights, I noticed that Mel was leapfrogging his way slightly downhill and to his left. He was moving 15 to 20 feet with each jump.

"Why are you going to the left?" I hollered.

"There's a big cliff over there. We're going to fall off of it and try to get enough air speed," Mel hollered back. "Once we do that, hopefully the machine will have enough forward speed so I can get us back to the hotel."

The word I didn't like was "hopefully."

But Mel timed it exactly right. We fell off the cliff, and instead of crashing, the helicopter gained airspeed, its human cargo of the world's two greatest skiers lashed to the skids. We made it safely back to the hotel, where we landed in total darkness. That night at dinner, dressed in our coats and ties, Killy said: "A mountain is like a beautiful woman.

You can go to her as often as you want, but she will only give you what she wants."

The Killy TV show aired on a Sunday afternoon up against an NFL football game. Only 3 percent of the people watching TV that day ever saw Killy and Lacroix on the Tasman. But Don and I and our entire staff all saw it, and we liked what we saw.

PART ONE

Growing Up

At age 4, before the Depression forever changed the Miller family.

CHAPTER ONE

1924–1930

How Old Would You Be If You Didn't Know When You Were Born?

ON OCTOBER 15, 1924, I WAS BORN ON A KITCHEN TABLE IN A SMALL house on Avocado Street below the then-tony Los Feliz Hills in East Hollywood, California. My father's mother was my mother's midwife. I don't remember ever seeing that grandmother but once more in my life.

In spite of the threadbare situation, I have always maintained that I was born lucky. First off, I survived my delivery. That was a good start, considering that at the time one out of 10 babies died during birth or shortly thereafter. My parents were perfectly fine as parents go, at least until I was age 4 or so. When I was no longer a cute baby, they stopped paying much attention to me. In a way, that was also good luck. Their neglect forced me to muscle up mentally and find the freedom to shape my own life.

My father, Albert Lincoln Miller, was 31 then and quite handsome in the fashion of the 1920s, with a toothbrush mustache like that of his fellow Hollywood citizen Charlie Chaplin, only my dad's was always gray, not black. He was 5-feet-8-inches tall and weighed 145 pounds, according to his Navy discharge papers. His Navy classification was as a printer. My father apparently was a man of many intentions. The collection of business cards that were discovered in his desk drawer showed he had sold real estate, built houses on spec, and started a number of one-man enterprises. His most successful gambit of all was that of an aspiring actor. In that, he was extremely lucky, for a while. There was a new entertainment industry growing up all around the country: No, not the movies—it was radio.

My mother, Helena Humphrey Miller, was also 31 when I was born. She was short, a bit under 5-feet tall, with a pretty face and a spirited gleam in her eyes. My two sisters, Mary Helen and Betty Jane, had been born in the couple of years before me, which made for three babies in three years, a bit too many over too short a time, especially after the family lost everything when the Depression hit.

My father's beginner's luck was just that. Between when I was born in 1924 and 1936, 500 new radio stations were licensed across America, and the first national radio networks were formed: ABC, NBC, and CBS. Soon, "radio sitcoms" were on their way to the homes of America. One of the first was "Amos 'n' Andy," which first aired in 1928 on more than 70 stations. The population of radio listeners boomed (there were already a million people living in the Los Angeles area alone and an estimated 300,000 radios), and the number of radio sitcoms increased, so employment for radio actors surged and gave Albert Miller his big opportunity. My father worked with friends who were actors to develop a radio sitcom with him as the star. The character he developed was "Cy Toosie," a gravel-voiced, pinchpenny, Yankee storekeeper whose ability was to resolve, in a humorous way, any problems that bothered his friends, neighbors, and customers. In the fall of 1928, my father signed with an Oakland, California, radio station as the star of his sitcom "Cy Toosie." I didn't know the difference, but things were looking good for my family.

The family took four days and half a dozen flat tires to drive the 400 miles to Oakland, camping along the way. In Oakland, we rented a home near Lake Merritt, which was a nice part of town then. My earliest fleeting recollections are of riding the ferryboats from Oakland across the bay to San Francisco. Ferryboats were the only way to cross the bay before the Oakland Bay Bridge was built. At one point, my family was flush enough to have a studio photographer pose me for pictures. A couple of them still survive in an old family photo album, showing me as a chubby, well-dressed 4-year-old. It looked as though the Millers had a fine future in store.

Then, two weeks after my fifth birthday, the New York Stock Exchange went into free fall on "Black Friday," October 29, 1929, causing the biggest financial crash in American history. Soon, 25 percent of the nation was out of work, unable to find a job of any kind. Radio stations, of course, were cutting costs.

My father's sitcom contract was cancelled, but he hung on, contacting people, trying to get his show back on the radio. My mother brought dinner home from the grocer's, needing only a small brown bag, often with only 5-cents-a-pound hamburger, a loaf of bread, and a jar of peanut butter in it. My father became a very angry, grumpy person. Permanently. The humorous part of his brain failed to survive. He sank into a depression of his own, blaming everything on foreign workers. From then on, he wanted only to get even with the Italians, the Hispanics, and others. Alternately, he blamed me. He became an inspired schemer but never was able to get back on the radio as an actor. When the bank foreclosed on the Oakland house owners we were renting from, we still had a car and enough money to drive it back to Hollywood, where my mother's parents cared for us while she and my father looked for a cheap rental. My grandmother, Edith Humphrey, and my grandfather, Walter Humphrey, stuck by their daughter and grandchildren—and to my father, only because he had married their daughter.

My grandparents had a fairly large three-bedroom home on Coronado Terrace. It sat on a steep hill off Sunset Boulevard near Echo Park, a suburban stretch of land on the crest overlooking Los Angeles and Hollywood. On a clear day, you could see the Pacific Ocean. We found refuge there, and we made do with temporary beds created by hauling mattresses and blankets to the Humphrey sunporch at the back of the house. It was comfortable enough in Southern California's mild, early-fall weather. We were luckier than those people spread out on the ground all over greater Los Angeles, where rows of families slept out in the fields. There was no "safety net": no unemployment insurance, no child welfare, no school lunch, and no food stamps.

Luckily, Grandfather Humphrey had the means to take care of us. He was a master machinist who built and invented complicated medical instruments in the workshop on the downhill end of the backyard. His brother and business partner, my great-uncle Charlie, was a bachelor who lived in the house, too, and he was just as good a machinist as my grandfather.

My grandmother Edith was a wonderful woman who took good care of her three grandchildren. Within a week or so, my parents found something sufficiently inexpensive, a house (to put it into a category it probably did not deserve) northwest of Los Angeles along the Pacific in the oceanfront village of Topanga Canyon, where it came out of the Santa Monica Mountains. The main street, Canyon Road, ran for a quarter of a mile toward the Pacific before it joined the two-lane, blacktop Pacific Coast Highway. At this junction was a little neighborhood grocery store, which was all that existed of "downtown Topanga." Any serious shopping had to be done in Santa Monica, six miles away. It was here I turned 6, in what became the dysfunctional family of an alcoholic.

In his mind, my father still saw himself as an actor. He ran in circles, trying to resurrect his glory days on Oakland radio without any success whatsoever. Our mother became the family breadwinner, having inherited Grandfather Walter's entrepreneurial genes. She disappeared during daylight hours, rushing about, adding one temp job on top of the other in Santa Monica. My father stayed home, loafed, and sort of took care of us, which in my case meant checking every once in a while to see that I was still alive so he could yell at me.

Our house was a $5-a-month, terminal fixer-upper, a one-story hut with four walls and one large room—the words "tar-paper shack" come to mind. The only plumbing was a cold-water tap over a sink. We ate whatever was the cheapest. For breakfast, we had oatmeal with sugar and diluted canned milk. Lunch consisted most often of just a mustard and mayonnaise or peanut butter sandwich, and I still have a peanut butter sandwich almost daily. Oatmeal and peanut butter are still my favorite comfort foods. At dinner, there was usually spaghetti on the table, mixed with 5-cents-a-pound hamburger. Wages, if you could find a job, were as low as 10 cents an hour.

As for the rest of our well-being, we did have electricity, but no bathroom. A hundred feet down a narrow, unlit path through brush and trees was a small outhouse that stood on the bank of the creek. The stress of living at a survival level made me cautious, with a twinge of paranoia. Whenever I walked to the outhouse on a windy, rainy night without a flashlight, I felt I was on a path of no return.

My grandmother Edith visited almost weekly and left a $5 check. This charity, plus my mother's occasional part-time earnings, were still barely enough for adequate food, especially when she had to buy my father whiskey to keep him from complaining about the lack of a drink.

We three Miller kids boarded the bus five mornings a week when it stopped at the grocery store on the Pacific Coast Highway to give us our six-mile ride to Santa Monica. First grade, it turned out, was mostly about reading out loud from uninteresting books. I was too bored and too hungry to pay much attention. There was no such thing as school lunch or food stamps in the Depression, at least not in Topanga or Santa Monica. I settled for my brown bag from home with two slices of bread inside, smeared lightly with peanut butter or oleomargarine.

The family situation only got worse. At that age, I was the one who would always receive my father's hair-trigger bursts of temper. Other than that, my father showed no positive interest in me, his only son. He never sat down to talk with me: What happened in school or outside school was of no interest to him. He ignored me unless I happened to annoy him. The cruelty of silence can be as devastating an abuse as being beaten. Being at home was like living in a vacuum. There was never any laughter. None of us three kids ever had a birthday party.

My mother, Helena, never shielded me from this abuse. Her Eleventh Commandment was that my father would always have his way, no matter what. And he believed that any sort of everyday scramble to bring home some money was beneath him. My mother, on the other hand, did pay a lot of attention to my sisters. She got up early every morning to dress and primp them. She set their hair and ironed their skirts and blouses to wear to school. My father favored them with lots of attention. He loved women in general, and his daughters were pretty and responsive to him.

My response was to flee to the sanctuary of the outdoors. Southern California's climate is wonderful for anyone wanting to stay outside as much as possible. It was fun climbing and exploring through the scrub brush in the foothills of the Santa Monica Mountains that rose up across the creek behind our shack.

The beach was a magical place. I had a collection of weird-looking driftwood. I turned over big rocks to observe snails and other little creatures. I would spend hours out in the waves trying to outguess the surf by diving through the foaming, incoming waves to get under them and swim around with the dog-paddle stroke copied from the other kids. Life was wonderful as long as I was not at home.

My early life did help me grow one talent: It sharpened my sense of finding ways to make money through entrepreneurship, though we didn't know the word at that time. Hunger is a great training tool. My first-ever stab at enterprise was in the form of food. On weekends, I would scrounge around on the beach in the afternoons to look for empty Coca-Cola bottles to take back to the grocery store. Each bottle was worth 2 cents. I traded them all in, and one bottle was good for a two-penny candy bar to assuage my hunger.

On the other hand, the sea could bring in harmful things. One night that first winter, a cargo came in from the sea that made our lives a lot worse.

Topanga Beach at night was the scene of a good many bootleggers driving by in speedboats loaded with illegal booze that was taken ashore and transferred to trucks on the nearby Pacific Coast Highway. One rainy November night, asleep on my thin mattress in our combination kitchen-dining-room-living-room bedroom, my father and two of his card-playing friends barged in, each carrying a gunnysack filled with bottles. They stood the bottles in rows against one wall as I fell asleep again.

The next morning, I woke up from the noise of my father prying the fiberboard panels off the wall, standing the bottles between the studs, and then nailing the panels back in place. Getting up for breakfast, I gulped down my oatmeal, left the house early, and headed for the beach as usual. It had dawned a crystal-clear November morning as I waded down the middle of the creek toward the ocean, setting off flights of shorebirds; sloshing along in the warm water always felt great on my bare feet and skinny legs. At the beach, a speedboat was lying half-sunk in the waves beyond the last cottages. There was a beautiful but damaged hull lying half in shallow water. Last night's high-tide waves had broken apart one side of the boat, and the engine was almost completely covered with sand.

The bootleggers must have run aground at full speed and fled into the night, abandoning the boat, but there was no sign of cargo. Sitting behind the wheel, I pretended to drive the boat. It took me years to figure out that it must have been my father and his two pals who carried off the cargo of whiskey. My father soon got in the habit of getting out of bed between 10 and noon every morning and starting his day by mixing up a bracing cup of coffee and whiskey over the sink.

Then came an even worse time at home: My father had run through his stash of liquor but now demanded a sizeable daily quota of whiskey. My mother was willing to give my father, whom she still adored, anything he wanted. She bought the liquor he wanted out of our food money, such as it was. Our grocery supplies shrank down occasionally to salad dressing sandwiches. My father walked about our one room, glass in hand, unemployed, unwilling to work, and enraged because he could persuade no one to revive "Cy Toosie" as a radio show. In his frustration and intoxication, he often turned on me. But I got so I could see this behavior before it erupted and easily escape.

Rather than face the fact that my family was very strange, I made the assumption that the way our family lived was much the way that every family lived. After all, we were still a family. With hairdos for my sisters, whiskey for my father, and some food saved from dinner for me, my mother kept us together. After the first winter was over and summer rolled around, I got a glimpse of what life really could be like by meeting a very different kind of man on the beach.

Topanga Beach was blessed with a stretch of superb surf. And while surfboarding had not yet come to Topanga, there was such a thing as bodysurfing, where all you needed was a body and a bathing suit.

The Topanga Yacht Club's caretaker had come all the way from Hawaii. It was fascinating, watching him catch a wave and ride it all the way to the beach. I wanted to bodysurf just like this fantastic man. Every day there was any surf, I tried to copy exactly what the Hawaiian was doing. First, I plopped my body down in back of the breaking crest and, of course, I was quickly left behind as the wave went on its way. It was probably a pretty funny sight, my trying to jump up ahead of the curl of the wave and getting hammered. At the end of, say, my 600th attempt, I got sucked under once more and came up, gagging for breath. The Hawaiian, concerned that I might run out of gas while in the grip of the wave and drown, came over and gave me a few pointers. He showed me that the trick to catching a wave was to hunker down just slightly under the breaking crest, and then straighten up fast to let the crest hit your back just as gravity kicks in and gives the wave real carrying power. By early summer, timing my push-off just right (at least occasionally), I would get the wave to carry me on that long, fun ride to the beach. Older kids from the families owning cottages on the beach also copied the Hawaiian, but thanks to his pointers, I could hold my own. It was the first time in my life that I could match anyone else in a sport. It gave me a surge of confidence every time the wave took me all the way to the beach.

The Hawaiian and I became good friends. We spent time together in his small commercial fishing dory, laying out and retrieving set lines, sometimes with a fish on them. Realizing that it was possible to have a real friend, even for someone like me, and making that real friend because of surfing gave me the first glimpse of what real freedom is all about.

CHAPTER TWO

1931–1932

Living like Millionaires in Marble Halls on a Diet of Peanut Butter

EARLY ONE DAY IN THE FALL OF 1931, MY FATHER ANNOUNCED THAT HE'D gotten an option deal that would let the family move to a place called the Encino Country Club Hotel in the west San Fernando Valley, some 15 miles north of Topanga Canyon, as the crow flies. Of course, none of us kids had any idea what all this meant, but everyone else was excited. My father had heard about the financial collapse of the Country Club and Hotel, which had been built in the early 1920s and was now standing vacant because the Club could not make mortgage payments. My father had somehow convinced the chairman that he could put on nightly entertainment that would attract enough guests to make a go of the hotel. He persuaded the owners to give him a 12-month option to buy the hotel and the surrounding 640 acres for $10,000 and house his family in the hotel rooms for a small monthly rent over the one-year duration of the option. My father could give potential investors a tour of the place, and he was certain he could come up with enough money in a year to finance it. In the meantime, the family would move into the empty rooms.

It amazes me that my father managed to convince the owners that there was a way of making money out of this elegant, empty building. A part of me envies his scheme—a presentation so convincing and smooth that the owners gave him the one-year lease option for $1. From the owners' point of view, they had nothing to lose. No one else was going to lease the hotel and, who knows, maybe this guy from Topanga might just pull it off.

The format for the planned show, called "At Cy Toosie's Farm," consisted of the hotel guests coming up on stage to present Cy Toosie (my father) with tales of strange, over-the-top "problems" they had concocted in their imaginations. Their "problems" would be resolved instantly in the course of my father's comic improvisations. The audience would applaud this character spinning out funny solutions. My father's thinking went something like this: This show would help him recoup his entertainer status and enable him to get Cy Toosie back on radio, broadcasting from the hotel.

After almost two years in our one-room, $5-a-month shack, this seemed fantastic, and it was going to happen right away. We drove slowly up the long driveway to the front of the huge building, and there we stopped: a rag-tag gypsy family with a net worth of less than zero, now walking through the richly decorated halls of our new home. On the second floor, up the handsome stairs, we peered wide-eyed down a long hallway and then into 30 or 40 luxuriously appointed bedrooms with hardwood floors, running water, and electric lights. Each of us kids would have our own bedroom with its own bathroom—no more walking through the woods in the rain to the outhouse. On the ground floor, we had a giant kitchen—a considerable improvement over no kitchen at all—and we had a family day room of our own, too. It was Cinderella time.

From the family's side, there were certain major problems. We were without any income, and my father had a monthly rent to pay. My grandmother lived too far away to leave checks, and my mother was no longer working. The surrounding rural country had no temp jobs—except picking fruit in season and wrangling horses that were boarded in the area. We were living on the money my father had gotten from those bedazzled into thinking that his scheme would work.

The hotel stood in the middle of the magnificent countryside of the San Fernando Valley, where in the spring, lush grass grew as far as the eye could see. I entertained myself by exploring the entire building complex and then scouting out the 640-acre property surrounding it. Any number of trails wound out of the grassland into the nearby foothills. All the buildings—the hotel, athletic club, stables, and swimming pool—were themselves interesting. While sitting in various chairs around the beautiful main dining room, I pretended to be a millionaire with waiters hovering about to serve my every whim. Investigating the empty clubhouse with its athletic equipment still standing about, I tried to build myself up (still one of my goals) by pumping the abandoned barbells once or twice to muscle up my arms. I balanced along the fancy tile rim around the edge of the empty Olympic-size swimming pool and climbed the ladder of the 30-foot diving platform.

The next day I'd be Daniel Boone, stalking a bear a mile from the Club on gravel driveways that connected half a dozen big, shuttered homes. It was fun to climb up on the porches and peer into the opulent interiors through cracks in the shutters. I had enough to keep me busy until dark, when it was time to go home to my big bedroom and sleep in privacy—an entirely new and slightly scary experience.

I spent most of the daytime hours that fall at school. I had entered the third grade of Encino Grammar in the fall semester, and I made a few casual friends among my classmates. We used our imaginations: a lot of playing cowboys and Indians or secret agents against the Germans, aka "the Krauts." Encino Grammar held 10 grades: K through nine. Three grades were squeezed into each room, with one teacher instructing all three grades at once. This saved money. The county's income from property taxes had plunged as the property prices decreased. In each classroom, some pupils recited while others read quietly. The teachers soon decided that I was reading so far ahead of my class that they promoted me, as per the California three-semester system. They wanted to move me up an entire year, to the fourth grade. However, when the school talked with my parents, who paid some attention to my life for once—albeit negative attention—they decided for some reason not to jump ahead further than the second semester or one-half of a grade. This meant that my graduation to the fourth grade was in January 1933 rather than June 1933. From then on, I would always move up from class to class in January instead of June.

Back then Tom Mix was my cowboy hero. He always got his man and never kissed the girl. Cowboys were great. One of the wranglers regularly herding horses around the Club became friendly with me and gave me his old cowboy hat. The hat was far too big for my head, but I stuffed folded newspaper inside the headband to make it stay snugly on my head. My father was not impressed. He walked into the family sitting room, yanked the hat off my head, and threw it in the fireplace, yelling, "No kid of mine is going to be a cowboy."

I roamed about the Encino Country Club Lake hoping to see one or two of the cowboys herding horses across the meadows. They often came past the hotel in the morning, with their dogs nipping at the horses' heels to keep the herd together. No one stopped the wranglers from running their herd near the hotel, despite the fact that their dogs were not necessarily friendly. The danger of having dogs herding horses around the hotel area had never been a problem.

On a warm spring Saturday afternoon, I was walking around the lake when a wrangler and his herd of 20 or so horses showed up, along with three mangy dogs. Suddenly the dog at the rear of the herd swerved and ran at me like a vicious wolf. He leaped at my chest, knocking me down. I desperately tried to hold off this crazed dog, but it had me by the throat, the shoulder, and my ribs, snarling and tearing at my skinny body. The wrangler jumped off his horse, grabbed a 2-by-4, and beat the dog off.

The wrangler picked me up and carried me to the hotel, while I yelled from the pain of dozens of rips and tears in the flesh around my neck, shoulders, and head. Blood had soaked through my dirty, torn shirt. My mother opened the door and half-fainted at the sight. My father was drinking already but was sober enough to get in the car and drive me, held by my mother, to the nearest clinic in Burbank.

Fortunately, the dog's teeth had not punctured any veins or arteries, but by the time we reached the hospital, I had screamed myself hoarse. My father carried me in and laid me on a cold, stainless-steel table. A man in a white coat showed up while I was writhing and howling, on the edge of hysteria. Almost 80 years later, it dawned on me that my father had taken me to a veterinarian's examination room rather than a regular hospital emergency room. A stainless-steel table is the examination table used by veterinarians, not hospitals. With no antibiotics yet invented, the veterinarian made do by sterilizing my many slash and puncture wounds with an acid of some kind. The acid hurt worse than the wounds it was supposed to sterilize.

It took four people to hold me down on the table: my father on one leg, a male attendant on the other; a large lady attendant held one arm down while my mother held the other. I screamed and strained to get up as each drop of acid fell in the wounds, releasing a puff of acrid smoke. It was the most pain all at once I was ever to experience, until my horrendous broken leg roughly 60 years later. I was still groaning in agony when the veterinarian said, "You can let him up. Make sure that the dog is tied up for 30 days to see if it gets rabies. If it does, then there will be further treatment of your son."

I moaned all the way to the hotel, where we discovered someone had already shot the dog so we couldn't find out if it was rabid. Apparently it wasn't, but I still exhibit a lot of stress whenever a strange dog comes trotting my way. My wounds soon healed, and after a couple of weeks, I was running around as much as ever.

My father's option on the Encino Country Club Hotel ran out before he was able to raise the $10,000 to exercise his option, ending our dream life in a first-class hotel. My father also owed some rent money to the owners for our quarters. So once again, we were on the run, throwing our stuff into the car in the pitch black of night, driving off like thieves. We drove south through the San Fernando Valley, heading for my grandparents' house on Coronado Terrace in Hollywood, where we arrived the next morning. They made up beds for all five of us on their back sunporch. We had lived half-rich for a brief while, but we were still dirt poor. I had lost the ocean and then the countryside. Over the next 10 years, I had to sink or swim as a city boy. It wasn't until later, when I discovered how to hitchhike to the beach, that I was able to satisfy my need for freedom.

CHAPTER THREE

1933–1935

Hollywood: Dodging the Rent in the Dark of Night

MY GRANDMOTHER EDITH WAS A WISE WOMAN. TO KEEP MY FATHER from overstaying his welcome at Coronado Terrace, she found a rental house for us, afraid that otherwise we would end up living in a shack again like the one in Topanga Canyon. She found a reasonably priced three-bedroom home on Hollywood's Finley Avenue and "loaned" our family a month's rent and a month's security so we could move right in.

She must have thought it obvious that one of the bedrooms at the Finley Avenue house was to be mine. However, shortly after we moved in, my parents put my bedroom space to better use by renting it to a distant relative who was willing to pay $5 a month for a place for his son to stay while he was in college in L.A. Once again, my thin mattress at the end of the upstairs hall indicated my pecking order in the family.

Until now, a great natural environment had helped me cope with my father's drinking. Could I survive in this suburban environment and hold on to the little bit of self-confidence I had found in the great outdoor life at Topanga and Encino? When I, silently as possible, went out the front door of the Finley Avenue house, I was face-to-face with endless houses sitting on both sides of blacktop—no sand, no open hills, no lush green grass, no real woods in Hollywood. I sensed a choice: find something that could be fun or turn in on myself and become a negative-thinking kid.

Franklin Avenue Grammar School was not the answer. It was hard for me to make friends because my scrawny, uncoordinated body was of no use when it came to sports—the natural catalyst among kids my age. Because I had entered fourth grade several weeks after school had opened, I was an outsider. I was left out from the beginning and too shy to ask anyone why.

My clear-eyed grandmother saw that my morale was dropping, so she did something about it. On my eighth birthday in October 1932, she gave me a big, red, wooden wagon that went like blazes. I quickly learned how to get up speed by adopting the basic wagon stance: left leg kneeling in the wagon while my right leg propelled the machine with short, hard, backward pushes that sped me rapidly along the sidewalks, among and around slow-moving pedestrians, never grazing even one of them. I pulled the wagon up every steep street within a mile of Finley Avenue and managed to invent my own dangerous sport.

The wagon by itself might not have been enough, but another stroke of good luck came my way. I got a job—a very little job, but it ramped up my spirits. On the first rainy Saturday in November, I was unable to use my wagon so I hung out in the small Hillhurst Grocery Store around the corner from the Finley Avenue house for about half an hour, moving around the counters as if looking for something to buy. Mr. Foster, the store's sole proprietor, knew I was from the family who had just moved into the neighborhood and realized that I had nothing to do with my time. He looked straight at me and said, "Warren, if you are going to hang around, you might as well do some work." He had no idea how much I needed that. I had found a refuge and also a job when 25 percent of American men were out of work.

That day I transferred eggs from large to small cartons, polished the fruit on display stands, and swept the floor. At closing time, Mr. Foster asked if I would like to come back the next Saturday. He held up a shiny dime and put it in my hand. Then he gave me some sage advice. "Warren," he said, "Whatever you do, don't spend all of this in one place." I had a job! I was the only kid in my fourth grade class who had one, and this made me feel a lot better, though self-esteem wasn't even recognized back then.

As for spending, Mr. Foster's advice taught me to buy one single penny candy every day on my walk home from school and that is all. (A delicious penny candy was a sure cure for low energy or low spirits.)

At the end of the first week, a nickel of my salary remained in my pocket. At the end of the second week, there were two nickels in my pocket. Just feeling the nickels in my pocket gave me a sense of well-being. One or the other of my sisters took me to the neighborhood theater where I spent 10 cents to get into the matinee double feature. For the first time, I was operating in the market economy—earning, saving, and spending, while my sisters got their money from my mother.

At home, my mother got her first permanent job—at the Federal Works Project Administration, which the U.S. Department had set up that year to provide jobs for the jobless. She earned $12.50 a week as the organizer for a dozen women in a quilting co-op.

Twelve dollars a week was a lot of money back then, but my mother put it into rent and drink for my father, still neglecting adequate food for the family. We ate what amounted at best to hamburger, potatoes, and bread with mustard or oleomargarine, but we had some food, when a lot of families didn't.

Our family was miraculously staying afloat, and living on Finley Avenue let me earn my 10 cents every Saturday. It also meant viewing two-year-old movies, such as "King Kong"—I loved the scene when the Air Force shot King Kong off the Empire State Building. Still, even with the movies every other week, I missed Topanga and the beach, as well as Encino and the freedom I found there. After a few months, even riding the wagon became more work than fun.

Then my guardian angel came through again. My grandmother Edith gave me a pair of brand-new, shiny roller skates. I was so excited I could hardly sleep. I woke up at 5:30 A.M. and snuck outside in the dark to strap on my new skates. An hour after sunup, I had learned enough that I could circle our block at decent speed without falling. My skinned knees bled a bit, but those roller skates were now the center of my life. Climbing the city streets that I had already found for coasting for my wagon, I was soon racing down every one of them on my magic, silver roller skates.

The skates gave me a chance to add to the family income, working for my mother. Twice a week, she brought home 12 pairs of scissors used by the ladies at the quilting co-op—the government allotted 10 cents a pair to have them sharpened twice a week. Every "sharpening day," my mother woke me up at 4 A.M. and handed me the bag of scissors. I headed out the door for my grandparents' house on Coronado Terrace, about two miles away.

Then came the best part: Back in 1915, when Sunset Boulevard was paved, the street crew put very little gravel in the asphalt so it was glassy smooth. There was almost no traffic, so I could build up a lot of speed and skate right down alongside the streetcar tracks. On those clear, cold, winter mornings, racing down Sunset Boulevard at what seemed a hundred miles an hour was a wonderful scary feeling, and all the while I was earning money for the family.

The income from the scissor sharpening brought in an additional $2.40 a week, on top of my mother's pay and the stratospheric $5 a month for renting out my room. Yet even with this much money coming in, the family hit a financial wall again. Possibly my father had tried some new scam that had failed, or else his demand for whiskey and cigarettes had grown out of proportion. So the Miller family jumped the rent at the Finley Avenue house, sneaked out with all our earthly belongings in the middle of the night, and moved to a house a good distance away on a street called Alexandria, south of Santa Monica Boulevard.

I had to switch schools again from Franklin Avenue Grammar to Ramona Grammar School, and worse yet, I had to give up my job at the Hillhurst Grocery Store. I no longer had the money to go to the movies, and my favorite skating streets were too far off except on weekends. My world was again shrinking.

On March 10, the 1933 Southern California earthquake occurred, measuring 6.4 on the Richter scale. The quake's center was out in the Pacific, but it killed 115 people and brought down buildings all over Southern California, including my school. (We ended up going to school in tents.) I was still feeling dislocated by our recent move, and now even the earth underfoot was also no longer dependable.

Six months later, my father suddenly called another "Miller Family Scramble." We skipped out on the rent once again and, as usual, moved in the night to another cheap rental my father had discovered on Manzanita Street, near the Sanborn streetcar junction. My sisters and I switched schools once again, this time to Micheltorena Grammar School, my fourth in the course of a single school year.

Then I found a way to make money again. During the Depression, people bought magazines one issue at a time from "magazine boys" because it was hard to find enough money to buy a year's subscription. I had heard that magazine-boy jobs were being offered by the local agent for the *Saturday Evening Post* and persuaded him to hire me. The agent handed me 10 *Posts* a week. I sold them at 5 cents each and made a penny and a half per copy, 15 cents total for the week if I sold all my copies. I made sure I sold them all. Persistence was the key, and I was definitely persistent. Evening after evening, I made cold calls on practically every house in my neighborhood and learned that success in selling is all about handling rejection. It took at least 20 turndowns for every single sale before I sold out 10 copies of the issue.

Then there was a second franchise for the *Ladies' Home Journal*, selling for 10 cents per monthly issue. I was to make 3 cents a sale—that sounded good, but I found that most housewives underwent "sticker shock," as 10 cents was sky-high for a mere magazine. Still, my take from both magazines averaged 75 cents a month. For the first time, I could afford an occasional hot dog from a deli to hold off daytime hunger pangs until dinner. My self-confidence thrived on the independence that my new 75-cents-a-month job provided. It didn't take much.

My career as a magazine distributor ended abruptly when another disaster hit the family. My mother had been promoted up the WPA job ladder to social caseworker, where her job was to carry out the country's first federal child welfare law passed earlier that year. Her salary was $25 a week, so we were rolling in dough. It was 30 years later before I learned what really happened. My father, unable to resist a scam, urged my mother to enroll a number of nonexistent families and cash the child welfare checks as they came in. Within a short time, she was caught, indicted, tried in Los Angeles County Court, and sentenced to two years in prison.

Consequently, my father faced a problem: My mother's income stopped. He could not pay the rent, let alone buy food. So he had another brilliant idea: He would take out a $500 loan from a loan-shark outfit, though he had no way to repay it. He could simply make himself scarce and let them take whatever they wanted from the house we could no longer afford to rent—or maybe he didn't think that far ahead.

The first time the three of us kids knew any of this came when we were walking home together one afternoon from school. As we approached the house on Manzanita Street, we could see that it was empty. There was no furniture inside. My mattress, my blanket, and my pillow were gone. My only piece of furniture, a rickety chest of drawers, was gone. All my clothes except those I was wearing were gone. The stove, the icebox, the pots and pans, the dishes, every bit of our house not nailed down had been stripped clean by the loan-shark company, leaving only bare floors and bare walls.

Our father came home soon after and said, "Your mother has landed a job in San Diego and will be away for several months." He did not explain why our belongings had disappeared. He simply handed us 5 cents each and told us to take the streetcar to our grandparents' house and stay there until our mother got back from San Diego, as if he had made some sort of rational plan to take care of us. I don't remember whether we even asked him questions. We headed for the streetcar, mute and bewildered.

We were in a daze as we climbed on the big red streetcar and rode the few miles to Coronado Terrace. I was never sure just how much, if anything, my grandparents knew about the situation by the time we got there. They never talked about the whole matter, either then or later. We told them that our mother was now working in San Diego, our house had been cleaned out, and we did not know where our father was. At the very least, the Humphreys knew that something really bad had happened and that it involved their daughter, so they did their best to make us feel welcome in their home. They set up mattresses for us in the back sunroom, and in the week that followed, Grandfather Walter and Great-uncle Charlie installed wood bed frames for the mattresses and solid windows to replace the screens and built a regular door to take the place of the screen door. The three of us would live in that room for the next two years.

It got more crowded when our father arrived, having spent the last of the $500 loan. The Humphreys must have had the whole story by then. They were certain of one thing: This rather intelligent-looking, 40-year-old man, Albert Miller, their son-in-law, was incapable of looking out for himself, much less his children. So they had to take him in, despite his refusal to look for a job. No matter what.

CHAPTER FOUR

1935–1936

Living with Good People Can Produce Good Results

SPENDING NEARLY TWO YEARS LIVING WITH MY GRANDPARENTS WAS THE best thing that happened to me. My whole life changed. It began first thing in the morning with genuine fresh milk on my breakfast oatmeal and with real sandwiches with real ingredients packed into my school lunch bag. My grandparents encouraged conversation, and they were really interested in what I was doing and thinking—an entirely new sensation for me.

Then a miracle happened. I was no longer the no-good kid of the family. My grandparents told my father to stop harassing me, and they made it stick. My father then went into a permanent snit, refusing to eat with the rest of us, insisting on having his meals in his bedroom alone. My oldest sister, Mary Helen, carried his meals to him and returned his dirty dishes to the kitchen. My father spent all of his days in his room, which gave me a chance to gradually start feeling safe.

Grandfather Walter was the quiet tower of strength in the family; he talked to me in a few well-chosen words and gave me some of his time. Great-uncle Charlie had the same steady temperament, although they had different amusements. Great-uncle Charlie played gin rummy with one close friend on Tuesday evenings and smoked his once-a-week cigar.

Grandfather Walter did not smoke or play cards, but he raised box turtles. One evening while Uncle Charlie was playing cards, he gave me a strong piece of health advice that I followed for the rest of my life. He turned to me, saying, "Warren, don't ever smoke one of these." He took a linen handkerchief out of his pocket, took a deep drag on his cigar, and slowly blew a lungful of smoke through the handkerchief, leaving a big, brown stain across the white cloth. "See, Warren, that's what happens in your stomach when you smoke this stuff." He was off on his anatomy, but thanks to Uncle Charlie, I never smoked anything in my life.

Grandmother Edith was calm, smart, firm, and always kind. She seemed psychic about whatever was going through my brain. She was also super-organized, taking care of the Millers, who doubled the size of her family, without breaking stride.

Her steady state of mind may have come from the Christian Science Church. She was one of the church's practitioners, helping teach others to successfully live through church rules, one of which was to love your family. Grandmother Edith practiced that faithfully. I now had a family in my life that supported me all around. Being with older people who loved me was something so far from what I'd experienced before that I felt as if I were in the hands of angels. Edith and Walter were the grandparents from heaven, and I thrived under their watchful eyes.

My grandparents calmly steered me in the right direction with a few quiet words that were easy to obey because I wanted to. Grandfather Walter gave me two simple rules to live by that I never forgot. The first was, "Never tell a lie, because you don't have a good enough memory." The second was, "Never steal anything, because two policemen are smarter than one crook." Obeying these two short rules saved me a great deal of trouble.

Grandfather Walter was a certified genius and a man of many interests. He quit school in the third grade in Wilmington, Delaware; apprenticed to a metalwork designer; and eventually became a brilliant machinist and inventor in his own right. He trekked west to Los Angeles, bringing his brother Charlie with him, and married Edith, a good deal for him.

My grandfather and great-uncle Charlie became famous in medical and dental circles in Los Angeles for their wizardry in manufacturing one-of-a-kind precision machines. Doctors, dentists, engineers, and scientists who came in with a rough diagram for an invention scratched out on the back of an envelope would have their crude drawings transformed into metal reality in my grandfather's machine shop. Their inventions included the intricate "escape boxes" that Houdini used onstage during his performances, the monster mask designed for Boris Karloff in the original 1931 movie "Frankenstein," and a dental tool named the "Hollenback Condenser," which is still used today.

The machine shop where all this intricate creation took place was only about 20 feet by 12 feet, but it had plenty of windows. All the power tools ran off a single, two-horsepower electric motor through a series of overhead leather belts, pulleys, and shafts. It was wonderful to hear the 30-foot main belt hum over the shiny steel wheels and hear the joint that tied the belt ends together click loudly each time it passed over the drive wheel. All of this came into good use rather soon in the matter of finding a reasonable way to attend school.

Coronado Terrace was in the same school district as Micheltorena Grammar School, so I thankfully did not have to change schools again. However, the door-to-door distance to school was now about a mile. There were no free city school buses, and the streetcar route that did make the right connections would have cost my grandparents 5 cents a day each way. On top of that, my life would be ruled by the streetcar schedule.

One of my schoolmates owned an old single roller skate. He sold it to me for 25 cents, and I fastened two wheels to the front of a 2-foot-long piece of 2-by-4 and the other two wheels to the back of it. Then I nailed a piece of 2-by-4 vertically on the front and a handle on the top of that, and I had great free transportation to and from school.

Once I had built my skate-coaster, which my grandfather Walter described as a pretty good job, he and Charlie started giving me lessons in shop work. This was another terrific morale boost: Two talented adults were showing faith in my ability to learn something useful. I enjoyed learning how to run the lathe and the drill press and how to buff castings. Based on my increasing skills, my grandfather began to pay me to help him.

After a while, I was doing much of the repetitive, mechanical jig work in the shop. Grandfather Walter paid 10 cents an hour, 10 times the money I had earned at the Hillhurst Grocery. I would try to complete routine jig work within two clicks of the drive belt on the overhead drive shaft, and sometimes I could finish one piece within one click. I was able to accelerate routine jobs and still maintain high quality. Later, after I'd graduated from high school, they were paying me 25 cents an hour.

My grandfather had become my hero, replacing cowboys entirely. I was in awe of this simple, honest, hardworking descendent of Dutch immigrants. Grandfather Walter became a model for my future work ethic. In the long run, it was easy to become a true, proud follower of Walter Humphrey.

Grandfather Walter's work amply fed all seven of us at Coronado Terrace, but his latest invention, an "ozone generator," was going to do more than that. Ozone is a rare gas that circulates freely in the atmosphere. At sea level, the air is 98 percent oxygen, and the nitrogen and ozone in it adds up to less than one-tenth of 1 percent. My grandfather's generator actually created ozone by drawing air across an internal ultraviolet lamp and out through a flexible metal hose. It was a beautifully functional machine, and ozone is a potent healing gas. Five minutes of breathing pure ozone through a mask attached to the metal hose, followed by 25 minutes of inhaling ozone blown through a eucalyptus oil, which was a new medical treatment back then, was all it took to get rid of a cold or lung infection.

My grandfather tested its potency on his volunteer patients. It worked so well that soon he had plenty of volunteers. Before ozone use was restricted to doctors, the Humphrey ozone generator played a big role in securing the future of the entire Miller family.

My own mind also tilted a bit toward chemical invention, although my first attempt turned out to be a disaster. As much as I wouldn't have wanted to admit it, at least once in a while a bit of my father's sneaky, destructive character popped up in my own behavior.

One rainy day with not much else to do, I took to exploring the basement of the Coronado Terrace house. Way back in a corner, in near darkness, I found a small nail keg standing next to a big earthen crock. Inside the crock, Grandfather Walter fermented his own wine, and my Christian Scientist grandmother always pretended not to know. Inside the nail keg were several reels of 35-MM nitrate movie film.

Curious, I wound off about 3 feet from one roll and wondered if the film would burn. Like most kids, I liked playing with matches, and I decided I had to find out. I cut the loose end of the film and wound it tightly into a 1-inch-diameter roll. I took the roll into the backyard and put a match to it. The little roll caught on fire right away, but instead of flaring up, it just smoldered away, making an awful lot of smoke with a terrible smell. I stamped on the burning roll, until it stopped burning. Here was a product any number of my schoolmates would like to have.

I went back to the basement and secretly cut a half dozen pieces off the end of the film, making six tight, 1-inch-diameter rolls (destroying forever, perhaps, the only copy of a long-lost, potential Academy Award winner). I wrapped each roll of inflammable film in plain, white paper held by a rubber band, and printed in capitals "STINK BOMB." I decided to sell this artistic, creative, smoky chaos for only 5 cents each.

The next morning, stepping aboard my skate-coaster carrying a pocketful of my new product, I was off to Micheltorena Grammar School. Once I hit the playground, I told my friends to gather around and lit one of the rolls of film in a far corner of the playground. The column of smoke that rose was surprisingly thick and gigantic, and the stench was overwhelming, irresistible for any stink bomb aficionado. Four rolls sold right away for my first-ever solo entrepreneurial adventure. Soon I would have another first: my first-ever travel adventure, a ride in the backseat of a big, black police car.

Naturally, teachers spotted the plume of smoke and called the Los Angeles police and fire departments. Then came the law, looking grim, bringing their shiny, black patrol car to a screeching halt and quickly catching me in the act of selling my next-to-last stink bomb. The evidence was the remaining stink bomb in my pocket. The cops marched me to their patrol car and gave me my first and last ride under police detention. Two unsmiling cops (maybe I saw one briefly hiding a grin) drove me about a mile to the office of the district superintendent of schools. And there I stood, sweaty with guilt, before the desk of the mighty superintendent.

He was a grumpy-looking guy with a grumpy tone. He shot me a half-dozen questions, such as where did I get the stuff and how much did I sell the bombs for? I guess I must have come off as just another normally irresponsible 11-year-old. Besides, by now it was getting late in the day, so the superintendent wound it all up by confiscating my last smoke bomb and giving me a dressing-down for contributing to the delinquency of minors. He concluded with a loud "Don't ever do this again!" The superintendent entered a reprimand on my permanent school record and let me go. I was very relieved because now my grandfather would not have to know I had violated rule number two, the one about stealing—and stealing his stuff, besides.

My little stink bomb episode took me almost directly to a real milestone in my life. Twenty cents from my hot and torrid "film venture," plus my accumulated hourly wages from my grandfather, allowed me to buy something horribly expensive—my first camera. It was a genuine, black Bakelite "Univex Camera with a Sports View Finder" displayed in a drug store. It cost 39 cents. I just had to have that camera—why, I am not sure. This purchase marked only the beginning of what was to be a very, very expensive habit of documenting my world.

One morning, my mother magically reappeared after 18 months of absence. She just stepped in through the front door of Coronado Terrace as big as life and gave us kisses all around as if just coming back from a little weekend trip, and then disappeared to be with my father in his back room. No one talked about her San Diego job, and it was never discussed during the rest of my sisters' lives or the following 60 years. I never knew the truth until I started digging deeper for this book.

The truth about my mother's supposed "job in San Diego," I learned many years later, was that she had been granted "compassionate overnight release" in order to give her the chance to see her three children. She had to go back every morning on the streetcar to the Los Angeles County Jail until she finished her sentence several months later. We kids still believed our father's explanation: Our mother, who had left her job in San Diego, now had come back to take a job in Los Angeles. Our grandparents never discussed their daughter's absence. Possibly they felt that the less talk about my mother, the better. Plus, it was a different era: People rarely spoke of personal or difficult things, even within a family.

Then came another positive change in my life: In October 1936, I joined the Boy Scouts. My 12th birthday had arrived, and I was finally eligible. I had wanted to spend time in the outdoors in the worst way, to recapture some of that freedom I'd had at Topanga and Encino.

Making it into local Boy Scout Troup 20 was just what I had hoped it would be. Again, my grandmother came to my rescue. When the troop was about to go on its first parade, she gave me enough money to buy the entire scout uniform: tan shirt, red kerchief, tan hat, tan pants, and tan socks—in all, $10 retail.

After joining, I was eligible to stay for 25 cents a night at Boy Scout Camp Arthur Letts, run by the City of Los Angeles Department of Recreation and Parks since 1924. I had the money saved from working for my grandfather. So without further fuss, wearing my Scout pin and neckerchief, without checking with my grandparents, I hopped on my skate-coaster and push-footed five miles from Coronado Terrace to Griffith Park and made camp under a tree, although rather minimally with my single, thin blanket and one can of beans. I was getting very hungry, because I had forgotten to take a can opener. After dark, it got really cold in the chill of the October evening. So I decided that instead of freezing to death that night, I would push my skate-coaster in the dark back to where my grandparents were beginning to worry about me.

My Scout career had begun with misadventure, but I later attended a Scout meeting every Friday evening and went on hikes and outings during weekends every chance that I got. My scoutmaster was a real traveler, and he took us on a trip somewhere every other weekend. On my first trip with Troop 20, he took us to the San Gabriel Mountains, about an hour's drive eastward and upward.

The San Gabriels are the barrier-mountains between Los Angeles and the Mojave Desert, and they're easily the most scenic nature preserve near the city, with rugged, tall, beautiful peaks. The highest, Mt. San Antonio, best known as "Mt. Baldy," rises to 10,000 feet. The San Gabriels also include four 9,000 footers, and Mt. Waterman, a perfect natural ski area with a road running right up to the base of the 8,000-foot peak.

We had been prepped at Scout meetings as to suitable clothing and shoes and how to stuff a backpack and how to hike as a troop. Once we got into the San Gabriels, we bunked in rustic cabins in Big Tujunga Canyon, where we took turns half the night feeding a wood fire in the stove. During the day, we took a couple of short hikes. Not having been out of the city for a long time, this felt like a homecoming. It was great to be walking through mountain woods once again. Beginning with my life in the Boy Scouts, good things started happening to me that changed my life forever.

Of course, I took my 39-cent camera on the hikes. I had shot an entire roll with my Univex and now had enough experience under my belt to know roughly how to avoid chopping subjects' heads off and that what you see in the viewfinder and what is recorded on the film is not always the same. The whole process of finding the proper scene had really hooked me.

On the San Gabriel hike, I went overboard and shot two whole rolls of film. Then I took the prints to my next Scout meeting so they could share the fun of the hike all over again. At the following meeting, my patrol leader, Johnny, asked me if he could get some copies. He was about four years older and came from a well-to-do family. He wanted the photos to prove to his parents that he really was going backpacking and not off to a Newport Beach party. To recoup some of the cost of the film and the developing, I told Johnny I would ask for 25 cents over the cost of his print order, and he was fine with that. I was excited to earn enough to buy and process my roll of film. It was plain enough that if I took interesting pictures, I could turn a profit by plowing earnings back in. Making money for shooting film on a trip that was fun to do anyway seemed almost too good to believe. This was the kernel of the idea that taking pictures of great places would be a good way to make a living. Fifteen years later, in 1950, I was able to begin doing just that.

CHAPTER FIVE

1936–1937

Discovering Skiing with an Open Mind and a Rubber Band around My Wallet

IN THE FALL OF 1936, THERE WAS, ONCE AGAIN, A CRISIS IN MY LIFE. The Millers all living in the Humphrey home had a built-in time limit. Five Millers sleeping in the sunporch bedroom was inadequate, along with eating the grandparents' food three meals a day. My father's job situation had remained the same: nonexistent.

Grandmother Edith believed that my parents had the responsibility for feeding and raising their three children. But she had delayed sending us out on our own because she wanted to give the smallest Miller, me, a chance to gain some self-confidence before facing my dysfunctional family alone. I now had a strong relationship with my grandparents and great-uncle, as well as friends in the Boy Scouts, so my grandmother thought that I would be OK if she activated step two of her plan. She cosigned a rental agreement that put our family into our own house. And it was just in time. To have all of us, myself as a 12-year-old kid, along with my two teenage sisters, 13 and 15, spending their entire childhood in the same bedroom in the Humphrey home was not ideal. My grandmother and grandfather were making a common-sense decision, and it would give me a chance to stand on my own in the family group.

But I still felt totally abandoned, with the only nurturing I'd had in my life taken from me.

Setting up my parents to make a go of things on their own was a situation that called for divine intervention. Grandfather Walter was on the side of the angels and had come up with step three of the plan. My mother, he felt, was capable of heading the household—if she hadn't had a prison record as part of her resume. The next step involved the ozone machine. Many health practitioners in Europe had begun healing with ozone. The result was a well-documented medical protocol for ailments such as infected cuts, parasites, staph infections, fungus infections, and other ills. German and Swiss doctors were prescribing ozone routinely. However, in America, ozone healing had just barely begun to take hold.

I experienced first-hand the power of ozone. I had a deep cut in one hand that was refusing to heal properly until my grandfather said, "Let's try some ozone on that." He took me into his workshop and ran a little jet of ozone slowly along the cut. Within 10 minutes, the infected cut dried up. The germs couldn't live in ozone, so they all died. I was amazed at how quickly it healed.

Grandfather Walter led the field of ozone generating, at least in the Hollywood–Los Angeles area. My mother had learned how to get consistently good results with my grandfather's run of volunteer patients, and he was getting more requests for treatment every day. Now here was a machine you could make a living with. You would just need eight or 10 of them.

Grandmother Edith located an appropriately roomy, single-story house on Franklin Avenue in Hollywood. The street was a busy thoroughfare with a bus route, and there was a stoplight right at the intersection with a cross street a hundred feet from the house, so there was a lot of traffic noise. However, the price was right. It had two bedrooms: My sisters would get one, my parents the other. I would get the small breakfast nook, but at least it had a door that I could close, and that was a lot more than many Depression children had.

My grandmother put down the first and the last month's rent on the house and cosigned the lease. In October 1936, all five Millers moved out of our crowded, free space at Coronado Terrace into the much less crowded house on Franklin Avenue. Grandfather Walter then moved an ozone generator into the house.

I agonized over having to part with my grandparents, but after all, they lived only a few miles away, and it was always possible to visit them on my roller skates—as I often did. After almost two years of no privacy, it was great to have my own room, which had a sizeable window that let in good light from the backyard. I was able to store my few belongings and had a place to study for school, something not done often, and here I could stay safely out of my father's presence, which was something I tried to do all the time. Except for our brief time at the Encino hotel, this was the first bedroom alone I had ever had. However, it was not the last of my grandmother's gifts to me that year.

For my birthday in 1936, Grandmother Edith gave me a brand-new bicycle. It was like giving me a pair of wings. I could make my getaway from home whenever I felt like it. My magnificent gift cost my grandmother $24.95 and was by far the most valuable present anyone had ever given to me.

The bike was a Schwinn Excelsior, the cutting-edge of bike technology of the day, weighing in at 40 pounds, much more than double the weight of a road bike today. It had fat bike tires and the first spring steel fork, and it was strong enough to absorb the shock of riding over curbs, potholes, and other kinds of bike torture I would surely invent. The bike went a long way toward giving me an escape from my father, who had resumed his usual combination of alternately ignoring my existence and making it miserable.

Because of my lucky bike, I landed a job delivering newspapers. Having a bike let me hang out with other kids while they rode their bikes. I pedaled my bike with my friends when they picked up the *Hollywood Citizen News* to deliver in the afternoon. One day, one of the guys quit while I was there, so I got the job and earned $9 a month delivering 80 papers, six afternoons a week.

The paper cost 60 cents a month or about 2 cents a day. It was a daily except Sunday. However, if all the money was collected at the end of the month from the customers to whom I delivered, I got to keep part of it. If somebody moved out in the middle of the night, I got stuck for the loss. So I learned early on to notice when the grass wasn't being mowed or the mail wasn't being picked up or the last two days' papers were still on the porch.

Still needing solid escape options, I always went to the Scout meetings, on Friday evenings and every other weekend I went on a Scout hike or outing. Weekday afternoons, if I wasn't delivering papers, I could stay after school at Thomas Starr King Junior High and play softball or tag football until it got dark. My coordination had improved. I was no longer the last kid chosen in pickup games. I was next to last.

Boy Scout Troop 20's leaders had scheduled a five-day Christmas week trip to Big Pines in the San Gabriel Mountains. I hoped there would be a lot of snow, real deep snow, not just skidding-on-a-sheet-of-ice snow. I was so excited by the idea of getting into deep snow I decided to build my own toboggan for the occasion.

The Thomas Starr King Junior High woodshop teacher, Mr. Breymeyer, a really good guy, gave me whatever help I needed. He had me steam and bend oak boards and rivet the boards to cross pieces. There it was: a two-man toboggan all my own!

When we got to the Big Pines Lodge, Troop 20 occupied a dorm that was bare and basic—two rows of two-tier metal bunk beds with thin mattresses on which we rolled out our bedrolls. My toboggan was a hit. A half-dozen of us spent much of our time during the five days at Big Pines taking turns running down our now hard-packed, straight, fast toboggan trail.

The high point came the day I saw my first alpine skiers. We were standing around on the hill, soaking wet again from wading around in the snow, when four skiers appeared over the top of our slope doing long, slow snowplow turns down the hill—graceful, godlike creatures with tasseled ski hats, yellow goggles, poplin jackets, and billowing pants tucked inside their boots. They were friendly and stopped and talked with us for a while. We decided this was a great way to enjoy snow and stay dry at the same time.

I wanted a pair of skis. I had given up delivering the *Hollywood Citizen News* because it required being there six afternoons a week and broke up my entire day. The $9 a month wasn't worth it anymore. So a few weeks after getting back to Hollywood, I landed another newspaper delivery job at $2 a week for delivering 300 copies of the *Los Angeles Downtown Shopping News* twice a week. I would have to get up at 4:30 so I could start delivering by 5:00 to every house in the area, but that was better than having every afternoon broken up. Those 4:30 wake-up calls shaped the rest of my life; I still bounce out of bed early every morning, ready to tackle the world.

One of the houses on my route happened to belong to Walt Disney. Disney had a black-and-white Great Dane as big as a horse behind his fence—the biggest dog I had ever seen. Fortunately, Disney's fence was an 8-footer.

One Saturday, I rode my bike up to the house of a friend, Julius Butler, who lived in Los Feliz, the ritzy part of my old neighborhood, to play some version of the cops-and-robbers chase game. I was a robber running full tilt around the house when I braked to a full stop. Julius had a pair of skis hanging in his garage. The skis were made of pine by Spalding, the best-known equipment maker for practically every popular sport in America at the time. They were less than 5 feet long, with genuine leather toe straps but without any extras like metal bindings and metal edges.

I bought the skis for $2. Julius threw in the bamboo poles because, he said, he was probably never going to go skiing again. The other kids thought I was crazy to fork over a week's pay, but I had already decided that I wanted to be on skis, not riding on a toboggan, the next time there was a chance to get up to the snow. The chance came two weeks later.

My Troop 20 patrol leader Johnny had recently turned 16 and celebrated by getting his driver's license and buying a Model A Ford for $32. He invited me to go skiing with him for a day on Mt. Waterman in the San Gabriels, and he was the perfect guy to go with for my first ski experience. He had taken a week's worth of ski lessons with his parents the prior Christmas at the Grand Hotel Ahwahnee in Yosemite and nearby Badger Pass, the only ski resort in California at the time.

Johnny took his lessons from the Badger Pass ski school director, a fantastic Austrian racer named Hannes Schroll. He had been hired by Ahwahnee after winning the first combined American National Alpine Championships in downhill, slalom, and combined on Mt. Rainier in the previous spring of 1935. No question—Johnny had an excellent teacher. All I had to do to get down the hill was to follow and copy Johnny.

I could also study the new book Johnny brought with him—*Downhill Skiing*, written by another Austrian, Otto Lang. Lang had also come to America the year before, another one of the top Austrian ski instructors who were immigrating to the U.S. in the 1930s because there were so many Americans wanting to pay to learn to ski. All of the above was sheer good luck. Lang's book and Johnny's lessons from Schroll had connected me with two of the best alpine ski instructors in America, even if secondhand.

We drove east from Hollywood in Johnny's 1932 Model A in the early-morning darkness. It was cold sitting in the open backseat, the "rumble seat," as it was called. I contributed 50 cents, enough to buy five gallons of the gas, but I still had to share my rumble seat with all the poles and skis. I spent most of the trip hunkered down under a thin blanket, with skis and poles digging into my chilled, skinny 13-year-old body.

We finally hit the 6,000-foot line where the snow began. Johnny put the bumper up against a snowbank and set the hand brake. I threw off my blanket, sat up, and there it was—the most beautiful sight I had ever seen: my first view of an untracked snowfield. Every tree, every shadow is still there in my mind more than 75 years later.

Can you remember what your first day on skis was like?

Mt. Waterman was the basic 1937 ski area: no lifts, no warming hut, no storm shelter, no outhouse. But the price was right: the cost of the gas to get there and back. And the timing was right: We had the mountain to ourselves. I was wearing my pajamas underneath my Sear's Levis for warmth. My leather hiking boots doubled as ski boots: knee-high and with a pocket on the side for my Boy Scout knife. In case of a rattlesnake bite, you had the chance to cut an "X" into each puncture wound, suck out the poison by mouth, and if you did it fast, you could probably save your life. The chance of a poisonous snake slithering through the snow and nailing me on Mt. Waterman was somewhat slight, but I felt secure knowing my knife was there.

My $2, flattop, nonlaminated pine skis looked puny compared to Johnny's ridge tops with toe irons, spring-heel bindings, and metal edges. Plus, Johnny had some idea how to begin. To show me how it was done, Johnny sidestepped up, pointed his skis down, and began to glide, while making three snowplow turns in a wide V-stance. I climbed up behind Johnny on his second ascent, but then he skied away and left me standing there. I was almost frozen in place, but I finally pointed both my skis slightly down as Johnny had done and tried to turn my heels out to get the skis into the snowplow position.

In my simple, leather toe strap bindings and rubber galoshes for boots, turning my heels out just turned my boots and not my skis. My heels hung out over the snow outside the skis, but the skis stayed pretty much parallel. It was all I could do to force the skis into a very thin V and proceed. Once I had traversed the slope, I came to the far side of the snowfield, where I skidded onto a gravel patch and came to a stop. I climbed out of the bindings, turned the skis around, put my boots back in the toe straps, and traversed back the other way.

Eventually, I could stand on my downhill ski and push the tail of the uphill ski out far enough so it steered me part way around the turn. Of course, I was leaning inward, as every beginner does, so I crashed to the inside of my turn before I was halfway through. Then I stood up, pointed my skis in the other direction, and got under way, eventually reaching the bottom of the slope. I climbed up again at least 900 times. At about the 870th time, I managed to turn far enough to reach the fall line before falling or running off the side into the dirt.

By the end of the day, I almost had the skis turning all the way around 180 degrees before crashing. I traded my entire lunch to Johnny in return for the use of his skis and boots for just one run down. On that run, I made two connected, very slow, swinging snowplow turns just like the ones in Otto Lang's book. It was not a very steep hill, of course. The memory of those first two complete turns on skis is almost as vivid as any memory in my life.

I've often asked people if they can remember their first day on skis, and if they learned to ski after the age of 5, they will remember almost everything about that day: what time they got up, the socks they wore, what time they started off, what that first turn was like, what they had for lunch, who they met on the trip—everything about it. I can remember to this day what the weather was like when we started, how long it took us to get there, how I paid 50 cents for five gallons of gas, and the view that day across the San Gabriel range.

People remember their first day on skis because it comes as such a mental rush. When you come down the mountain from your first time on skis, you are a different person. The weariness in the mind slips away, and there's that wonderful feeling of being powered by that huge force called total freedom. I had just now experienced that feeling, if only for half a minute; it was step one in the direction I would follow the rest of my life.

CHAPTER SIX

1937–1938

Freedom Is Always Located Just Outside of the Box

IN 1937, THE GOOD NEWS WAS THAT MY GRANDPARENTS' PLAN WAS working. My parents, for the first time since we lost our house two years before, were on their own and had remained solvent for a number of months. Grandfather Walter installed a second ozone machine in the house, and my mother administered the treatments. Our make-do living room/clinic doubled the number of patients treated daily. Their health problems often went away during the first half-hour treatment, or at least got noticeably better. The word was out. There were now always 10 or 12 walk-in patients sitting around the living room, waiting for a turn at one of the magic machines. My father, with nothing much else to do, spent a lot of time happily sitting about our living room, trying out his radio comedian charm on the patients.

My mother had no medical license, but she got around that by running her business as a charity accepting donations. Patients "donated" on their way out, by dropping an unspecified number of nickels, dimes, quarters, and even dollar bills into the bowl on the small table in the middle of the room. The coins rattled in noisily, and the dollar bills fluttered like leaves falling, encouraging patients to drop in a quiet dollar bill instead of a noisy couple of quarters, which was probably the average donation. At 16 patients a day, my mother was not getting rich, but her take did add up. She took in about $30 a week, and the Miller family was inching slowly toward middle class. The change would have been more noticeable if a quarter of the income every week was not being spent on booze to keep my father happy.

My mother shopped and cooked dinner—she and my father usually ate first, while, like the teenagers we were, we often drifted in late and helped ourselves to whatever was left. A Norman Rockwell *Saturday Evening Post* magazine cover of a family dinner it was not. Neither Mary Helen nor Betty Jane ever brought home groceries or cooked a meal or washed dishes. I stayed away until after dinner, but even if I happened to be there, I never offered help for fear my father would seize the opportunity to make fun of my effort. *Good Housekeeping* would not have given its seal of approval. Dirty dishes filled the sink. No one ever ran a vacuum cleaner. The floors had a permanent coating of dust. Shoes, clothing, laundry, and personal stuff lay around where it had been left. My mother had no time to deal with any of this, and she never asked or taught us kids to pitch in and help. Coming home late and raiding the refrigerator, I retreated to my room. I lived in a family of silence, but I always had my bicycle—and weekends to ride it in nearby Griffith Park. I had a bed, clothes, food to eat, and school to go to. Relative to many others, I was a very lucky young teenager.

My bike became my escape vehicle. I rode down almost every country road to the perimeters of East Hollywood, Griffith Park, and the San Fernando Valley. I pedaled the 10 miles to Pop's Willow Lake in the northeast end of the San Fernando Valley to go swimming in fresh water, and I pedaled the 20-miles-plus down to Santa Monica and Malibu to watch the surf and the pioneer Southern California surfers. Several times I spent the day riding the three miles to the top of Mt. Lee, the highest ridge in the town where I could get a good look at the huge white letters spelling out "Hollywoodland" that were visible even 25 miles away. It took me an hour and a half of hard pedaling on Griffith Park fire roads and up steep terrain to the place near the top where stood that strange and wonderful piece of work of telephone poles, metal, and lightbulbs that were the "Hollywoodland" sign.

The great white letters were 50 feet high by 30 feet wide, fastened to horizontal boards nailed across half-buried telephone poles. The sign was built in 1923, the year before I was born, by a real estate development firm named, naturally, "Hollywoodland." Each letter was studded with lightbulb sockets, thousands of sockets. However, the sign's glory days were long gone. There were no longer any bulbs in the sockets. The real estate firm developing "Hollywoodland" went bankrupt during the Depression.

The giant letters stood as if erected by a vanished race of giants. The letters were rusty, and the whole sign was leaning dangerously forward on its legs, ready to topple. However, as the sign raised a sort of magic glow of civic pride—and Hollywood was a show town, after all—civic-minded groups, one after the other, propped the sign back up. Finally, the city itself took over, shortened the letters to "Hollywood," and shored up the sign's legs. Though the Depression had hit, and people irregularly looked after it, the sign never died. Rescuers always arrived.

My bike exploration gave me lifetime bragging rights to have seen the sign up close and personal. It fit my natural delight in telling stories that eventually led me to a life of adventure and collecting stories for my films.

The biggest adventure that summer was my first trip to Yosemite National Park. Most people have seen on postcards the huge cliffs of Sentinel and Half Dome. It is some of America's most spectacular mountain scenery, with the sheer granite faces rising as much as 4,800 feet above the Yosemite Valley. My Scout Troop offered a weeklong trip in June to Yosemite, and I had to go on that trip.

We had to earn our way by racking up points for going to church or going to school wearing our Scout uniforms or passing Scout merit badge tests, such as making a fire by twirling a wood drill in a notch in a dry board to get a friction spark. Also, we could become skilled at metalwork by hammering out a copper ashtray as a gift to our parents who, in those days, invariably smoked.

I busted my buns and made my quota of points. On top of that, it cost me $6 for the week's trip—less than $1 per day including transportation and food. I paid my $6 out of the $2 a week I was saving from delivering *The Shopping News.* Some of the other kids' parents drove us there for free.

Once we got out of our crowded, cramped cars at Yosemite, we were directed to bed down in Camp 9, reserved for organized groups. Our first act the next morning was a bit of typical kid insanity that the adult scoutmasters watched carefully but let us enjoy. We slid down the banks of the Merced River, a torrent of ice-cold water from a snowfield a few miles upstream. We jumped in and shivered our way downstream through the white foam of the rapids until we were too frozen to stay in. Then we climbed out, ran back up the river to our starting point, and did it again. Only kids under 14 years old are that dumb.

There were no crowds in Yosemite in 1937. Our spectacular four-mile climb to Glacier Point was on a trail with plenty of elbow room. We half-ran all the way back down even as it was getting dark. Then we heard someone holler from the bottom of Glacier Point, "Let the fire fall!" In those days, the park concessionaire, Yosemite Park and Curry Company, always had a couple of employees start a bonfire on top of Glacier Point sometime in the afternoon. At precisely nine o'clock at night, they shoved their pile of burning embers over the edge into a several thousand-foot drop, a blazing free fall as spectacular as any Fourth of July display—but going down instead of up.

On another day, we climbed up Vernal and Nevada Falls and then up the back of Half Dome, where two steel cables strung from solid posts formed the steep route to the top. We climbed up, pulling ourselves along hand-over-hand on the cables, and when we got to the top, we were allowed to crawl on our stomachs out to the very edge and look down the nearly 5,000 feet to the Yosemite Valley floor. It was a 16-mile round trip to the top and back. This was a long hike for skinny 13-year-olds.

Yosemite had seemed a mystical zone, a mountain heaven of faraway places where I had never been and would never go without joining the Boy Scouts. It was within the reach of an ordinary family, but my family was not ordinary. Exploring Yosemite was the sort of adventure I wanted, visiting the fantastic places of the world.

Living in Southern California offered many great adventures, and it was a lucky place to be born. Having been in the mountains a week, when we got back to Hollywood, I started exploring the Pacific beaches and their surf, riding my bike out to Malibu several times and then spending the day bodysurfing in Santa Monica, using techniques learned when I lived at Topanga. Surfboards would not arrive, but for a few, until three or four years later. When they did, riding a board seemed like more fun than hurtling along half underwater while bodysurfing.

During my next semester at Thomas Starr King Junior High School, I asked my friendly woodshop teacher, Mr. Breymeyer, to help me build a surfboard. He found a plan for one in *Popular Mechanics.* It took me a month or more during shop class to build the "hollow" board.

It was made of plywood, 5 feet long and 2 feet wide, with square corners, not curved and shaped like later boards. It was 4 inches thick a third of the way back from the nose and tapered down to 2 inches at the nose and tail. On each side was a sturdy wooden handle. I could lie on my belly, hang on to the handles, kick my feet really hard to try to catch the wave, or kneel and hang on to the handles to catch a wave that usually had already broken. Once the board got going and caught the wave, I could then try to stand up, although standing up was theoretical.

The big practical problem was getting the board to the beach. Most of the surfers were old enough to have a driver's license, but my 16th birthday was still two years away. It took me a couple of weeks of daily begging to get my mother to car-top my board to the beach. She drove me out one Sunday afternoon: The ozone clinic was closed, but she would only take me to the bay behind the Santa Monica breakwater where most waves were never more than a foot or so high.

I already knew how to catch a wave from bodysurfing and did manage to catch these little waves while kneeling on the board and hanging on to the handles. Near the end of the day, I could stand up for 20 feet or so before falling off. It wasn't stylish, but it was an accomplishment. I managed to get my surfboard to the beach only twice more that summer. On one of those days, I rode my board for 50 feet without falling, and that was all it took me to get hooked. Surfing became my second sport full of "freedom feelings."

The next summer, I was soon busy building a second board. It was a "paddleboard," a bigger and longer board without handles to get in the way. The basic goal of surfing is to ride at an angle across the face of a wave to get the longest and fastest possible ride, much longer than you get going at right angles to the wave or straight toward the beach. My plans called for a "Tom Blake hollow surfboard," 12 feet long and 16 inches wide—my first light, hollow board, according to the thinking of the times.

Luckily, the first "light" board had been invented in 1926 by the American surfer Tom Blake while he was living in Hawaii, where he eventually became one of the most famous surfers in history. Blake built the board out of laminated redwood and drilled hundreds of holes through the redwood to lighten it. He then encased the redwood in thin wood sheets on the top and bottom. Blake's first "light" board weighed a mere 100 pounds. There was already a big group of Hawaiian surfers using much heavier boards. The theory of the heavy board had been that when a wave rolled forward over the board, it would not straighten it out to head straight for the beach as easily or quickly as a light board. A friend of mine, Gard Chapin, actually built in a 20-pound slug of lead in the nose of his board so that when the wave broke on him, it wouldn't straighten out so easily. The experts made fun of Blake's new design by calling it the "Cigar Box Board," meaning as breakable as a cigar box, until they saw how much faster the hollow board ran across the face of a wave, giving a much longer ride than the heavy board. Plus, it was easier to paddle.

Blake's hollow surfboard was such a great success that by 1930, it became the first surfboard to be mass-produced. In 1935, Blake was the first to attach a fin to the bottom of a board so that it would not skid sideways so easily down the face of a breaking wave. I had all the advantages of Blake's breakthroughs building my surfboard. Fiberglass and foam had not yet been applied to surfboards, maybe not even invented yet, so my hollow paddleboard still weighed 30 pounds. In today's fiberglass age, this is way too heavy. It was another two decades before surfers got it: The lighter the board, the easier it is to steer. Now surfers ride boards as light as 6 pounds, doing things on them that back then, in my wildest imagination, I had never envisioned.

During my first summer as a paddleboard owner, I hit up everyone for a ride to the beach but only made it four times. However, during those four times, I did make a few great rides—for me. I was only a young teen, and it was frustrating to watch the other guys doing things that I really wanted to do.

CHAPTER SEVEN

1939

Berendo Street: Round Was the Shape of My Basketball But Not My Body

1939 BROUGHT DRASTIC CHANGES TO THE MILLER FAMILY LIFE: WE became closer and moved farther apart in different ways, most of them strange, a few of them normal.

The ozone machines kept bringing in money for the family. My sisters were now buying better clothes with the money my mother gave them.

For my birthday in October 1938, my grandmother once again changed my life. She gave me a four-month membership to the Hollywood YMCA and a basketball. The first time I played on a hardwood floor and heard the squeak of my shoes as I changed directions, basketball became my addiction. I started riding my bicycle the two miles each way after school and had a lot of coaching help from a man named Jewels Runyan. Riding home in the dark after playing for two hours on the hardwood floor, I was thinking about doing the same thing the next day instead of doing my homework. I was lousy, but eager to learn. Some Saturdays that winter we played for three or four hours at Griffith Park. I was hooked.

During Christmas 1938, my parents gave my sisters fur coats, and me two new pairs of Levi's and a punching bag. My standing with my parents was very much like my standing with my classmates: I was mostly invisible to them. In January 1939, at age 14, I graduated from Thomas Starr King Junior High on a Friday. On Monday, walking alone into John Marshall High School and being thrown into the middle of hundreds of older kids was something I was not prepared for: walking down the high school hallways with crowds of kids whose lives were mostly about after-school dates at soda fountains, activities in student clubs, and school dances was alien to me.

I didn't know how to get along with my classmates, so I retreated into my withdrawn mode—still the little kid from Topanga Canyon. I never volunteered for anything. I had a couple of friends from Scout Troop 20, but that was pretty much my circle of acquaintances.

As I began to gain more confidence on an ice-skating rink, on a ski slope, or on a breaking wave, I became reasonably talkative. Starting in a basketball game helped me feel accepted. On weekday afternoons, I played pickup basketball at the Hollywood YMCA. On Fridays, I skated at the Pan Pacific ice rink on Beverly Boulevard. On Saturdays and Sundays, I hitchhiked to the beach or played basketball all day at Griffith Park.

Football was not for me: I didn't like other guys ramming into me and giving me body bruises. The game also meant standing around after every play, longer if someone got hurt. In baseball, you spent most of your time on the bench or in the field waiting for the batter to hit the ball to you. I liked basketball because it was practically a nonstop game, and I was a wired kid.

The downside was that the YMCA had no spectators standing around to cheer when anyone made a good play. I was 14 and would have responded if someone had taken notice. My father was not interested; my mother was too busy at her ozone clinic and feeding the family to give me 10 seconds to listen to a replay of my basketball games. At this point in my life, scouting got left behind. Hiking was fun, but basketball was more fun, and it took over my afternoons. Surfing was fantastic and took over my weekends. As I gradually learned, girls had attractions scouting couldn't match, and after a while, I geared up my courage to ask girls out on movie dates—though I never got into "going steady."

At the same time, my mother no longer was available to even make our school lunches. Every morning, it was a toss-up whether or not the refrigerator had leftovers of any kind. It was often empty, except for breakfast cereal and milk. My sisters solved their own lunch problem with their weekly allowances by buying lunch at school, but my mother had never given me an allowance. I was still getting up at 4:30 two mornings a week to deliver the *Los Angeles Downtown Shopping News* before going to school, earning $2 a week so I could buy lunch if I wanted.

I must have read something about balanced nutrition for athletes because I stopped indulging in milkshakes and started eating white-bread sandwiches—bread that cost 10 cents a loaf and was called "Wonder Bread." Back then, it was high praise to call something "the greatest thing since sliced bread." A loaf of Wonder Bread, combined with slices of bologna sausage costing 20 cents, lasted me five days. To go with the daily Wonder Bread sandwiches was a 10-cents-a-quart carton of milk that I wrapped in a wet towel to keep it cool by evaporation in my locker until lunchtime.

Every day in the schoolyard at lunch, I polished off my quart of milk and my two Wonder Bread-bologna-and-mustard sandwiches, and ate my way out of what could have been a slowly growing case of malnutrition. My daily afternoon basketball sessions began to get more energetic.

Back at Franklin Avenue, however, the biggest change in our family life came as my mother lifted the family into the middle class by gearing up her ozone clinic treatments with the help of my grandfather. He brought a new ozone generator in every so often. Each new machine gave my mother the chance to treat at least two more patients every hour, 16 more patients every day. Ailing middle-class patients and the desperate poor lined up shoulder-to-shoulder from early morning on. Inside, patients filled every chair in the living room and the den. My mother was fine in the midst of this disorder, but it depressed everyone else in the house, especially my father.

He was upset because he could no longer spend his day pulling up a chair and talking to patients. He must have complained, because my mother started giving him walking-around money so he could go out and have a good time. For my father, that meant going elsewhere to impress people with his wit and wisdom, bending the ears of Hollywood neighbors in cafes and bars, coming home only when it was dinnertime. My sisters also began to go missing at dinner. They were now dating without fail each Friday and Saturday night and sometimes weeknights as well. It was easy to not get home until after dinner and make my own dinner out of leftovers. During the three years of high school, the whole family seldom sat down to dinner together other than at Thanksgiving and Christmas. We never did celebrate anyone's birthday.

But still, life was very good for me: a room of my own, a bicycle, basketball shoes, a YMCA membership, and a $2 a week job delivering the *Shopping News.*

By January 1939, my mother had 10 ozone generators running at the same time, each with a patient attached. The house looked like a sci-fi film. None of the family hung around during the day—it was too weird: From 8:30 A.M. to 9:30 at night, patients were in our house. My mother now proceeded to change that.

Late in 1939, she purchased the Albert Miller family's very first house. Apart from giving my father all the money he wanted for liquor, my mother had always been smart about money, and house prices in the Depression had bottomed out. In time, my mother's modest cash flow was enough to buy a house. I'm sure that my grandmother Edith cosigned the purchase papers. The family moved from an overcrowded one-story, two-bedroom clinic/house on a noisy street to a four-bedroom, one-bath, two-story house on Berendo Street in a quiet, suburban part of Hollywood, with shade trees and large lawns and no patients. It was a buyer's market. My mother got the house for $500 down and $50 a month, a total price of $5,000.

It was just in time. Mary Helen and Betty Jane, or "BJ," were going on 17 and 16 respectively, gliding into the marriageable age bracket. This stage of their lives called for testing various beauty aids and clothing fashions in privacy. This fit in with my mother's long-term plan for enhancing the Miller family status, which pivoted on having both daughters marry well. My mother was definitely not counting on me to raise the family social status by marrying a rich girl.

My room was only half the size of my sisters' rooms but had a big closet that held all my former Boy Scout camping gear, ski equipment, swim fins, belly board, beach towels, straw hat, and the tools necessary to repair my bicycle. Plus, I was outside most of the time, so I didn't need much room.

My mother was not through with her surprises yet. She leased a store on Vermont Avenue, a 10-minute drive from Berendo Street, moved all 10 of her ozone generators there, and put up a sign over the door advertising the "Miller-Ray Ozone Clinic." She kept the door open from nine in the morning until nine at night. She bought herself a new car so she could commute. Then, as a pacifier, she bought my father his own car, so he would not complain about the fact that she was hardly ever home. The Berendo Street house had a detached garage where my father parked his car to keep rain from spotting it. My mother parked her car alongside the garage. This made it official. The Millers were now living the American Dream: a two-car family with a garage and a lawn.

Did my father now sign on to become an upstanding middle-class head of the household? Not at all. He still earned no paycheck, of course—and he outdid himself in destructive behavior. Just as I had begun courting my first girlfriends by riding them on my bicycle, my father began courting his first (I assume) extra-marital "girlfriend" by taking her riding in his own car. He began to drive every day at four in the afternoon to pick up his new friend at a streetcar stop after her day as a clerk in a downtown department store. It was an education knowing this in detail at the time, but it was better when it appeared my mother was apparently relieved rather than upset at my father's daily disappearance. With my father out from underfoot, my mother could concentrate on the ozone healing business. She had become a businesswoman. She must have felt my father would be around whenever she needed him. He had no one else to buy his clothes and give him walking-around money to support his drinking habit.

During the winter of 1939–1940, I took my second trip skiing. It had been a whole year since my first ski trip to Mt. Waterman. On this trip, five members of my Boy Scout troop and I decided we just had to go play in the snow before it all melted. One of them had a driver's license and borrowed his father's car to take us to the mountains. We stuffed our gear in the car and tied our skis and sleds behind the two side tire mounts of the car. Side mounts on the front fenders of a car's running boards held spare tires because flat tires were a frequent occurrence. It had been a minimal snow winter in Southern California, so we drove almost a hundred miles southeast to the village of Hemet at the base of the 10,000-foot San

Jacinto, which is the huge ridge that rises over Palm Springs, one of the few Southern California mountains with any patches of real snow left on it that year. It was a three-mile hike from Hemet up to the snowline, but in the days before lifts in Southern California, climbing was the only way to gain real altitude. Only about five resorts in the U.S. had ski lifts that winter—skiing was still in its infancy.

The six of us started climbing toward a patch of snow on San Jacinto that turned out to be about 75 yards long and 20 yards wide. But it could definitely be skied, if you knew how. This was my second ski day with my primitive, secondhand skis, and I was still struggling with those 4-footers with leather toe-strap bindings, no edges, and no heel bindings. I had a sketchy idea of how to get around a 90-degree turn from my first ski outing, at Mt. Waterman. However, we had a great time skiing, riding sleds, and razzing each other. The sun started to drop to the horizon as we hiked back down to the car, getting there at sunset. The driver said he was fine, not tired, and ready to drive. We all got in and promptly fell asleep, each tucked into one corner of the sedan.

The next thing I heard was screaming, and I was pinned against the roof of the car, which was flying through the air upside down. The driver had been going too fast through a sharp left turn and had flipped the car so it landed on its roof. After all the broken glass settled, someone asked if everyone was OK. I said, "I'm OK, but I think my arm is broken. It looks weird, and I can't move it." The others managed to squeeze out of the car and open the back door. They slowly hauled my body out onto the grass, piling their jackets around me for warmth.

It was obvious that I had broken my left arm and dislocated my wrist. I lay there in the moonlight, telling them not to let anybody move me until they were able to get a doctor. I got really lucky when a car drove up the road and stopped. The driver was a veterinarian who had just finished delivering half a dozen lambs at a nearby sheep ranch.

He took a look at how my arm and wrist were lying and said, "It's not a problem. Why don't you guys hold his elbow back and I'll pull on his hand and that will reset the dislocated wrist, and the broken bone in the arm should just fall into place." They held my elbow, the vet pulled my hand, and accompanied by a sharp pain, the bone in my arm and my dislocated wrist indeed slipped into place. The adrenaline rush must have eased the pain. He brought out a roll of bandage and splinted my arm, made a temporary sling, and tied the sling against my body, telling me to avoid banging the arm against anything hard.

This was my second encounter with a veterinarian. They were much cheaper than regular doctors!

In the meantime, my five friends were addressing the upside-down car problem. Pushing, lifting, and grunting, they managed to tip the car back up onto all four wheels—no worse for wear but with big dents here and there and a lot of grass and mud stuck on the roof. The driver got in, turned the key, and amazingly the engine started, and the car humped its way back onto the road. The rest of us got in, and we drove cautiously back to Hollywood, arriving at Berendo Street about three o'clock in the morning. As I walked to the front door, every light inside the house went on.

My mother had been worried about me and was still up. She opened the door and took a step back, asking, "What happened?" I said our car had flipped over and that I had broken my arm, but that it was now set and splinted. I then projectile-vomited all over her. She was steady as could be. She wiped off the worst of it, led me up to my room, and after I lowered myself carefully into bed, she pulled the sheet and blanket over me without a word of reproach. So far in my life, I never had a pill of any kind, not even an aspirin. That was because of my grandmother's Christian Science influence. In her own strange way, my mother cared for me. However, she was so driven to make a living, so driven to please my father whenever he was around, and so driven to please my two sisters when they were around, she only got around to me when she had any time left over, which was hardly ever. She truly had no time for herself.

But I was living a fantastic life of undisciplined freedom.

CHAPTER EIGHT

1939–1941

Surfing, Basketball, Skating, and Dating; Just Get Up and Try

My YMCA basketball sessions ended in the spring of 1940. Summer vacation was on the horizon, and the weather was getting hot. I wanted to surf.

Learning to surf is a lot harder than learning to ski. You can start out learning to ski by going down an almost-flat slope and proceeding toward the bottom at a slow speed, while you figure out how to make your skis turn or stop. However, waves run at a speed of 12 to 15 miles an hour, and there is no slowing them down. Once you are on a wave, you have to turn on the wave and go across it without the nose of your board burying itself in the bottom of the wave, or your ride is going to be short and possibly disastrous. The face of a wave is a shakier platform than solid, packed snow.

Luckily for us high school kids from Hollywood, falling off the board at San Onofre and Palos Verdes was not a problem, because there were underlying reefs so the water depth remained shallow a long way out. At low tide, you have to paddle a hundred yards out before the water gets 8 feet deep. The idea is to get a long, fast ride. The waves that form over a reef become steep and then break. When you catch a big wave and turn across it, you have a chance to ride that wave a long distance.

When the word was passed that the surf was up at San Onofre, and one of us who had reached 16 (I was still a few months away) had a license and the loan of a car, we all met somewhere in Hollywood late on Friday nights. Carrying sleeping bags and committing to splitting the cost of gas plus the cost of parking at the beach, we drove the 60 miles south to San Onofre. Back then, it was OK to sleep on the beach, but it cost a dollar for a parking sticker good for 24 hours. The man who leased the beach from the state patrolled occasionally, and if your car did not have today's sticker, he'd confiscate your sleeping bag.

We usually got to the beach at 2 A.M. and stretched out in the sand in our sleeping bags. In the morning, with luck, we woke up to the sound of big waves breaking way outside on the reef. Most of that summer, I paddled my board out to where the waves were breaking and tried to catch one and fell off at least 973 times. Then one day I caught one way outside, and Ted Nicholson shouted, "You've caught it! Stand up." I stood up and rode the wave all the way to the beach. I had never done that before, and it was an awesome feeling. Meeting Ted in junior high was a stroke of luck; after he introduced me to surfing, we've stayed friends through all the years, with both of us now in our 90s.

I'll remember that ride forever. The sun was hot, the water was glassy, and the board seemed to go forever across the face of the wave. I had just done something that very few people in the world had ever done. In 1939, there were fewer than 300 surfers in all of California.

IN THE FALL OF 1939, BASKETBALL PRACTICE BEGAN AT MY HIGH SCHOOL, and I found out the school teams had a point system: to play varsity you had to weigh a minimum number of pounds for your height. At 14 years old, 5-foot-8, and 130 pounds, I was too skinny to meet the minimum mark. There still was the junior varsity, or B team. Three full years of riding my bicycle everywhere and two months of playing basketball pickup games at the YMCA had given me legs and wind. That fall, I became a member of the John Marshall B team. The B team played against the other schools' junior varsities before the varsity games.

One Saturday when we had heard that the surf at San Onofre was flat, instead of surfing I rode my bicycle to Griffith Park. There I got into a half-court basketball game on asphalt. In Los Angeles, you can comfortably play basketball outside in the winter. A couple of players from the John Marshall varsity were playing on the other side, but after half an hour, it was fairly even. Both sides took a five-minute break, and one of the varsity players lit up a cigarette. I remembered what my great-uncle Charlie had told me about smoking and what it did to your lungs and stomach. My thought was, "Next year I'm going to go after that guy's place on the varsity team."

That same winter, I started serious ice-skating. I could never seem to get enough sports in my life. Friday evenings, I went on skates I'd bought with my paper route money. It cost 25 cents a night, but what a great feeling of building speed around the rink, going very fast. I had nothing waiting for me at home besides homework. No contest there.

However, my grandmother Edith, as always, was keeping tabs on me. She remembered that during the two years I had lived at Coronado Terrace with her, I had fun drawing Mickey Mouse and Donald Duck figures from the Sunday funnies. So for my 1939 Christmas present, she gave me *Fun with a Pencil*, a book just published by Andrew Loomis dedicated to "all those who love the pencil." I began to draw cartoons, depicting students and teachers in situations that were good for a laugh.

That next month, January 1940, at the beginning of my second year at John Marshall, I enjoyed sketching cartoons so much that I switched from my class of engineering drawing to commercial art. It was a no-brainer for me. My grandmother had changed my life once more. Unlike schoolwork, drawing gave me a lot of enjoyment.

Once when our social studies teacher assigned us to write two speeches and give them in class, I chose the ongoing war in Europe as my first speech topic. Germany had just frightened the world by occupying Denmark and Norway, and World War II had started. Despite that fact, I really did not feel strongly about a war on another continent; I barely got a passing grade. When I finished, the social studies teacher suggested I find a topic that really interested me for the second speech.

I chose bodysurfing. I drew a diagram on the blackboard, showing how waves worked and how you held your body to take advantage of them. The teacher and our class were all impressed—many of them had never even been to the beach. I got an "A."

THAT FALL, MY OLDEST SISTER, MARY HELEN, WHO WAS THREE CLASSES ahead of me at John Marshall High, entered the University of Southern California in the center of Los Angeles. California's state university, the University of California at Los Angeles (UCLA), was much bigger and a lot less expensive. However, USC definitely had more social cachet. My mother liked that. Her profit from the ozone business had been rising, so she could enroll her daughter in the more expensive university. It cost a whopping $10 per unit or about $150 per semester. Add two zeros to that amount for today's tuition.

The campus was six miles from home, which was a trek with a couple of transfers by bus and streetcar. So my mother bought a 1937 Buick Phaeton convertible for the commute. As I recall, she paid $125 for it, a fairly high price for a three-year-old car, but it was already a classic, as only a couple hundred Phaetons were ever built. It was a racy, four-door convertible that carried a lot of status. On this one, my mother was not just going middle class, but ritzy middle class. She wanted her daughters to one-up the other kids.

Basketball season began at John Marshall in September 1940, and I had bulked up enough to hold my own against anyone else trying out for the varsity team. It was easy to outrun my cigarette-smoking friend from a year ago at Griffith Park. By midseason, I had taken over his place as first-string guard on the varsity team, and was on my way to earning my high school varsity letterman's sweater as a junior.

Basketball then had no status. The big deal was football. Our basketball coach was not even a former player, but a geometry teacher who was paid $5 a week extra to keep us in line. He knew less about basketball than his players did. We didn't have any plays; we just played as if every game were a pickup game. That season, Hollywood High beat Belmont High, John Marshall beat Hollywood High, and Belmont High beat John Marshall, so the season ended in a three-way tie. There was no playoff. What mattered was that I had gotten in hours of exciting play against the top players in the league, which was what turned me on.

In October 1940, I turned 16. My life was brightened by a blaze of light that occurs only once in a lifetime: passing my driver's license test. With that, my mother told my sisters that rights to the Buick were mine when they were not using it, as if my mother had suddenly recognized me as nearly an adult. Both my sisters were out on dates every Friday and Saturday evening and sometimes a couple of nights a week, so there were many chances to drive the Phaeton. Neither one of my sisters ever had a job of any kind, so they didn't need the car to drive to work on weekends.

Having the use of my sisters' car proved magic. Any girl I asked out said "yes" if she were free. My social life accelerated like a rocket, from occasionally riding a date on my bicycle handlebars to at least one date per weekend.

There was a huge public ballroom, the Glendale Civic Auditorium, six miles from Berendo Street and the Pasadena Civic Auditorium just a bit farther. These auditoriums were converted to huge dance halls on weekends and normally had one of the famous "Big Bands" of the Swing Era. California kids danced weekly to the music of Artie Shaw, Glenn Miller, and Stan Kenton at 25 cents a head. When I went, I usually followed that by heading for a drive-in restaurant in Glendale. Bob's Big Boy Restaurant had good-looking carhops in short skirts who brought out double-decker hamburgers at 15 cents and giant, extra-thick milkshakes for another 15 cents.

It was a bargain if I took a date: We each had hamburgers, milkshakes, and a whole night of dancing for $1.10, not including gas. (Gas was now up to between 11 and 15 cents a gallon; I might burn 20 cents worth on a date.) I replaced the gas except when I didn't have the money, but my mother covered my sisters' gas costs.

Norway's Sonja Henie had won the Olympic figure-skating gold in 1928, 1932, and 1936, and then very successfully went on to star in the movies. In 1940, my interest in skating picked up another notch when Hollywood's Sonja built the area's first outdoor ice rink in Westwood Village. It was different skating around the Westwood rink in the bright, warm California sun.

In 1940, I had custom-made racing skates with offset blades, allowing me to lean farther to the inside of the track without hitting the ice and releasing the blade. The more you could lean without slipping, the faster you could go. The skates cost me an enormous $28, the most expensive item I had ever bought in my life. I really wanted to become a faster speed skater.

I paid for those skates by unloading Railway Express freight cars at the

Los Angeles rail yards during my Christmas vacation in 1940. I looked less liable to keel over than the drunks standing next to me in the hiring line, so I was put to work unloading 100-pound boxes of salmon shipped by rail from Seattle. The pay was so good, 25 cents an hour, that I covered the price of my $28 skates in three weeks.

This was just the beginning of "the Buick and I" era that brought me a whole new chapter of my surfing life. There were always other surfing friends willing to pay the gas and parking fee at the beach. In effect, the barrier separating me from surfing—lack of transportation—had dropped to zero. I now surfed almost every weekend.

I got to know some of the older surfers who became great friends, several lasting my lifetime. I was grateful to my sisters for bringing that Buick into my life.

ALL THROUGH THE YEAR 1940, THE NEWS FROM EUROPE WAS GRIM, AND the U.S. was in no shape to wage war. Our standing Army consisted of 174,000 regulars and 200,000 National Guardsmen, and at that time, we had only the 17th largest army in the world. In 1940, Congress passed the "U.S. Selective Training and Service Act," aka "the draft," to begin to build the U.S. armed forces to a size that was consistent with the nation's status. All U.S. males between 21 and 36 had to register with their local draft boards. The names that were picked in the lotteries got a year's training in the U.S. Army and became standby Army reserves. However, none of the kids or their older brothers whom I knew thought America would ever go to war. First, it was not a popular idea, and second, Europe was too far away. The isolationists of the time remained the most powerful bloc of men in Congress.

My own mind was completely tuned to surfing that summer of 1941. Thanks to my sisters' infrequent use of the Buick, I was out surfing at least once or sometimes twice a week. A few times I took the Buick to Manhattan Beach, where I met Ward Baker, the same age and just as quiet and surf-crazy as I was. We became great friends and would spend future winters together as full-time ski bums.

That summer was the first in which I had a chance to watch Pete Peterson, a great surfer and stuntman. In the 1930s, Peterson had won a couple of surfing championships at Malibu and one at San Onofre and was starring in "Pete Smith Specialties," a series of comic movie shorts, featuring stunts. Pete lived in Santa Monica where he worked as a lifeguard, but he often surfed at Malibu. He was so smooth and elegant on the board; he became for surfing in the 1940s the sort of figure Stein Eriksen became for skiing in the 1950s.

In the fall of 1941, my sister BJ enrolled at USC just as I was nearing my senior year at John Marshall. Dating had become more interesting, and girls were pretty neat. There had been a lot of great ice-skating. I was able to play varsity basketball during both my junior and senior years. There was not much missing from my life other than the lack of family attention, but not knowing the difference, I was having a great time.

However, the news coming from Europe on the war was so bad that even a Congress that was politically determined to keep the U.S. neutral voted for more war readiness and revised the Selective Service Act in 1941. In a year, I would have to register for the draft, but I was not worried. I felt, along with most Americans, that war with Germany was never going to happen unless the U.S. was planning to take over the whole of Western Europe. That feeling disappeared in a flash one Sunday morning early in the winter.

I had taken my surfboard to the beach at Malibu in the Buick, and it was strange that no one else was there. I surfed on knee-high waves until I got tired and went to sleep in the hot sand. As the sun began to sink and the wind came up, I awoke. I had my usual gallon jug of water on the hood of the Buick so that the sun could heat the water enough to take a quick shower to wash off the sand and salt.

I loaded my 100-pound, solid-redwood surfboard and took my warm shower, put a shirt on, and swung the Buick onto the Pacific Coast Highway, heading south toward Santa Monica en route to Hollywood. There was not a single car in sight. Something was wrong. Turning on the car radio, I heard the rebroadcast of President Roosevelt's speech from earlier that day. Japanese planes had bombed Pearl Harbor in Hawaii early that morning of December 7, 1941.

America was at war.

CHAPTER NINE

1942

Since I Didn't Know Where I Was Going, I Knew I Would End Up There

HIGH SCHOOL GRADUATION CAME A MONTH AND A HALF AFTER PEARL Harbor, and the shock waves were still reverberating. A very strange, new phase of my life began. For the first time, my mother had begun talking about my schooling, something she had never mentioned before. She was insisting that I go to college. I had just barely made it through high school. Until then, I had taken my cue from my parents and thought I was probably just a dumb kid, so why all this fuss about college all of a sudden?

High school classes bored me. Homework was worse, and I rarely did it, because it took time away from the good things, like basketball and surfing. I ended up in the bottom third of the class. There were no cheers if I got an "A" anyway, which I almost never did, so why try? From my point of view, I had done my duty: I had graduated, and in October 1942, I would be registering for the draft, so what was the point? I thought college was for those who wanted to be attorneys, engineers, and schoolteachers or to meet and marry someone. Not me. I wanted to become an animator at Disney studios—better still, go to Hawaii and surf every day.

After I loudly declared "No college for me," my mother began to fear that I completely lacked middle-class goals. BJ and Mary Helen were the good examples, both of them at USC studying for their B.A. degrees while I was headed toward being a nonachieving younger brother. My mother insisted I had to change my attitude. "You have to go to college. Everyone who becomes anyone goes to college," she explained. She then pulled out her ace in the hole and alerted my grandmother.

The two of them put their heads together and underwrote a student loan for $125, cosigned by my grandfather and covering the tuition for my first semester at USC. Whether I wanted to or not, I was going to go to college.

At USC, I was no longer able to slide by with minimal effort as I had done in high school, giving me at best a mass of C's. USC was a lot harder. They gave me two or three quizzes every week to prove how much I had absorbed. The quizzes killed me, but I didn't dare fail them. I slaved away in my room night after night actually reading my assigned lessons, goaded by the guilt of being put through school at my mother's, and especially grandmother's, expense. I discovered I wasn't as dumb as I thought.

THE WINTER OF 1942 WAS MY BREAKTHROUGH SEASON FOR SKIING: learning to connect my turns, to ski 40 feet on an intermediate slope without braking in an awkward, leg-splitting snowplow or falling down in a dumb body-stop on a nearly flat slope. Also, the snow was unusually good for Southern California that year.

To put this in context: In order to enjoy skiing in Southern California, you had to be crazy. At sea level, Southern California is a land of palms and coconut trees, a subtropical zone where onshore winds bring in rain some of the winter time. To ski, you first had to be at least 7,000 feet above sea level, where it was reliably cold, and with luck, where it had snowed enough to cover the ice patches. Before snowmaking, Southern California skiers prayed for snow, asking that they be allowed to ski for at least two weekends in a row before the snow was rained out or melted.

Southern California's low latitude was not the only problem. The other was that the U.S. was fighting a World War on two fronts, and at that time, losing on both. The enormous American effort straining to reverse the situation led to rationing. The military was burning a lot of gasoline, so it had to be rationed. There was no rubber, so tires were rationed. The Japanese had cut off our sources from across the Pacific.

Despite rationing, I had the biggest ski winter of my life to date, and we skied Mt. Waterman almost every weekend. I bought myself top-of-the-line gear at the one ski shop in town, Hollywood Tennis and Golf. The new skis had "micro-matic" toe irons, featuring adjustment screws so the sides of the toe iron could be widened to fit different boots, much like old-fashioned metal roller skates. The heel springs pushed the boot hard enough into the toe irons to keep the toe from coming out. At the same time, they allowed the boot heel to rise up, so walking on the flat was easy compared to walking with bindings of today. Many ski areas did not have lifts—or if there were a lift, the trail layouts were primitive. If the trail did not go back to the lift base, and many trails didn't, you had to cross-country ski back to the base of the lift to get your next ride; therefore, being able to "walk" on skis was important.

Because of the lack of reliable release bindings, the injury rate was about six times the rate of today. Depending on how tough the trails were, the injury rate at a given ski area could be as high as 10 percent over the course of a day. If you skied 10 days at a given area, statistically you had a 100 percent chance of getting hurt. (So statistically, the best thing to do was to ski as many different places as possible. Yeah, OK, that's probably not how it works.)

My brand-new hickory skis cost a hefty $19.95. Considering the magnitude of my purchase, Hollywood Tennis and Golf threw in a pair of bamboo poles. They had the standard curved iron points needed to hold when scrambling over the large patches of ice typical for Southern California trail skiing in the era before ice could be broken up with grooming.

Nor was there any snowmaking: That wouldn't come for decades. So, the day before a weekend, a snow report either kicked off a ski trip or canceled it. Hollywood Tennis and Golf phoned the ski areas every Friday and chalked reports on the blackboard hung on its back wall. The closest sizeable ski area to Hollywood was Mt. Waterman, and it now had the only chairlift in Southern California. The other California chairlift was at the Sugar Bowl on Donner Summit in northern California, too far away for a day trip from Hollywood. Lodging at a ski area was way over our budget, so it was Waterman or nothing. (There were fewer than 15 chairlifts in North America: Sun Valley had six, and there was one each at Stowe, Timberline in Oregon, and Mt. Tremblant, and Alta had two. That's 13—gotta figure out the others when my brain gets back.)

The Mt. Waterman chair had been built in 1941 by Lynn Newcomb, the owner and founder. Newcomb saw a chance for profit in the new sport if he could build a chairlift. He visited Sun Valley and Timberline, making sketches of Sun Valley's Dollar Mountain chair and Timberline's Magic Mile chair. He then got the Forest Service to give him a permit and proceeded to hire someone to bolt his lift design together. The resulting chairlift was rickety. It creaked and swayed. Today, you might be afraid to ride it. It was slow, with 300 passengers an hour, and only if running regularly, which it usually didn't. Getting to the top without having the lift stop twice was pure luck, but it sure beat climbing.

The trail design lacked variety. The main lift slope ran at a fairly steep angle all the way to the top. One trail ran under the lift and was too steep for most skiers. Up top, there was a rope tow installed on the easier slopes. There was no cafeteria, flush toilets, or outdoor tables; you ate your lunch in the car or standing or squatting outside. Still the Los Angeles and Hollywood skiers came by the droves, parking on the two-lane, dead-end road leading to Mt. Waterman.

On our typical trip, having set my alarm for 4 A.M., I walked quietly downstairs to start my sisters' car. Their 1937 Buick Phaeton convertible was a sports car designed for four, but we were nearly always six or seven. Needing elbow room to steer, the other two in front took turns sitting on top of each other's lap. The three or four in back had to find clever ways to pack themselves in without having an arm or any other body part fall asleep.

We stopped at the first gas station that was open. Rationing allotments were tight, so gas stations often ran out of fuel. Once we started up the mountain, I drove slowly to prevent our bald tires from fishtailing on the hairpin, ice-covered turns and steep switchbacks. Fender-benders were common. Skiing was a risk sport, even before you got there.

The total combined ski knowledge of all of us in the car still added up to almost zero. We were surfers, but not real skiers—yet. We'd all been at least bodysurfers since we were old enough to beg someone to haul our skinny bodies to the beach. We had not spent 15 cents on ski lessons. We could understand equipment, though. Our conversations were about the latest hickory and laminated ash skis, the different kinds of base wax we had, and the choice of running wax we were rubbing on bases from our little waxing tubes, all depending on the kind of snow that we had when we got there.

We had saved up enough money to buy the all-day ticket for $2.50. Then, there was the standard minimum half-hour wait in the lift line. We took advantage of it to chat with attractive girls in line. Once we got on, it was a fun but masochistic ride. Every time the cable-grip weld above your seat rode across the small wheels on each tower arm, a sharp, jarring shock ran through the metal chair and into your sitting bones. But did we complain? Never. Any uphill device, no matter how slow and painful, was so much better than climbing.

There were a couple of instructors at Mt. Waterman, but we didn't have money to spend on lessons. We would occasionally stop where we could overhear what instructors were telling their classes. Then we would try to do it. Our 7-foot-3-inch-long wood skis were stiff, with minimum side cut, and it was easy for the terrain to twist the front of the ski so the edge would not hang on.

At lunchtime, we stood around munching peanut butter sandwiches with jam or mayonnaise—anything to give the flavor of peanut butter a little diversity. (None of us would have survived the Depression and World War II without showing signs of malnutrition had not peanut butter been available as a mainstream protein when butter and meat were so tightly rationed.)

At 4 P.M. when the lift closed, we skied down slowly as if to lengthen the day, but actually, getting back down the steep slopes to the bottom of the ski area was an exercise in controlled terror. We tried to make the turns we had practiced, but getting into the fall line for the first turn down the steep trail kept spooking us. We would sometimes traverse until we ended up on the uphill side of a tree. We leaned against the tree for balance and did an uphill kick turn. Then we traversed in the opposite direction.

After skiing, going down the access road was a test of courage and arm strength. When the California sun came out, the snowbanks on the sides of the road started to melt around noon even at 7,000 feet, layering a thin film of water on the road. The water froze again by late afternoon, turning the road into a slanted skating rink. The ride back to Hollywood was two hours of being half-asleep in close quarters, inhaling the reek of wet wool and drying sweat. Before splitting, everyone agreed, "Next weekend, same time, same place, only leave earlier so we can park closer to the mountain." We'd just had a great day of skiing. We couldn't wait to do it again.

Then came the dull, weekday classes at USC. Most of us were dealing with the small difficulties caused by rationing, but suddenly, some of our fellow Californians were losing everything, with government help. That April, U.S. Federal Agents rounded up all citizens or immigrants of Japanese blood on the West Coast. All 120,000 Japanese on the West Coast were sent to "relocation centers" inland, without a shred of evidence that a single Japanese person had ever shown any interest in spying or sabotage on behalf of their relatives across the Pacific. I knew one of them well—a Japanese gardener I befriended who lived in a room over a garage in the Franklin Avenue neighborhood. One day that spring, I happened to ride my bike past the garage and saw that his car was no longer parked there. The owner of the house told me, "They came and got him." This friendly little guy was as harmless as could be, but it didn't matter.

We were at war, and war is irrational. And fighting in the war was where I was headed. In the meantime, I was industriously following my plan to make the most of the time left by getting in as much surfing, skiing, and ice-skating as possible and keeping my grades as high as possible so I could put off the inevitable for as long as possible. The active part of my life balanced the negatives: I learned finally that studying was worthwhile so I could get a better position in the armed forces. I had, however, signed up for courses whose classes all ended by noon so that if the surf was good, we could head for the beach in the Buick and get in a couple of hours surfing or hang around playing pickup basketball with the other gym rats. I did think about going out for varsity basketball but lacked the confidence to get out there on the floor during tryouts that fall. As a "walk-on" I would have to replace someone who was already on the team on a scholarship because of his outstanding high school playing and scholastic record.

I saved my serious athletic effort for speed skating at the Pan Pacific Auditorium, sometimes twice a week. I was aiming for the Southern California speed skating championship, sponsored by the Los Angeles evening paper, *The Herald Examiner*. My skating efforts came to a climax at midwinter, soon after going to a ballet costume store on Hollywood Boulevard and laying out a big $4.50 for a pair of black ballet tights that hugged my skinny legs. My legs were so skinny everyone laughed when I skated out onto the ice. Nevertheless, I managed to qualify for the finals in the "B" division with the help of my form-fitting pants, finishing third in a field of 10 in the final "B" division elimination race of a dozen laps. It was the first trophy I had ever won.

PART TWO

Growing Out

At Pre-Midshipmen's School at USC in 1943. U.S. NAVY PHOTO

CHAPTER TEN

1942–1943

USC; a Surfer Joins the Navy; the Major Cause of Accidents Is the Stupidity of the Victim

In May, at the end of my first freshman semester at USC, I needed to earn more money. The summer and fall might be the last time I could go surfing before being called into the military, and I wanted to make sure I had enough money on hand to go every weekend. I was able to get a job with the Arrowhead and Puritas Water Company in Los Angeles, which turned out bottled drinking water delivered in 5-gallon glass bottles to their residential customers. Thousands of gallons of mountain spring water from Lake Arrowhead 60 miles south was trucked twice a week to the bottling works in huge tank trucks.

By the end of the summer, I had saved up $200. I quit a week before the fall semester started at USC, borrowed my sisters' Buick, and rented a cabin at Topanga Beach for a dollar a day. I cooked on my Coleman stove and shopped at the grocery store on the Pacific Coast Highway, the same store where I traded Coke bottles for penny candy as a 6-year-old.

There was a hurricane off of the west coast of Mexico, and the surf got bigger every day. I had only been there a day when Pete Peterson, the super waterman, stopped on his way from Santa Monica. We saw a P-38

Army Air Force interceptor with its twin-bodied fuselage flying so low that it was obvious something had gone very wrong.

The plane was probably on a test flight from Lockheed in Burbank when one engine started failing. Whatever the problem, the pilot dropped the big plane flat onto the water and managed to skid it along on the surface. It threw up a huge wake and then stopped dead in the water about 100 yards out in front of my cabin. Pete immediately raced into the water with his surfboard, paddled out, and pulled the pilot, wearing his life jacket, onto his surfboard.

We walked him up to the phone booth at the Topanga grocery, knowing that he was in trouble. As the pilot called his boss, we snuck away to the beach and paddled back out to where the waves were breaking.

I wondered what a guy says to his commander when he has sunk an airplane worth a ton of money. The P-38 was a great design, the first aircraft ever to fly over 400 miles an hour, and it already had a fine record for sending Japanese planes into the ocean. I wondered if they would be able to get it out of the water … maybe it's still there.

The next day the surf was bigger and shaped better at Malibu than at Topanga, but the beach always had a big wire fence keeping us from using it. The owners wanted to keep everyone out. Pete came prepared. He took out a pair of giant pliers, cut a hole in the fence, reconnected the fence wires, and we spent the day riding the really good Malibu waves. We saw no one guarding the beach, and as long as we stayed out in the water, even if the legal owner's guards had been around, there was nothing they could do about us.

After a great day of surfing, Peterson left to get some sleep before he had to start his job as a lifeguard. Those big waves rolled in all week, which brought a lot of other surfers. It was the best surfing and the most freedom that I had ever had. There was no one to answer to—no parents, no sisters, no teachers. I realized again how good just plain freedom was.

I RETURNED TO BERENDO STREET ON THE FIRST OF SEPTEMBER AND, OF course, that feeling of freedom and independence vanished. However, I did make use of my new stash of cash to buy access to the beach and surfing. For $25, I bought a trailer from a neighbor whose son had built it on the rear axle and wheels from a Model T Ford. Then came a clamp-on trailer hitch from Sears and Roebuck, and I rebuilt the trailer to hold surfboards. I could now haul as many as six friends and their 80-pound surfboards to the beach in one Buick-load.

Looking back on all this, I recall much of it quite clearly: I was driven to spend so much time active in sports to the point where it could seem a crazy life. This might possibly be the same drive that later tied me so tightly to filming and my show circuit, but a much more stressful kind of life. Deep down, somehow I must have needed all the pressure, the personal connections, the sports and the waves, the snow and all the excitement involved. Possibly it was growing up so alone and sad, in a houseful of silence. I was making sure on some level, hidden from me, that I would never again be without attention. Years later, when I became an entertainer, I was guaranteeing myself that intoxicant I needed so much—attention. In reality, I was a co-alcoholic of the worst kind ... doing many things so people might like me.

On October 15, 1942, I registered with my local Hollywood draft board. Registering did not mean that the military would send me off to the war front the next day; there was usually a gap between registering and being assigned to train with one of the armed services. Nineteen out of 20 draftees were assigned to the Army.

My surfing friend Ward Baker was going to USC, so we started researching military options that offered more than life in the trenches. The Navy's V-12 officers' training program was available to anyone who had gone to or was going to college. Figuring that in the Navy if your bed got wet, that meant everyone's bed was getting wet, Ward and I decided we preferred being on a ship dodging Japanese bombs and torpedoes to fighting the Germans in the trenches. Not that the Navy was such a safe place. By the time I had to register, almost a year after Pearl Harbor, Japanese planes, ships, and submarines had sunk three U.S. Navy aircraft carriers, three cruisers, and one battleship, with a loss of many thousands of American lives.

I made the decision to sign up for V-12 on my own, without any advice from my parents. At the time, the V-12 was almost full. The Navy allowed anyone who had been accepted to remain in college until called into active duty. The Navy paid the tuition, so I continued going to USC classes until being called for active duty.

During my second semester at USC in the fall of 1942, I changed my major to astrophysics and stellar astronomy. I took analytical geometry, but it was not the complicated astrophysics of today. I also took surveying, an outdoor job that I could work at without being cooped up in an office in case I ever wanted to pursue it as a profession.

Seriously considering a postwar career as an illustrator, I took a few life art classes but could not stop myself from drawing cartoons in the margin alongside my serious attempts to sketch the nude models posed on the stand in front of the class. One day my art teacher came over and said, "Warren, you've got to quit drawing those cartoons. You're never going to be able to make a living as a cartoonist. You've got to get more involved in fine art." I replied, "If fine art is such a high-paying profession, how come you're teaching school?"

This got me a very bad grade from the teacher. It did show, however, that there were a few times that I didn't allow someone to run over me. Furthermore, my cartoons were accepted for a campus magazine called *Wampus.* At some later date, the humor writer Art Buchwald was the editor. Freelancing for the campus magazine started me creating cartoons about life around me, something I have continued to do the rest of my life—usually for fun but sometimes I was paid for them, too.

Loading myself down with these activities made me a very busy guy. In 1942–1943, one of those extracurricular tasks I took on was to design the card stunts for the USC football games. This involved directing the color and placement of placards in the "card stunt section" of 400 students in the USC bleachers. On a signal, this big section of students held up various colored 24-by-24 cards that when viewed from across the field became a picture. We see the stunt all the time on television, now done by a computer. Back then it was laid out physically, following my drawing.

I designed the card stunts for two football seasons: One of them was a portrait of Knute Rockne, the famous coach; another was a P-38 fighter plane. The stunts got a big hoot and holler from the spectators.

The Navy notified me that I would not be called up during the January semester of 1943, the first semester of my sophomore year. So I split my weekends that winter and spring between surfing and skiing.

My gas-rationing situation had eased. Even if I could not round up four friends, I could still go. I had begun dating the daughter of one of the members of the Hollywood rationing board. When I submitted my application for extra gas for my Coleman stove, which used only about a pint a day when it operated at the beach or the mountain, my girlfriend's father made a mistake in his arithmetic, and the card was good for 8 gallons a week instead of 1 gallon a month.

This was a bit on the shady side, but because people used their "E" cards for their outboard gas so they could go fishing, I felt that I, too, ought to be given enough gas to cook on the beach. It was a bit complicated, because it was illegal to pump "E" card gas into a car. I drove to the station and gave the attendant two 5-gallon gas cans for the 8 gallons of gas. After I got around the corner, I poured the gas into the Buick's gas tank. I didn't worry anymore about running short of gas or finding surfers who had an "A" card.

THE SKIING WAS GOOD THAT WINTER. WE WERE AT MT. WATERMAN every Sunday when we were not surfing, thanks to the gas ration cards as well as my summer bankroll. One Sunday in 1943, we drove to Mt. Waterman, but the good weather didn't last. The snow began falling thick and fast about noon. It was terrific skiing, but by 1:30, the owner's son, also named Lynn Newcomb, started telling us to get our cars off the mountain because a huge blizzard was on the way. We managed to get the Buick through the snow, which was already packed into slippery ice from cars spinning out. No one had put chains on, and snow tires would not be invented for another decade. It snowed 24 feet in the next 24 hours, burying cars that could not get out in time. The cars stayed buried for the rest of the winter, all within 50 miles of the Los Angeles City Hall, where the storm arrived in the form of a deluge, causing floods all over the city.

Once back in Hollywood, we all wanted to go skiing the next weekend on all the new snow. Once you were up at snow level, the scenery appeared to be somewhere just north of the South Pole. Some of the roads had been plowed, but the ski resorts were still buried. Instead, we drove up the ridge route toward Bakersfield on Highway 99. Even at that lower elevation, it had still snowed about 8 feet. We found a plowed place to park alongside an abandoned gas station, where the roof had caved in under the weight of the wet snow.

We hacked some steps up the side of the 8-foot snowbank left by the rotary snowplow. On top, we found good terrain, and by this time, after reading my copy of Otto Lang's *Downhill Skiing* at least 10 times, I was able to translate what he wrote in the book to my own muscles to make snowplow turns and bring the skis almost parallel between turns. We climbed and skied what seemed to be miles and miles of this easy, rolling terrain. As it started to get late, we skied back and got into the car for the ride home. I felt slightly different driving, but I could not figure out why.

At about 1 A.M., I woke up in my room at Berendo Street, and my eyes felt as if somebody was dripping grains of hot sand into them. I was snow blind! This is what happens when ultraviolet rays burn the cornea. I lived at home between semesters in a state of total darkness for four days. I wore ski goggles with tape stuck over the eyepieces. If a little ray of light managed to get through, it was as if someone had stabbed my eyes with an ice pick. It was five days before I could go around without taped-up ski goggles. Fortunately, this all occurred during the Christmas holidays, so I didn't miss any classes. I managed to get to Mt. Waterman a couple more times that season to take advantage of the deep snowpack, but I had learned a big lesson: From then on, I always wore dark glasses when the sun was out. (Unfortunately, I didn't learn as much as I should have. After decades of skiing and surfing without sunglasses in the sun's glare, I now have macular degeneration—a terribly debilitating problem if you ever want to read again.)

One weekend, I took a trip to Big Bear in the San Bernardinos with four friends. We skied on the rope tow on a Saturday. At night, the others all went out to dinner, but to save my stash of cash, I had brought along my Coleman stove and cooked a couple of hamburger patties in the motel room before turning in early. The next day we were skiing at Snow Valley, down the road from Big Bear.

Snow Valley had a "sling lift" where eight people standing side-by-side at the bottom hooked themselves up to a sling that hung from a long piece of angle iron that was fastened to the overhead cable. It was a jig-back lift, so that when the lift operator put the engine in gear, it hauled eight skiers up one side of the lift to the top. If one of those eight people fell, he or she would crawl off to the side to let the others continue. Then the fallen skier could ski down and wait their turn in line once again. Picture a T-bar with enough room for eight people at a time.

Surfing, on the other hand, had its own challenges. The National Civil Defense office had ordered a blackout along the Pacific Coast. This was to shield it from Japanese submarines looking for American ships clearly silhouetted against bright background lights. As we approached the coast, signs warned drivers to shut off their headlights and run under parking lights only. As many as 10 Japanese subs were out there, patrolling the Pacific Coast, something that no one mentioned in public at the time for fear of encouraging the Japanese or panicking people. Sub warfare had paid off for Japan already. Within months after Pearl Harbor, the Japanese had torpedoed two freighters, one off of Los Angeles and one off of Santa Barbara.

Although the blackout made it difficult to locate the freighters offshore, the Japanese managed to sink 10 freighters off the coast before the war was over. Without the blackout, there would have been many more losses. Streetlights were turned off, and lights in buildings were blocked by "blackout curtains." Civil Defense wardens patrolled the streets to enforce the blackout, and there were very few civilian cars out at night. It was a dark and lonely coast during the war.

As we would near San Onofre at 2 A.M., often with the pea-soup fog rolling in, the parking lights illuminated no more than 50 feet of the road. It's a miracle that we never had an accident in the dark with the Buick.

During the day, it was a different matter. The Japanese were not out to sink surfboards, so we surfed from dawn to dusk, particularly at San Onofre. Everybody knew everyone else, and the culture had ripened to the point where everyone went by a nickname. Ted was Teddy, Richard was Richie, Bernard was Barney, Tom was Tommy, Bill was Billy, Robert was Bobby, and so on. It went to extremes. One day I was stuck with the name Warnie, and it was printed on my surfboard. My oldest friends still use it today.

FINALLY, ON JUNE 1, 1943, THE NAVY NOTIFIED ME THAT I WAS BEING called to active duty, along with everyone else in the university's V-12 program. This did not mean I was going to be sent to midshipmen's school right away—the Navy had still not worked through its previous batch of recruits. However, my life did change considerably. I was now a student operating under contract to the Navy to take, and pass, courses at USC. I was now a seaman third class, wearing a Naval uniform at all times and subject to all Navy regulations. It was the Navy's attempt to instill discipline in us recruits, but having no discipline required of me while growing up, they had a tough nut to crack. I was given orders to take a month's leave, as required by regulations, to wind up my civilian affairs, say farewell to one and all, and then report back to the Navy's office at USC on July 1.

It was simple. Having no affairs to wind up, I spent the month surfing. Most of the time I was at San Onofre with Gard Chapin and Dorian Paskowitz, two of the best surfers of that era. One really hot day, Gard and I decided to dig a cave in the cliff overlooking the beach to get out of the sun. It turned out to be a wonderfully cool place to sit out the summer heat.

Strange, the things I remember.

CHAPTER ELEVEN

1943

Life in the Navy Becomes a Book

On July 1, 1943, my month of freedom was up. I reported for duty with the Navy at the USC campus, where they assigned me to a platoon, and I was given quarters to share with seven other V-12 officer candidates in a campus apartment. The eight of us slept in four double bunks, in a two-person college dorm room, with one bathroom for all eight of us. Other than an occasional study session at the room's only desk, none of us spent much time there except to sleep after 10 o'clock, our lights-out curfew. This cut into our social life heavily, except Saturday night and all day Sunday when we had liberty until 10 P.M. that night. My first week dealing with active duty was educational in that all branches of the military periodically run into what is known as "SNAFU," politely translated as "Situation Normal, All Fouled Up."

My first encounter with SNAFU came the first day in July when we reported to the college gym, where we were to receive all our uniforms including regulation blues, summer whites, and outdoor gear. There was a crowd of about 500 men called to active duty from four military reserve programs on campus: the Navy V-12 officer training program, the Marine Corps Reserve Officer Training Program, the

Army's ROTC, and the Navy's ROTC. The ROTC guys were already in their uniforms.

The rest of us lined up for the Navy yeomen who gave out uniforms by just looking each of us up and down for a moment and, without asking for clothing or shoe sizes, gathered a set of jackets, shirts, shoes, and pants that had been allotted to each of us. After we got back to our dorms, now called barracks, and tried the stuff on, some of us were walking around wearing uniforms that fit like bathrobes, while others could not get into their uniforms at all. I was in the middle, tall but thin. I could put on my assigned clothing, but my shirt and pants hung in draping folds.

The Navy enlisted man's uniform descended from the one developed in the early Navy after the American Revolutionary War. Instead of a normal fly and zipper, the bell-bottom trousers had 13 buttons, standing for the 13 colonies. The collar piece, a flap at the back of the neck from a much earlier British era, was a reverse bib those same sailors wore so that they would not soil the uniform with the tar that kept their ponytails together. Why the bell-bottoms? I have never heard an explanation.

Some of the V-12 guys rushed out to buy tailor-made uniforms so that when they went on a date they were "Mr. Charming," while the rest of us settled for these bad-fitting suits. I was so skinny that on my first trip to Berendo Street to pick up some of my things, my mother insisted on putting my pants and top on her sewing machine. My mother had a way of becoming a fully normal mother when I was with her by myself. She trimmed the waist of the pants by at least 4 inches, and the fit was just right. I wore that uniform proudly until I exchanged it for my officer's uniform a year and a half later.

The deal with the Navy boiled down to a trade-off: We obeyed the rules, and they paid our tuition, gave us a place to live, and fed us in the Navy mess hall on campus. For the first time in my life, it was great eating three big, square meals a day without having to buy my own food and cook it. The Navy also paid us $21 a month walking-around money, and we didn't have to work for it, so I gladly gave up a $1-a-day job at the Student Union soda fountain.

There were a few other rules. We were at the beck and call of our captain, the USC Navy commandant, and he ordered that during football season that fall of 1943, Saturday leave was postponed during a home game until after the game was over. The V-12 companies marched in formation in summer dress whites, about 500 men in all, into the Los Angeles Coliseum, home stadium for the USC Trojans. We sat together in the bleachers, except for me. I marched into the stadium and, instead of sitting down with the other guys in white, I just kept on walking out the gate on the ground tier and stopped by my dorm to pick up my swim trunks and swim fins. Then I thumbed a ride to the beach. A sailor in uniform had no trouble getting rides to spend Saturday afternoons bodysurfing.

On balance, my Navy life was an expansion of my freedom. For the first time, I was independent of my mother and father's loud arguing. Except to visit, I never went back home for an extended stay again. Getting out from under the family roof was bringing more freedom into my life, despite the inconveniences of Navy regulations.

There was also time to pull off a new entrepreneurial project. My experience drawing cartoons for the campus magazine inspired me to draw cartoons about the Navy life around me. Some of the other guys thought them funny enough to ask for copies—and offer to pay for them. So I eventually published a cartoon book and sold copies for $2.

The father of one of my surfer friends taught the print shop class at a local junior college. So I asked him, "Why don't you make publishing my book a class project for your students? Your pupils can use their skills to make plates of my cartoons and do the lead typesetting, the layout, and the printing. I will put up the $200 to buy the paper and spiral binding for a thousand copies. And your class has a successful project to help them get a job sooner when they finish school."

The Navy Goes To College was an 8½-by-11-inch horizontally bound book with one of my sarcastically captioned cartoons on each page. It was the first collection of my humor in print, detailing the trials of the V-12 program: You study whether it's 2 A.M. or not, go to class whether you did the homework or not, swim the length of the pool whether you are afraid of water or not, jump off the high-dive platform whether you are afraid of heights or not, go through the obstacle course in a hurry whether you are athletic or not, do fitness exercises at dawn whether you are awake or not, walk across campus with your body permanently bent to the left because you always carry all your books under the left arm so your right hand is free to salute. The cartoons struck close to home with the other V-12 students.

After *The Navy Goes To College* was off the presses in September 1943, I sold a copy to more than 300 fellow officer candidates right away and over time to another 500 students on campus. I sold about 200 more to other officer reserve outfits. I took in almost $2,000 and had a profit of about $800, a big chunk of cash for me. This was almost four times the amount I had made handling 5 gallon bottles of water all summer long.

It was yet another lesson in how much money could be made under the right circumstances, while doing something that was fun. You also may notice a recurring theme in my life: The ever-present concern about my finances continually drove me to develop entrepreneurial ideas.

CHAPTER TWELVE

1943–1944

I Knew There Was a Lot More to Life Than I Had Experienced So Far

THE INITIAL SIGNS OF SUCCESS FOR *THE NAVY GOES TO COLLEGE* GAVE me the self-confidence to try out for the USC varsity basketball team against a number of players who were on basketball scholarships. I did have the advantage of being 6-foot-2, tall for that era, but I was a walk-on, that is, a player without a sports scholarship. Also, I was not exactly the picture of a pro: I wore the same well-worn, kangaroo-skin, high-top shoes that I had bought in high school.

Occasionally during practice, the coach yelled over to me on the far end of the bench, "All right, Miller. Get in there at left guard, and let's see how you do." Usually, by the time I had warmed up, I was benched again, but my time on the floor grew longer by the week. The two-hand set shot was universal: You got set in a two-footed stance and fired the ball with two hands aiming carefully at the basket. I had a one-handed running shot, pioneered by Hank Luisetti at Stanford, but the coach gave me a black look every time I used it. However, I was getting the hang of it, and a single shot counted a lot back when game scores ranged between 40 and 50.

Tall players were in short supply. So whenever I was on the floor, I collected more than my share of rebounds. I was nervous the first time I was sent out on the court in a real game, wearing the flashy USC varsity uniform while I was still only a sophomore with no scholarship, no previous record, no anything. I thought I had it made.

The coach picked me for the traveling team during the Christmas week tour of 1943, scheduled for Phoenix, Salt Lake City, Berkeley, and Palo Alto. Then I blew it. A deep layer of snow had collected on the San Bernardinos, and I was having a hard time giving up skiing during an entire Christmas vacation in order to tour with the basketball team because I knew I would be sitting on the bench most of the time.

I organized a Sunday trip to Mt. Waterman a couple of days before I was supposed to go off with the team. The skiing was so good that I figured out an excuse to skip the tour and still play for the varsity the rest of the season. I persuaded my mother to call the coach and say I had the flu and had to stay in bed. My mother got the message a little mixed up. She said I had caught a cold when I had gone skiing and therefore could not go on the trip. I could imagine the coach asking himself why I had gone skiing when I should have been practicing. Now I was never going to get more than a few minutes' time out there on the playing floor, if any at all.

After Christmas week, I went to Shelby Calhoun, the junior varsity coach, and told him I would like to play for his JVs rather than the varsity—I wanted to maximize my playing time to get enough experience to play varsity ball the following season. Calhoun was happy to add me to his roster, and I played the majority of the minutes of every game.

USC games were played at the Shrine Auditorium in Los Angeles, which seated 6,000 spectators. It was the same space where the Shriners held their annual charity circus, and later the site for the Academy Awards. During the winter of 1943, I spent a lot of time on that huge stage with the USC JVs in front of a thousand or so USC fans who would show up early before the varsity games that later filled all of the seats.

I skied more that winter than I ever had before. However, skiing was not all about getting down the slopes in good snow: It was also about the girls who had begun to discover skiing. They were out there by the dozens. The whole point of the sport went from the macho male skiing at top speed to boy-meets-girl in the lift line. As it happened, I didn't need to meet a girl skiing or anywhere else. I already had one. My life had taken a swing to the normal direction, even if late in the game. My hormones had finally outmatched my focus on sports. I met a great-looking girl who was also a good bodysurfer (very few women were at the time). She was my girlfriend for a short, happy time. She will remain anonymous as she is now a well-known family matriarch. We hit it off, and it all worked out beautifully. I thought I had fallen in love. And, of course, as in every wartime drama, after much too short a time, I would be sent off to war, or so I thought.

Everyone who could read the newspapers knew the invasion of Europe was coming. On June 6, 1944, known as "D-Day," the Allied Forces, 160,000 strong, invaded France across the English Channel and drove deep into Normandy. The U.S. launched extensive submarine warfare against Japan, the Air Force's B-24 Liberators were bombing the Japanese on Wake Island, and the Army had taken New Georgia in the Solomon Islands. A month after D-Day, my orders were handed to me: I was to report to "pre-midshipmen's school" in Asbury Park, N.J., on July 1. There was nothing left to do but to say good-bye to my girlfriend. I gave her my fraternity pin as a secret engagement. She said she would wait for me. Of course, I had no idea what I was doing, but I did have a girlfriend to come back home to.

One morning, we stood on a train platform full of military men with their wives, parents, and girlfriends. We kissed, the train whistle blew, and I climbed aboard the train, stuck my head out a window, and waved good-bye. She waved back from the crowd as the train gathered speed.

This was the first train ride in my life. In 1944, to travel by air with the military, you had to have overseas orders. Rail was the only way to move the mass of military men and women across the country. From my seat, I stayed nose to the window as we crossed the Mojave Desert and out of California to where I would see the rest of America.

At Asbury Park, we spent more time on close-order drill than in learning about ships. We were learning to obey commands instantly—getting away from the freedom of our earlier lives and the college atmosphere by instilling a sense of rules. We did get classes on basics such as compass dead reckoning. Few pre-midshipmen knew the difference between a square knot and a granny. They needed all the terminology lectures: "The pointy end is the bow, and the square end is the stern."

I graduated from Pre-Midshipmen's School in early September 1944 with orders to report to Midshipmen's School in Chicago in late September. Even though that left me two weeks' leave, it would take nine days to travel by train to the West Coast and back to Chicago, leaving six days in Los Angeles. I still went and met my girlfriend at the train depot, but things had changed. We talked for a long time. Neither of us was ready to marry. I was about to go off for another three months and then who knows how long after that. Although we were sure our feelings would survive that kind of separation, she gave me back my fraternity pin, and we parted as friends. I spent the rest of my six days surfing and seeing friends.

Getting ready to head back to Chicago, I made sure my ice skates fit in my sea-bag. It gets cold in Chicago in the winter, and I had met many good-looking girls at the Polar Ice Palace during my high school days. Now I was 19 and had a little money and a uniform, and if the Navy would let me have the time, I was sure there were plenty of pretty ice-skaters in Chicago.

CHAPTER THIRTEEN

1944–1945

Everyone on Board Received a Death Threat

AFTER ARRIVING IN CHICAGO AT THE END OF SEPTEMBER 1944, I TOOK one of the elevators in the Water Tower Hotel, a 10-floor hotel on Michigan Avenue that was the home of the Navy Midshipmen's School, run by Northwestern University. My room was on the ninth floor. The Navy assigned us what was for the Navy a lavish living space—only two men to a room.

Two weeks after classes began I was appointed company commander, based on my academic record at Asbury Park. Now I had to be on my toes in my studies and set an example in learning and in deportment. My job during close-order drill was to count cadence and shout the commands to maneuver 150 men, hoping to not run them into a wall or over civilians. Classes were more advanced and dealt not only with seamanship but also with gunnery and damage control. We also had a chance to play with a recently invented, mechanically driven computer, the "Mark 16 Rangefinder." We typed in fictitious target locations and wind directions, and from there, the computer in real life would feed the direction and elevation of the gun. Interesting, but I could not quite believe a gear-based computer on a battleship rocking and rolling at sea could direct the fire of 16-inch guns accurately enough so its shells would hit a target eight or 10 miles away.

On Sunday nights, the company marched to a chapel a few blocks away. One beautiful Sunday winter night, the chaplain gave us a nondenominational sermon about loving our fellow man, and then we marched back through beautiful, light powder snow to our rooms to learn more about how to kill people. I had trouble with that.

The ski area in Wilmot, Wisconsin, had not yet been founded, unfortunately, so I had no place to get away and take advantage of the snow. But some private tennis clubs flooded their courts to give members ice-skating, and I skated for hours on one flooded tennis court or another on Saturday afternoons and Sundays. People were very generous and welcoming.

After 90 days at Midshipmen's School and just before Christmas week 1944, I was commissioned as an ensign in the U.S. Navy. The narrow stripe on my jacket sleeve was replaced by a wider stripe. My pay was raised to $175 a month. I had $150 of it automatically shipped to my Hollywood bank account. At the end of a year, I'd put away $1,800. For the first time in my life, I had money in a bank account.

As the class company commander, they let me choose my next duty station. My choices were a destroyer escort, a sub-chaser, or a minesweeper, considered by the Navy as Small Craft, versus battleships and aircraft carriers. The Miami Small Craft Training Center was my next duty station. My orders once again gave me two weeks leave before reporting to Miami. Going back to Southern California was a two-night, three-day exercise in discomfort, but it was worth it.

Three days later, I got off the train in Los Angeles and got a ride to Berendo Street, where my sisters' Buick was still available. One of my longtime 4-F surfing friends and I went to Palos Verdes. The surf was small but perfect. The next day, a skiing friend and I drove up to Mt. Waterman. There was plenty of snow, but it had thawed and frozen as hard as concrete, and the lift was not running during the week. With difficulty, we climbed to the top. The top half of the mountain was full of Volkswagen-size bumps. We made our way down slowly, one turn at a time, and got to the bottom with only a few scrapes from falling on the icy hill. It was still a great, sunny ski day.

In early January 1944, I was off to Florida. After the train change in New York City, the Miami train headed south into the Great Smoky

Mountains, where it stopped at a station to take on water for the steam engine. I climbed out of the train and was walking through the station when I saw a sign over one door reading "White Men Only" and a second door reading "Colored Men Only." I had met segregation for the first time. I didn't understand it, after growing up in Hollywood in a completely white community. During my entire school career, I had never experienced segregation: There were no black students where I went to school. But I knew this was wrong.

Reaching the Miami Small Craft Training Center (sub-chasers are about the smallest ships in the Navy and are considered small craft at only 110 feet long) located in Biscayne Bay opposite Miami Beach, I was not ready for class again so soon. School had been ongoing without any sizeable break for nearly three years, but still I was very lucky to be able to join the officer's training. The Training Center was holding classes in Quonset huts at the end of a pier where it was really hot, even hotter than Chicago in July. I slept a lot during the hot classes, because I had played basketball the night before or stayed out too late at a USO dance.

Once again, there was little hands-on training in small craft, but mostly a lot of book study. So I eased up on the studying. I had my commission—the Navy was not going to throw me out if my grades sagged, I hoped.

We finally got to see the workings of a real ship on a day's cruise aboard a 110-foot wooden-hulled sub-chaser with a single 40-MM gun on the bow, a machine gun for general use, and depth charges on the stern. We were given a chance to handle the ship, stop the engine and start it up again, and do a few simple maneuvers. The ship's company was 27 men, including three officers—my preference for size.

As part of our final physical tests, we ran an obstacle course. My finish time had broken the course record by 10 seconds. The timing officer didn't believe it. He said, "Warren, you skipped a couple of obstacles." I disagreed and said I would run it again, with the timer tagging along to watch. He did, and I improved my time. All my basketball experience had me in the best shape of my life.

My obstacle course run got me the only "A" on my report card for the Miami Small Craft Training Center the day I graduated in March 1945. When I told the assigning officer I wanted to serve on a sub-chaser, he said, "That's nuts! But if that is what you want, then fine." My orders came through three weeks later. They read, "Ensign Warren A. Miller, report to COMSINCPAC San Francisco to await further transfer to SUB-CHASER #521. Proceed on your own to San Francisco to arrive within seven days of this date and await first available transportation to the aforementioned ship." There was no mention of where Sub-chaser 521 was stationed, but with overseas orders, a plane reservation was available to me.

When I arrived in San Francisco, the Navy put me up in the very exclusive St. Francis Hotel to await further available transportation to somewhere in the South Pacific. After checking in, I slept around the clock in a deluxe suite that had been converted to a Bachelor Officers' Quarters. Seven other newly commissioned Navy officers were also living in a deluxe room with a great view of the park, but we slept on folding Army cots. My further orders were almost a month in coming, but there were a lot of USO dances to go to. Every morning at 9, we had to stand by a telephone while the Treasure Island Naval Base informed us whether there was available transportation for any of us to our unknown destinations. If no orders came, we had nothing to do until the same time the next morning.

During my lengthy stay in Florida, the gold braid on my hat and on the sleeves of my dress blues had become tarnished, and the sun had given me a tropical tan, the very picture of a veteran who just returned from the South Pacific. The young ladies at USO dances commented on my tropical tan and rusty gold braid. After our second or third dance, they would always ask, "Why don't you wear your campaign bars?" I'd look at the floor and quietly say, "I'd rather not talk about it," as if I'd been in some horrendous fight on the beaches of the South Pacific. That answer worked every time.

Five weeks of USO dances later, my transportation finally arrived. I packed my stuff and grabbed a taxi to Treasure Island where a big Navy Patrol Bomber Medium (PBM), a four-engine amphibian as big as a Pan American Clipper, was waiting to take me on the second leg of my journey to Sub-chaser 521, wherever it was.

On a cold, overcast, blustery morning near the middle of April, we climbed aboard and were briefed on crash procedures by a chief petty officer, who told us we had a 17-hour journey ahead of us on a plane making its first transpacific flight. We donned our inflatable life jackets as we taxied out into the bay—it was only the second airplane ride of my life.

South of the Oakland Bay Bridge, the pilot jammed all four throttles forward. There was a deafening roar as the big radial engines shook the huge flying boat.

I don't think Navy Aircraft insulation had been invented yet. At least there was none on this plane—just olive drab paint covering bare aluminum, with exposed wires running almost everywhere. Some of the rivets had already begun to rattle in their holes. Some of the holes were drilled too large, so it was easy to remove an occasional rattling rivet with my fingernails, but I didn't. Honest.

We could peek out of 8-inch-diameter windows or sit in the same uncomfortable DC-3 bucket seats that were designed for 3-year-old children with 10-inch-wide shoulders. It looked to me as though every part on the plane had been designed and built by the low bidder.

Thanks to the "need to know" restrictions of the military, none of us knew where we were going. I did know my next destination was somewhere in the tropics, so it made sense to leave all of my cold-weather clothes at home. My dress blues, my overcoat, every warm piece of clothing that the Navy gave me, I had shipped in boxes to Berendo Street. My seabag was somewhere in the cargo hold of this giant flying boat, and I had nothing else in the cabin with me except my shaving kit, a change of underwear, and my mimeographed instructions on what to do in the event of a crash at sea or anywhere else. At about 10,000 feet in early April, it was freezing cold inside the loud, cavernous seaplane.

About an hour after becoming airborne, my body was shivering so badly that it forced me to get up and do some jumping jacks in the back of the plane to warm up. While doing my jumping jacks about 75 feet from the center of gravity of the plane, my 180 pounds jumping up and down were magnified to about a ton or so of impact, or so I was informed later. The door to the pilot's cabin burst open. Our copilot-navigator and the engineer came running aft to find out how much of the horizontal stabilizer had fallen off.

No more exercises were allowed.

The crew finally calmed down while the copilot-navigator and the engineer finished chewing me out and returned to their duty stations. When they disappeared, I started scrounging around for something to wrap myself in so I wouldn't freeze to death en route to the tropics.

In front of an amidships bulkhead, hidden under a couple of cardboard boxes full of Spam, there was a bundle of *San Francisco Chronicle* Sunday papers. The papers were going same-day, free airmail delivery to about a dozen big shots stationed in Pearl Harbor. I decided to use the Sunday funny papers first by putting them between my T-shirt and my khaki shirt. That worked so well I next wrapped the want ads around my legs. But I found that the society pages felt a little warmer.

Walking back to my seat with a stiff-legged gait, I fell sound asleep for the next few hours. Waking up with a start, I was wondering what would happen if we crashed: What would the rescuers think when they found a body floating in the middle of the Pacific Ocean wrapped in the *San Francisco Chronicle* funny papers?

Every hour or so, my sleep would be rudely interrupted as the pilot brought the big plane down to about 500 feet above the waves. The navigator then staggered back to where I was huddled with the other three passengers. Alongside my seat, he opened a small hatch in the floor, and even more noise and howling wind came roaring and crashing through the bowels of our flying machine. Then the navigator dropped a 2-pound bag of yellow dye onto the waves below. As the bag burst and spread its dye over the water, the navigator used the yellow splotch as a fixed point. Then he held up a navigational instrument of some kind that could measure the angle of drift to determine how far the plane was being blown off course. The whole process kept the hatch open for about 15 minutes.

Because we were traveling an awesome 130 miles an hour, the slow airspeed gave him plenty of time to figure out what course would eventually get us to one of the Hawaiian Islands. When and if someone in the crew finally spotted one of the Islands, the pilot could then navigate by sight to Pearl Harbor on Oahu, our just-revealed destination.

As it happened, the pilot assumed the lights he finally spotted below were on the island of Kauai, so he turned left around to head back to Oahu and Pearl Harbor. The chief petty officer came back from the cockpit and shouted reassuringly, "The navigator finally knows exactly where we are on the planet, and it sure looks like we have almost enough fuel to get all the way back to Pearl Harbor!" Reassuring.

When we finally landed, I found a spare bunk in a Quonset hut. The next morning I checked the Navy desk to see if my orders had come. They had not, but being finally warm, I hitchhiked to Waikiki Beach and rented a Tom Blake paddleboard for $1 an hour and surfed at "Queens," a special break toward Diamond Head, where the surf was steep and fun. The surfers there were all Hawaiians, except for me, the only *haole* (foreigner) in the water.

I surfed every day until my orders came, informing me that Sub-chaser 521 was expecting me at Guadalcanal. I got into a DC-4 cargo plane with 30 others, and eight hours later, we set down at the airport on Guadalcanal. A Navy launch took me out to where Sub-chaser 521 was patrolling off Lunga Point. It was a tired-looking, wooden-hulled ship.

I soon got into the routine onboard. The skipper, Lieutenant Partridge, was a good guy. The weather was an even 90-plus degrees Fahrenheit with the humidity at about the same. It was more comfortable when Sub-Chaser 521 was at sea, and a slight breeze caused by the ship's speed through the water took away some of the heat. Sub-chaser 521 was currently patrolling the coast, steaming back and forth off Lunga Point along a "ping line" that ran six or eight miles in one direction, with our sonar underwater detection device "pinging" all the way. Then we would make a U-turn and go six or eight miles along the same route back to the starting point. It was explained to me that two years earlier, a munitions ship had been blown up near Lunga Point, and the military had decided that a Japanese sub had snuck in close to shore and torpedoed the munitions ship. The Navy had stationed a sub-chaser here in spite of the fact that for two years they had never found a sign of a submarine or even an oil slick.

After patrolling for a week, Sub-chaser 521 went back to port to take on water and supplies. That was the sum total of the ship's duties. It was not the kind of sub-hunting that I had imagined. On the other hand, it allowed me to get familiar with handling the orders to the helm and to figure out how everything worked aboard, compartment by compartment. I felt safe in April 1945 because the fighting in the Pacific was a long way from Guadalcanal.

Guadalcanal had been retaken from the Japanese two and a half years earlier and marked the farthest point of the Japanese advance. It had become a key airbase for the fleets of B-29s now bombing Japan almost nonstop, but there was not much to Guadalcanal except B-29s and coconut plantations. At any rate, Rodgers and Hammerstein's South Pacific it was not. As junior officer, it was my duty when we came back from patrol to order groceries at the Navy's onshore ships' stores to feed the entire crew for the next seven-day patrol. I went "native." I was 20 years old and had grown a full beard and handlebar moustache, both blond.

In May, there was great news: The Germans had surrendered to the Allies on May 8, 1945—VE-Day, "Victory in Europe Day." The full attention of the American military was now turned to the Pacific. The admirals conferred, set plans in motion, and in late July 1945, Partridge got new orders: Proceed in convoy to sail Sub-chaser 521 on the first leg to the island of Funafuti in the Central Pacific, there to take on fuel and supplies for the second leg to Pearl Harbor. Once at Pearl, Sub-chaser 521 was to be converted to a shallow-water minesweeper for the coming invasion of Japan. The U.S. Combined Chiefs of Staff had set the invasion under the name Operation Olympic for November 1. The estimated cost in blood of invading Japan was a quarter of a million American casualties. Among the first likely casualties were the crews of the sub-chasers and minesweepers clearing the minefields for U.S. landing craft. We were fairly certain we had been committed to death.

CHAPTER FOURTEEN

1945

A Sinking at Sea: The Rest of My Life Is All I Would Get

IN EARLY JULY 1945, A CONVOY OF SIX SUB-CHASERS GATHERED AT LUNGA Point, on Guadalcanal. As soon as the sixth sub-chaser showed up, the Guadalcanal dispatch officer sent all six of us in convoy eastward to Funafuti in the Gilbert Islands, southeast of Tarawa in the Central Pacific. This was to be our first leg on a long trip to Pearl Harbor, where the ships would be converted into shallow-water minesweepers giving us 50-yard-line, front-row seats for the invasion of Japan. However, nothing is ever guaranteed.

Instead, our fate was to sail into a typhoon. The wind started out disguised as an ordinary blow, but the barometer plunged, and the wind reached 50 or 60 miles an hour. Waves 10-feet high became 20-feet high, then 30-feet high, and by the third day, the top 6 to 10 feet were being blown off at 60 and 70 mph. The wind blew sheets of spume off the wave tops, lashing our faces like a whip, and we were in for a significant storm. The 360-degree view from Sub-chaser 521's open flying bridge showed the huge waves playing with the other five sub-chasers like toys. The ships, including their radar masts, disappeared in a trough and reappeared on the next crest, and it seemed like it took a long time between crests. The ordinary typhoon wave was hard to handle, but it was the rogue wave that could cause the real trouble—a 50- or 60-footer that could come at us without warning. Rogue waves came from a buildup of very tall waves that creep up on each other—the energy of them all combines to be a killer. We realized what kind of trouble we were in when the first rogue wave hit the convoy. The sub-chaser to one side of our ship rose so high up on the crest of a wave that the ship's sound dome next to the keel was seen clear out of the water. Next our ship slid down the face of the wave, slamming into the trough with a shock that sent vibrations through the ship.

Even the regular waves as they crested were now lifting over half of the front of the ships' hulls almost entirely out of the water. The wind was getting stronger, judging by its rising, ominous howl. Black, scudding clouds blotted out the sky. It was twilight before noon, and we were in a full-blown typhoon, deflecting our sub-chasers to a zigzag course that was almost uncontrollable. For several days, we had not been able to take navigational sightings of the sun at noon. We could be about to run ashore on an atoll, with a crash that could bend the hull in half. Then a small break in the clouds allowed the skipper and me, as we braced on deck to get a noon sun sighting with a sextant, to measure the distance of the sun over the horizon. The angle, together with the time of measurement, would hopefully give us our position.

We staggered into the chart station and began working the numbers. The ship rolled so violently we both had to brace our feet against the bulkhead to keep from sliding down the slanted deck. We watched as the inclinometer needle in front of us swung farther and farther until it rested at 62 degrees. (At 90 degrees, the deck on which we had been standing would become vertical, and we would sink.) Luckily, the ship paused at that 62-degree point for what seemed like forever before it began to roll back onto its keel while the wave rolled under us, and we both began to breathe again. This kind of wave could make the ship "turn turtle," a capsizing of the sort that usually leads to a 100-percent casualty rate for all those aboard. We didn't need another wave that big and breaking.

At noon, the executive officer had come on duty to take over the afternoon watch while the captain and I went below to try to sleep. It's impossible to adequately describe what it is like to try to rest below deck in a storm like this. You lie in your bunk on your stomach, with a pillow stuffed under one shoulder, and draw your knee toward your chest to provide some sort of horizontal stability. There is no way to get vertical stability (that is to stay down on the bed) except to tie yourself to the bed frame. I was contemplating the tie-down method of getting some rest when a set of sharp whistles over the intercom signaled general quarters, every man to his emergency station, followed by the shout, "Man overboard!"

Scrambling topside, I poked my head out of the hatch, and heard the executive officer scream to the helmsman, "Full right rudder! All ahead, flank!" The wind would now be from the bow, and the ship responded by turning to head us back where we had come from. However, as the twin engines screamed, and the ship started climbing the face of the breaking wave, we were hit by another huge wave breaking. White water 8 feet thick slammed our 110-foot ship to a standstill, as the wave carried us back into the trough again—and farther away from our man overboard. The skipper took over command, but each of the next three breaking waves slammed us right back into the trough, and each time forced us farther from where one of our men had been washed overboard.

The skipper tried a new tactic. With full right rudder with the starboard engine in maximum rpm reverse and the port engine full ahead, our ship finally turned rapidly enough to get the momentum that enabled us to break bow, first through that thick wall of white water on top of the wave, and we were finally headed back the way we came. Our man overboard was somewhere out there, but the odds of spotting him, let alone being able to get him aboard, were a hundred to one. We were saved this hopeless task, as coming toward us was the sub-chaser that had been 500 yards behind in the convoy. Its blinking signal light spelled out in Morse code that it had spotted our man and had him safely aboard.

Now we had to turn 180 degrees to get back to our place in the convoy, which meant turning our stern to the waves. As a surfboarder, I knew that was going to be a difficult challenge. Catching a wave coming from behind is how surfers start their ride. The helmsman managed to time our turn with my directions on how to do it exactly right so that we caught the wave. We were about to have the ride of our lives. Had we continued down the wave at full throttle, we would have buried the bow in the bottom of the trough, forcing the ship's bow to turn abruptly one way or another until the ship was breached, possibly rolling over in a capsize. We just rode the wave until it rolled under us.

Our ship settled down on its station in the convoy, once again headed for Funafuti. The skipper turned the command back over to the executive officer, and he and I went below to grab what little sack time was left before the next watch at four o'clock, about two hours away.

Half an hour later, our cabin door burst open, and the chief bosun's mate hollered, "Captain, you and Miller better get up here right away. The ship is sinking!" And it was.

It was tough making my way toward the forward hatch and going below deck to check things out. The forward magazine where we kept the 40-MM and machine gun ammo was 3 feet deep in water, which was pouring in through where one of the planks had rotted and dislodged. Every time we hit the bottom of a wave, the water spurted through the hole as if from a pressure hose. Every time a wave rolled under us and the bow came out of the water, the water gushed back into the rest of the ship. We were in real trouble, taking on water faster than the crew could bail it. Our two motor mechanics were trying to make the portable auxiliary pump run. They never did. We found out later that the pumps hadn't been overhauled and run in two years. The skipper ordered the rest of the crew to start carrying our ammo up the ladder onto the deck and back to the stern to keep the props in the water and the bow lighter. Instead of signaling the other ships to reduce rpms and stay with us, the executive officer on watch had increased our rpms to stay with the convoy. This just increased the size of the hole in the bow.

It was getting dark when I joined the rest of the crew hauling the ammo to the back of the boat or throwing it overboard. Staggering along a rocking, rolling, pitching wet deck in the dark, cuddling live ammunition in your arms is not exactly comforting. It certainly increases your alertness. The wind was still howling when I took a few minutes off to go below to my quarters and pack survival equipment in case we had to abandon ship. We had only one life raft, and it could carry only six men with room for six others to tie onto the sides and float in the water.

Packing a baseball hat and dark glasses (because I did not want to go sun blind again), a signaling mirror, and a dozen chocolate candy bars of the sort that no man should be without, I found a sizeable bag and added swim fins, a fishing line, and 20 fishhooks. Then I put on my life jacket and foul-weather gear. I grabbed the Bible my grandmother Edith had given me as a going-overseas present. Never having read it, I had the fleeting thought that if we were stranded on a desert island, I would definitely have time to read. I knew I never would have time after the war. I tied the bag around my waist in case the ship sank.

Once I got on deck, it looked as if we'd lightened the bow enough so that the ship might stay afloat until daylight. I went to the navigation station and put the sextant and charts of the area in a place where they could be grabbed at the last moment. I nested the ship's chronometer into the bag, and then it was back to helping move the ammo to the stern. The night wore on. Fatigue was making us slow and clumsy. We staggered under our loads. By the time daylight crept into the sky, the hull's movements had become increasingly sluggish, as the water inside the hull rose steadily. It was plain to me that the ship was going to sink. It was only a matter of how soon.

It was now time to have a little chat with the captain and the crew, gathering them for a short break from their work moving the ammo. The worst case was another sub-chaser would stand by so we could dive over the rail and swim for it. The only trouble was that 11 of the ship's company couldn't swim a stroke, as they abruptly confessed. All of them had faked their swimming tests in boot camp. As an alternative, we could tie a couple of 100-foot heaving lines together, tie one end to the raft, lower the only raft over the side, and let the port watch crew get aboard and play out the line over the side until the raft had drifted downwind far enough so that one of the other sub-chasers could haul the crew off the raft to safety. Then we would haul our raft back and the starboard watch would get into it, repeating the process. The few of us remaining aboard could haul the raft back and be picked up later. We could, in that way, save everyone. I suggested my plan and told the skipper about our nonswimmers. The skipper approved my plan.

In the early morning, there was a noticeable drop in the wind. It was apparent that the worst of the typhoon had finally passed. Now all we had to do was continue to bail and move anything that wasn't bolted down to the back of the ship to keep the bow as high as possible for the next few hours. Then we could start abandoning ship. At about 7:30, the 11 men from the port watch went over the side and climbed into the balsa-wood life raft. Each man had a short line tied to the raft to keep him from being washed away during the rescue. The raft was released and went floating downwind toward the next rescue sub-chaser that had moved into our lee. This had all been organized by the blinking signal light. In case it turned out my idea worked, we could haul the raft back alongside and load it again. The rescue sub-chaser came slowly and carefully alongside the raft, and in spite of the raft's bobbing up and down in waves, the rescue ship's crew dragged all 11 men safely aboard. The raft and the sub-chaser rose and fell side by side in the still-mountainous waves.

Though the waves were starting to subside and the wind had dropped to a 30-mile-per-hour range, our Sub-chaser 521 was now so far down by the bow that the only way we could steer the ship was to run the engines in reverse and steer it backward. The water was creeping along the deck and was 4 or 5 inches deep under the feet of the helmsman. I said "Good luck" to the starboard watch as one by one they stepped off into the water and hauled themselves aboard or tied onto the raft we had hauled back. It worked again. Most of our crew was safe aboard the rescue sub-chasers, except for four of us left on board. We had hauled the raft back to get us off the boat. Then we had a crazy idea. The chief bosun's mate showed us on a chart that there was a small atoll about 80 miles from where he thought our position was. If we could keep the ship afloat for 20 hours steering it backward at four knots, we could possibly beach it on the leeward side of the atoll at high tide and salvage most of it.

So we tried to turn the ship, now half full of water, stern first. Twenty minutes later, a 50-foot rogue wave rolled under the hull, bringing the ship's propellers clear out of the water. With no water for the props to dig into, the engines revved up, screaming; then the "over-speed trip mechanism" kicked in and shut the engines down. After a moment's silence, the chief motor mechanic said very simply, "Captain, this ain't gonna' work. Now, how do we get ourselves off this sinkin' wreck?"

A next sub-chaser in the convoy came astern and approached our now-derelict hull, slowing down within hailing distance as the skipper on the bridge hollered, "Stand by! I am coming alongside." He was risking his ship, of course. If something went wrong and he collided with our all-but-sunken hull, he could be in as bad a shape as we were, but he handled his ship as neatly as if it were a dinghy. He eased his ship slowly up our leeward side, watching the rise and fall of both ships to time his approach so that his ship came within 3 feet of ours. He shouted, "Are you ready, because I am not doing this twice!" His deck came down almost even with ours for a second or two and his crew reached over their rail, locked arms with us, and yanked all four of us safely aboard.

The skipper and I, the bosun's mate, and the motor mechanic from our ship joined the captain on the bridge. After thanking him, I took off my life jacket; untied my bagful of swim fins, fishhooks, fishing line, and candy bars; and laid it all in a corner with my grandmother Edith's Bible on top. I sat and leaned gratefully against a bulkhead, finally off my feet for the first time in almost 20 hours. The ship's cook brought up some coffee and hot tea for us, as the signalman on the bridge blinked out messages to tell the rest of the convoy that we were safe and all accounted for. I didn't drink coffee, but found I could use a bit of nourishment, so I dug around in my survival bag and got out a candy bar. I was halfway through eating it when, less than 200 yards away, Sub-chaser 521 sank slowly out of sight, leaving a trail of bubbles as it disappeared. No more than an hour had passed since the first raft full of survivors had left the ship.

We were invited to the ship's mess for breakfast. I thought it only appropriate at that time to present our chief bosun's mate, who had kept us afloat for almost 18 hours, with my grandmother Edith's Bible as a token of my gratitude.

CHAPTER FIFTEEN

1945–1946

Experience Is All You Have Left When Everything Else Is Gone

FOUR HOURS AFTER SUB-CHASER 521 SANK IN THE TYPHOON, THE remaining convoy received orders to head back to Guadalcanal for an official Naval Board of Inquiry. The Board heard witnesses for two weeks and then went into seclusion to decide in mid-July whether anyone was at fault in the loss. Before it was my turn to testify, I made sure to shave off my beard and handlebar mustache.

At the end of July, the Naval Board of Inquiry announced that the sinking was due to natural causes. Everyone was off the hook. I kept it to myself, but I thought our sub-chaser should never have left the dock, considering its hull was so obviously weakened by dry rot and worms. In the meantime, the crew had been housed in barracks ashore for over a month, awaiting orders, very likely on some sort of small craft for that final, lethal showdown with Japan. Then in a flash the whole world changed, forever.

On August 6, the Army Air Forces dropped the first atomic bomb on Hiroshima. It took a second atomic bomb three days later on Nagasaki before the Japanese quit. The Emperor of Japan broadcast his nation's surrender on August 15, nine days after the Hiroshima bomb, six days after the Nagasaki bomb. The war was over. There wasn't going to be an invasion. That last and bloodiest battle of the Pacific war was not going to be fought. I was not yet 21 years old on "VJ-Day," a huge turning point in the history of the world. We all celebrated on Guadalcanal.

However, I had another problem. I had lost all my clothes and records in the sinking except what I was wearing. It was impossible to get the Navy to buy me any new uniforms or clothes of any kind, including shoes, until a new set of records arrived. So I spent considerable time scrounging a shirt, pants, and slogging boots from the U.S. Army's "Lucky Bag"—the "You lost it; I found it" department. I could at least wear a long-sleeved shirt and long pants to meals, even if the Army shirt I found was two sizes too small and the pants barely made it to the top of my used boots. Also, I had hung onto my regulation Navy "baseball hat" with the officers' gold pin on it.

Scrounging for clothing was about the most exciting thing I did while waiting around for more than a month for my next orders to show up. Finally, the first week of October 1945, I received instructions to fly to Pearl Harbor Naval Base, in the then Territory of Hawaii, to await further orders.

Once I landed on Oahu I was eager to wander around Honolulu, a relaxed city that I enjoyed. Still, it was a bit awkward, because my records had not caught up, and I still couldn't get new clothes. On my 21st birthday, I hitchhiked to Waikiki in my trunks with a towel over my shoulders to rent one of the beach boys' heavy, redwood surfboards without a fin and spend the day trying to catch waves. It didn't matter that I was out of practice; it felt like returning from the dead to be back surfing. To make my birthday a celebration, friends I'd run into took me out for a steak dinner. Life was good.

Two months after I had survived the sinking of Sub-chaser 521, my new orders caught up with me. The Navy sent me to a sub-chaser in Guam in the Mariana Islands south of Japan. The Navy was now a great vacuum cleaner, inhaling sailors at one point and exhaling them to faraway places—a ship or a base in some semi-inhabitable place far from reality. My new ship was stationed at Apra Harbor on Guam's northwestern shore. The only redeeming feature: It was headed in the right direction, to San Francisco, as part of a convoy of small craft scheduled to be decommissioned. With hundreds of other small craft no longer needed, the biggest Navy in the history of the world was being mothballed.

Flying into Guam, I reported to the officer of the day aboard ship at

Apra Harbor. He immediately warned me in a low voice not to swear, not one naughty word. The captain had forbidden the crew to take God's name in vain, ever. I used very little profanity, but practically all the other men onboard were used to swearing a lot. However, uttering a single "damn" could sentence the offender to two days of dishwashing duty in the galley in order to reflect on his lapse from good Christian behavior. The other thing about the ship was that it was so poorly maintained it carried at least 200 million cockroaches. I learned this when I sat down in the mess hall and had to squash six or eight hungry roaches racing each other to be first on my plate. Thereafter, I ate my meals standing up, occasionally shaking off the cockroaches crawling up over my boots.

At Guam, my records caught up with me, so I went to ship's stores and requisitioned khakis and underwear. In the 90-degree heat and humidity, changes of clean clothes were welcome. Finally, a sufficient number of war-weary, worn-out sub-chasers showed up to make up a convoy. At the end of the month, our convoy put out to sea, headed by a 327-foot LST as the "mother ship;" sub-chasers did not have the fuel capacity to reach San Francisco and had to be refueled by the LST en route. The initials, we young officers decided, stood for "long, slow transport."

On our 47th day at sea, a month and a half on the hot Pacific, our convoy slowly slipped under the Golden Gate Bridge in San Francisco. Never had I ever seen a bridge that looked so good. Treasure Island was a huge Navy installation where decommissioning a small vessel should have been no big deal. It meant taking apart the sonar and radar gear, unbolting the 40-MM gun, and getting some of Treasure Island's heavy forklift equipment to take this equipment off the boat and ashore. More than that, we needed someone to tell us what to take where. It could have been completed in three days, but the officer in charge was too busy to get to ships as small as ours. We stayed at dockside all through November and half of December 1945. The only change in our inactivity aboard came after the crew sprayed a deadly liquid throughout the ship. We were off for the rest of the day, and when we got back, no more cockroaches.

THE SECOND SATURDAY AFTER LANDING, I GOT WEEKEND LEAVE AND hitchhiked the 375 miles to Hollywood. Every time I stuck out my thumb, a driver stopped to pick me up because servicemen were heroes. My last ride dropped me at Berendo Street, and no one was home. My two sisters lived in their own homes, my mother was out making real estate deals, and my father was with his girlfriend. Leaving a note for my mother on the kitchen table (though my parents hadn't written me a single letter while I was in the service), I went to bed in my old room and dropped into deep sleep. I got up at 5 A.M., transferred my ski equipment and my Navy dress uniform into the Buick, and drove back to San Francisco.

The following week, after five days of duty, I headed off for a three-day weekend to ski Donner Summit, one of the two nearest sizeable ski areas to San Francisco, the other being Yosemite's Badger Pass. The trip marked the beginning of my change from a day skier dabbling in the sport to a totally hooked skier. I now had more than $2,000 in my bank account, so I could finally afford to become a real skier, even paying for overnight accommodations. Although, of course, I would always look for the cheapest bed available. My true ski life began on this three-day December weekend at Donner Summit, at a cost I would have considered exorbitant before getting "rich" in the Navy.

Donner Pass is 200 miles east of San Francisco. City skiers could catch the Central Pacific after work and be at the unloading platform in Truckee in time to get a good night's sleep at one of the lodges. I planned to do the same only by car, taking along an old surfing friend, Reggie Chambers. It took us three hours to get to Sacramento on a two-lane road. Then we drove up the western side of the Sierras, trapped behind 18-wheel trucks traveling six miles an hour up the steep, two-lane road. We reached Donner Summit Lodge after midnight. The only remaining room available was in the deluxe class, $8 a night. That struck me as a lot of money, never having spent that much for overnight lodging anywhere.

The next morning, we bought all-day tickets on the rope tow across the Central Pacific tracks from the hotel. Donner had become a rope-tow heaven, with at least a half-dozen ropes going all the time. Two instructors from Austria, brothers Bill and Fred Klein had started a ski school at the Sierra Club's Clair Tappaan Lodge in 1936, a decade earlier, when alpine skiing was first beginning to take hold in the U.S. These two Austrians sparked the great surge in early alpine skiing on Donner Summit. Having only been on a rope tow a few times, I had my first really intense day "riding the rope" and not even stopping for lunch.

"The Rope Tow," to quote one of the leading ski writers of the day, "is man's most economical way of getting more people up more hills in less time than with any other means of transportation." This winter, hundreds of rope tows across America were bringing skiing to the people, the largest stimulant on the ski scene at the time.

One of the realities of the rope-tow experience was that my arms carried the weight of 20 to 50 feet of thick, wet Manila hemp, the space between me and the skiers behind and in front. Additionally, my arms were dragging all of my body weight on the ride up. After about a half a day of riding, while my arms were tired, I was astounded to see pretty girls who kept on riding the rope. Chatting up one of the girls, she said she had no trouble hanging on, but confessed that after her first winter, her right arm was an inch longer than her left.

Back at Treasure Island, I got up my courage to meet with the commandant, a vice-admiral, telling him how long our sub-chaser had been tied up waiting for the heavy equipment to carry the 40-MM gun and other material off the ship. The vice-admiral reached for the phone and made one call. The heavy machinery, along with someone who knew where all the detached stuff was to be stored, appeared the next day. We completely decommissioned our ship by the end of the third day.

Now I had done my duty, and I no longer had to live on a ship. This was a bad situation because there was no way to control where the Navy was going to shuffle me off to next. My first assignment was to "ship's company" at Treasure Island Naval Base to be available for a ship in the Pacific needing an officer with sub-chaser experience.

Meanwhile, it was time to enjoy life in San Francisco. There was a good side to being in ship's company. The Navy provided me with a $7 per diem, which amounted to an additional $200 a month, doubling my pay. The Navy also gave me a place to live. San Francisco has many good restaurants where I ate well, while still saving money for my bank account in Hollywood.

Every morning, I checked with the secretary at the desk in the department to see if I had received any orders. On the third morning, I received new orders: Report to a destroyer at dock in San Diego by midnight December 31, 1945. Before then, I could spend a couple of days skiing Yosemite.

I got in touch with Ward Baker at his home in Manhattan Beach. Ward had survived the war in good shape, partly because he had been discharged early. He had a physical disability in both knees from so many hours kneeling on his surfboard. Ward was by now a commercial fisherman off Catalina Island, concentrating on anything that would take a hook and eating enough of his catch to sustain himself, as well as selling mackerel to fish markets and occasionally shooting a wild goat on the Catalina cliffs. Ward said he would be glad to spend a few days at Yosemite skiing, and we were off in his Plymouth Coupe. Ward was an extraordinary guy, expert at surviving on his own hook, and he was also a talented auto mechanic.

SET IN THE MOUNTAINS 200 HUNDRED MILES EAST OF SAN FRANCISCO, Yosemite or Badger Pass was, at the time, the leading ski resort in the nation, except for Sun Valley. As many as 2,000 skiers a week enjoyed Yosemite's terrain. Former Olympic skier Charley Proctor managed the resort, a main reason for its success.

Ward and I rented a place available on the cheap in Yosemite Valley's "cabin city." First thing in the morning, we headed for the resort's only lift skiing at Badger Pass, a 15-minute drive. Badger was essentially a long and wide slope served by the current version of Yosemite's "upski," as it was called—nothing like any lift existing today. It was a big jig-back, flat-bottomed "boat tow" that had two sled-like hulls about 20-feet long and 5-feet wide, with a rack in the middle to hold the skis. Everyone stood up during the ride, which was a great chance to meet interesting ladies at a cost of 25 cents per ride. When the boat stopped on top, everyone got off, while the other boat that had been going down at the same time was loading at the bottom. The "upski" was not fast. There was a much faster rope tow on the slope, where an all-day ticket was $2.50. Comparison shopping and the girl-availability factor told us to take the boat tow. Before getting in for my first ride, I waxed my skis with "klister," an extra-special Norwegian ski wax, or so I thought. Ski conditions that day were unusually deep: cold powder snow quite different from the wet snow for which the Norwegians had invented the wax.

I took off down the slope, but the skis didn't. I did a forward face-plant. "Wrong wax," a ski instructor standing there looking down at me said, as if it weren't obvious. The bottom of my skis had huge wads of snow clinging to them. From there, I walked down the hill on the skis, which were steady as snowshoes. At the bottom, I borrowed a scraper and scraped off most of the wax, but not enough to give me a fast ride. In the cabin that night with Ward, we sat around thinking about how to get my skis back into slick condition. I knew gasoline took bubble gum off anything. Maybe it would do that with sticky wax. I siphoned half a root beer bottle of gas out of Ward's Plymouth. Then I removed the klister by absorbing it in gasoline-soaked rags. After I finished with each rag, I threw it into the burning wood stove that heated the cabin, fanning the flames. "Can't leave gasoline-soaked rags lying around," Ward said. "Oily rags set off spontaneous combustion, you know."

Seven rags had gone into the stove before the cabin got so hot my sweater had to come off. Then it was my off with my T-shirt, off with my pants, and off with my long johns. Before long, Ward opened the door to let in some cool air. The sky outside was red from the flames shooting out our chimney. In the distance I saw the figures of a couple of park employees and two rangers rapidly approaching, as I stood in the doorway wearing nothing but jockey shorts.

The next morning, there was a required talk with the district Ranger in his office. My alibi, which did not go over well, was that I had never thought that gasoline-soaked rags would fly up into the Yosemite night sky on heat waves streaming out of the stovepipe, frightening various members of the Yosemite Park and Curry Company staff and a number of skiers who thought they might have to vacate their cabins. Despite the fact I was wearing a Navy shirt with campaign bars for Marksmanship, Pacific Theater, and Good Conduct, I found it necessary and desirable to contribute a number of dollars in support of something called the Yosemite Park Rangers' Emergency Contingency Fund (probably for their end-of-the-season beer party).

The next day, both Badger Pass lift operators refused to let me ride their lifts because they had heard about what had happened the night before. So I made 11 ascents on skis, climbing up the steep part of the big hill at Badger Pass. Even with the right wax, I still knew nothing about powder snow skiing technique and fell more frequently than usual.

When my boots came off in Ward's car, I discovered a large set of blisters on both feet, thanks to all my climbing. My feet hurt so much that putting on my sneakers was impossible. Instead I wrapped my feet in soft, absorbent bandaging material donated by the Park Ski Patrol and then bought a pair of oversized ski socks to go over the bandages. Ward drove us the 300 miles to Berendo Street, where we arrived a couple of hours after midnight.

The next day, New Year's Eve, was the deadline when I had to be in San Diego to get on the destroyer. The blisters were still there, but I was determined to ride a few waves at Malibu. Even if I arrived late, I couldn't pass up the chance to surf, as I might soon be several thousand miles out in the Pacific again.

Malibu on the last day of the year was a classic winter day. It served up glassy, knee-high waves, hot sand, and no one else there to ride them with me. The cold water soothed my burning blisters, and the world was still a great place. However, when it was time to go, I had to walk across the dry, warm sand that filled up every one of my blisters. It was a memorable but not too comfortable end to 1945.

I drove the Buick back to the Berendo Street house and stashed my surfboard, deciding that the destroyer would probably not leave San Diego on short notice and was probably already waiting for a spot in the Naval yard for decommissioning. I parked the car on the dock and walked up the gangway in my bare feet full of blisters and sand. The duty officer signed me aboard and said, "Find an empty bunk somewhere and report to the captain at 0800."

THE OFFICER OF THE DAY TOLD ME THAT, BY THE WAY, THE SHIP PROBABLY didn't need me to fill out the officers staff after all. He said that in the morning, the captain would probably write me new orders. That was fine by me, especially because I was invited to celebrate the rest of New Year's Eve with the ship's crew. From his desk on New Year's Day 1946, the skipper wrote new orders for me. He had a considerable hangover and sent me on my way back to Treasure Island. I drove the 450 miles north to Treasure Island with slowly healing blisters on my still-bare feet.

I reported back to the Navy desk at Treasure Island, where my papers would be held. Every weekend they gave me liberty. Monday through Friday, they made me attend more training classes. The classes were on damage control, seamanship, communications, and so forth—the same stuff that I had already studied four times in four different schools. The whole thing made me crazy, and I had to figure a way out.

A good-looking, young Navy WAVE (lady sailor) presided over the desk where my file was kept, so why not invite her to breakfast at a nice restaurant, where I made my case over waffles and scrambled eggs. I told her that I had already taken all the classes that would be assigned to me at Treasure Island—back in USC Pre-Midshipmen's school and at Asbury Park and had repeated these same studies at Midshipmen's School in Chicago and had studied them again at the Small-Craft Training Center in Miami. On top of that, my ship had been sunk by a typhoon. I didn't need to try and stay awake in class five days a week until I was sent to some other place in the Pacific. That afternoon, I invited my new lady friend out to dinner on Fisherman's Wharf. Three dinners later, I had her complete sympathy. I convinced her that if she slipped my papers into the bottom drawer of her desk, the mere absence of my papers from the desk files consulted every morning by the officer in charge of ship's company would free me from all unnecessary daily classes, by giving the appearance of a presumed assignment elsewhere. And after all, the war was over, so how important were all those classes, anyway?

I promised to phone my new lady friend every morning during the week, at exactly 9:30 A.M., to hear if new orders had been issued to go somewhere besides her bottom drawer. I convinced her that "trustworthy" was my middle name and that I would honor my promise to stay close enough to get back to Treasure Island within 48 hours.

On a Tuesday, I called my new girlfriend from a pay phone on Treasure Island. No orders, so I asked her if I could call from Carmel the next morning. "Not a problem." On Wednesday I called her from Carmel; again no orders. She gave me permission to call from Yosemite the next day. No orders. From then on, the daily call was from Yosemite to my Navy WAVE friend at Treasure Island. By some sort of miracle, no new orders arrived during the next seven weeks, right through to the second week of March. This amounted to a fine seven-week vacation (sometimes called AWOL) that became yet another turning point in my life of skiing.

CHAPTER SIXTEEN

1946

You Don't Need a Lot of Money to Make a Major Change in Your Life

I WAS BACK SKIING AT YOSEMITE, AND MY CONTRIBUTION TO THE Yosemite Park Rangers' Emergency Contingency Fund had evidently made up for my frightening the rangers with my flaming rags flying all over the valley. This was a day-by-day ski vacation. The Navy reassigned officers according to boat type, and its outdated sub-chasers were being decommissioned, so the number of sub-chaser berths needing crews was dwindling.

Of course, every morning I awoke in a sweat with the thought that my new orders would arrive, and somehow the Navy would figure out what I was doing. Pushing the thought aside, I dressed in time to be the first to arrive at the Badger Pass parking lot, drank the first cup of hot chocolate at the cafeteria, made my long-distance phone call from the lodge, and stood first in line at the rope tow, waiting for it to open. After skiing all morning, I bought lunch in the cafeteria and had dinner at the Yosemite Lodge, where a great buffet cost a couple of dollars: a baked potato, meat loaf with gravy, and lemon meringue pie that would fill up anyone. All of my meals were covered by my Navy $7 per diem. It was good to be eating high on the hog.

No orders arrived during the first month of my AWOL ski vacation. I know this was wrong to do, and it bothers my sense of honor whenever

I think about it 70 years later, but the war was over. I think I was so scared that I would be killed in the war that I did stuff that wasn't OK.

My other concern was how to cover the $2.50 rope-tow cost for skiing at Badger Pass. If I paid full fare, it would cost me $75 in lift tickets for a month. True to my tight ways, I worked out a deal: Renting a bed for a dollar a day from the guy who operated the rope tow was less than renting a cabin by myself. As for the rope-tow tickets, they came in seven different colors, one for each day of the week. After I had bought seven tickets for the first week, I could show my landlord, the rope-tow operator, whichever color ticket was the right one for the day. The scam worked, and so did my arrangement with my new best girlfriend at Treasure Island.

My Yosemite "vacation" was the first time I had ever been able to concentrate on skiing every day. I made a new friend who became important to me for life: Bill Janss was six or seven years older and was the Winter Sports Director at Badger Pass. Bill was a fine instructor in a day when good instructors were scarce. The instructors were good because the manager, Charley Proctor, had acquired three of the first Austrian instructors escaping to America from the threat of German occupation in the 1930s. Hannes Schroll was the first, hired after he won the initial U.S. Alpine Combined Championship in 1935. Then came Sigi Engl, who was hired at Yosemite in 1937. He had made the Austrian National Team for two years running. Luggi Foeger arrived in 1938 in the nick of time, the year the Germans invaded Austria. None of the three were still at Yosemite when I got there, showing how quickly they spread themselves around, building the sport in America. Hannes Schroll had left to found Sugar Bowl in California, and Sigi had joined the school at Sun Valley, which he later headed. Luggi was designing ski areas in the Sierras. All three had trained young instructors at Yosemite in the Austrian Technique that was being adopted all over the U.S. Bill Janss, too, became a big man in the sport, eventually developing Snowmass in Colorado and buying Sun Valley. Almost everyone with a good ski resort job I met in those days later would become famous in the sport.

One day, Janss asked me, "Do you know how to do a correct snowplow turn?" The truth was I had never had a ski lesson in my life. So Janss taught me the classic Arlberg snowplow turn that was standard in America at the time.

A bunch of Tenth Mountain Division veterans came up from Monterey on weekends and held an informal slalom race every Sunday. By the third week, I somehow won a race. Yosemite also sponsored a weekly downhill from the top of Badger Pass to the bottom. I foolishly entered one, and halfway down, I really crashed. The first successful release binding had been invented several years earlier by a Norwegian downhiller in Portland named Hjalmar Hvam, but I was not using it and severely tweaked my knee. I skied favoring my other knee for the next week or two.

I began cartooning again. *The Navy Goes To College* had been a successful business project, so every lunchtime, if the weather was good, I sketched with my trusty No. 2 pencil on a table on the sundeck of the Badger Pass base lodge. Skiers on the slopes right in front of me often fell on their behinds or face-planted just 50 yards away. Most skiers never took lessons, and the equipment was primitive: one-strap heel bindings and soft leather boots. The slope always had an epidemic of holes from simple sit-down falls that created sizeable "sitzmarks," or bathtubs, in the snow, which of course went unpacked in those days. "Sitzmarks" were so common that signs were later posted around beginner areas urging skiers to "fill in your sitzmarks." By the end of the day, even the beginner slopes could look as if they were shelled by light artillery.

From then on, I drew and sold cartoons for $1 each during lunch hours, and during après ski I would sell some more. I don't remember how many, but enough that it proved I could turn out cartoons of skiers, and I could remember some of them once I was back on duty in the Navy. The best of these cartoons, along with some newer sketches, became finished drawings for my first cartoon book on skiing, which I called *Are My Skis On Straight?*

One lady friend at Yosemite that winter of 1946 was a 16-year-old junior racer named Brynhild Grasmoen. She lived with her family in nearby Merced. She attracted my attention because she skied so fast I could not keep up with her. She was a leggy, bright, fearless young lady, full of confidence and a nice smile. I was five years older, but that didn't matter; Brynhild and I hit it off nicely. She was still in high school, and her father, also a skier, took Brynhild with him and his wife on weekends skiing at Yosemite, and that very nearly changed my life forever.

Most times when I skied with Brynhild, I joined her by cleverly taking a line that caught up with her on the slopes. The main hill at Badger Pass was small enough, and you could nearly always spot someone you were looking for. We'd ski together for a run or two, which was all she could stand because she would always have to wait for me at the bottom.

Sometimes we had lunch with her parents. Her mother had an eagle eye when it came to her daughter, and in spite of the age differences between Brynhild and myself, her family was very cordial and even had me for dinner at their home in Merced a couple of times.

Bill Janss continued my ski lessons, taking me up through the standard Arlberg teaching progression during the week. The Arlberg teaching system is structured to go from steered snowplow turns with skis on the inside edges into sliding stem-christie turns. The whole key to the sliding turn, Janss showed me, was to get the skis off their edges and flat enough to slide through the turning arc, but not so flat that the outside edge of the ski catches in the snow, sending the skier sprawling.

I skied every day as if it could be my last, and had a farewell party with my friends in the Park every night. By my 29th farewell party, I was definitely a tired skier. The wise-guy standard of the day was that a veteran skier was one who knew the difference between a broken rib and a cracked rib, between a torn ankle cartilage and a broken ankle, and between a flirtatious girl wearing a tight sweater and one wearing a wedding ring under her ski glove.

I saw my first genuine ski film one day. Luggi Foeger had left a copy of one of his films that was occasionally shown at the Yosemite Lodge. The film was about a backcountry trip to the Ostrander Lake Hut, six miles off in the wilderness from Badger Pass, and about climbing and skiing the untracked steeps of Horse Ridge, a glacial cirque in which the Ostrander Hut stood. I had no idea that a film could bring home the feeling of skiing so well.

During the seventh week at Yosemite, in early March, my orders arrived on my Navy WAVE girlfriend's desk at Treasure Island. Unfortunately, she was not able to reach me on the Thursday when the orders arrived, because that was one of the days when I was not scheduled to call in. When she answered my usual Friday call, she was very upset and told me in a not-very-friendly tone that I was under orders to report aboard a troop transport in Oakland, which was to leave at 16:30 for Honolulu. From there, I was to take the first available transportation to Kwajalein Atoll. I told her not to worry and that I would be there before the ship left.

I broke the speed limit all the way from Yosemite to Hollywood, dropped off my ski gear, put the Buick away at Berendo Street, picked up my duffel bag with all my Naval belongings, caught the all-night bus to Oakland, grabbed a cab, and reported to the officer of the day just a few minutes before 4:30 the next afternoon. Thirty minutes later, and I could have been court-martialed. There was no time to pick up my orders at Treasure Island, so it took me a while to get the officer of the day to believe my convoluted story explaining why I did not carry orders. Finally, he allowed me aboard, and soon the ship was on its way to Honolulu.

The war had been over for about seven months, so I had packed only my khaki uniforms, figuring that any officer going overseas as a passenger on a troop ship at this late postwar stage would be another junior officer, like me. I had completely ignored the probable presence of senior career officers who had re-enlisted. It was embarrassing when I sat down to dinner aboard the troop transport and found the other officers all in dress blues, neckties, and white shirts, each with a dozen campaign bars on their jackets. I had on my khakis with the three campaign bars. I soon made it known I had lost my dress blues when my ship had sunk, but in this select company, I was the dufus. It was a long trip to Honolulu.

From there, I flew to take my place as junior officer on a minesweeper stationed on Kwajalein Atoll, some 2,000 miles southwest of Honolulu. The ship was a shallow-water minesweeper on permanent station 500 miles or so northeast of Kwajalein, steaming in a five-mile-diameter circle around an invisible, fixed longitude and latitude mark in mid-ocean. The radio techs manned a radar 24/7. Whenever the radar picked up an airplane at night, the crew shone searchlights straight up, giving the plane's navigator a "semi-conditional navigational point" en route to wherever the plane was headed. Pilots still relied on sextants and star fixes for finding locations, and there were times when there were no stars to shoot because of very high clouds.

Officers aboard stood on duty four hours on and eight off, around the clock, circling this invisible point in the Pacific while the flat-bottomed minesweeper rocked and rolled in the waves. As the junior officer, my watch was midnight to four in the morning, and then noon to four in the afternoon. During my night watch, I sometimes found myself wondering what Brynhild Grasmoen was doing. I kept reminding myself that my enlistment was over in a few months—at noon on June 1, 1946, to be precise.

When June 1 arrived, I was in luck, as our ship was back at Kwajalein for refueling. I walked off the ship, my last duty station in the Navy, and waited for transportation to San Francisco. Two weeks later, I was back in San Francisco, but the Navy WAVE who had aided and abetted my several-week ski holiday was mustered out while I was on the minesweeper. She had returned home to Philadelphia, so I couldn't thank her for all she did for my psyche.

I was walking down Market Street with my honorable discharge in the inside pocket of my jacket. At 21, I had completed almost four years of schooling and duty with the U.S. Navy without getting shot or shooting at anyone, But I did have the excitement of a ship sinking under me in a typhoon.

While I was walking by a camera-store window, I saw a Bell & Howell "Sportster" 8-MM movie camera for $77. The $100 mustering-out pay was burning a hole in my pocket. I had to have that camera, so I walked in and bought it, along with three rolls of film, even though I had no idea where the camera would take me. It was June in California, and it was time to go surfing.

After taking the train to Los Angeles, I made myself at home in my old room on Berendo Street. Without a job and not particularly wanting one, I decided living a short time with my parents was a good way to save money. I felt that there was a life for me somewhere out toward the horizon, but that it would take a bunch of money to get there. I saw my next job as publishing my first ski cartoon book, but it would cost me a lot to get it into print.

Both of my sisters had gotten married while I was in the Navy so my mother gave me a homecoming present: my sisters' old Buick. Obviously, neither of my married sisters had any use for a racy, old convertible four-seater, but even so, the gift showed my mother's good side.

As a thank-you, I went down to the local appliance store to buy my mother a new-model Whirlpool washer and dryer. All she had to do was pick them up when they arrived. However, she kept reporting that the appliances had not arrived. I finally went down myself, and the salesman told me my mother had canceled the order and taken the money instead. I should have been really angry with her, but there were other things to do. She had bought an old office building while I was overseas and had unsuccessfully tried to get it fixed up to rent the top floors as offices. Evidently, she needed the money to keep the household going, so I didn't say anything.

Within a month of arriving home, I was able to contract with a print shop in Los Angeles to turn out 1,000 copies of *Are My Skis On Straight?* My optimism ran high based on my success with selling my pen and ink cartoons for $1 each at Yosemite. I believed I could sell almost anything. That belief has persisted throughout my life, for among many other things, I sold ski cartoons, ski bootlaces, glasses painted with ski cartoons, and ski films. To sell *Are My Skis On Straight?*, I went around to the two or three ski shops that existed in Los Angeles in those days and tried pre-selling the book. The presentations went fairly well, each shop ordered, and thereafter, I brought the shops more books every so often. I was sure I'd make my money back and then some. And I did.

It was also time to build a new surfboard because my old one had been slashed deeply by rocks whenever I'd fallen off, leaving it to wash ashore on its own. This was before the ankle leash everyone wears today. I started building it in Bob Simmons' garage in Pasadena. Bob was a surfing friend, who was a pioneer board builder and designer. Buying the lightest redwood slabs available and using Bob's clamps and tools as needed, it took about 20 clamps to glue the boards together into "a blank," measuring 24 inches wide, 3.5 inches thick, and 11 feet long. I thought it was going to be the greatest surfboard in the world. It weighed almost 100 pounds. Simmons had already become the first to fiberglass a surfboard and the first to put a plywood deck on top of a foam core, but at that time he was keeping his ideas under wraps. Eventually boards would weigh less than 10 pounds, but I was perfectly and stupidly happy with my heavy board for the next five years.

DURING THAT SUMMER OF 1946, I RECONNECTED WITH BRYNHILD BY visiting her in Merced. She was now a grown-up 17-year-old, more beautiful than ever. I was very naïve. She had won the California women's downhill championship and would later win the 1947 Women's Olympic trials. I was still not sure what direction I was going to turn as far as my college degree. Mrs. Grasmoen's idea of a proper man for her daughter involved one who went to law school or business school to eventually earn the kind of money it takes to raise a family. However, I was not into status at all. I didn't need a bigger car, tailored suits, expensive restaurants—I just wasn't interested in those things.

Still, the family remained cordial and invited me to go with them one weekend to the ski resort that Brynhild's father, Arnold, a banker, was building at the base of San Francisco Peak just outside of Flagstaff, Arizona. Mr. Grasmoen had been awarded a lease that covered the skiable part of the mountain. The place certainly had potential. The mountain was a towering, ancient volcano that rose out of the flatlands to 12,000 feet and had an interior crater that could become a huge snow bowl in winter. A dirt access road through the Forest Service land to the bottom of the ski area, built by the Civilian Conservation Corps, connected the base of the mountain to the outside world. The CCC had also built a big log base hut six years before that could serve cafeteria food to a sizeable crowd. Arnold Grasmoen had bought a 100-acre ranch just outside the Forest Service land, where he was building a modest ski lodge with accommodations for about a dozen skiers.

At the mountain itself, Mr. Grasmoen had built a couple of beginner rope tows down on the volcanic plain, one of them 3,000 feet long. He was not going to run the lodge himself but was going to have his brother take it over. He hinted that there was a job for me next winter if I wanted to help finish off the lodge and run the tows on weekends. I was not quite ready to settle down to a mundane job. The Arizona Snow Bowl was a long way from being properly developed, even as a basic ski area. If you wanted to ski on steeper stuff, you had to climb above the rope tows. At the very least, the ski area needed another rope tow going up to steeper terrain. As another consideration, the local town called Flagstaff was very far from any type of surfing, which I needed to be happy in warm weather. So I said, "I will think it over."

As fall came around, I decided, possibly with an eye to pleasing Mrs. Grasmoen, to take advantage of the GI Bill and sign up at USC to get enough credits to finish my bachelor's degree. I was only a semester or two short of earning it. School, however, quickly became a real struggle. Hundreds of thousands of other discharged servicemen were also trying to cash in on the GI Bill. College classrooms everywhere were flooded with eager, older pupils who had survived military service. One of my classes was so crowded that it was standing-room-only at the back of the classroom and along the sides. I was able to attend the lecture only by standing outside leaning against a windowsill and trying to get my head far enough through the window to hear. This was not how I had pictured my return to college, but I hung in there for a while.

The best thing about returning to Hollywood was getting in touch with Ward Baker in Manhattan Beach. That fall, Ward and I surfed together a lot. We took movies with our 8-MM cameras of each other surfing —my first movies. Eventually, I bought an 8-MM projector so I could watch the films and learn the best angles for shooting surfing.

Ward and I talked about taking a weeklong ski trip together. I began figuring out how to do it without deeply denting my savings account. Ever since I had rented a bed in a cabin at Yosemite, I had realized that this was an expensive way of staying at a first-rate resort. All we really needed was a house trailer to be pulled by my car.

I began looking at the *Los Angeles Times* classifieds for a bargain, and finally I found it. It was a homebuilt, aerodynamic, "teardrop" design aimed at short trips for two to the country, with a huge flip-up door in the back that opened the whole width of the trailer—a very smart invention. This lift-door formed a roof that gave the "kitchen" overhead weather protection. The kitchen itself consisted of a small cupboard for the pots and pans, plus a Coleman stove—all within easy reach. The lift-door made it possible to cook outdoors and have a tailgate party of the sort that people now have at football games. This meant we could flip open the lift-door, stand outside, and cook on a stove set in the back of a trailer beside the icebox. The trailer was only 8 feet long, 4 feet wide, and 5 feet high. The lift-gate curved from the top of the trailer down to the back end to give it a streamlined effect. The front 6 feet, 6 inches of the trailer was taken up by the double bed. To crawl out of the bed, you had to wiggle around and push your legs out the door. Living in it at length was crowded for two guys over 6 feet tall, but the trade-off was that it was very cheap for a house trailer. Plus the trailer was light enough and streamlined enough so the old 1937 Buick could tow it at a decent cruising speed. It was certainly possible to live and ski out of this rig. The price was right, too, at $200.

CHAPTER SEVENTEEN

1946

In Alta, We Discovered Powder Skiing for Only $2.50 a Week

IN EARLY NOVEMBER 1946, WARD BAKER AND I HEADED FOR ALTA, UTAH, towing our 8-foot teardrop, sleep-inside, cook-outside trailer. I had given up trying to get my college degree and was happy to be free of the crowded classrooms. What was supposed to be a thrifty, weeklong skiing trip morphed into a three-week skiing trip. Out of my Navy savings, I bought four Army-surplus, down-filled, "mummy-style" sleeping bags, two for each of us. Two mummy bags, one stuffed inside the other, could keep anyone warm on a slab of ice at the North Pole. The plan was to sleep in the trailer, and eat, and then perhaps even socialize, at the trailer's open-kitchen area under its hatchback and tarp.

Then there was the goal of the trip: to have a good time, one day at a time, and while we were at it, to learn to ski powder. The winter before at Yosemite, skiing the not-too-deep, or occasionally very light powder, made Ward and I believers. Deep powder was beautiful and made packed snow second-class. We chose Alta because it was the first place it snowed that season; we later discovered its reputation for the deepest and lightest powder within driving distance. We set aside enough time to learn what Alta could teach us at our level of disposable income. We had collected as much economical food as we could in the trailer: a lot of oatmeal, 10 pounds of frozen mackerel that Ward had caught off Catalina Island, and 10 pounds of frozen goat meat that he acquired when we shot two goats on the same island. We packed our frozen fish and the goat meat deep in the bottom of our mummy bags as insulation against defrosting during the day. However, it all had to come out at night for us to sleep. I won't even mention how it and we smelled. No one we'd heard of had skied from his own private trailer parked at the lifts of a first-class ski resort. Also, no one told us it could not be done.

Additionally, we each brought our 8-MM movie cameras, my 8-MM projector, and the 8-MM films Ward and I had shot while surfing to show skiers at Alta—none of whom, it turned out, had ever seen surfing. We saw the film as an icebreaker in what would surely be a tight social circle at Alta. We were all set to go on a 700-mile road trip on what was then a two-lane, winding road.

The old Buick could only be pushed to about 45 miles an hour towing the trailer without heating up, so we only made 300 miles a day. The wear and tear since I first got the use of the car back in high school was beginning to show. The rear springs groaned under the weight of the rear seat, packed to the roof with our gear.

When we reached the Great Salt Lake area, we drove around the town, and then began to climb slowly into the black skyline of the Wasatch and up Little Cottonwood Canyon. As the steep road began slowing down the Buick, our headlights lit up a sign reading "Alta 12 Miles." The snow on the road was getting deeper. We put our skid chains on our bald back tires. The bailing-wire-spliced skid chains gripped pretty well. We did not have to get out more than three or four times to push the car up the steeper stretches. The headlights, one of which had started pointing more toward the sky instead of at the road, proved that we were driving up Little Cottonwood Canyon. Then the road ended in a flat meadow, and we were surrounded by snowbanks of feathery-light powder snow, 3 feet deep. Ward looked around and said, "This is the place."

We had parked below the employees' dorm for Alta Lifts and Lodge. The temperature was dropping fast. Inside the trailer, our breath condensed on the ceiling, and flakes of snow began drifting down on us as we fell asleep. Think of putting a sleeping bag and ski clothes into an empty, top-loading deep freeze, climbing in, removing some of your clothes, shutting the lid, wriggling into the bag, and going to sleep.

In the morning, we were under a dusting of light powder inside the trailer, condensation from our breath that had frozen on the ceiling. Brushing the snow off was easy, but getting dressed in the cold of morning without opening the trailer door was technically impossible. My first move was to put on my wool shirt and ski jacket over my long johns and turtleneck shirt I slept in, shove myself into ski pants, open the trailer door, and put on Army-surplus flight boots. And all the while Ward was struggling into his clothes, taking up his half of the trailer. I would then shuffle off and get into "the kitchen" outside in the back of the trailer. One morning there were eight little mice that had just been born in my right flight boot.

My routine was to light the Coleman, take frozen milk from the icebox, bang it against the trailer to chop out the frozen milk, drop the chunks into the pan, add the dry oatmeal, stick the pan on the burner, and wait for the chunks to melt and the oatmeal to cook. The last move was to change into frozen, ice-hard ski boots that we hoped would warm up as we walked to the lift. We were full of oatmeal and ready to ski.

In Southern California, skiers are grateful no matter what type of snow falls because it may melt by tomorrow. At Alta, 2 to 4 feet of powder seemed to fall every few days. Among all of the Alta skiers, there weren't many of them skiing in the powder back then; instead they skied on a cut-up run full of bumps.

There was room for only four lodges because the floor of Little Cottonwood Canyon was so narrow and had so many avalanche paths running across it that there were few building envelopes. And more beds were not necessary in those days, because most skiers drove up from Salt Lake for the day. Instead of rope tows, Alta had two of the nation's earliest chairlifts, made out of parts cannibalized from old mine hoists. Only Alta and Sun Valley at the time had as many as two chairlifts, one above the other. It was their multiple stacked chairs that made Alta and Sun Valley the two best skiing experiences in America. (Aspen's chairlifts were in the process of being built.) Looming over the scene at Alta was High Rustler, which was a long climb to reach—the high point along the canyon wall and the steepest skiing anywhere in a U.S. resort, with a 45-degree drop that looked impossible. That's why we were at Alta. We had gotten hooked on powder snow—and a challenge.

All-day lift tickets cost $2.50, which we considered expensive. Fortunately, some girls steered us toward Snowpine Lodge, where we found we could get weekend jobs frying hamburgers, as well as much-needed showers. It was the oldest lodge, originally built as a miners' shelter and now serving as a skiers' dorm. They gave us each $10 a weekend, plus all the hamburgers we could eat. Ten dollars gave me four-days' worth of lift tickets, and the fifth day would cost us $2.50 in cash, but that was our entire expense for skiing at Alta.

We were running out of mackerel and goat meat, so we carried the hamburgers that had fallen on the floor or were overcooked away in our small rucksacks in order to leave the kitchen clean. We were heavier when we left work each night. Hamburger mixed with oatmeal extender for dinner kept us full. We never woke up hungry because we made two or three hamburger mistakes each day that we worked.

Once we tried cooking an unlucky porcupine killed on the road. I don't recommend it to anyone: Porcupine tastes just like the last tree bark it ate.

I discovered *Are My Skis On Straight?* sold well to Alta skiers. The manager at Snowpine let me leave a copy on a side table during weekends, with a sign saying "To Buy, See Warren in the Kitchen." I sold 56 copies of the book for $2 each during our three-week stay.

The powder was great. Prevailing winds swept into California from the Pacific, dried out over the desert in Nevada, and were forced up into the cold, high altitudes over the Wasatch to provide the dry snow that powder skiers dream about. As a result, American deep powder technique was pioneered at Alta, beginning in the 1940s with a series of early ski-school directors. The first was Dick Durrance, the first U.S. racer who could match the Europeans. Dick arrived at Alta in 1942 and gave lessons out of the Snowpine Lodge that he and his wife, Miggs, were running. Dick came up with the first technique to handle the short powder turns needed in Alta's narrow couloirs. He angled his inside ski out a bit as he stepped on it, and then stepped onto the other inside ski for the next turn, a two-step move Dick called "the Dipsy Doodle." Dick and Miggs Durrance would become great friends of mine through the rest of my life.

During our second week, Ward and I organized a showing of our surfing movie. I had brought out my film projector and used a screen set up in the Alta Lodge lobby. The films were silent, of course, so I put in a few ironic comments that came automatically from my weird view of life, the sort of humor that saves the day when things go wrong. My commentary drew some laughs, and after the lights went on, a bit of applause. The audience saw surfing they had never seen before—and I was doing something I had never done before—narrating it. I discovered that I really enjoyed doing it, way back in November 1946.

On our final day at Alta, Ward and I both took our 8-MM cameras up with us and filmed each other. We wanted to see what we'd learned. Then we had to load up and head back to Hollywood. Thanksgiving was coming. On day three of the trip, we talked all the way through Las Vegas, and driving through the night, we reached Los Angeles as the sun rose behind us in the east.

CHAPTER EIGHTEEN

1946–1947

Six Months of Powder, Sunny Days, and Cold Nights

THE DAY AFTER I CAME BACK FROM ALTA, MY MOTHER COOKED Thanksgiving dinner. She was still scrambling to fix up and rent space in the office building that wasn't producing much revenue, except as space for the ozone business. Still, she served a whole turkey with all the trimmings.

The day after Thanksgiving, Arnold Grasmoen, Brynhild's father, was on the phone again, asking if I wanted to work at the Arizona Snow Bowl as a general handyman and operate one of his rope tows that was open weekends. He had almost finished building the lodge and needed help finishing it off. He offered reasonable pay and free room and board—the best and only job offer I had at the moment. I also found out that while I was in Flagstaff, I could sign up for classes, including life drawing, during the week at the nearby Northern Arizona University to finish my degree. (I, of course, was hoping Brynhild would be around some of the time.) I told Mr. Grasmoen that if I could bring Ward Baker to work along with me and get paid, then I would come. He said OK, and it was a deal. Ward wanted to take some courses at the university, too, where both of us would have full tuition under the GI Bill.

Years later, I figured out that a lot of my interest in Brynhild was because her father, the president of a small bank in Merced, and her mother had a 100-percent normal life, something I had never seen before. He even walked home every day for lunch, which his wife prepared for him. The only out-of-the-ordinary behavior he had was that he really liked to ski, but his wife didn't.

Driving the Buick to pick up Ward in Manhattan Beach, I was not really surprised when the engine conked out, luckily near a garage a few blocks from Ward's house. The mechanic took a long look and gave me an estimate of $250 to bring it back to life, roughly the value of the car when it was running well. The garage owner got my down payment, and I said the rest of the money would be paid when he got the car running.

Meanwhile, we drove to Arizona in Ward's Plymouth Coupe. When we got to the Grasmoen Lodge, the first thing we did was look at the ski area. It had a foot or two of snow at the bottom, but the vertical rise of the two rope tows was only about 100 feet; the hill was almost flat. The upper slopes did not have enough snow to cover the rocks, making skiing impossible even if we climbed up there. The developed skiing had zero interest for us. Arnold Grasmoen's brother and his wife were running the lodge. They must have gotten a very low price on a large supply of potatoes because they served us potatoes three times a day and not much else.

Brynhild never did show up, because she was busy trying to make the U.S. Ski Team. After a week or so, Ward and I were tired of potatoes and unhappy in general, so we packed our gear, went to see Mr. Grasmoen's brother, and told him, "We are heading back to Hollywood, but thanks anyway for thinking of us."

Life in Los Angeles was dull after three weeks of skiing Alta. So we decided we had to get back there. This time we planned to stay awhile, and then take off to visit the ski resorts of the West to ski and sell more copies of *Are My Skis on Straight?* My book sales were important because they could help pay for my share of the gas and food.

To resupply us, Ward went fishing off Catalina Island for anything he could catch and shot goats on a cliff above the ocean so they then would tumble into the water, and he could pick them up from the boat. I washed and fumigated the trailer. The two of us left for Alta on December 26,

1946. We hit Yosemite on New Year's Day, 1947, for a few days and stayed awhile, earning lift tickets working as extras on the Ski Patrol.

The Grand Hotel Ahwahnee provided its guests with huge, luxurious lunch boxes, from which there were many leftovers. My subsequent lifelong friend Bob Maynard saved the leftovers for us. He was a busboy back then, courting Nancy, to whom he's been married ever since. Maynard went on to start Keystone Resort in Colorado, run Sundance, and then become the president of the Aspen Skiing Co., among many other achievements.

Yosemite's luxury hotel was a dozen miles from Badger Pass. The Ahwahnee became the ideal blueprint for the Sun Valley Lodge, introducing the concept of a grand lodge with a bar, a cocktail room, après-ski dancing, and first-class service. After learning the value of this level of service, Bob Maynard set the standard for top ski resort managers for years.

One day while shoveling snow for Charley Proctor, we told him that we wanted to become ski racers. His answer was a wake-up call, "If you guys get paid to do any kind of work on skis, you will be professional skiers and unable to race, except against ski instructors and other professional skiers." We quit shoveling the mogul we were leveling at the time. That's how tough it was to stay amateur in those days, but those days didn't last very long.

AFTER A WEEK OF SKIING AT YOSEMITE, WE WERE ON OUR WAY TO ALTA, this time via the Donner Summit and Reno. The remaining miles to Salt Lake City flew by with only a few problems. A good distance into Nevada, on the road somewhere east of Winnemucca, we hit some marshlands that had a lot of ducks. We started shooting ducks from the moving Buick, which was not easy. The ducks were in a number of ponds on either side of the road, so I drove with my right hand on the wheel and my left hand out the window holding onto Ward's belt to keep him from falling off the running board. If the next pond was on his side, Ward became one with the car until he raised his shotgun. If the pond was on the far side of the car, Ward crouched out of sight, like an Indian hanging on the far side of his horse in an attack on covered wagons. Ward would pop up and take his shot over the roof of the car as the ducks took off. Before we reached the end of the marsh, we stopped to wade out and retrieve the eight ducks he shot.

Warren's parents, Albert Lincoln Miller and Helena Humphrey Miller, in 1929 on the beach at Topanga Canyon, near the small shack they lived in for two years.

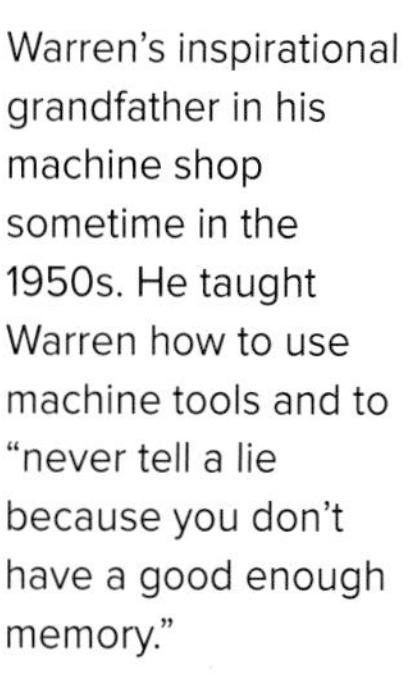

Warren's inspirational grandfather in his machine shop sometime in the 1950s. He taught Warren how to use machine tools and to "never tell a lie because you don't have a good enough memory."

Warren's first understanding of a dysfunctional childhood came when his father worked a deal for the family to live in the abandoned Encino Country Club. It was a short occupancy, with the Millers departing under the cover of darkness. ENCINO COUNTRY CLUB PHOTO

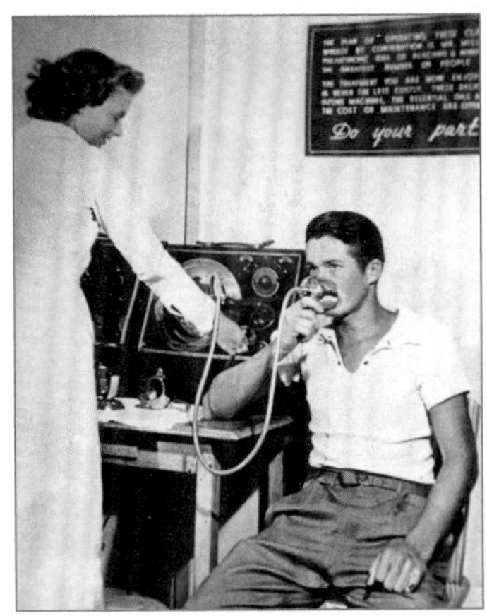

Ozone paid the bills for the Miller family. Warren's sister, Mary Helen, then a freshman at USC, administering to a "patient" in 1941.

Warren's first photo of a skier, David Heiser, at Idyllwild above Palm Springs, in January 1940. David was also a member of Boy Scout Troop 20.

WARREN MILLER PHOTO

Warren and his sister, Mary Helen, while they were both at USC.

Commissioned as an ensign in the U.S. Navy in December 1944, Warren's orders sent him to Guadalcanal and Sub-chaser 521, which was sunk in a typhoon.

After skiing every day for three weeks at Badger Pass while awaiting his next orders from the Navy, Warren won his first slalom race, holding off the Tenth Mountain Division veterans up from Monterey for the weekend.

Ward Baker camping out in the Alta parking two weeks before Thanksgiving in 1946. No one told them they were supposed to be cold, so they weren't. WARREN MILLER PHOTO

Testing the first chairlift design in the world for Sun Valley. The "test dummy" would later don roller skates to simulate skis on snow. UNION PACIFIC RAILROAD PHOTO

During the Sun Valley winter of 1946–47, Warren befriends Ernest Hemingway and Gary Cooper. In the Duchin Room, Hemingway tosses martini olives at Cooper, who was a strong skier.
UNION PACIFIC RAILROAD PHOTOS

The best view of the Sun Valley Lodge was from Warren's Buick and trailer in the parking lot. WARD BAKER PHOTO

Warren and Ward "fumigating" the trailer in the spring of 1947. The mattress was frozen to the floor of the trailer.

The famous end-of-season "farewell to the parking lot" party.
SUN VALLEY PR PHOTO

Ward and Warren in the spring of 1947 on the weeklong Ostrander Lake backcountry trip, and the figure-8s they left on Horse Ridge.

Warren, nicknamed "Warnie" by his surfing buddies, with the broken-nosed surfboard he built in 1947 after leaving the Navy. It was 11-feet long and weighed more than 100 pounds when waterlogged. The Malibu Pier is in the background.

Warren launched his ski career as an instructor. He's pictured top right in 1948 with the Sun Valley Ski School, attired in their Andre of New York gabardine ski pants with matching nylon windbreakers. Johnny Litchfield, the assistant director, is far left in the first row; Otto Lang, the director, is fourth from left; and Sigi Engl, who would later take over the school, is far right. SUN VALLEY PR PHOTO

Warren with the Squaw Valley Ski School in November 1949, the resort's first season of operation. The instructors had no uniforms, and on a good day they each had one student. Warren is flanked by Dodie Post, director Émile Allais, Charlie Cole, and Alfred Hauser. SQUAW VALLEY PR PHOTO

Warren during the production of his first surfing film at San Onofre in July 1949. With his waterproof box, the camera never got wet. Here it was aimed at Myra Roche, a mother of five children at the time. The next winter, he was painting casts on the deck at Squaw Valley. He earned $1 each and sometimes got a free meal, too.

WARREN MILLER PHOTOS

The Bell & Howell camera that Chuck Percy and Hal Geneen loaned to Warren in 1949. It's attached to the base of the water box that Warren built the following summer.

WARREN MILLER PHOTO

Seattle's Metropolitan Theater, with Warren's first film on the marquee. It's now the porte cochere for the Olympic Hotel. The film tour has returned to Seattle for 65-plus years.

WARREN MILLER PHOTO

The first film, and several to follow, starred Warren's mentor, Émile Allais.

WARREN MILLER PHOTO

Warren, posing and then waxing at Sun Valley in 1951, wears his signature bighorn sheep sweater. It was knitted by a waitress he had taught to ski.
SUN VALLEY PR PHOTOS

Warren and Jean married in June 1951. The wedding reception was held in their one-bedroom apartment over a garage in Glendale; note the surfboard hanging on the wall.

Jean, on the beach at San Onofre, was a model, avid skier, and supportive business partner for Warren.

WARREN MILLER PHOTO

Warren editing his second film in 1951; the spare bedroom was turned into a film studio.

JEAN MILLER PHOTO

Warren's popularity grew beyond the ski world after he was recruited by Jantzen as a spokesperson in 1956, modeling the apparel brand's sweaters along with star mainstream athletes such as Frank Gifford. The national ad campaign also had Warren posing prior to the 1960 Olympics in Squaw Valley with ski school director Jo Marillac and his wife, Margaret Ann. JANTZEN PR/TOM KELLEY PHOTOS

Zurs was a favorite location for filming powder and scenery, as well as for the hospitality of innkeeper Herbert Jochum. In bottom photo, Warren with his rucksack plans the next powder shot. Jochum is hidden in front of Warren; double-Olympic-gold-medalist Andrea Mead Lawrence is to the right, her husband Dave is on the left.

Warren sailing his P-Cat at Dana Point in the mid-1960s and surfing in the late 1960s at Malibu. DON BROLIN, LEROY GRANNIS PHOTOS

The legal limit in the state of Nevada was five ducks, assuming that you had a hunting license (we didn't), that you did not shoot from a moving car (we did), and that you shot during duck season (it wasn't). A warden coming along would have insisted we spend a few days inside a warm county jail, but we were 22-year-olds out for a winter of low-budget skiing and had lucked into a low-budget bonanza. I ran through so much adrenaline hunting the Winnemucca ducks that some unwinding was needed. There are worse ways than duck hunting to undo postwar mental trauma, not that it was even recognized back then.

We went into the local hotel to use their washroom to shave and get cleaned up. With mud up to our knees from breaking through the frozen marshes, it was easy to follow our path from the car, through the lobby to the 5-cent slot machine, and on to the men's room and the 10-cent toilets.

It was nice in the men's room: steam heat, hot water, and the first warm water shave in days. We mixed up a little warm water with some salt and ketchup we brought along and topped off our sponge bath with a nice warm cup of tomato soup. Ward then crawled under the door of the 10-cent toilet and removed two of the ducks from his coat pockets as I stood and watched. While I pretended to take a half hour to shave, he took the same length of time to remove the feathers from the ducks. He was just about through the second one when he decided to flush the feathers down the drain. Apparently, these birds had their winter coats because the feathers jammed up the drain and 2 pounds of feathers started trickling across the floor, headed for the lowest point in the men's room which, in this case, happened to be the door.

We folded up our gear, Ward stuffed the ducks back into his pockets, and we sauntered toward the door. I felt a little conspicuous, but Ward really looked that way, especially from behind, as the remaining duck with head intact stuck out of a hole in his pocket. With every step he took, it bounced along behind him.

We were, by this time, fairly clean, so we put the ducks back into the trailer and went down the street to spend our ill-gotten gambling funds on hot bowls of chili. (We had made 85 cents on the nickel machine.)

Driving down the street an hour later, headed east for Salt Lake City, I was starting to unload our guns when a car behind us honked. We waved it around, because our top speed was 34 mph and we thought he was trying to pass. He honked again. We waved again. By this time, I turned around and watched the car begin to pass us. I leaned over to give forth with some of the dialogue I had learned in the Navy. Just then the window of the car rolled down and an officer of the law sat behind a .38-caliber revolver. Since we were sitting on the wrong side of this particular .38, Ward pulled over and stopped so fast that the ski rack broke. The skis kept right on going up the highway. Their actual distance traveled varied with the individual wax jobs.

The police parked on an angle in front of us so we couldn't get away while they were walking to the car. I began to wonder what we had done. One deputy came around to my side of the car, with revolver drawn, while the other stood 4 feet away from Ward's side and said: "Let's see your driver's license."

They were looking for car thieves. However, the peculiar fragrance of oil, cooking grease, goat, and mackerel wafting out of our car window made locking us up in the clean cell at the sheriff's office their last choice. Luckily for us, poor grooming wasn't such a bad idea.

"I don't have one," Ward said. It had expired a couple of years ago.

"Where is the registration for your license plates?"

"I just sent it in for new ones," I lied. I'd forgotten that I'd left it in the men's room with a map of Elko, on which I had made a notation of the bank's location, when we made our getaway after the feather-flushing flood.

"Where are your new license tabs?"

"We didn't get them in the mail yet."

"Are those guns loaded?"

"Yes."

"Why?"

"In case we get held up."

Tactician that he was, Ward came forth with: "If you fellows are going to be so belligerent, why don't you just take us to jail?"

So they did.

We got truly warm for the first time since Christmas. Bars or no bars, this place really had it. We sat for half an hour on the two steam heaters in the lobby. As the heat began to creep through our clothes and into our bodies, the odor of the mackerel and goat meat we had been sleeping with was unleashed. Like a tidal wave, I could see that it was turning the law enforcement officers against us with each passing moment. During the day, we always put the mackerel and goat meat in our sleeping bags to keep them frozen. At night, leaving them in the car, they would stay frozen. But it did make our sleeping bags, and consequently us, a little ripe.

The booking sergeant finally came back from his afternoon game of pool and had a good heart-to-heart talk with us. I could have understood him better if he had stopped squirting his bottle of Airwick at us with every other word.

We had been picked up because someone matching our descriptions had stolen a car like mine in Reno. We identified ourselves conclusively by telling them what was in the bottom of our sleeping bags. Goat meat, mackerel, and chickens. Old chickens.

"Where did all the duck feathers come from?"

"Down sleeping bags."

"Make them out of mallards, do they now?"

"Army surplus, you know."

He let us out, and we got out of town as fast as our car's limited speed would allow. Fueled by duck breasts and duck soup, we made good time between Elko and Alta. On arrival, we were rehired at the Snowpine Lodge to fry hamburgers. We were definitely less fortunate with the weather than before. Alta was having a deep cold spell, and frostbite continually threatened to become a permanent part of our faces. The skiing was great, but we had to take the runs in short bursts and check each other's faces for white spots every time we stopped. Back then, the only protection was using a neckerchief under goggles; this was way before face masks. During the week, we met several good-looking girls in the lift line who were good skiers. Two of them invited us to the Alta Lodge, where we sat around in comfortable chairs while we told war stories from our checkered pasts.

The girls had just come from Sun Valley. Their report made it seem much more luxurious than Alta. Sun Valley had a big main lodge with a cocktail lounge with après-ski dancing and a connected outdoor, round, heated swimming pool. Who had ever heard of such a thing? After the cold, cold skiing at Alta, just thinking about soaking ourselves in the hot water of the Sun Valley swimming pool made up our minds.

That evening, we decided to pack up and head for Sun Valley. We went north through Ogden, reached Shoshone, Idaho, where we saw lots of rabbits on the run on both sides of the road. Ward said we should get some groceries. He got out his shotgun, and before long we had six rabbits. In the center of a frozen irrigation ditch, we chopped a hole in the ice, cleaned the rabbits, and drove on to Ketchum, an old mining and sheep ranching town now full of skiers, thanks to Sun Valley a mile up the road.

THE FIRST THING WE DID IN KETCHUM WAS TO GO INTO THE LOCAL photo store and sell the owner a dozen copies of *Are My Skis On Straight?* When we asked where we should park our car and trailer in order to ski, the owner said to go up to Sun Valley and park in the lot between the Skier's Chalet and the garage. We found a spot out of the way of other cars and settled the Buick into what would become its permanent winter parking place. Sun Valley was in its sixth year of operation, not counting the two years when it was shut down during the war, when the Lodge was turned into a hospital for recovering sailors. The resort buildings were the only structures in a 4,000-acre field, including the Sun Valley Lodge and its round, outdoor swimming pool. The Challenger Inn and the Skiers' Chalet were the only inns; there were no condos in that era.

There was a movie theater called the Opera House and Pete Lane's ski store, with such a savvy clientele that I sold over a hundred copies of my book there that winter. A half-mile off was Dollar Mountain, with one chairlift to the top, and Proctor Mountain, also with one chairlift, which wasn't running at the time. Closer was Ruud Mountain, with another single-person chairlift. All were smooth, open-sloped mountains of about 1,000 vertical feet. On the other side of Ketchum was Mt. Baldy, with steeper, longer ski trails served by three chairlifts, one above the other, which in itself was enough to ensure that Sun Valley had no competition as the best destination resort in America.

Ward and I had to start our Sun Valley experience by swimming in the warm outdoor pool. As soon as we'd parked the car and trailer, I went into Pete Lane's ski shop and traded 10 copies of my book for two pairs of swimming trunks. Sun Valley was so relaxed in those days that we just walked in the door of the pool dressing room with our trunks in hand, and the attendant gave us a towel. We weren't even asked to show our room key—a good thing because we didn't have one. We eased our bodies into that deliciously warm water while the high, glass walls around the pool deflected the cold wind.

In order to hang around the pool, or anywhere else in the resort, we needed the approval of Sun Valley's general manager, Pappy Rogers, who knew most guests and nearly every employee by name. Someone once wrote that he had the "geniality that held the Sun Valley style together." But he was also a high-flying character who fired employees who irritated him one day and sometimes hired them back the next. It was necessary to get on his good side as soon as possible.

When we met Pappy, we introduced ourselves as the ex-Naval-officer-trailer-dwellers sleeping in his parking lot. Rogers decided in one long look that we could become local color, with good manners. Rogers let us keep our car and trailer in back of the Challenger Inn for as long as we wanted to stay. He let us know we were expected to show up from time to time at the pool and bars in the lodges, watching out for ladies who were alone and might need some help. We promised to perform diligently.

The season was already well under way, so an at-least 10-minute search told us that the ski-bum jobs had all been taken. We had a gross of cocktail glasses with us that I hand-painted with ski cartoons during rainy days at Berendo Street. Every one of them sold. The stash of my $2 cartoon books was in the back seat of the Buick. My individual cartoons sold for $1 apiece, and for $2, I decorated plaster casts of hospital patients. My financial endeavors proved to be a success in Idaho.

We found a good way to get on the lifts at Baldy without having to pay. Just how we did it has never been revealed and will go to our graves with us, out of gratitude to Pappy Rogers. My decorated glassware, cartoons, and book profits added up to a sum that, along with free meals of rabbits and ducks, didn't require us to take part-time jobs. Ward did take a part-time job at a photo shop developing pictures at night toward the end of our stay, but having no work gave us more time to ski Baldy, swim in the pool, and attend après-ski dances in the Lodge to live music, just as in the European resorts.

The atmosphere was not always refined, however. The day that Sun Valley officially opened in December 1936, a fistfight had broken out between two celebrities in the cocktail lounge. Newspapers across the country jumped on the scandal, writing headlines like "Ski Resort Opens with a Bang!" Steve Hannagan, the resort's New York PR man, made sure that the story got out on the Associated Press wire with the name Sun Valley spelled right. Hannagan knew it would get huge coverage.

Sun Valley was founded by Averell Harriman, chairman of the board of the Union Pacific Railroad and a partner in Brown Brothers Harriman & Company on Wall Street. He built the ski resort where he did because a Union Pacific spur ran into Ketchum, bringing in cattle cars to load up on local lamb for distribution throughout the country. That meant he could at least partly write off the resort as a business expense.

Harriman had already built El Tovar Lodge on another Union Pacific line at the Grand Canyon, but there was a personal reason to develop Sun Valley: Harriman's European businessmen friends took winter vacations to ski resorts in the Alps. Whether they skied or not, they wanted to relax in surrounding mountain scenery, posh accommodations, first-class restaurants, and a friendly atmosphere, among beautiful people, though that phrase had not been coined as yet. There was only one current ski resort close to filling that bill in America and that was the Grand Hotel Ahwahnee at Yosemite. But the Ahwahnee's location was on the far edge of the continent and not on a Union Pacific line. In those days of limited air travel, Harriman found that to attract moneyed skiers, it made more sense to build a resort easier to get to from New York and Chicago via the Union Pacific. Sun Valley was Harriman's own winter retreat, and it attracted socialites, celebrities, actors, and actresses. Harriman's continental friends enjoyed it, too, and he imported charming European ski instructors to teach in the ski school, most recently headed by Friedl Pfeifer, who came from the St. Anton ski school in the Austrian Arlberg. During our first year, Friedl had left to start his own ski school at Aspen, splitting direction at Sun Valley with Otto Lang, who also came from the famous Hannes Schneider's St. Anton Ski School.

The real genius behind Sun Valley's popularity was the great pitchman, Steve Hannagan, famous for making Miami Beach into the top resort destination in Florida, "starting with a sand dune," as he put it. Hannagan's yearly flood of pictures of pretty women on the beach in their swimsuits was sensational in its day. Every winter, newspapers carried them.

It was Hannagan who had insisted on the name "Sun Valley" rather than a place-name like Ketchum, Alta, or Yosemite. It was Hannagan who insisted on the round, outdoor swimming pool for the same reason. Girls in their swimsuits at the pool's edge in Sun Valley in the winter were displayed in newspapers all over the world every year, announcing that Sun Valley was in business. Hannagan had continent-wide contacts, especially among Hollywood bigwigs, actresses, and wannabes. He managed to get a good number of the wannabes to Sun Valley for swimsuit shots. He also arranged to have Errol Flynn, Clark Gable, Claudette Colbert, Robert Young, and Sam Goldwyn there for the grand Christmas Day opening, with a celebration in the eventually world-famous Duchin Room. And he was the one who knew that the resort needed better uphill transportation than rope tows.

Because of the genius of Steve Hannagan, Sun Valley pulled Americans into the age of high-mountain, luxury resort living. The chairlift, the eventual backbone of American destination-resort skiing, debuted at Sun Valley at the same time, designed by a Union Pacific engineer as a civilized replacement for the arm-stretching, wringing-wet or icy rope tows. The chairs standing on Sun Valley's Proctor and Dollar Mountains at the resort's opening in 1936 were the world's first chairlifts.

The chairlift was invented in a railroad yard in Omaha in the middle of July 1936. Charley Proctor, former Dartmouth ski coach and 1932 Olympic skier, showed up with a couple of ski friends to figure out a replacement for the rope tow. A young engineer had built overhead moving cables with hooks to transport bananas from the fields to the trucks without bruising them, and he suggested that they could replace the hooks with chairs to haul people up the mountain.

Two days later they had built a scaffold in the back of a pickup truck and were scooping up Charley Proctor's friend, who was dressed in his heavy wool ski clothes, standing on a pile of straw in his boots and skis and sweating in the hot July sun. The straw was not slippery so they added train oil to it, and as the truck took faster and faster trips, trying to scoop up the skier, the chair finally started to hurt the back of his legs. They quit for the day.

Later over a beer or two, someone said, "There's a lot of concrete out behind the roundhouse, so why don't we find a pair of roller skates and see if that friction is more like skis on snow?" It worked, and the speed that the pickup truck scooped up the roller-skating, wool-clad skier is the same speed that a fixed-grip chairlift runs at today.

In the middle of July, the Union Pacific Railroad engineers were told to finish designing the chairlift, build it, and then ship it to Sun Valley, where it would be running on Dollar by December 15. No permits needed; no problem in those days. They just did it.

The lifts were operating by December 15, but the snow did not show up until February 15. Pappy Rogers said, "Anyone who wants to stay until it snows can stay free until it does." A lot of out-of-work Hollywood-wannabe-types stuck around freeloading until it snowed, and then left the next day when they had to start paying for their room and meals.

The three lifts on Baldy were not built until 1940, because no one was a good enough skier yet to handle such a steep mountain, plus the ski equipment was so terrible it wouldn't have worked on Baldy's steep runs.

Harriman brought in four more chairlifts in 1940 to be installed, one on Ruud, where Harriman had built a big ski jump just so Sun Valley could be on the national all-around championship circuit, which then included slalom, downhill, cross-country, and jumping. Harriman wanted his resort to be first-class in everything, and it was—except for the trailer in the parking lot in the winter of 1946–1947.

Harriman had another brilliant idea. I have been asked many times, "Why was the Sun Valley Lodge built so far out in the middle of a wide valley instead of nestled on the side of a hill somewhere?" When Harriman bought the 4,000-acre ranch for $4 an acre, Harriman asked the seller, Ernest Brass, where his cattle spent the winter. Since cattle always stay in the warmest part of a valley, this is where the lodge was built. Some long-time Sun Valley skiers say, "The lodge was built on the largest pile of manure in Idaho." But I know it was built in the warmest part of the Wood River Valley and it's now completely surrounded by condominiums, some of which sold for less than $10,000 when my friend Bill Janss started building them in the mid-1960s.

Sun Valley was a casual place, where meeting an upper-class young lady like Josephine Abercrombie was not impossible for an ordinary guy like me. I met her skiing on Dollar Mountain, a beautiful 22-year-old with a good sense of humor and, by her outfit, not worried about its cost. I learned that she was a champion horsewoman—an athletic, graceful young woman who I thought was very attractive. After I had timed my stop to seem casual near Josephine on the side of Dollar Mountain, we rapidly became good friends. She spent every day on Dollar Mountain under the guidance of a private ski instructor, and every one of her ski vacation evenings with me.

Our relationship might have blossomed, but she was from Texas and I was from California, and I didn't even have a job—we were GU (geographically undesirable). That didn't keep the two of us from enjoying Sun Valley while she was there: dancing to live music, bowling in the lodge alley, or going down to Ketchum for an evening of wandering in and out of the gambling halls and watching the high rollers play with their money. Josephine was staying in the most expensive rooms in the Sun Valley Lodge—$18 dollars a night—while I was staying in the parking lot for zero dollars a night. The nice thing about being in Sun Valley was that our differences didn't matter while we were there.

Usually I climbed on my skis to the restaurant that then stood on the top of Dollar to meet Josephine for lunch with her friend Audrey Beck. (I still did not have a legal lift ticket.) When Josephine decided she would rather go swimming than skiing, that's what we did. After that, we met for Cokes at the Sun Valley Lodge, and we danced to Hap Miller's band in the Duchin Room. The romance topped out on the dance floor. It was a very Sun Valley story, and I would be lucky enough to have another Sun Valley romance later in my life. That is what Sun Valley is known for—romance, besides the excellent skiing. We took in movies at the Opera House where they showed "Sun Valley Serenade." We went there on the days the doorman, a friend, fed the tickets back into my palm, and I stuck them in my pocket. If Josephine noticed, she never said a word.

Finally, Josephine and Audrey had to leave; they asked Ward and me to drive them to the Hailey Airport to meet their plane. Of course I would. I was a little apprehensive about starting the solidly frozen car, which hadn't been moved for at least three weeks, so I began preparations for the 12-mile drive a couple of hours before the scheduled departure. I used "the coffee can gas trick" for starting frozen cars: First puncture holes around the side of a coffee can about one-third of the way up from the bottom; then pour gas in up to the holes and light it. The can works like a chimney so that the gasoline burns hot, and the can is then shoved under the frozen engine and radiator. In theory, the flames will be just high enough and burn just long enough to warm up the oil in the engine. It will also set your engine on fire if the flames are too high. I thought I had the equation for the right amount of gasoline against a given temperature. I had a long wire connected to the can to drag it out from under the car if the flames got high enough to scare me. I would use a ski pole to move the flaming can around under the car to warm the radiator as well as the engine. Most importantly, the hood was open, and I had a big shovel ready to throw snow on the engine if the fire got out of control.

After the car started, it was a short drive to the front of the Sun Valley Lodge to let the bell captain figure out how to get Josephine and Audrey's eleven-teen suitcases stashed in the Buick's trunk, the back seat, and tied to the front fenders. We managed to drive safely to the Hailey Airport, skidding no more than half a dozen times.

In 1947, the Hailey Airport was a grass field that the owner took care of when he had a couple of days off from working on the highway. There were a couple of small hangars but no control tower. There was something that barely resembled a runway. Standing out there all by itself on two wheelbarrow wheels was a ramp that had four or five steps.

The ramp apparently was available for the occasional two-engine planes that flew up from Hollywood, bringing movie stars to Sun Valley. Alongside the ramp was a 4-by-4 wooden post with the required small first-aid kit and a large fire extinguisher. Someone must have believed this was enough to handle a crash landing. There was also a telephone number to call in case of an emergency. There were, however, no phones this far out of Hailey.

We sat there together in the car and waited for the plane. We were the only people at the airport, and there wasn't another car to be seen except for the occasional one driving past on the road south toward Shoshone. I assumed Josephine and Audrey would fly out on a commercial flight but found out later there were no regular commercial flights into Hailey.

About an hour later, we heard the sound of an engine. The sun flashed off an almost-invisible plane above the snow-covered hills to the southeast, forming a backdrop that only a movie director could have dreamed up. It was a scene out of the old 1937 movie "Lost Horizon."

The plane slowly got bigger and became a twin engine DC-3. When it was close enough to lower the wheels, you still couldn't make out any commercial markings, because there were none. I had never seen a private plane this big. My sense of Josephine's family escalated to the very, very successful. Instead of my sneaking Josephine into the Opera House to see movies for free, she could have asked her father to buy the theater for us, and he could have easily obliged. (I learned later that Josephine's father invented the blow-out valve needed on all oil rigs to prevent fires. She was an only child, and her father taught her all the business principles he would have taught a son. She became a very successful business person in her own right, establishing a respected and successful thoroughbred-breeding farm called Pin Oak, among many other ventures.)

The DC-3 kicked up a giant cloud of snow as it touched down on the runway. The pilot turned the DC-3 around, creating another giant cloud of propeller-driven snow as it taxied up to the Buick.

The rear cabin door opened, and steps swung down from hinges. The pilot and copilot climbed out, bringing greetings from Josephine's father, who owned the plane. They unloaded a table and four chairs, three picnic baskets full of food, a couple of bottles of wine, crystal glasses, and sterling-silver place settings. We sat there warm and toasty in the reflection of the sun off the aircraft's shiny aluminum, while we munched on roast beef sandwiches and seafood cocktails, sampled a great salad, and divided a chocolate cake. Too soon, all the plates and silver were put back in the picnic baskets and lifted aboard. Hugs and kisses all around, and "I'll write and phone!" promises exchanged. The pilot took me aside and told me where to stand and what to do with the fire extinguisher if a fire erupted as he started the engines. Fire quite often erupted when starting a radial engine airplane.

As the engines started up without any major fire, the pilot saluted with two fingers, just as John Wayne used to do in war movies. I backed out of the way with the fire extinguisher at the ready. The pilot taxied the plane north, while Josephine and Audrey waved good-bye and blew kisses through the miniature windows.

It was the end of my first, very Sun Valley love story.

CHAPTER NINETEEN

1947–1948

The Rich, the Famous, and Us: The Beginning of What Became My Eventual Career

WHEN SUN VALLEY OPENED FOR THE 1947–48 SEASON, THE HANNAGAN machine was up and running. At the top of Sun Valley's guest list were names that ran from the merely famous to the unbelievably famous. Hannagan had outdone himself when he got Mohammad Reza Shah Pahlavi—the Shah of Iran. He arrived with four bodyguards, but none could ski. Nelson Bennett, head of the ski patrol, provided four ski patrolmen with prior service in the Tenth Mountain, who declared they knew how to handle the .45 Colt revolvers used by the Shah's bodyguards. The Shah skied in the center of these four, revolver-toting Tenth Mountain vets—two about 50 feet out in front and two 30 feet back—with the co-director of the ski school, Otto Lang, just in front of the Shah. Possibly Otto was there to keep the Shah from colliding with the circle of bodyguards, but more likely he was a royally appointed ski buddy, one of four Americans the Shah met daily at lunch in the Roundhouse, at a table reserved for them and their ski patrol–bodyguards.

When you got on the River Run chairlift, you hunkered down as you glided silently across and above the Big Wood River. You knew it was below zero when the water was steaming, and it was indeed a magical entry for me every morning to ski on Baldy. Three single chairlifts ran to the top, and there was sometimes powder on River Run from one storm to the next. Much of the beautiful terrain was fairly steep and full of big moguls, lined by curtains of dense trees; it required skills and control above and beyond most of the skiers of the day.

Ward and I spent the mornings going to the top and all the way back down, finishing on River Run as fast as we dared. We sometimes took a long, slow traverse over to Lookout Bowl, where there was always powder, but it was also a long, slow traverse back to the chairlifts at the Roundhouse. The run from the top of Baldy to the bottom of River Run was the longest fall-line run in the U.S. at the time.

We got off at the top of the Exhibition chair and climbed to the Roundhouse, where there were usually people such as the Shah, Otto Lang, Gary Cooper, Cooper's wife, Rocky, and Ernest Hemingway—a celebrity network only Sun Valley could knit together. The Shah's love of Hollywood films was well-known. He had every year's best releases sent to his palace, and he held a firm opinion that the best film of all was "Sun Valley Serenade," produced in 1941. This was why the Shah was at Sun Valley. Otto Lang was a friend of the Shah's and had directed the film's ski sequences.

By the time the Shah's lunch was over, Hemingway had usually worked his way through a bottle of wine and had ridden back down the two bottom lifts, while the Shah and his ski buddies and the patrol rode the other lift to the top of Baldy. Ward and I usually tagged along to the top, where everyone was equal. We skied down at a good distance from the Shah but often right on the tail of Gary Cooper, a pretty good skier. He was 20 years older than us and one of my movie heroes. To stand boot-to-boot with a figure that I had only seen in the movies was amazing. He was always eager to chat about what wax we were using on any given day, because he knew nothing about the subject. (He didn't know that we didn't either.) Cooper was friendly, inviting me to drop in any time he was on the set in Hollywood.

The Shah's ski patrol–bodyguards were all good skiers, but during lunch in the Roundhouse, we noticed that they hung their guns, holsters, and belts on clothes pegs on the wall near the door, and they could have been easily snatched up by anyone. I thought it was strange, and Jack

Simpson (who later with his wife, Mary Lou, developed the once-famous-but-now-gone Warm Springs Ranch), came over to say hello and then in a low voice whispered, "Warren, you see where those bodyguards are sitting?" I said, "Yes." He said, "See where their guns are?" I nodded, and Jack said, "If you stand up between the bodyguards at their table and the door, the bodyguards can't see the guns. You stand there, and I'll steal a couple of the guns and walk outside. Then we'll ski down and leave the guns at the bottom."

It was hard to resist because I would be able to tell this story the rest of my life. With me standing in direct line between the guards and the guns, Jack snuck out the door with two of the four guns inside his ski jacket. Walking out, Jack pushed one of the guns into my jacket pocket.

We skied to the bottom of River Run and handed the guns over to the chairlift crew, saying they had been overlooked at the Roundhouse by the Shah's bodyguards. We told them to slip the guns to the bodyguards, very quietly without any fuss, when they came down with the Shah. That didn't happen until the end of the skiing day. The bodyguards must have very quietly accepted the loss, still wondering how it had all happened. The Shah never found out that half of his bodyguards were unarmed. In fact, nobody found out. You read it here in print for the first time. Iran was a completely different place in 1947, as was Sun Valley.

Sun Valley attracted everyone from ski bums such as ourselves to the top end of the celebrity chain. Ernest Hemingway had written *For Whom the Bell Tolls* in his room at the Sun Valley Lodge, with Steve Hannagan picking up his tab.

On cold and windy days on Baldy, Ward and I took longer lunch breaks at the Roundhouse in order to warm our insides thoroughly with "homemade" hot tomato bisque. We would fill our Dixie Cups with hot water freely given from the kitchen for tea, add ketchup that was sitting on the table, crumble copious amounts of oyster crackers that floated as a mass just below the surface, and add salt and pepper to taste. Tomato bisque a la Warren was filling, tasted good, and was free.

Still grateful for all the free ketchup–tomato bisque that warmed my stomach throughout my early ski life, I dedicated my future story-and-cartoon book *Wine, Women, Warren, & Skis* "To Miss Abigail Nicelunchowski, the inventor of the oyster cracker, without whose foresight I might not have survived the terrible winter of 1947."

My ski technique grew slowly with hundreds of lift rides. As a measurement of achievement, the steep Canyon Run was skied with no turns, stops, or traverses. This was the ski patrol's macho marker, separating the men from the boys. The trick was to pick a line through the intersections of the big bumps in the narrows instead of over them. Of course, I stood up straight and spread my arms wide to slow down by increasing my wind resistance. Still, it was very fast for what seemed like forever.

The attractions of Sun Valley did not end with good skiing, but included a large population of good-looking girls and guys, either guests or employees, and especially the confident young ladies in the lift line who came from all over America. I managed to meet lots of ladies. Ward and I each spent a time teaching two very pretty girls working at Sun Valley how to ski, and both of them knitted each of us a thick winter sweater. Those sweaters were a welcome gift and very warm. (Decades later, my eventual wife Laurie had mine, the one with bighorn sheep on it, copied and reknitted by our dear friend Lila Corrock in Sun Valley.)

I spent bad weather days drawing cartoons at a table in the Challenger Inn. I was getting low on my book inventory and kept my best cartoons for what would be my next book.

Sun Valley was a very hard place to leave. As our stay lengthened, word spread that two strange and primitive but not dangerous guys lived in the Sun Valley parking lot. Occasionally people would come walking through the parking lot to look, talk, and watch us cook rabbit on the Coleman stove in our outdoor kitchen.

Sun Valley didn't have as many deep-powder days as Alta, but then it had a hot-water swimming pool and free protein with the rabbits, and with nearly constant sunshine, every day was a new adventure. Productive Shoshone hunting trips lasted us two weeks, at a rabbit a day on the Coleman stove. We had rabbits fixed almost every way possible on the outdoor stove: fried, stewed, boiled, and singed close to burnt.

During our first winter, a low spot came one early, sunny morning when the parking lot had about 3 feet of snow, all tracked up with deep tire tracks. The management had evidently ordered it to be plowed, so cars could park there without getting stuck. A giant rotary plow chugged into sight, stopped a few feet from us, and the driver asked us politely to move our car and trailer so they could completely plow the lot. This was a problem for us.

Originally, we planned to only stay a week, so we had buried our trash by kicking holes in the snowbank behind the trailer, burying our garbage, and then throwing in more snow, figuring we would be long gone before it melted. There was nothing we could say. We spent the next few minutes getting the Buick started and moving everything except the trash.

We watched silently as the snowplow carved a deep, clean path through our private trash-disposal area. The wheel of the giant rotary threw a river of snow, curving through the air and into the trees. Then there was a *schmoosh* sound as the rotary hit our trash holes, throwing bits and pieces of trash onto both the low and high branches of trees at the edge of the parking lot. The snowplow driver waved good-bye and moved on. He left our trash hanging from the tree limbs, including, but not limited to, a half-dozen rabbit skins, milk-carton shards, a pink napkin or two, polka-dot Wonder Bread wrappers, and a lot of other unidentifiable shreds. The trees looked as if a small tornado had gone by, or there had been a very odd Christmas celebration. Most of the trash dropped off, but one of the rabbit skins stayed stuck high up in the tree, so that when anyone asked for directions to our trailer, we just said, "Go to the parking lot and look around for the tree with the rabbit skin and milk cartons. That's where we are parked."

The picture magazine *Look* arrived to do a story on Sun Valley and included a picture of Ward and me standing, grinning outside our trailer—strangely because our trailer life was the exact opposite of the Sun Valley image in the Steve Hannagan world.

I always enjoyed standing in the snow in our outdoor kitchen after a good day of skiing on Baldy, on a below-zero January night, listening to the hiss of the gasoline-fueled Coleman stove and trying to soak in some of its warmth at the same time.

I liked the smell of rabbit frying above the totally silent evening. At the same time, I could look up and see the constellation of Orion high in the black canopy of winter nights. Twice we even got to see the Northern

Lights this far south. No one has ever had it as good as I did then, except Ward Baker, who was cooking the rabbit.

One night in the Lodge, Ward and I got dressed up again to sit in the audience watching the East Coast ski filmmaker John Jay narrate his fourth-annual ski lecture film, "Skis in the Sky," covering, among other things, the chairlifts we had ridden so often. Jay showed his film in the Duchin Room, spinning his background music on a 78-rpm platter while he narrated expertly along, complementing the scenes. It didn't look that hard. I had the thought, "Hey, I can do that." Except I didn't have a 16-MM camera, film, or projector, or the money to buy it and finance a movie. However, I was smart enough to realize that his offbeat humor was what the audiences liked the most.

Ward and I woke up one morning to the sound of rain on the trailer roof. Suddenly, it was April, and the snow was melting. It was time for us to leave. We decided to have a big, friendly farewell party and rabbit roast around a bonfire beside our trailer for all our Sun Valley friends. We drove down to Shoshone and shot about 20 rabbits. We got back around 10:30 and walked into the Skiers' Chalet, figuring that everyone had already gone to bed. In the men's shower room, Ward skinned the rabbits, and I did the cleaning in the washbasins. We had rabbits lying in every washbasin when an obviously drunk guest staggered in with his towel to take a shower. After one look at us with blood up to our elbows, he turned and ran out the door to report the carnage to the house detectives. By the time he woke up the detectives and led them back, we had everything cleaned up and were out of there.

The evidence was all gone except for some blood and hair left in one of the showers. The detectives thought the guest was lying, possibly to cover up a murder here in the Skiers' Chalet men's room, so they hauled the rapidly sobering guest down to the Hailey police station for questioning. He didn't get out until noon the next day.

The next day, we began cooking the 20 rabbits. A couple of guests brought eight heads of lettuce and salad dressing. Somebody brought firewood. Others brought beer and Cokes. It was one great, memorable evening. The manager of the resort's camera shop took photos, and the next morning he gave me blowups of the pictures, which I still have. Sixteen guests are in one of the photos, but there were twice that many. Well after midnight, the bonfire was dying and people full of beer, rabbit, and fun began to leave. It had been a good finale to what we both agreed, up until then, was easily the best winter of our lives. We also agreed, considering all the noise our party made, that early the next day would be a good time to leave.

We still wanted to continue our trip and see as much of Western skiing as possible. However, we were very, very low on gas money, or any other kind of money, so we were open to having anyone come along who was willing to pay for the gas on the road to Los Angeles via Jackson, Wyoming, and south to Colorado to Pikes Peak, Berthoud Pass, and Aspen. Two waitresses at the Lodge were at our party and volunteered to make the trip with us. We made a deal to split the cost of food between us; the waitresses would buy the gas and sleep in the car. We would supply the transportation, sleep in the trailer, and provide a running commentary on the passing scenery during the day. By noon the next day, we had shoved all our gear into the trailer and fitted the two waitresses and their bags into the back of the car. We fired up the Buick and headed for Jackson Hole on four bald tires with two waitresses and three leftover fried rabbits.

CHAPTER TWENTY

1948

Back and Forth across the Great Continental Divide

WHEN WE HIT THE SMALL TOWN OF DRIGGS, IDAHO, WE REALIZED WE'D forgotten to bring sugar and milk for breakfast. We stopped at a restaurant, and once back in the car we discovered that three of us had each swiped a sugar packet, so we had sugar for the rest of the trip and then some. Then we stopped at the only grocery store to buy milk. The store did not sell milk, because almost everyone in town owned a cow or bought milk from their neighbors.

From Driggs, the Buick struggled over 8,000-foot Teton Pass and then coasted and slid down into Jackson, surrounded by beautiful peaks. The Storm King ski area lay right at the edge of town, the only one in Wyoming at that time with a chairlift; Jackson Hole wouldn't open until 1965. The town of Jackson was still suffering from the Depression. Vacant lots were selling for $300 to $500.

From there it was on to Denver, and the girls told us that this was as far as they would tolerate sleeping in the back seat. They decided to take a train out, satisfied at having at least seen something of the Rocky Mountains. We drove 60 miles south to Colorado Springs and maneuvered the Buick up nearly to the top of Pikes Peak to see the second ski area on our list. The Pikes Peak Ski Club's rope tow was already shut down for the season.

We had come too late for the skiing, but we were into our "nothing matters" mood. Whatever happened, it was OK. After Pikes Peak, we drove down to about the 5,000-foot level, drove north to Denver again, and turned west to drive up 11,000-foot Berthoud Pass.

Again we were on the Continental Divide. There was plenty of snow but not much in the way of facilities. A couple of surplus Army barracks served as skiers' shelters, and for lifts there were two rope tows, each one running up to opposite sides of the road for a few hundred vertical feet. Almost no one was skiing, so one of the tows was not running. The operator started up the rope tow that had been idle, and we skied down in fresh snow. He had a photographer at the bottom and he filmed us as if we knew what we were doing, making short turns side-by-side. We did this several times, moving across the hill a little farther each time to get fresh snow. I don't believe the photographer got anything close to a usable picture: Our tracks were more like figure-sevens than figure-eights, but we had gotten in some free skiing in powder snow in the Rockies.

After Berthoud Pass, we headed for Aspen to see the world's longest single chairlift and to visit Friedl Pfeifer. We drove south along the Rockies, and after about 25 miles, turned west over Loveland Pass. At 11,000 feet, we crossed the Continental Divide for the third time. The Buick complained all the way up about having to do 180s on the steep switchbacks. (The double-bore Eisenhower Tunnel wouldn't open until 1973.)

Going down the western side of the Divide, we passed Arapahoe Basin, scheduled to open in 1948. We were now in Summit County, which would eventually be home to the most intense concentration of ski resorts in the nation. Breckenridge opened there in 1961, Keystone in 1970, and Copper Mountain in 1972. After another 50 miles, we climbed Vail Pass and coasted down the far side through the valley with sheep ranches on both sides. This would become Vail, developed in 1962 as the largest ski area in the U.S., and to the west, Beaver Creek, opened in 1980. Today, between East Vail and the Vail airport in Eagle there are some 35,000 residents and the jobs and infrastructure to support them. If there were no skiing, these people would all be in front of you on a freeway somewhere.

We arrived in Aspen in mid-afternoon, as it was winding down its first season as an emerging major resort. Friedl, who owned the ski school and was general manager of the ski corporation (before Dick Durrance took over), had already built two chairlifts. One was the longest in the world, rising up from the streets of the old mining town to the top of Ajax Mountain. The mountain was spectacular, the town not quite as appealing. There were blocks of empty, run-down, 1890s Victorian houses left over from the silver boomtown days, and not all that many decent places to stay. However, we had our trailer, so it was OK with us.

We found Friedl at the base of the No. 1 chair. We asked if he'd sit down with us for a cup of coffee at The Jerome, the classic hotel on Main Street that was built during the days of the silver-mining boom. Friedl said, "OK, but first take your derelict car and trailer and hide it somewhere before the sheriff comes and takes you to jail."

We met later at the long, long bar in the Hotel Jerome, and Friedl told us that real estate in town was dirt-cheap. "Warren, you and Ward ought to buy a couple of these houses or vacant lots while you're here. Last year, I bought 10 for $10 each." I should have listened.

We stayed overnight to ski Ajax in the morning. We didn't have enough money to buy day-tickets at $4 each, so we climbed instead. We had one great top-to-bottom run, the one shining ski memory of our Rocky Mountain spring skiing tour.

After a quick stop at Alta, we headed for Yosemite, hoping there was still skiing at Badger Pass. But at only at 7,000 feet, the snow was so patchy that the lifts were shut down. No matter. Bill Janss was still there. We got together with him for dinner at the Yosemite Lodge cafeteria and talked about our winter, including taking the ski films with our 8-MM cameras at Sun Valley and Alta. We'd always had our rolls of film developed right away, because we were excited to see what we'd shot; plus, the cost of the film included developing. We were obviously happy with the progress we'd made, and Janss said he would really like to see our films. One thing led to another.

Janss found an empty room at the Ahwahnee where we could show our footage, and he also found a way for us to make all our 50-foot rolls of 8-MM film into one long movie. He rounded up splicing equipment, and we put two big reels together, making a 40-minute show for 20 ski friends.

I ad-libbed the narration for the footage. Whenever there were only

5 feet or so left on a reel, not enough to shoot another subject or sequence, I had always found something different to shoot, oddball stuff. A flock of chickens running around in the middle of a road with a hefty farm lady trying to round them up became a fat ski-school director lining up her pupils for morning class. Every time a scene like that came up on the screen at the Ahwahnee, it was easy to ad-lib some way-out remark. To my surprise, the audience laughed each time. That taught me something. My offbeat observation would match the sort of remark Groucho Marx might make on his television show. In short, a film that shows nothing but skiing, skiing, and more skiing can lose its audience, but funny footage brings the audience's attention back. We'd screened surfing footage at Alta earlier in the year, but Ahwahnee was the first ski show we had done, and it was a success. The whole process was fun, and it hit a nerve, with an unanticipated consequence: It sent me on a 55-year career of making movies.

SHOWING THAT FILM AT THE AHWAHNEE BROUGHT TO MIND THE LUGGI Foeger ski film on backcountry skiing at the Ostrander Hut above Badger Pass. At 8,500 feet, the country around the Ostrander Hut ought to still have spring skiing. The trailhead for the path to the Hut started four miles up from Badger Pass. If we got a ride to the trailhead, we could climb on our skis with skins the six miles to the Hut at the base of Horse Ridge. The ridge itself went up to 9,000 feet and should freeze at night and then give us corn snow. That was the idea.

Ward agreed, and we began our first backcountry expedition. We didn't contact the Yosemite management people. We were afraid they would not let us go for one reason or another. So we bought a week's worth of food, packed it into rucksacks, tied our sleeping bags on top of them, and inserted our still cameras, our 8-MM movie cameras, and a bar of soap into the side pockets. We persuaded a friend of Ward's, a pretty waitress at Yosemite Lodge, to drive us in the Buick to the trailhead, where we asked her to meet us one week later.

To ski in, we just unhooked the heel spring of our bindings from the downhill hitch and put on our sealskins. It was a six-mile, steady-uphill climb to the 8,500 feet. As we went along, the snow got deeper. We arrived to find a good-looking, two-story structure built of native stone and native timbers by the country's Civilian Conservation Corps during the Depression. The lodge stood on the shores of the frozen Ostrander Lake. The huge bulk of Horse Ridge rose behind the Lodge to 9,000 feet. The whole scene was postcard beautiful. There was no one at the Lodge, so we laid out our sleeping bags on the plywood beds and took over the place.

Horse Ridge cirque, with steep terrain, was just as Luggi's movie had shown it. The corn snow was perfect, but we were so naïve that we didn't worry about avalanches. The base was solid enough to hold our weight, yet soft enough so we could climb in our boots and carry our skis over our shoulders—much easier than having to zigzag up icy-hard, steep slopes on skis. On the seventh day, we cleaned up the cabin, skied the six miles out, and were at the trailhead with our sunburned faces, sore shoulders, and tired legs. Right on time, we heard the coughing of the Buick engine as it struggled up the steep hill to pick us up.

If anyone had asked if we had gotten our fill of skiing that winter, we would have said "maybe." That night at dinner in the Yosemite Lodge Cafeteria, we asked where all the Badger Pass ski instructors went when the lifts closed. They said the instructors had all gone to Mammoth Mountain, where there was still 15 feet of snow. They were riding the rope tow put up by Dave McCoy for the first-annual California ski-instructor's certification exam.

The top of Mammoth is 11,000 feet and has 3,000 vertical feet of skiing to the lodge level. It would be about 10 years before Dave McCoy built a gondola to the summit. This winter, there was snow almost right down to 8,000 feet. Even though we had enough money for gas to drive to Mammoth, we would then have to hit someone up to cash yet another $25 check from my Navy savings to get back to Los Angeles.

The town had very few people and was practically deserted all winter. Like Aspen, there were buildings left over from the mining days. Developing Mammoth Mountain itself was Dave McCoy's dream. He had been licensed to put in the first permanent rope tow that same year. He and his volunteers had dug the tow out again and again, after it had been buried by 3- and 4-foot snowstorms. Mammoth had more snow than any other ski area in the state. The next year, he moved his rope tows farther up the mountain and bought two Army-surplus weasels to tow the skiers over the snow, in from the parking at the main highway to the rope tow. He did this while holding down a day job as a state hydrologist, but his heart was in skiing. He would eventually make Mammoth into one of the two largest ski resorts in America, but in the 1940s, no one had any idea of how big skiing would eventually get.

We had several good days skiing on the one tow. We also watched a dozen or so instructors from Yosemite and Donner Summit creating and then taking the Far West Ski Instructors Association certification test. The FWSIA was the first professional ski-teaching group incorporated in the U.S. and was in the process of trying to blend the teaching methods like the Arlberg used at Yosemite, Aspen, and Sun Valley and the Swiss technique taught by Hans Georg near Mammoth. There were even a few renegades already teaching the French technique at a few ski schools in the East and in Canada. But the fact that the rope tow had been set up for the instructors gave Ward and me a chance to ski for the better part of a week. Dave McCoy was not charging anyone to ride his rope tow, yet. He was also happy to cash a $25 check, the money we needed to get home, and this was the beginning of what would become decades of his never-ending support.

To this day, Dave and I are still very good friends. Nearly 70 years later, I'm 90 and he turned 100 in August 2015. He's still going strong, riding all over the high desert on his electric motorcycle, taking wildlife photos along with his wife, Roma, riding on her own Swiss electric motorcycle.

CHAPTER TWENTY-ONE

1947–1948

Discovering Nylon among the Snowflakes

IN THE SUMMER OF MY 23RD YEAR, IT WAS GETTING A BIT LATE TO DECIDE what kind of life I was going to live: go along making skiing my priority, or follow the course most of my friends took. My friends were either going to law school, attending business school, or working for a corporation with a regular job; some were married, some not; all were looking forward to a family with 2.5 children and a three-bedroom home with two baths and a double garage. The rewards of the standard life were multiple: having a family life, buying a brand-new car every few years, eating out at good restaurants, taking expensive vacations, and moving to a bigger house every so often. With no obvious goals, I just couldn't picture spending my life confined to the four walls of an office eight hours a day.

I had already gone through that structured kind of life in my Navy career in college and then in Midshipmen's courses. Skiing and surfing were great; too much to give up for a life like that again. Another force operating here was that I never had a role model of a normal working parent or a normal family life. My mother had a grinding, underpaid working life, but my father had never brought a paycheck home in my entire life. Both had lived a chaotic, unattractive life that excluded me. I felt deep discouragement from viewing my mother's life as an example of what marriage was to be.

Ever since I had left the Navy in June 1946, I had happily spent 90 percent of my time unconsciously running along the path to freedom. I had just spent my first full winter skiing at Alta, Sun Valley, Yosemite, and other points west. Now that I had come back in the late spring of 1947 to my old room on Berendo Street, my parents as usual made no comment about my future or my past. They left it up to me to decide, and this, as it turns out, was a great gift.

My decision came right out of skiing. Even without trying very hard in the past two years, I had self-published and sold a thousand copies of my ski cartoon book *Are My Skis On Straight?*, earning a $1,000 profit. So I decided to self-publish my third cartoon book that could earn me another $1,000 and give me time to look around before taking my next step. While $1,000 in 1948 was not a full living wage, it amounted to one-third of the average annual middle-class salary. It would carry me well into the next winter at Sun Valley if I lived out of my trailer. In the long run, I had to find satisfying work that still left time open to go surfing and skiing.

I freshened up my freehand drawing skills by signing up for a life art drawing class, not so much to learn to draw better nudes as to expand my ability to capture on paper the comic essence of funny scenes that popped into my head when watching skiers. The class cost $3 a session and was held in a classroom on North Vermont Avenue, just off Sunset Boulevard.

One evening, I was galvanized by a particularly beautiful, well-endowed woman who was our model, one with an original personality who, during her rest breaks, threw a towel around her waist and roamed the classroom, checking on how we were doing. During her last two breaks, she managed to embarrass me by coming directly to my easel, leaning over my shoulder, and complimenting me on my sketch. That was like an emotional jet-assist to make my decision. I took a large chunk of money out of my Navy bank account to cover the cost of printing my second ski-cartoon book.

After a couple of weeks bargaining with various printers, spaced out by weekends of surfing, I pulled out the pencil sketches I had made during the past winter at Sun Valley and got to work in my room at Berendo Street, turning the sketches into finished ink cartoons. I made a rough layout for the book, wrote the captions to go with the 40 pen-and-ink drawings, and the printer soon delivered my second ski-cartoon book, *Nice Try George.* The 1,000 copies cost me $1,000. I loaded 200 of them into the back seat of the wheezy old Buick and drove around to the five or so Southern California ski stores in existence at the time, convincing the management at each one that this might be their only chance to buy copies of this limited edition. The ski shops bought just over 100 copies at $3 each, less 40 percent, an instant profit of $80, bankrolling my next trip to Sun Valley.

Next problem: The old 1937 Buick Phaeton convertible was no longer reliable. I had to have a better car. I looked through the classifieds and found a 1946 Ford business coupe with 4,000 miles on it. It had been knocked down to an even $1,000 because the mileage was considered high in those days. It was just a standard Ford Coupe, minus the back seat plus a fiberboard floor running from the front seat to the hatchback door-cargo space. I could convert it easily into an 8-foot-long double bed and have storage space left over, enough to hold all the unsold copies of my new cartoon book. I had to have that car.

So I went to my grandmother Edith, one more time, persuading her that getting this car was crucial for my career. She came through, again. She loaned me the $400 down payment. The other $600 I arranged with my bank to pay off at $20 a month. I also negotiated the use of a new, factory-built, teardrop trailer for next winter. I had run across an ad for one from the Kit Manufacturing Company in Long Beach, 25 miles away. It had two side doors, a propane cook stove, and fenders, advantages that would ease life in the winter.

I drove out to meet the CEO, Bill Worman, and I showed him the story from *Look* magazine with the picture of my homemade teardrop trailer buried in snow in the Sun Valley parking lot. My sales pitch was that Ward and I were repeating the trip this coming winter, and wouldn't it be great if his trailer appeared in a national magazine? I pointed out that the trailer would be exposed to a lot of potential customers. Worman let me have one of his new teardrop trailers for the winter. All that was required of me was to bring it back to the Kit Company by late spring, along with any pictures and publicity stories.

Another surprise development: One day when I was out filming surfers at Malibu to show to my Sun Valley ski friends, a surfer came up to ask if I made films. When I told him I had done a 40-minute ski film, he insisted I come to his home soon for dinner and show it to his friends, who had never seen a skier in action. At his house, I enjoyed his wife's tuna casserole and showed the film. The guests laughed during the mindless, disconnected footage and gave me a decent round of applause at the end. A second invitation then arrived from some surfers at San Onofre. Then another request for a show came through for Manhattan Beach, and I was starting to wonder if doing all this for a tuna casserole dinner was worth it. Then the host passed the hat and handed me $8.35 for an easy evening's work. All that was standing in the way of drawing a much larger audience was a big screen and very expensive 16-MM equipment, more money than I had available.

THE DAY AFTER CHRISTMAS 1947, WARD AND I DROVE OFF IN THE HIGH-mileage, new-to-me Ford, towing the newly loaned Kit Kamper trailer. The Ford cruised at 45 mph, which was faster than the old Buick. Ward and I stopped at Yosemite for a day of skiing with our friends, and then went on to Sun Valley, arriving on December 29, parking in the same spot. We were astonished to see only 2 inches of snow on the ground. That was not good. The first night, we woke up to the sound of rain on the roof. That wasn't good either.

The next morning, Baldy was a sheet of ice from the bottom of River Run up to the Roundhouse. All the Mt. Baldy skiers, including the instructors, rode down at the end of the day on the chairlifts from the Roundhouse to the bottom of River Run rather than ski the sheet ice. These bad conditions caused me to spend part of the time socializing at the Challenger Inn, and this seemed to alert that little part of my brain that was always looking for another income opportunity. A few cartoon murals on the cafeteria walls would liven up what was now just empty, light-brown space. Making a proposition to Sun Valley's general manager, my friend Pappy Rogers, I offered to paint 10 cartoon murals on the cafeteria walls in exchange for a season's ski pass, worth $250. This might also result in selling more of my cartoons.

Pappy liked the idea, but first he had to ask Max Barsis if he wanted to do it. Max was an early ski cartoonist and writer who had published his first and only ski cartoon book, "Bottoms Up," nine years earlier, about the time Sun Valley opened. He socialized brilliantly in the Lodge cocktail lounge and was now a celebrity in residence—like Hemingway, but not nearly as famous. As it turned out, Max did want to paint the murals. Pappy asked if I would paint murals on the walls of the employee cafeteria for the same season's pass and three meals a day for as long as it took me to do the work. This was my first commission in the ski world or in my life, for that matter, and with free meals for the duration of the job, it took me an amazingly long time to finish them.

Sitting down at a table in front of a breakfast tray of ham and eggs in a warm dining room was a lot better and warmer than standing around with Ward under the trailer hatchback in subzero weather, breaking up frozen milk to put on our dish of hot oatmeal. To compensate Ward for the loss of my company, I took enough food in the cafeteria line to stow away a good deal in waxed paper-lined ski jacket pockets to relieve Ward of his dependence on the rabbits of Shoshone for protein.

Next, a store owner in Ketchum asked me to do ski cartoons for his store, and that really helped shore up my available cash.

Snow finally did arrive in Sun Valley at the end of the second week of January. My meals and lift tickets were taken care of, so we skied all day. The snow on Baldy was good, so it was easy to ignore finding a full-time money-making job of any kind.

The U.S. men's Olympic team was training at Sun Valley for the 1948 St. Moritz Olympics under Walter Prager of Dartmouth, so Ward and I spent some time watching the country's best racers, including Dev Jennings, Jack Reddish, Barney McLean, and Dick Movitz. During February, those top skiers were off racing in St. Moritz, which would give us a better chance to make our mark racing. The two of us first entered the Sun Valley guest races on Dollar Mountain, where we always finished well up among skiers who had raced a lot more than we had. We spent a lot of time practicing slalom on the Roundhouse Hill, where the Sun Valley Ski Team set courses for themselves and guests.

Our first big race was the Paul Brooks Giant Slalom at Bogus Basin in Boise, 150 miles west. We went to the secretary of the Sun Valley Ski Club and asked if the club would buy our gas if we represented it at Bogus Basin. The club secretary replied, "Sorry, but we have already picked our team." She had never seen us ski, but she had seen where we lived. So we went to Boise with our trailer and entered as the Sun Valley Parking Lot Ski Team.

Rocks and stumps were sticking out everywhere on the course because of so little snowfall. Bamboo was not yet required for race gates, so Bogus Basin's giant slalom flags were attached to square pine 2-by-2 lumber that probably would have felt like fence posts if you hit one of them, but rarely did any racer get that close. The course was lumpy, bumpy, and icy: There were no grooming vehicles in those days. However, a rough track was not as much of a problem for the survival technique we specialized in. Before the race, the slick skiwear the Sun Valley Ski Team sported made Ward and me look like the poor relatives from down in the hollow: $3 Army-surplus ski pants, $17 Chippewa ski boots, and $19 Northland skis that Pete Lane had traded me for a sign I painted for his store. We had no racing record, so we were assigned start numbers at the back of the pack. Stan Tomlinson from Boise won the race, and I finished number two. Ward was not far behind in fifth. The Sun Valley Parking Lot Ski Team had beaten the Sun Valley Ski Team, and the Sun Valley racers couldn't believe it.

We were raised to the category of Class C racers, and we were off to a good start, doing much better than I thought we would. Our next race was the 1948 Sun Valley Ski Club Championships. Somewhere I have a piece of 8-MM film showing Averell Harriman handing me the Amateur Class second-place trophy on the Challenger Inn front porch. Jack Simpson had beaten me. (He had doubled for Sonja Henie in some of the skiing sequences in "Sun Valley Serenade.") The overall winner that day was Toni Matt, racing in Open Class (instructors could not race against amateurs back then). Matt was an Austrian downhill champion from St. Anton who had escaped to the U.S. as the Germans marched in to annex Austria and was now teaching at Sun Valley.

During the week before our next race, Ward and I decided to take a day off from skiing and drove the 60 miles to Twin Falls to look at outdoor kitchen gear in the Army-surplus store. Our visit started a step up in my business career. There, sitting between the 20-MM cartridge cases and a pile of army training rifles, hand-grenades, 40-MM shells, and mess kits was a small barrel of surplus nylon parachute shroud lines that lay jumbled like a bunch of boiled spaghetti. I thought that maybe the nylon would make good ski bootlaces. The standard, cotton-weave bootlaces started shredding and breaking after a week of use, because the ends were drawn through several pairs of flat but sharp-edged boot hooks. If that nylon line could keep Army parachute troopers from falling out of the sky, it should be tough enough to stand up to sharp boot-hook edges.

I bought 50 cents worth of random lengths from the store. Back at our trailer, I cut off two pieces that were about right for my ski boots and found that nylon cord is made up of a woven sheath wrapped around 10 smaller strands of spun nylon. I found out that the cords become fuzzy when the sheath is cut. So I just burnt the ends, and I had tips on them. That pair of nylon laces lasted me the rest of the winter, about 75 days of skiing, and showed little wear.

CHAPTER TWENTY-TWO

1948

Sun Valley, Ski Races, and Bootlaces

IN LATE JANUARY 1948, WARD SUDDENLY BEGAN TO RUN A FEVER. A ski patrol friend diagnosed him with the flu, and the freezing, midwinter temperatures made our trailer a very poor place to recover. Ward decided to head home to Southern California to recuperate. I drove him to Hailey, and he caught the Trailways bus on his first leg to Manhattan Beach, where he would soon shake the flu in the winter warmth of that world.

We had been practicing slalom with two good racers, Dean Perkins from Ogden, Utah, and Don McDonald from Seattle, Washington. The challenge was to beat Perkins; obviously, he was headed for the top on the 1952 FIS (International Ski Federation) team. This is the international governing body of ski racing. Every four years, they have a world championship that falls midway between the Olympics. Being on the FIS ski team is the equivalent of being on an Olympic team in alternate years.

Our two-man parking lot ski team was down to one man, and the next big race was the Eccles Cup, an important, annual giant slalom held at Snowbasin outside Ogden, Utah. Don, Dean, and I drove down together. We split responsibilities for the necessities. I furnished the car, McDonald bought the gas, and Perkins got us sleeping bag space in Ogden in his mother's basement.

We reached the Perkins' house in Ogden at 2:30 in the morning, curled up for a few hours in sleeping bags in the basement, had breakfast, and drove up to Snowbasin. I showed up with my Class C racing credentials and paid the $2 entry fee at the sign-up desk. In return, I got a lift ticket, a bottle of Coke and a hot dog, plus a racing bib, along with the other 125 racers, including the entire UCLA ski team, coached by Wolfgang Lert. Lert became famous in the ski industry after founding Hagemeister-Lert with his partner Hans Hagemeister and selling ski sweaters for years.

The Snowbasin race was a much bigger event than I had anticipated. Although I was a Class C racer by now, they gave me a starting number well back in the pack. My run was more like a super-fast fun run than it was an all-out effort to win the race. My $19 skis were working great, and I had the right wax for a change, but I figured one of the better-known racers from the Salt Lake Team would beat my time.

A half-hour after the race, while I was sitting around eating my hot dog at the base lodge, a race official finally stood up, and every one quieted down. He announced, "The winner of the Eccles Cup Giant Slalom, racing for the Sun Valley Parking Lot Ski Team, is Warren Miller!" Boy, was I (and everyone else) surprised!

The next big race was the U.S. Ski Association's Intermountain Championships at Storm King in Jackson Hole. I remember coming in second or third in the slalom and doing lousy in the downhill.

Ward came back from Southern California before the next race, recovered from his bout with the flu, so we drove to the Far West Ski Association's Championships at Donner Summit. There was a raging blizzard at the Donner Ski Ranch, and it snowed 3 or more feet during the race. In those days, the officials didn't cancel a race because of a little snow on the course. The ruts on the slalom course were knee-deep, and the snow kept on dumping. Again I did lousy in the downhill, but I think I won the slalom. From there we entered the Silver Dollar Derby on nearby Mt. Rose, 22 miles southwest of Reno.

We made a good chunk of money there, but not from racing, of course. The snow was so deep on the downhill course that the race committee paid skiers to pack it by sidestepping the course on their skis. The first successful mechanical grooming machine, the Bradley Packer, wasn't invented until Steve Bradley put one on the slopes of Winter Park, Colorado, three winters later. So we ordinary, poverty-stricken amateur racers were happy for the chance to be paid for packing the Mt. Rose downhill course. The sponsors or possibly their friends in casino management appeared to have a lot of money. We sidestepped up and down the course and earned $20 for each round trip on the almost 3,000 vertical feet. Sidestepping down, of course, was much easier than sidestepping up. Ward and I each did two round trips three days running, and each ended up $120 richer. During the races, I managed a second place in the GS, as I remember it, and Dave McCoy won the downhill, slalom, and the combined in our amateur class.

All the winners were in for a mild disappointment: Previous seasons' trophies were beautiful belts, with a silver dollar set in the buckle. This season, strict amateur status prevailed. As far as the Far West Ski Association officials were concerned, anyone who won, or even competed for a prize of "usable currency," would never be allowed to race as an amateur again. The sponsors of the 1948 Silver Dollar Derby removed the real silver dollar from every buckle on the trophy belts and replaced them with fake silver dollars made of stamped aluminum.

Later, back at Sun Valley, the points I had earned over the season qualified me for the Harriman Cup Races, the big final event on the circuit. Though the competition was stiff, we wanted to enter it. The U.S. Olympic team was back from St. Moritz, and the Harriman Cup entrants had nearly doubled. Placing in the top 50 in the U.S. National Downhill my first year of racing would be doing very well, I thought. Jack Reddish swept the men's races. Suzy Harris Rytting took the women's races. I was 47th over the course, which ran right down the steep fall-line slope to the bottom on the Warm Springs side of Baldy. My $19 skis, by then, had lost several of the rivets holding the edges in place. The wooden bottom of one ski had a big, worn groove on the inside of the metal edges. The edges stood out from the bottom of the skis by the thickness of the edges, as if they were flat rails on each side of the ski tip.

That was my last official race. I had learned a lot about technique, but racing was never going to compensate anyone involved for the amount of time and money spent. Compared to the racing scene today, where Olympic gold medalists reap handsome cash rewards for endorsing products, racing in 1948 was truly amateur. This was also only my third year on skis, and it would be impossible to catch up.

When the racing season was over, it was back to skiing every day on Baldy. The neglected murals finally got finished in the employees' cafeteria by my working an hour or two on them each evening after dinner. I was looking forward to having some time free for socializing. Then on my first evening free, Chuck Helm, who had the only full ski shop in Ketchum, told me he had sold a dozen copies of my ski cartoon book. We were sitting on the Challenger Inn front deck, and Chuck asked me if I could paint cartoon murals on the bond beams along the walls of his shop. Chuck offered me $200 and, naturally, it was a done deal. This provided me going-home money and refilled my savings for the money I'd spent for travel during the racing circuit. I spent the evenings the next three weeks painting murals. And those murals stayed up there in his shop for about 50 years.

I MET A VERY INTERESTING YOUNG LADY NAMED LYNN RENNICK IN THE lift line on Baldy. She was pretty, intelligent, a college graduate, and a fair skier, but Lynn lived in San Francisco, which, in those days, was considered GU (as I've said before, geographically undesirable) because of its 400-mile distance from Hollywood. This made it unlikely we were going to see each other longer than the traditional Sun Valley romance—good for the duration of the vacation—but we did have a good time together that spring in Sun Valley. We even made a few dinners together using the handy propane stove on the new teardrop trailer.

Ward and I stayed until the lifts closed right after Easter, which arrived in mid-April that year. However, the snow was so good in the high mountains that we didn't want to quit, so we arranged to stay up at Pioneer Cabin. Built by the Sun Valley Company the year after the resort opened, the cabin had a great scenic location in the mountains back of Sun Valley and was a three- or four-hour climb on skis to get there. It had decent beds, a full camp kitchen, and great snow conditions. We stayed three or four days, climbing up and enjoying the corn snow going down.

After a few days, it was time to start to worry about making enough money to get me through the summer, so I left Ward and spent the next four or five days at an empty corner table in the Challenger Inn, drawing finished pen-and-ink drawings from pencil sketches of skiers I had made during the winter. I wanted to sell copies of them as individual prints that I would hand-paint and autograph numbered to the buyer, as soon as I had enough money to print them. (I did not get around to doing this until 1990.)

Ward headed home early, again taking the bus. He had signed up to try out as a lifeguard at Manhattan Beach, and wanted some swimming practice to get in shape for his test. Even after Ward left, it was hard to leave Sun Valley, a place that had begun to feel like home. I had started to save enough money to think about building a cabin of my own in Ketchum. However, it was time to leave: The guests had gone, and the lifts had been shut down. Loading the trailer, it was easy to cover the 850 miles to Hollywood in two very long days, sleeping at night in the Ford's roomy double bed.

Once back in Hollywood, I took the teardrop trailer back to Kit Company and gave Bill Worman, the CEO, my sincerest thanks and some good pictures Ward had taken and enlarged, showing the trailer 3 feet deep in snow. It was not national publicity but would make for good advertising shots. Years later, when I moved to Orcas Island, we renewed our friendship; he'd retired to the island as well. Small world.

A week or two after I got home, I drove to San Francisco to see Lynn. I learned quickly that she had a very wealthy grandmother. Soon thereafter, the grandmother invited Lynn to Los Angeles to stay at her cottage at the Huntington, a luxury hotel in Pasadena. At this close range, it was easy to see Lynn, so I took her surfing at San Onofre one weekend, even though her grandmother insisted that Lynn book a motel room while I slept on the beach in my Ford. Lynn's grandmother did seem to want the two of us to stay involved. Every time I arrived at her cottage to pick up Lynn, the three of us spent a lot of time talking—among other things about my dream of building a log cabin in Sun Valley. I had already designed the cabin and had figured out that it would cost $3,500 (excluding the land) to do it myself.

One night, the three of us had dinner at the hotel's renowned Langham Restaurant, and Lynn's grandmother offered to loan me the $3,500. She would hold a $3,500 mortgage that I would pay off by the month, and was obviously hoping her offer would help keep Lynn and me in contact.

Even so, this was an incredible offer that I was not about to turn down. The check for $3,500 and the mortgage papers were signed within a week, and I started buying the plumbing supplies and tools needed to build my log house in the Wood River Valley. The tools included a "shake froe," a rare, old-fashioned hand-splitter to make cedar shakes. This was going to be a totally made-by-Warren house, though there wasn't a cedar tree within 500 miles of Sun Valley. I was either incredibly naïve, young, or just plain stupid—maybe all three.

I planned to finish the cabin by winter so I could start my newest enterprise, a nylon bootlace business. So after wedging all my newly acquired hardware and tools into the Ford and the old teardrop trailer, I left early in July and drove back to Ketchum for the first time without Ward, who had gotten the job lifeguarding at Manhattan Beach. Ward soon became a full-time commercial fisherman, his life centering on the sea, while mine was centered on the mountains, but we still remained good friends, now going on 75 years.

The first thing I needed in Ketchum was a place to store all the plumbing. A 15-by-30-foot garage with a dirt floor on a side street was available. Perfect. The owner was a friend, Austin Lightfoot, a retired fishing and hunting guide, who rented it to me for $5 a month.

Renting the garage turned out to be a good move, because later it would become my Ketchum apartment. Next I started looking for a vacant lot and made one of the dumbest moves I ever made in my life—not the dumbest, but close. I met an architect building a house for himself. I was a bit uncertain about building a log cabin by myself, but the architect, who shall remain nameless, convinced me to help him build his cabin; in return, he would help me design and build mine. It seemed like an excellent idea. It wasn't.

Of course, I never put anything on paper. We worked like fiends on his cabin all through July, August, and part of September, and I enjoyed learning while I was doing the work. As the cabin neared completion, the architect sold it, left town, and I never saw him again. It was a disaster. I had just spent three months of my time and had nothing to show for it. Now I knew how to build a log cabin, and most of the $3,500 from Lynn's grandmother was still in the bank, but it was too late to start a foundation before frost set in. Building my cabin would have to wait until next spring.

I did find a lot, however. Years ago, Austin Lightfoot had bought what I thought was a choice triangular-shaped lot on Trail Creek that he sold to me for $350. It had Trail Creek along two sides and the highway to Hailey on the other, forming a perfect location for a small log cabin. I bought it on the spot.

In August, I had to start focusing on the nylon parachute-shroud ski bootlace business to make some money. Otherwise, I was in big trouble. I owed my own grandmother for the car payments and Lynn's grandmother a mortgage on a cabin. My romance with Lynn was on the decline. Not only had I screwed up with her grandmother's loan by not starting the cabin as early as I'd planned, I felt I was a loser. As much as Lynn and I had been attracted to each other that fall of 1948, our romance dwindled to the occasional letter back and forth, but I'm glad we remained good friends.

I was at a low point: The Woes of Warren were all over me. Yet I did find some company. Austin introduced me to his good-looking granddaughter, a very attractive Southern California brunette a few years younger than I, Marci Luring. She was spending some time with her grandparents in Ketchum but would soon be going home. Companionship always meant quite a lot to me: Knowing that someone was on my side made the days go better.

I perked up when I began fixing up the garage, which was fun to do. I bought enough lumber to build a floor over the dirt floor. Insulation? Of course not! The garage had exterior siding of ¼-inch-thick lapstrake and bare studs inside. I nailed a tarp from the ceiling, thinking it might help retain the heat. I was afraid that all winter the garage's temperature would remain the same inside as the outside except colder because it was always shady inside. So I bought an oil heater at the Salvation Army store in Hailey for $12, so I could work and sleep in the garage. I bought a $10 bike to run around Ketchum and Sun Valley. Austin Lightfoot really changed my life with that $5-a-month garage. I built a drawing board for my mural- and sign-painting and was in business.

In the first week of September 1948, I ran my first bootlace tests in my garage laboratory, so things began to look up for future business. I rode my bike up to Sun Valley to see if Pete Lane wanted to order laces for the coming ski season. He wanted to know if I had any other colors besides olive drab.

I asked, "What colors would you like?"

He asked, "What colors do you have?"

"I'll be back in the morning with my color chart."

Leather ski boots were soft and offered little support, but with my new laces you could tighten them up. I jumped on my bicycle and headed for the Ketchum grocery store. I walked straight to the back where there was a small 4-by-8-inch color chart for Rit Dye thumbtacked on a post between the Brillo pads and shoe-shine polish. If Pete Lane ordered, other ski shops would follow. So, contrary to the rule that my grandfather had taught me about never stealing anything, I detached the Rit Dye chart from the post, tucked it under my jacket, bought an ice cream bar, and rode my bicycle back to the garage, where I went to work at my drawing table.

I created a professionally hand-lettered, 8-by-8-inch sign, with the headlines "MILLER'S MARVELOUS BOOTLACE COLOR CHART" and "THE SKI BOOTLACE OF THE FUTURE" painted over the original Rit headlines. I rode my bicycle back up to Sun Valley, showed the chart to Pete Lane, and said, "Pick the colors you would like." Pete said "I want a gross of deep red and a gross of bright yellow!" I had hit the jackpot. Pete had just ordered 288 pairs, $172 worth, of my ski bootlaces of the future. There was still one move to go.

Looking at the bright red and deep yellow on the color chart, I knew that the olive-drab laces would dull these bright Rit colors. I needed white nylon. Up to this point, I had just assumed that Army-surplus nylon parachute lines came only in the U.S. Army's favorite color—olive drab. I called a friend of mine in Los Angeles, who would become my source for Army-surplus nylon, and he said, "Certainly there is white nylon parachute line." He could guarantee me any number of thousand-foot rolls of what I needed. I said, "Send me two rolls."

My next step was to figure out how much it would cost to cut the laces and burn the four tips of each pair. I gathered three married lady friends from the Ketchum community interested in making some extra money and told them I wanted to run a time test for cutting and burning the ends of the nylon line. We set up the first Nylon Bootlace Burning Party at the garage the next evening. Bringing along four candles, we cut 100 pairs of laces, each taking enough for 25 pairs. We timed how long it took us to burn their tips. We left the doors open to let the fumes escape, and from the street, we must have looked like an assembly of mediums sitting around in candlelight calling up the spirits. Candle-burning parties later became something of a Ketchum underground urban legend.

The results of our test showed that a speedy burner could burn a pair every minute, or 60 pairs an hour, assuming we burned one tip every 15 seconds or so. I also did a quality-control analysis by figuring how many pairs I could expect to lose through poor burning. I calculated that if I paid the relatively small sum of 2 cents per pair, burners could make $1.20 an hour while sitting and listening to the radio for relaxation. Minimum wages were roughly 25 cents an hour in 1948.

Dyeing the bootlaces was more of a kitchen-recipe challenge. A gross of laces could be dyed by starting with cold water and bringing it to a boil briefly in a 5-gallon can. A 25-cent package of Rit Dye, distributed between two cans of water, would do the job. So a gross, 144 laces, cost 25 cents for the dye, plus I had scrounged the 5-gallon cans from the trash. To avoid spending next winter at Sun Valley over a hot stove, I needed to find someone willing to do the dyeing at a price that would still leave a good profit.

The dyeing expert turned out to be "Mrs. Flush," the nice wife of a Ketchum tradesman known as "Flush the Plumber," the town's leading plumber. The sign on his truck read "Flush the Plumber," and I never heard him called by any other name. The Flush cabin had a large living room with wood rafters and a big kitchen stove, a perfect setup to dye and dry new nylon bootlaces. I immediately began negotiating with Mrs. Flush to name her price per gross. She agreed to dye them for 1 cent a pair. At 2 cents a pair for the nylon, 2 cents for burning the ends, and 1 cent a pair for dyeing, I would have a profit of almost 45 cents on each pair of high-tech, high-fashion, color-coordinated, never-wear-out ski bootlaces. I had the happy thought that there were now almost 200,000 skiers in the U.S., every one of them a potential customer. I stood to make a small fortune if I could get to them.

The next logical step was to go on a road trip to get orders for the laces. The best sales territory consisted of the "ski cities" along the 1,000-mile stretch of the West Coast from Seattle to Los Angeles, hitting every ski shop on the way and taking orders. In my euphoria, I had forgotten to include the cost of gasoline in my calculations. At 15 to 20 cents a gallon, gas was a big cost. The Ford got 10 miles to the gallon: My trip at a minimum would be 3,000 miles and would take 300 gallons at a cost of about $60, and that was my profit on a gross of laces. That was a bit daunting.

When I told Flush of my concerns, he said he had someone working for him whom I should meet, someone who also had a product to sell. We got into the Flush plumbing truck, drove toward Ketchum, and stopped at a vacant lot with a great big hole in the back of it. Dirt was flying out by the shovelful. Flush went over and looked down into the hole, saying, "Klaus, I want you to meet Warren Miller." Klaus climbed out; he was a big guy with a really big smile on his face.

Klaus Obermeyer had recently arrived from Oberstaufen in Bavaria with $10 in his pocket and two pair of lederhosen in his pack, along with five shirts and a pair of mountain boots. Klaus had prospered by selling Authentic Imported Bavarian Koogie Ties and was looking to sell "Koogies" all over the West. We all went back to Flush's place, and his wife served tea while we talked.

Back in his hometown in the Bavarian Alps, Klaus was a mountaineer, guide, ski instructor, and ski racer who had come from such a poor family that he said as a child he had made his own skis, bending the shovel of the skis upward by skiing with a rope going from each leg to the tip of the ski.

In the continuing postwar drought of skiing clients in Europe, Klaus decided to check out America, so he applied for a visa, got on a boat to New York, and hitchhiked to Sun Valley, where he'd heard there were a lot of wealthy skiers. Klaus had something to sell them, and he soon made many friends through his enormous good humor, his charm, his yodeling, his rich Bavarian accent, and by wearing a strange device around his neck that he managed to convince guests to buy. He insisted that "Koogie Ties" were the craze at all the premier Bavarian mountain resorts. He showed me a Koogie Tie, which had two white pom-poms connected by a round string of white yarn that went around the neck and tied in front to give the wearer something like a bolo tie. Silly, but perfect for American skiers who loved fads and wanted to be part of the "in" crowd. When Gary Cooper showed up with his Koogie Tie in the Duchin Room, that was all it took. Klaus had sold enough Koogie Ties at $3 each wholesale to make it worthwhile to pay Mrs. Flush to make them up while he dug septic tank holes for Mr. Flush.

The fact that no self-respecting Bavarian would have been caught dead in a Koogie Tie was beside the point. Any photo taken of guests in the Duchin Room in the late 1940s will likely show at least one or two Koogie Ties. Mrs. Flush could produce a dozen a day for 15 cents worth of yarn and 50 cents for the pom-pom labor. Klaus had sold his Koogies to the stores in Ketchum and Sun Valley, and now had dreams of a tomorrow when the whole world would be wearing his Koogie Ties. In a short discussion, Klaus and I decided to join forces to execute a Koogie Tie/Miller Ski Bootlace marathon sales trip in early November.

CHAPTER TWENTY-THREE

1948–1949

The Rise (Before the Fall) of the Bootlace Mogul

OUR AMBITIOUS PLAN FOR A MONTH-LONG, ALMOST-3,000-MILE SALES trip up and down the West Coast hinged on sleeping in the back of the Ford and splitting the cost of gas and food. Together, we would sell our products at every ski shop from Idaho to Seattle to Los Angeles and back to Idaho via Salt Lake City. We didn't quite make 100 percent sales, but we came close. We got the ski-shop addresses out of the yellow pages in phone booths in every city. We piled stuff into my luggage trailer, along with my Coleman stove, a jug for drinking water, a few loaves of bread, an insulated ice chest containing six frozen trout, 2 pounds of elk meat, and a couple pounds of venison, a jar of peanut butter (insurance against starvation after the shops closed), and a bag of oatmeal along with plenty of sugar. We'd buy milk along the way. We loaded cooking utensils, road maps, sleeping bags, a couple of pillows, a display box carrying nine gross of Miller's Marvelous Ski Bootlaces, my color chart, and a cardboard suitcase of the Genuine Imported Obermeyer Bavarian Koogie Ties. We each loaded in our skis, boots, and poles, just in case there was early snow when we got to Utah. We were ready to sell.

We left Sun Valley heading west to Boise. The first ski shop we called on had just been opened by the ski racer, Bob Greenwood, who had finished third behind me in the giant slalom at Bogus Basin the year before. We were already friends. I let Klaus show his "imports" first. Bob placed an order for two-dozen Genuine Imported Obermeyer Bavarian Koogie Ties. Then I went through my sales pitch, spread my rainbow of colored samples on the counter, and he ordered a gross of them, in six different colors. This was too many colors for one order. It would make Mrs. Flush dye 10 to a pot instead of a gross to a pot. I told the owner that Pete Lane of Sun Valley had ordered only red and yellow for his most prestigious ski shop. Bob Greenwood decided to do the same. We then had success at every shop in Spokane and Bellingham, and then Seattle and Tacoma. Everyone was ordering at least a gross of laces.

We refined our ultra-cheapskate travel mode as we went. We began driving to the next town as soon as the last ski shops closed in our current town, sometimes driving most of the night. We found that the safest and easiest places to park and sleep were in church parking lots with lights or right next to a police station. We parked facing east so the sun shining in the windshield in the morning warmed the car. If there was a YMCA nearby, we took our morning shower there (for 75 cents, including a towel and soap). If there was a local motel row, we would cruise it hoping to spot a cleaning lady entering a unit. Klaus would get out, introduce himself, displaying his big, friendly grin and thick accent, and relate a story with varied elements about him enduring Hitler's Germany, being forced to fight on the Russian front, being captured at Stalingrad, and finally escaping to America in search of a dream. He would work up to the fact that he was now a traveling salesman trying to make a go of it in the U.S. and ask, "Possibly could my friend and I take a shower in the room you're making up? We would like to give you 50 cents so you and your husband can have a beer after work." It almost always worked. One of the cleaning ladies even gave Klaus a dollar to help him get his start in America.

Unfortunately, I had no idea about volume discounts, C.O.D., credit checks, or end-of-month payments. I had never taken business courses in college, never thinking I'd have a business to run. Selling bootlaces was a piece of cake, but I had a lot to learn about running a business—you'll note this is a common theme in my life. So I just took the orders and told the shopkeepers, "I will ship your laces in a week and assume you will pay your bill when you receive the shipment of laces."

"Sure, Warren!"

Later there was time to worry about collecting and getting paid, which I did, because many of them didn't. We drove south from the Bay Area, through the San Joaquin Valley, calling on every ski shop we could find in Modesto, Merced, Fresno, Bakersfield, and finally, at the end of the 400 miles of this last leg, Los Angeles, which we hit on November 23.

Calling in at Berendo Street, my family invited Klaus and me to Thanksgiving dinner. We ate dinner with my family, including my two married sisters. Unfortunately, my father was once again drinking heavily. Screaming and shouting at everyone, he was back again as his favorite character, an inebriated racist, blaming his failed life on "those people," threatening violence and verbal garbage of the sort that I had to live with as a child. The family was embarrassed, and I could hardly wait to leave.

Back on the road, we eventually ended up in Salt Lake City, where we took orders from each of the four ski shops. Then we declared an end to the selling, and took two days off to ski at Alta. We shoveled out a spot in the parking lot across from the Alta Lodge for the car and bedded down in the back for the night. It snowed nonstop for the next two days, while we skied deep powder snow and didn't have to sell anything to anyone. Klaus was a much better skier than I was, but he always waited for me to catch up.

The third morning we got up early to find the snowplow had piled up a 6-foot bank around the car, entrapping the trailer. It took until 10 A.M. to dig out and start down the canyon, where I left Klaus standing at the bus station with his big smile and his backpack containing his worldly possessions. He was carrying his skis over his shoulder, with his other hand clutching the beat-up, cardboard suitcase with the remaining stock of Genuine Imported Obermeyer Bavarian Koogie Ties (from Ketchum). In a short while, he was teaching skiing for Friedl Pfeifer in Aspen. It wasn't long before he was selling equipment and clothing to Aspen stores on the side with irrepressible salesmanship: Anyone who could sell Koogie Ties could sell anything. He is still in Aspen, at this writing, after a career he capped by becoming the largest ski-apparel manufacturer in America. Klaus had the magic touch, backed up by ambition and hard work. In 2013, Obermeyer generated between $30 million and $40 million in ski-apparel sales.

It was early December when I returned to Ketchum. It was so cold the oil heater in the garage wouldn't warm up enough to melt the ice in the pan of water on top of it. I had to fill orders for 6,000 pair of bootlaces at a potential net of $3,000. All I had to do was get the laces manufactured, ship them, and collect all the money—something I'd been pretty naïve about by not preparing proper agreements with the shop owners.

My Ketchum Trail Creek cabin was getting closer to reality, even though I had spent some of Lynn's grandmother's money in "start-up costs" on the sales trip, and she was beginning to ask me about making monthly payments even though the cabin had not yet been built. I needed some income before the bootlace revenue started to flow. Nelson Bennett, who knew my situation, suggested trying out for the Sun Valley Ski School on Dollar Mountain. Pete Lane let me buy on credit some great gabardine ski pants and new ridge-top hickory skis. I arrived at Dollar Mountain sporting a very big smile to deny the butterflies in my stomach, because no one had ever taught me how to teach skiing.

They were all there: The Gods of Ski Instruction, the leaders of the Sun Valley Ski School, men you read about and watched from afar: Ski School Director Otto Lang, Assistant Director Johnny Litchfield, and Supervisors Sigi Engl and Sepp Froelich. I really wanted the job. Sun Valley treated its instructors well. Becoming an instructor meant being given a warm room in the instructors' chalet, three square meals a day at the Challenger Inn Dining Room, and a monthly check for $125, plus a percentage of all the private lessons.

Being allowed to try out for a ski instructor's job my fourth real winter on skis made me feel pretty good. My ski-bootlace manufacturing start-up was on hold for three days while I learned how to demonstrate carbon copies of the Sun Valley Ski School turns in the manner invented in St. Anton. First there were the very important snowplow turns. Then came the stem turn with weight shifted to the outside of the ski partway through the turn. Then the stem-Christie turn with skis parallel in the last part, and then came the turn to end all turns: the parallel Christie, in which the skis are continuously parallel throughout.

Getting hired would mean teaching beginners, often "never-evers," on their first day on skis. I made sure that my beginner snowplow turns were demonstrated with my skis held at the widest angle, and my weight shift was more pronounced than anyone else's.

Besides the turns, we were asked to demonstrate how to climb with a sidestep, and then climb with the herringbone step, facing directly uphill; how to glide while walking on the flats, traversing across the slope; how to carry skis; how to put them on; how to take them off; and the directions to the men's and ladies' rooms at Dollar Mountain.

Then there was the diplomatic part of ski instruction: An instructor was expected in the evenings to do his best to lend atmosphere (and ski-lesson hustling) to the Lodge and the Challenger Inn after-ski cocktail time by at least having a bottle of Pepsi and showing up after dinner in the bars. We were told to ask for separate checks, so we wouldn't get stuck with some little bright-eyed, sexy tourist's evening tab. By the third and final day, I began to relax. If I succeeded, there would be no more mummy sleeping bags, no more flight boots with squashed mice in them, no more oatmeal and frozen milk breakfasts, no more frigid post-date routine of getting out of a suit and standing outside in a blizzard in my underwear and flight boots while hanging my suit up inside the Ford, before finally climbing half-frozen into bed in the teardrop trailer. However, I did miss Ward and sharing our times together.

Life was instantly better when Otto Lang came over to me at the end of day three, saying "OK, Warren, you can teach beginners, but you have to take a shower and get a haircut before you do." I was on the gravy train! Free food and $125 a month in pay! It would be easy to live on that paycheck. And I was really lucky to have Fritz Kramer as my roommate.

AFTER MY INSTRUCTION DAY WAS DONE, THERE WAS A WHOLE OTHER LIFE with a whole other job of filling the orders for all those laces. Christmas week was coming on fast, and that was when nearly half of all ski equipment was sold. Not only that, there were half a dozen different signs to paint. The oil stove was turned way up in my garage apartment, so I could paint signs in the evenings. It was so cold some nights that I had my two-burner Coleman stove on the floor under my drawing board to keep my fingers working. Occasionally, I pulled the stove out from under the drawing board so I could stand over it for a while to thaw out the rest of my body.

Until the money started coming in from the ski shops, I was going to have to generate a fairly big income stream. I needed to simultaneously pay off the two grandmothers, the bank that held the car loan, my nightly burning crews who burned the tips on the nylon laces, and the Army-surplus friend who provided the 1,000-foot reels of nylon. Not to mention Mrs. Flush, who dyed the finished laces, and the post office that sent off boxes of them almost daily to my many customers.

The lace business kept growing. It seemed as though almost everyone who walked into a ski shop in the West where my laces were on display would walk out with a pair. New ski shops were coming in by word of mouth. There soon were 45 shops selling my laces. Pete Lane's shop alone was selling almost 200 pairs a week. Thirty percent of the skiers in Sun Valley were replacing their last-a-week cotton laces with my guaranteed-for-a-season, choice-of-colors (red or yellow), magical, nylon ski bootlaces. Mrs. Flush was working my 5-gallon nylon-lace dye pots to the limit, and we were making the next-day shipping deadlines. By mid-January, we had begun filling reorders. Mr. Flush had organized a day shift of ski-bootlace burners to keep up with the demand coming from phone-in orders. The Flush log cabin was company headquarters: They were providing the phone, and they were doing very well. The Flushes were making as much as $24 a day. Back then, that was very good money.

I was becoming the American ski bootlace mogul.

CHAPTER TWENTY-FOUR

1949

The Most Frequent Cause for Divorce Is Marriage

BY MID-WINTER 1949, SUN VALLEY WAS BECOMING MY HOME. I WAS teaching skiing and giving private lessons, filling orders for ski bootlaces, having dinner with my friends in the employee cafeteria, having an occasional date for dinner at the Challenger Inn, supervising my friends burning nylon lace ends, painting signs, and checking with Mr. and Mrs. Flush in Ketchum, who were dyeing hundreds of bootlaces every day. With so many 52-inch yellow and red laces hanging and drying over their rafters, the cabin looked like an Italian spaghetti factory. Orders for laces were still coming in as of mid-February. So far I had banked some $4,000 in checks that got mailed to my mother to deposit in Hollywood. That was more than enough for me to live on for a year. I had never thought I would have enough money to need to know how to handle it. I never realized that to have a verifiable account, I should have had a bank in which I deposited my own money just for tax purposes, let alone for security. All those ideas were foreign to me. I also still had the money loaned to me to build a cabin on Trail Creek. I felt I had a comfortable cushion, until the crash.

One day I stopped in the Lodge lobby behind three men who were looking for something. They said they were from Fox Movietone News and asked for some help. One of the men held up a pair of fancy reading glasses without lenses in one hand and a Tyrolean hat in the other. "Try these on," he said. They were looking for a skier who could do a clown act, pretending to be a beginner taking lessons who takes a lot of falls. After I put on the glasses and the Tyrolean hat, they seemed to think that I might fit the bill. I told them that nobody in America had survived more falls than I.

I learned a lot for 20 days at $35 a day, while still getting my room and board paid by Sun Valley. I would have done the movie for nothing, just to get away from teaching on the baby slope on Half Dollar. The outfit had a big 35-MM camera on a heavy tripod; a supply of big, unexposed film reels; and a crew that included the cameraman, a producer, a director, and a grip to move all this heavy stuff around. There were two toboggan-loads of stuff. They hired Jim Patterson from the ski patrol (later, father of Susie Patterson, 1974 U.S. women's slalom champion) for the part of the instructor in the film. It was a no-brainer to fall in whatever position the director wanted, sliding on my back with skis waving over my head, if that was the shot they wanted.

One part I played was a skier out of control on Baldy, skiing off-trail through a split-rail fence built to come apart, and sailing off the jump on Ruud Mountain, wildly swinging my arms for balance (it wasn't an act). I also was learning a few things by asking the cameraman questions. He told me it was his 22nd year behind the camera. He also said that if you want to perform in front of the camera, you had the job for maybe five years. If you were behind the camera, he said, you could film the rest of your professional life. This sank into my mind. I ended up $700 richer and sent it all to my mother to deposit in the bank.

IN FEBRUARY, I MET TWO MEN WHO CHANGED MY LIFE. THOUGH THEY didn't look like what I thought VIPs should look like, I was assigned two from Chicago, Chuck Percy and Hal Geneen. Chuck showed up in his Navy bell-bottom pants with the 13-button fly, the nearest thing he owned to ski pants. Hal was out of shape. They both cheerfully put up with all of the mandatory three-day beginner's instruction at the bottom of the baby slope of Half Dollar. On the fourth day, I took Chuck and Hal for their first ride on the Half Dollar chairlift. It was a clear day, and I was carrying my 8-MM Bell & Howell Sportster movie camera in a belt holster. On the way up, on the left, I took some backlit shots of icicles on the towers, shining in the morning sun.

When we got off at the top, Chuck and Hal both wanted to know how I liked the camera. I said I thought it was great! Chuck said, "I'm glad you like it. I'm president of the company." (I'd never met the president of anything before in my life.) At lunch that day, they invited me to dinner at the Trail Creek Cabin.

Chuck and Hal were, respectively, president and the comptroller of the leading American manufacturer of 8- and 16-MM hand-winding movie cameras. The classic windup 16-MM Bell & Howell was the official Armed Forces combat camera during World War ll. It was so simple in design that it almost never malfunctioned. Chuck had become president that year at age 29. At Trail Creek that night, the entertainment was a ski film made by a couple of guys from Canada—a bad amateur job.

Riding back in the hay wagon after dinner, I reviewed what was lacking in the film, which was almost everything. Chuck said, "You seem to know something about making movies." I told him I'd already done a one-hour film on surfing and skiing, and I was going to make a travel lecture film about skiing. I had never said that before, but maybe it had been lurking in the back of my mind ever since I was a kid watching MGM's "FitzPatrick Traveltalks," each one ending with a romantic sunset over the final lines, "As the sun sinks slowly in the west." Chuck asked me why, if I wanted to make travel films, was I teaching skiing? I said that Otto Lang was paying me $125 a month, and I was saving up to buy the camera I wanted: a Model 70 DA Bell & Howell with a three-lens turret that cost $256.

The next afternoon, Hal showed up in my class again (Chuck had graduated to a more advanced class). Hal said he and Chuck had talked at lunch and had agreed they would have their factory send me the exact camera, and I could pay them back out of my earnings. He asked, "Now what were those lenses you wanted?" and I told him, while wondering why two high-up executives were bothering with me.

It was one of those gestures easy to make and easy to forget. When I went to the Sun Valley Post Office to get my mail two weeks later, the clerk handed me a box, along with my pile of orders for more ski bootlaces. Inside there was a brown-leather case with a red-velvet lining and a Bell & Howell

70 DA with the three lenses, two rolls of film, a booklet on how to thread and operate the camera, and a note signed by Hal Geneen and Chuck Percy: "Warren: Good Luck. Pay us for the camera out of your earnings."

Chuck Percy later became a senator from Illinois and Hal Geneen the CEO of ITT. We remained good friends for the next 40 years, skiing and dining with Chuck when he would come to Vail with Bob Galvin (whose father invented Motorola), and dining with Hal and his wife when they visited. Bob often brought interesting, successful people to Vail for fascinating talk sessions. Unfortunately, they have all passed away in recent years, after living long, amazing, and inspirational lives.

With this present of the camera, I realized that there was nothing stopping me from becoming a filmmaker. I began to think about filming skiing and surfing full-time. I wrote a letter of profound thanks to Chuck and Hal the next day. I was so inspired by their friendship that I began to build a waterproof box so I could start filming surfing as soon as the snow melted. It would be a long time before there was any skiing to film next winter, and this winter I didn't have the time.

A casual conversation can later have unanticipated consequences. In 1949, noted playwright and author Frederick Kohner, his wife, and his 8-year-old daughter, Kathy, were in my ski-school class. Frederick and his wife skied in Austria before escaping from Hitler's wrath in World War II. This was their first ski trip in America, and we had a great time reacquainting Frederick and his wife with skiing and getting their daughter started heading downhill properly.

We became friends as well and ate several lunches and a dinner or two together. We talked about what I did during the summer, and most of the conversation was about surfing at Malibu and San Onofre. By that time, I told them about my 8-MM surfing movies and my desire to make travel lecture ski films.

Frederick took his daughter to Malibu the next summer, and like me she got hooked on surfing. She was not even a teenager when she first appeared on the beach with her parents, lunch, bathing suit, and towel. She was not tall, and in those days everyone who could surf at all had to have a nickname: Kathy's became a mixture of "girl" and "midget"—hence the name that is still hers today, Gidget. She quickly became a mascot to the old-timers. Her father or mother would drop her off at Malibu in the morning and pick her up in the late afternoon. Gidget's surfing career and notoriety became the unintended consequence of my surfing stories about the beach as a place of freedom—like a ski hill, only a lot warmer. In about 1954 or 1955, Frederick finished writing his book *Gidget.*

In 1957, I got a surprise phone call from the film studios. They were producing a feature film called "Gidget." They needed help understanding surf culture and finding a good place to shoot the movie. I spent the next two weeks driving the producer up and down the coast from Ventura to San Diego so he could look at all of the potential beaches to film. Kathy's father sold the film rights for a lucrative price, and was generous enough to give his daughter 5 percent.

At the end of the winter, I found out that there could be a flip side to romance. The object of my friendship was a good-looking lady in my class who couldn't slide forward the length of her skis without sitting down on the snow. It took me three private lessons to get her to move at least 100 feet before going into a sitting fall. She was so impressed by my patient attention that she bought me a pair of $40 Molitor ski boots, a huge gift back then. She invited me to dinner at the Lodge several times, but she was not on my official girlfriend list as yet. I had been dating a couple of female employees for a longer time than I had known her. But she was interesting and well educated, with enough money to pay for a month's stay in the Sun Valley Lodge. We got along well, especially in company with a married couple who were her close friends, Jack and MaryLou Simpson. Then came the fatal night all four of us spent at a restaurant in Ketchum.

I still don't know exactly how it happened. I still had never taken a drink in my life so it wasn't liquor. No question I had been stretched out tight for four months of constant day and night work. I was close to physical and mental exhaustion, the point at which your body and mind begin to feel hollow, a feeling that luckily dissipates with a few nights' good sleep—but that's just what I was not getting.

Jack and MaryLou began asking why I looked sad. What I must need, they decided, was to settle down with someone like their friend, whom I was by then dating. She seemed a wonderful person to settle down with. "What have you got to lose?" asked Jack. My date added to the momentum, proposing we get married right now, this very night. For some reason, to my stretched-to-the-limit mind, this seemed logical. I had never married; in fact, I had never even really been with a woman. I thought maybe this was the way you got married: You just went ahead and did it. Never having discussed anything like this with my non–role model parents, I was exhausted and let myself be led by Jack and MaryLou.

Before I came to my senses, all four of us were in Jack and MaryLou's car on a long drive to Elko, Nevada, where all you had to do was show up at a minister's home at any hour—no blood tests, nothing. It was a long drive, but I was evidently past the point of asking myself what would happen if I didn't like being married. There was no reason at all for marrying this woman, or any woman at that time of my life. We arrived in Elko, woke up the minister, and were married, with Jack and MaryLou as witnesses.

My brand-new bride rented a duplex for us in Hailey the next day. After living with her for a couple of weeks with a gradual feeling of uneasiness, I had to face the hard fact that I had made a very large mistake.

She was perfectly nice, but I defined myself as a workaholic with only a little romance thrown in around the edges, while my wife thought life was one long romance. Somewhere deep down, the terrible recollections of my parents' wildly destructive marriage began to haunt my brain.

The morning after my last day of teaching, I bolted. I packed my bag, got in the Ford, drove to Boise, and actually paid to fly to Los Angeles. I made an appointment with an attorney who was a friend of my mother's. The first question he asked was if the marriage had been consummated. I said, "Yes, it had." He said the marriage could not be annulled. I had to get divorced, he said, and he told me how to do it. I wrote everything down and drove back to Berendo Street. This was the first time I'd ever met with an attorney.

Jack Simpson called me and said my wife was driving the 800 miles to Los Angeles to talk me out of going through with the divorce. The two of us had a long meeting, where I tried to convince her that I had to have a divorce. Then I flew back to Boise, and once back in Sun Valley, contacted a lawyer in Hailey, and at the same time, got a job as a dishwasher at the Challenger Inn, which had opened for spring guests. The job came with three meals in the employees' cafeteria, plus $125 a month and a bed in the ski patrol barracks. I could breathe easily once again, or so I thought.

There was still one more crisis. A day later, there was a phone call at the cafeteria from Jack, who told me my wife was in the emergency ward at the Twin Falls hospital. While driving back, she had missed a turn at 85 miles an hour, gone off the road, and wound up with a broken shoulder, a broken collarbone, and cracked ribs. She was lucky that she wasn't more badly injured, but she needed a blood transfusion, and the hospital asked that we donate.

Jack, MaryLou, and I drove down to Twin Falls, found the hospital, and each donated a pint of blood. I fainted shortly after giving blood, so they had to give me my pint back. That's how physically exhausted I must have been. I went in to the hospital room to see the woman who was still my wife and felt as guilty as could be. But I finally convinced her I was just not ready to marry her or anyone else, either emotionally or financially: I was not mature enough.

In due course, she got well and did not oppose the divorce. We appeared before a judge in Hailey in May, and the divorce was granted.

Even after all this turmoil, Sun Valley was where I wanted to be—and to build my cabin. The plan was for a one-story, one-bedroom cabin with about 800 square feet. I started working on it sunup to sundown, knocking off only to go back to the Challenger Inn to wash dishes and eat. I had drawn the plans from a book on building log cabins and asked a lot of questions.

BY THE MIDDLE OF JUNE, WITH THE CABIN'S FOUNDATION IN PLACE AND the walls going up, I was sitting on the creek bank, thinking about surfing at San Onofre. And asking myself why I was building a house in Ketchum. I really did not want to go back to teaching skiing on the flats of Half Dollar next winter. What I really wanted to do was make feature-length travel films. So the cabin building was stopped, and instead I put a "For Sale" sign on the road and sold the cabin and lot two days later for $900, $100 more than I had spent on materials and the vacant lot. (But $948,100 less than the property was listed for 65-plus years later, when it was described as a "one-of-a-kind" cabin built by me.) I packed up, left Ketchum behind, and drove back to Hollywood, where there was a lot of surfing available.

There, a great shock awaited me.

I asked my mother for the money that I had sent to her from my ski bootlace business, about $8,400, according to my figures. My mother looked me right in the eye and said, "Well, I never got more than $900 from you in the mail." That was all that was left in the bank account. My mother evidently had not been doing well in her ozone business and had been driven to the point where she lost sense of right and wrong. In truth, she and my father had been living on my money for a considerable time. To make myself feel less crazy, I kept reminding myself that it was my mother who had kept the family going through all those terrible years when we had no money. Now, at least I knew I'd helped out. If she only admitted she needed the money, I would have given it to her.

After closing the door on Sun Valley, it was all over for that era of my life, and I never looked back. So many other companies were producing nylon bootlaces now that I didn't really have an edge. I was now committed to a different goal: making films. With my Bell & Howell, I was off to the beach on weekends, sleeping and eating in my Ford, and learning how to film while riding a surfboard holding my waterproof camera box. My idea was to make a surfing comedy, featuring mostly a series of crash-and-burn falls. That summer I shot 12 100-foot rolls; it was all that I had time to shoot. I was able to ride my board alongside another board and film its rider from fairly close up. It ended up as a 15-minute film called "Surfing Daze." For this first attempt at editing, I bought some editing equipment and glued together the 16-MM film in my bedroom at Berendo Street. Borrowing a 16-MM projector, I thought my film looked good up there in a larger format.

After showing it informally to several audiences that fall, I got all kinds of encouragement. Once past that, I wanted to start making a feature ski lecture film. It was now time to find a ski area where I could work as an instructor and film in my time off, earning enough to keep on buying film and shooting all winter long.

THAT SUMMER, I VISITED MY FRIEND ERWIN LENKEIT, WHO OWNED Featherlike Pneumatic Products in Los Angeles, which produced air mattresses made of vulcanized, rubber-coated fabric. They had been introduced in 1940 and become very popular. I watched how they manufactured air mattresses. They had just lost their main leak-tester, and Erwin offered the job to me, so I became Featherlike's chief air mattress tester for the summer. My job was to find the leaks on any returned mattresses by dumping them in the immersion vat to see where the bubbles showed up. I'd circle the places with an indelible pencil, and then turn them over to be revulcanized. Erwin wanted me to join him in the business and treated me very well, considering I had just dropped out of the mountains into his operation. I was making 60 bucks a week, very good pay in those days.

Then I learned that a new resort called Squaw Valley was opening up in California just west of Lake Tahoe, with my hero and champion French ski racer Émile Allais as head of the ski school. Émile was also heading the ski school in Portillo, Chile, during the Southern Hemisphere's winter. I wrote asking for a job teaching under him at Squaw that next winter. It was a big surprise in September when a letter came back from Émile saying "yes." He would pay me the same as Otto Lang had. I went to Erwin and told him that I was going to have to quit on November 1. He understood that my career was in film, not in monitoring little bubbles in a big water tank.

Squaw Valley was slated to open for the Thanksgiving weekend. About 10 days before, I loaded up my skis, boots, and the 16-MM camera in my '46 Ford, and was on my way to Squaw Valley, about 480 miles straight north through Sacramento, east over Donner Summit to Truckee, and then 10 miles south to Squaw. As long as I was driving this far north, I made a side trip of about 80 miles, rented a board, and surfed the superb waves at Santa Cruz just south of San Francisco. It was my last surfing in 1949, and it was very cold without a wetsuit in 44-degree water.

The resort was still getting ready for its first season. The mile of access road into the valley was still dirt and bumpy. The accommodations offered to ski instructors were a bit bumpy, too. The president and owner of the resort, Alex Cushing, had bought some Navy-surplus barracks from a closed U.S. Navy depot north of Reno. They just chainsawed them down the middle of the roof along the ridge, put each half on a tractor trailer, hauled the halves to Squaw Valley, and nailed them back together. There was construction going on all over the place, and it was a little like living in a war zone—but that was not important. During the coming winter, I was going to ski more powder at Squaw Valley than I had ever thought possible in a single season.

And I also had my Bell & Howell 70 DA at the ready.

CHAPTER TWENTY-FIVE

1949–1950

Making a Living Is Not the Same as Making a Life

THE 1949–50 SEASON TURNED OUT TO BE MY TRANSITION WINTER. If everything worked right and I managed to shoot enough good footage to make my first feature film, my life would change forever, though I didn't know it at the time. Squaw Valley was stunningly beautiful—a broad valley surrounded on three sides by a ring of steep mountains.

The ski school also looked good. Émile was the director, and we would be teaching by his method. It would be nice instructing both beginners and advanced students, instead of being assigned to a baby slope as I had been at Sun Valley. My pay was $125 a month plus room and board, giving me enough extra income to buy the raw film to make my movie, which I hoped a lot of people would want to see. My future hung on that assumption. It was almost a given that Émile's name would draw enough pupils to the school, so there would be plenty of private lessons coming my way.

Émile was an extraordinary skier. He had won two FIS World Championships just before World War ll. He probably would have won his third in a row had he not broken an ankle in training. Émile had invented the French Method, the teaching system of France, and had already been a key factor in the initial design of three ski areas: Valcartier in Canada; Portillo in Chile; and currently, Squaw Valley. He later went on to influence more European resorts.

There were other powerful attractions at Squaw besides its beauty and Émile's presence. There was Squaw's mile-and-a-half-long double chair, replacing Aspen's chair as the world's longest at the time. It was designed by Bob Heron, the lift engineer who had built the Aspen chairs in 1946. It was only the third chairlift built in California. There were also two rope tows for beginners in front of the lodge, which was designed by architect Sandy McIlvaine. Behind all this was Alex Cushing. He was the one who had raised the $400,000 needed to open Squaw. Hailing from a wealthy New York City family, Alex had skied in Europe. He imagined Squaw as a place that could equal Europe's best, beginning with the biggest lift in America, the most modern lodge, and an amazing world champion as its ski-school director.

I had counted on Squaw's ski population being much like the one at Sun Valley, where nearly every guest stayed for a week. I had counted on extra money teaching private lessons and selling cartoons and photos to add to my income. Within a few days, it became obvious that the lack of skiers at Squaw meant my chances of making the money needed to finance the purchase of reels of 16-MM film was not very good, but I was motivated to run my new movie camera—"obsessed" might be a better word.

The first surprise came while riding Squaw's big chairlift. It went over a mile and a half of fairly easy terrain, but then stopped short of the headwall at the end of the valley. Squaw needed another lift. This giant headwall spanned the two peaks at the end of the valley, rising about 3,000 feet bottom to top. It was the biggest headwall at a ski area then, other than the Tuckerman Headwall on Mt. Washington in New Hampshire and the cornice at Mammoth.

This terrain held the sort of challenge that would have brought experts from everywhere to try it out, if it only had a lift. There was a lot of flatter, but equally beautiful, advanced terrain on all sides of the valley; but again, no lifts. This did not go over well with the skiers. During the season, the slopes were often deserted.

Squaw's other problem was a lack of beds. The lodge had room for 40 guests and space for another 30 skiers in its skiers' dorm converted from

Navy barracks. Although Squaw could draw from Reno, 40 miles away, and from nearby Truckee and Tahoe City, it needed hundreds more skiers daily, and they were available only from the big market on the other side of the Sierras: San Francisco, 200 miles away.

Unfortunately, the drive from San Francisco across Donner Summit remained an ordeal: 6-mph speeds on a two-lane road behind a row of 18-wheelers and up icy switchbacks. Skiers from San Francisco usually stayed only for a weekend rather than a week, as they typically did in Sun Valley. There wasn't enough variety of lift skiing to keep them interested that long. On weekdays Squaw averaged, at least in the first part of the winter, no more than 50 to 100 skiers, and on weekends often no more than 100 to 200. Luckily, those figures more than doubled by the end of the season.

Wayne Poulsen, an airline pilot, and Sun Valley ski instructor Marty Arrougé had bought the entire valley for $10,000. As longtime skiers and amateur competitors, they knew Squaw was an extraordinary place, but in order to get start-up money, they had to invite Cushing into the ski corporation and deed the corporation's 25 acres at the base of the chairlift over to him. However, Cushing and Poulsen had very different views on how to develop Squaw. Cushing had the muscle (money) on the board, so Poulsen was voted out as president.

That left Cushing running the resort. Cushing must have realized after a month or so into this first winter that he had to raise a good deal more money to get more skiers to Squaw, but that was not going to happen right away. During this first difficult winter, Cushing's active imagination often led him to plunge ahead without sufficient preparation on the ground. That September, when Émile arrived with his wife, Georgette, they had to be hauled into the valley in a truck for lack of a paved access road. On Thanksgiving weekend as the resort opened, Cushing and his wife, Justine, arrived, along with their children, their maid, and their butler. There was no cook in place at the lodge, so the butler wound up doing the cooking. He served meals cafeteria style. He was the only person I've ever seen carbonate Jell-O to make it go farther, probably at Cushing's direction.

At least Cushing's plan had plenty of instructors; the four of us were hardly ever overworked. The other three on the roster were Charlie Cole, my fellow instructor on Half Dollar at Sun Valley; Alfred Hauser, who had taught for Allais during the previous summer at Portillo; and Dodie Post from Reno. She had won the Silver Belt at Sugar Bowl and the Silver Dollar Derby at Mt. Rose, and captained the 1948 Olympic women's team at St. Moritz, where she broke an ankle in training. (Much later in life, after she married author Ernie Gann, we visited her frequently at her San Juan Island farm, but she just recently passed away.)

Émile gave the four of us a course in how to instruct *á la Ski Française.* I was very lucky: In fact, without Allais' invention of the French Method, I would not have been there at all. I first saw the book *Ski Française* in the winter of 1947. A couple of guys I skied with from Washington state had bought the book and were doing *ruades*, the French technique's very handy, short-braking jump turn, down the Canyon on Baldy. Earlier, Ward and I had bought a copy of the book and tried out its teaching sequences. I thought that Allais' system was much more effective than the Arlberg system being used everywhere else in the country. Arlberg uses the stem turn, with ski tips together and tails apart, as the basic turn. Once you made a thousand stem turns, you had to unlearn it in order to turn with the skis parallel. Everyone wanted to be a parallel skier in that era, yet only about one out of 20 ever got that good—the other 19 were hung up in the stem-turn stage, having developed a dependency on the stem too powerful to break. *Ski Française* avoided all that, because beginner turns were made from a forward sideslip with skis parallel. This was a simple stroke of genius from Émile Allais.

Allais was more than a teacher: Even at 31, he could leave any instructor in any ski school on the American continent far behind. Once, while coaching the U.S. team at Sun Valley, Allais blew the racers away by taking them to the top of Exhibition and straight-running the trail to inspire them to do the same. I don't think any of them followed.

Even though I liked teaching under Allais at Squaw, my goal that winter had been to shoot enough rolls of 16-MM to make a feature film—that was my real passion. I wanted to shoot at least 40 rolls, 4,000 feet, the minimum that was needed to make a 90-minute feature-length ski film. At $10 to $12 a roll, it would cost about $500 for film, 70 percent of my basic salary at Squaw. Even though I was getting room and board, setting $500 aside was not easy. At Sun Valley, I had been adding $5 to $10 a week to my income by giving a private lesson almost every day.

At Squaw, teaching the Allais way, I sometimes had a beginner ready to ski the chairlift on the second day: My students got a lot more for their money here than they had at Sun Valley. However, students happy with their progress were less likely to feel the need for private lessons. The Arlberg method produced results more slowly and could, therefore, generate more money for the ski school. There were so few pupils coming around early in the season that when all four of us instructors and Émile each had their own pupil, it was a big day.

My fallback for extra cash for several years had been drawing cartoons. In the evenings, I drew them in the room I shared with Alfred Hauser in one of the converted Navy barracks. When I finished a cartoon, I would hang it up by the ski shop in the lodge for sale for $1. In midseason, I was averaging $3 to $4 a week, and I would earn about $80 extra for the season from my cartoons. I also took my Speed Graphic out during the lunch hour to take photos of couples relaxing on the front porch. Sometimes, after dinner, I drove 10 miles down to Tahoe City, where a friend of mine had a darkroom. I paid him for the use of his chemicals, developed my negatives, and printed any picture worth enlarging to an 8-by-10. The next day at breakfast, I'd hunt the couples down in the lodge and offer them their Squaw Valley souvenir for a dollar. I probably made another $50 for the season selling photos, not counting the times when I found out that the man was with someone other than his wife. The price then became $10.

It wasn't hard to find time to shoot. Any instructor who did not have a pupil on any given day was free to go with Émile on his daily free-skiing tour, so I had plenty of opportunities to film Émile's group skiing in fresh powder. Of course, a lot of the footage was spent shooting Émile who, even with all the skiing he had done in his life, still loved to ski for fun. He would take off on different runs that would go on until I ran out of film, leading our group with his signature smoothness and enthusiasm. The fact that there were no lifts on Squaw's steep powder slopes gave me more time to shoot before the snow got tracked up, and I got a whole lot of deep and light footage. In fact, that was what I named the first film, "Deep and Light." Stan Tomlinson from Boise, who had beaten me for first place two years before in the race at Bogus Basin, was now on Squaw's ski patrol and skiing beautifully for my camera.

I made sure to shoot comic-relief footage, mostly of head-over-heels falls in the powder that everyone except Émile would occasionally pull off. Of course, I did a lot of deep powder skiing myself as part of the process. I was having a great time compared to teaching at Sun Valley the winter before. In the Allais ski school, I was on equal footing with every other instructor, not low man on the totem pole, suffering through a succession of three-day basic kindergarten courses on the slopes of Half Dollar.

PART THREE

Lifting Off

Earning renown as "the godfather of extreme sports."

CHAPTER TWENTY-SIX

1949–1950

Countdown to a Start-Up

ALTHOUGH THE IDEA OF BEING A FULL-TIME FILMMAKER HAD GROWN ON me as an ultimate goal, I was like somebody who wants to play pro basketball when he is in high school: He has to work into it because there is a long learning curve. In filmmaking, there is also a tough financial curve. Les Jay, of *Western Skiing* magazine, gave me a vote of confidence by telling me that my photography was plenty good enough to put a film together. From then on while at Squaw, I hustled, scraped, begged, and borrowed whatever money I could get to buy rolls of film until the season ended, but 3,700 feet is all I could afford to shoot.

Émile had a publicity agent named Mitch Hamelberg, who was the one who got Émile on the cover of *LIFE*. He wanted a ski technique film made of Émile. I was the guy on site, so Mitch said, "Why don't you do it for me? I'll pay you $35 a day." This was a huge amount of money, so I shot the whole French Technique in the wee hours of the morning, into the late spring, before the chairlifts opened. Émile and I would get up at 4:30 A.M. to film the various demonstrations. Mitch bought the film, paying me a total of $350, which gave me additional funding for my own first feature film.

Back in mid-February, I had met photographer Ray Atkeson, who was from Portland, Oregon, and became a lifelong friend. He was about 10 years older and came up to me carrying an Army-surplus rucksack. As we were ready to board the chairlift, he asked, "Would you make a few turns for my camera?" He was, I think, the best winter-sports black-and-white photographer in the history of skiing, with his perfect sense for composition, his right-on exposure, and his untiring efforts to climb to the best locations.

Atkeson usually began his day climbing in the early-morning hours to get that irreplaceable sunrise shot. His work ethic inspired me to make whatever effort was called for to reach the most spectacular locations, wherever they were.

I still have his pictures of me skiing in my collection, and it was Atkeson who made the famous shot of French World War ll hero Joe Marillac skiing the Squaw Valley headwall, perfectly relaxed, and using the French Technique. In the photograph, there is a big tree proving that the hill was at least 45 degrees steep.

In February 1950, Allais appointed me as temporary head of the ski school for a week. It was a milestone month in the history of American skiing. For the first time, the FIS Alpine World Ski Championships were held in North America, in Aspen. These were the first World Championships to be held outside of Europe, and the first official world championships held since 1939, when the War had suspended international ski racing. Most European nations except for Switzerland were still too strapped for cash to host the event after the devastation of the war, even five years after it had ended. The FIS, rather than giving the championship to the neutral Swiss or to the Austrians who were pushed to the wrong side, awarded it to its wartime ally. The addition of the giant slalom as the third alpine event also was a first.

Émile and his wife, Georgette, went off to Aspen for a week, leaving me in charge. They were invited to attend, I'm sure, as guests of the French National Ski Team. Dodie Post also took off for Aspen to visit with all her old racing friends on the international circuit. My job was to divide the pupils between those of us who were left: Charlie Cole, Alfred Hausser, Tyler Micelou (who had been hired recently), and me.

Sometime in March, the world's leading ski filmmaker, John Jay, showed up at Squaw. Émile formed an expedition to climb to the top of Squaw Peak so that John could film us all for his next season's feature film. Even Émile's wife came along. John did a lot of shooting that day. (He had no idea I was working on my own film.) That night, he showed his film to the lodge guests. I focused on the audience reactions, noticing the strongest reactions came during the comedy bits John had inserted in the film: John had a dry, New England satirical sense of humor, but I had my own brand of film humor by now. I exercised it the next weekend when we had a good crowd. As soon as I had finished with my class, I went out and shot footage of beginners fighting Squaw's two rope tows and losing, plus off-the-wall stuff to beef up the humor for my first-ever, feature-length film.

I came back to Squaw many times in later winters, particularly the winter when Cushing, on a particularly big binge of imagination, managed to sell the idea to the International Olympic Committee to hold the 1960 Winter Olympics there. That led directly to the Squaw of today. It has more than 30 lifts to the top of nearly every mountain in sight, making it quite a different place than it was in the winter of 1950. Even more importantly, Alex was able to convince the state to expand the two-lane highway over Donner Summit into a four-lane freeway. This opened the entire Lake Tahoe basin to development by cutting in half the commuting time from San Francisco.

CHAPTER TWENTY-SEVEN

1950–1951

Digging Ditches to Finance My Kodachrome Addiction

ABOUT THE TIME THE SNOW MELTED AT SQUAW VALLEY IN THE SPRING of 1950, I got some real encouragement again from Lester Jay. Lester and Wolfgang Lert were founders of *Western Skiing* and had sold it to *Ski Illustrated* in 1948 (a new owner merged the titles to create, or recreate, *SKI*, but that's another story). Lester came to Squaw just as I was starting to worry whether there was enough quality footage to put together a feature-length ski film. The truth was I really didn't know how to put one together.

Other than earlier surfing footage, I had never projected any of my footage after it was developed because a projector could leave scratches on the original ski film. I had no copy when I got into a conversation with Lester. I told him I had already shot 34 rolls that winter and was serious about putting together a feature film and having ski club sponsors book it. Lester said, "Well, can I see some of the film?" I decided to chance a scratch or two. I dug up a 16-MM projector, cleaned the gate thoroughly, set up a screen, and showed Lester five rolls of what I knew were my best untracked powder snow shots.

After the first three rolls, Lester seemed impressed. He said, "I've seen enough, but let's look at a couple more, just in case." I showed him two more 100-foot reels, and Lester said, "You know, John Jay is making a pretty good living with his annual feature-length ski films. From what I've seen here, you could also put together a feature film. Why don't you do that? And if I can help you, I will."

Besides Chuck Percy and Hal Geneen letting me buy the new camera on credit, this was the best thing that could have happened. Lester had the authority to vouch for the quality of my film. Now I had to figure out how to start editing my thousands of feet of film into this first of more than a half of century of Warren Miller feature films. I also had to get a summer job. After leaving Squaw at the end of the season in April, it was back to Berendo Street and a job digging ditches and pounding nails on a construction crew during the day and writing and editing at night.

However, I put editing off a bit. I certainly had to go surfing at San Onofre on my first weekend back in Los Angeles. I ran into a friend there who proudly showed me his new Chevy panel delivery truck that he had just bought to live in when he went surfing. The space inside was huge, much bigger than the back of my '46 Ford business coupe. I decided to get one of my own. It would provide a no-cost place to live in while I was traveling around showing my film and surfing, and one I could also use as an office. I was so optimistic I sold the Ford and threw in what was left of the $350 I made on the filming of Allais. The rest of the truck's $1,300 price tag was covered with a car loan that my grandmother cosigned. For the first time in my life, I was driving a new car. By this time, I had salvaged enough of my bootlace money from my mother to finish paying off Lynn's grandmother for the loan for the house in Ketchum and my grandmother for my '46 Ford loan. And I'd opened my own bank account in Hollywood, so any money that came in went directly to me and was deposited right away.

Recreational vehicles had just begun to show up in California, with full kitchens, showers, toilets, and middle five-figure prices. All I needed was an RV with a bunk, a counter workbench, a kitchen, and a low four-figure price. I built a bed on one side, a long counter on the other side, and a chest of drawers underneath. I built a "kitchen" next to the doors in back for my Coleman stove, pots and pans, dishes, pantry, and an insulated icebox, which a friend helped me make out of galvanized metal.

With a comfortable place of my own where I could make my own food, it was easy to stay on the beach all weekend. In the evenings, I began scripting my film on the long counter from my typewritten description of each scene. My next serious step was to cut the film and rearrange the sequences.

I had absolutely no training in motion-picture production, no idea of how to go from my 37 100-foot rolls now sitting in their cans to a final hour-and-a-half feature ski show on two 45-minute reels. I edited the film by blundering along. I logged each scene, with a brief description, plus a number for its position on the reel and another number that identified the reel. My logbook took me right to the scene I wanted.

It took three months before there was a final sequence for the entire film. For the next step, I had to retreat to Berendo Street and build 10-foot-long racks in my old bedroom, cut the scenes that would be used out of the rolls of film, and hang the scenes, like ties on a tie rack, in the order of their appearance. Next, I spliced them, until I had 45 minutes' worth of film designated as Reel One. Then I spliced the scenes for Reel Two. I started Reel Two with my 10-minute "Surfing Daze" movie to give it variety, while also making it longer. Next, I painted and photographed the title and screen credits on a ski and filmed it in a bed of soap flakes to look like it was on real snow: "Deep and Light" by Warren Miller was my title shot. I titled Reel Two: "The French Technique" and incorporated Allais' teaching sequence and the great skiing that resulted. Then I reviewed both reels by cranking them through the movie-scope in succession. It looked good to me.

I knew I needed $400 to buy a projector and to have a lab make a release print. I was out of money, and making $40 a week digging ditches at my construction job kept me alive but no more. None of my friends were anxious to make a loan. One weekend while surfing at San Onofre, some surfers I had known for years asked how it was going. I told them that it was time to show the film to potential sponsors, but I didn't have the $400 to buy a release print and a projector.

One of the guys said, "Warren, I'll lend you a hundred." He turned to the other three and said, "Why don't we help Warren show his film?" All four of them were successful businessmen, and they all knew that they would be paid out of my ticket sales. All movie tickets back then were a buck apiece to avoid the federal entertainment tax that kicked in when the theatrical admission fee went over a dollar. As soon as these guys came up with the $400, I ordered the print and bought the projector. (Those four "angels" who put up that money were John Levy, El Jordan, Jack Given, and George Gore. I hope they realize how grateful I am for their belief in me.)

Now there was only one thing missing: a music track. Music played such an important role in ski films that John Jay had set up his own recording studio in his house and cut his music track onto 78-rpm records. However, 78-rpm original discs deteriorate with use so rapidly that I wanted to avoid using them. The wire recorder had been around since 1946. The first truly fine tape recorder had just come out: The Ampex let you record and make a version of Scotch tape splices without pops. Grandmother Edith suddenly had one appear in her living room. She called me as if she just had a thought and said, "Well, I'm not using my tape recorder at all. Can you use it for your movie work?" I drove right over and picked it up. Grandmother Edith had come through once again.

Even with the right sound equipment, it was still difficult to create a music track from various selections of music available on 78-rpm records. Each new selection had its own feeling. A friend of my grandmother's, who played the organ in a neighborhood church, called me and said she would like to help. She said she could play various selections to make a music track with smooth transitions, but the only time we could use the church organ was from 4 to 8 in the morning. Several times I drove my projector, my print, and my screen to the church at 3:30 in the morning, projected the film, and practiced my narration off the top of my head. After three or four run-throughs, this talented lady said she had the selections all worked out in her head, and it made the film much more enjoyable.

I started calling my local skier friends who might belong to a ski club, and told them I had a great new movie. "I'd like to come show it to you, and I've got a moneymaking idea for your ski club." I said that Lester Jay would back my word that I had something worth seeing. I managed to get a bunch of dates to show the film for ski club officers. This was shoot-from-the-hip guerrilla marketing, at its best—and it was working. One of these ski club sample showings would get me a booking.

At this point, I have to back up a little to explain how I got my construction job. Dick Meine was just starting out on a career as a subcontractor for construction firms, and he took me on as a member of his crew, even though I knew little about construction. I was willing to work for $1 an hour, five days a week, $40 total. Dick was subcontracting a foundation and framing for a building in Redondo Beach, adjacent to Palos Verdes, a 40-minute drive from Berendo Street. I first dug the foundation ditches, and then helped pour the concrete. Sometimes I would take a cold shower on the beach, maybe go bodysurfing, park overnight, make my own dinner, work on the script in my Chevy truck, and then be all set to go to work in the morning after a good long sleep.

One day, while nailing down the 1-by-6 roofing shingles with another of Dick's crew working alongside me, we got to talking. I asked, "Out of curiosity, how much is Dick paying you?" and he said, "Two dollars and a quarter an hour." "Well, that's just great," I said. "He's paying me a dollar an hour, and I'm doing the same work." I learned that there was a carpenters' union headquarters in Beverly Hills, and that they'd let me in without even checking my experience if I paid an additional fee in cash with the first month's dues and if I promised not to take a job in their territory. (That cash was already known as graft.)

I went back to Dick and told him I'd just joined the union and now my rate should be $2.25 an hour. Dick said, "You've got two options. One, continue to get $1 an hour from me, or you can go elsewhere and try to get $2.25." So I continued to work very hard for Dick for a couple of months and became a very fast and efficient building framer. Thanks to the experience he gave me, we remained friends for years.

I was also able to apply at the union hall for work at union wages. On my first day at any job, my bosses saw quickly that I was still not very good as a carpenter, but because I was a hard worker, they'd keep me on for a week or two until the framing got more complicated than I could handle. Then they'd dump me. I ended up working for 32 different contractors in two years.

IN MY FIRST FILM, THERE WERE A LOT OF GOOD SKIERS: SQUAW VALLEY instructors, with Dodie Post one of the best of them, and members of the ski patrol, who were also excellent skiers, including Stan Tomlinson, Jack Nagle, Gar Robinson, and Jack Simpson. I also showed other ski patrolmen like Gordie Butterfield and Arnie Madsen making fine turns in deep powder, and there were two or three days' worth of shooting beginners on the rope tows that were inserted here and there for comic relief. There was also an extraordinary sequence of Émile and a totally blind skier. That was amazing footage on an icy rope-tow hill full of bumps.

Émile took him up on the rope tow. I was there with my camera before they got to the top, and I shot 100 feet, two and a half minutes. Never having seen anything like this made me want to share it, knowing that it would impress my future audiences as it did me—and it did. The rope-tow slope was full of ungroomed bumps, but Émile was able to talk the blind skier down the hill, teaching him uphill christies. Just the fact that this guy was blind and skiing with the two-time world champion was enough to excite any audience. Afterward, I almost always devoted part of the films to a segment showing someone who had overcome tough challenges to find his or her freedom on the side of a hill.

There were also shots of the guests from a high angle from the chairlift tower, mostly of the bad skiers coming down the mile and a half of Squaw's big, open slope. The film also had some scary shots of skiing on the steeps of the headwall. Of course, the best skiing in the film was the wizard himself, Émile Allais. No one skied as smoothly or effortlessly.

Now I was scrambling around most of Southern California in my new home on wheels, showing the film to ski club officials between construction jobs. I had set dates with 10 of them. These viewings were also lessons in learning how to narrate. I watched the club officers' expressions closely, noting where my ad-libbed narration was working and where it was not. My commentary got better and smoother at each showing, or so I thought. I also was less nervous; however, the first nine clubs all gave me the same answer: "We really like the photography, the music is OK, and we would sponsor it and give you a $200 guarantee if you get somebody else to narrate your film."

There was no way I could afford to pay a narrator. I just kept slugging away, learning how to handle almost-constant rejection, a lesson that helped throughout my life, as much as I hated it.

The short films of Pete Smith from an earlier era influenced my narration. Pete Smith was a pioneer filmmaker who produced short, candid films on everything from operating a drill press to bringing the cows in from pasture. He appropriated old movie clips, edited them down, and ran them over comments on the little stupidities shown. Pete Smith produced 160 specials through 20 years, twice winning Oscars for Best Short Film. They were usually shown at movie houses between double features.

While I was practicing to be as successful as Pete Smith, I was turned down by the Santa Monica Ski Club—and by the Santa Ana Ski Club and by seven others that have escaped my memory bank. The 10th was the Ski Club Alpine—a bunch of Southern California ski racers and the leading ski club in that part of the world at the time—and they said, "Let's do it!"

They booked me for a night in mid-October with a guarantee of $200, or 40 percent of the gross, whichever was higher. The showing was in the auditorium at John Marshall Junior High in Pasadena. The day of the showing, I was busy nailing on a roof from 8 until 4:30, constantly asking myself "Will anybody show up?" After work, I drove down to the beach to one of the freshwater showers that were there to give swimmers a chance to wash off the salt. I washed off all the sawdust and sweat and went back into my truck, put on clean clothes and my tweed suit, tied my bow tie in the rear-view mirror of the truck, and headed for Pasadena, 30 miles away to the east of Los Angeles.

I was really nervous. I had never given a speech to a crowd before. I was going to face hundreds of people who had hired babysitters and taken their wives or girlfriends or spousal equivalents to dinner before coming to spend $1 on me. When I saw that the auditorium was filling up, it was exciting but also intimidating. I had arranged to do a warm-up introduction, which turned out to be a good idea.

I walked out on the stage to face the crowd and started my introduction—a tale of the ski bum life: living in a small trailer in the Sun Valley parking lot, spending only $18 total for lift tickets for four month's skiing.

I talked about shooting rabbits in Shoshone for dinner and the rotary plow that threw our buried rabbit skins into the tree above the trailer and the intricate dance routine involved in getting undressed outside in the freezing night air in order to get into bed in the freezing cold teardrop trailer after a dinner date. The audience laughed at my stories, not just polite laughs, but loud laughter. So far, my ski movie night was working, and I hadn't shown the movie yet.

The film really worked, even though I had no script other than the one that was lodged in my brain. I took my cues from the images as they came up on the screen and ad-libbed my way through the film in a monotone. I was so new to the business I had stationed myself, my tape recorder, and my microphone up in the balcony by the projector, where I was talking to everyone's back. I didn't know enough to stand on the stage alongside the screen and talk toward the audience, but once the film got going, those nine practice sessions for the officers of the ski clubs that had turned me down had evidently polished my routine. I hoped I was going to be an acceptable feature filmmaker!

Ski Club Alpine had sold 836 tickets at $1 each, and that meant $334.40 was coming to me as my 40 percent. I had made more money in an hour and a half than I had in a month and a half of pounding nails. To look at it differently, my take was a little less than the amount spent on the 37 reels of raw film stock I had bought in order to film the movie in the first place.

The ski club received more than $500, the auditorium only cost them $25, and I supplied the posters for free. I expanded this same formula in many markets over the next 55 years with the same percentage as that first night in Pasadena in 1950.

CHAPTER TWENTY-EIGHT

1951–1952

Meeting Jean; My Future Was Going to Be Different from My Past

THUS, MY 55-YEAR-LONG JOURNEY BEGAN WITH THE SHOWING OF MY first ski film, "Deep and Light," in Pasadena on a Friday night. On Sunday, I went surfing, and on Monday, I was back to pounding nails. The ski club was happy and talking about the same proposition the following year. It was then that I realized I would have to make feature-length ski film No. 2.

On carpenter's wages? Not a chance. I was still parking my truck at the Berendo Street house and using my parents' phone as a point of contact, when on Wednesday night, a ski club president called from Seattle. He had gotten a phone call from his brother, who had watched my film in Pasadena and told him that he and his ski club should sponsor it. The ski club wanted to go head-to-head with the Penguin Ski Club, which sponsored John Jay. I didn't think I could drive that far for a one-night stand for the $200 guarantee, but I told him that I would call him back the next night.

I checked the mileage, and with two oil changes and gas as high as 20 cents a gallon plus a three- or four-day drive each way, if I charged him an extra $100 guarantee, I could make up for the lost carpenter's wages and get a little ahead financially. I called the ski club president the next night and told him that I would leave in two weeks; we then made a verbal deal of $300 or 40 percent of the gross, whichever was the greater. I also told him I would pay him a 15 percent commission if he got me another show date within a week of his show in the same area.

He called me the next night and said he had persuaded Sandy Martin (with whom I've stayed friends all these years), a partner in a ski shop in Vancouver, B.C., to sponsor the show for $200 or 40 percent of the gross. This became an easy price for the gamble of putting on the extra show, and I used that same financial formula for many years.

I continued to pound nails for the next two weeks while I pored over maps and finally figured out that Highway 99 was the only option. It would be a long drive on a two-lane road behind semitrucks, so I packed up my projector, film, tape recorder, tweed suit, and bow tie; stocked the kitchen in my truck; put a clean sheet in my sleeping bag; and made sure I had my YMCA membership card so I could take hot showers in any city. I left on my first road-show tour in late October 1950. I had gambled a year of my time at Squaw Valley, almost $400 worth of film, and six months of editing the film, along with my day job.

I drove north, and every mile was exciting and new to me—into Oregon and then Washington, and as I approached Seattle on Highway 99, the Smith Tower stood out against the skyline, then the tallest building west of the Mississippi.

I was the new guy in town, but I had some friends living there who had worked at Sun Valley and Squaw the previous winters, and they let me park my red truck in their driveways so I wouldn't get rousted by the police. I was three days early, so they got some friends together for one more rehearsal before the big night in the Metropolitan Theater. (Years later, the theater was converted into the porte cochere for the grand Olympic Hotel. Right next door was a small sport shop called Eddie Bauer. It was the first time my film was advertised on the marquee in front of a theater, so I used my Speed Graphic to snap a photo of it, which I still have in my collection.)

I improved this second showing of "Deep and Light" by putting the tape recorder on a table beside the screen and narrating from the stage. The ski club sponsors came within 23 seats of a sold-out house, and I got my 40 percent of the house's take of $877, or about $350. That was a big deal. A dollar would buy five or six gallons of gas back then.

After the show, the sponsors wanted a new film for the next year, as did Pasadena. I was concerned about painting myself into a tight corner in order to have enough time to get to ski areas to film, plus work every day as a carpenter, but I agreed anyway. I used the phrase, "Same place, same time, next year"—which I used for many years when ending the shows—and then drove north toward Vancouver for my next show, with Sandy Martin and his partner, sponsored by their shop, Two Skiers, Limited.

Canadian customs, however, had other ideas. They wanted to charge me duty on my film, musical tapes, projector, and tape recorder. I balked, drove back to Blaine, Washington, and called Sandy, who told me to just drive east to Sumas and not declare anything, to only answer questions and not volunteer any information. It worked, and I got to his ski shop about 4:30 for a 7:30 show the same night.

The show was in the stevedores' union hall, with canvas tarps covering a hardwood dance floor and once again a crowd just above 800 skiers. I used my own projector and gave the sponsors $3 in trade for having someone run the projector for me. Sandy and I went back to the ski shop to divvy up the money, and I had never seen such a pile of it in my life. Four dollars for me and six for him, and so it went, until I had another $300—and another request for a new film the following year.

Sandy had booked me another show in Port Angeles, Washington, but without the guarantee. I didn't realize I could have gotten there easily on a couple of ferries; instead, I snuck back across the border at Sumas and drove south all the way to Olympia before I could head back up on the west side of Puget Sound to Port Angeles.

I was excited as I drove into Port Angeles, after making three months' wages in the two previous shows. What wasn't to like about this? I would soon find out. After a showing in the Port Angeles American Legion Hall, the sponsors passed the hat, and I collected $8.35 and a National Ski Patrol pin. The sponsors generously gave me all the money in the hat instead of just 40 percent of it. When they asked me about a show date for the next year, I told them I'd get back to them. (It wasn't until the 1960s that they started renting the sound version of the film.)

After the Port Angeles show, I turned east and drove to Sun Valley with no previous promotions to show the film. I figured all my old ski instructors and employee friends would spend a dollar to see it. The long drive gave me a lot of time to think. When I reached Sun Valley, my first stop was Pappy Rogers' office, and I was happy when he said OK to my showing the film. I put up posters in Ketchum; it was slack time at Sun Valley with no guests, and I sold only 13 tickets.

After the show, the opera-house manager took me down to Ketchum for a late-night cup of hot chocolate and to divide up the $13. He graciously paid for my cocoa and a grilled cheese sandwich dinner and offered some advice I've never forgotten:

1. Entertain the people who show up, and feel sorry for the people who missed your show. They probably hadn't heard about it.
2. You will work all of your life to be a success overnight.

That advice helped me through a lot of nearly empty auditoriums during the early years. For this show, I'd gambled and lost. However, I did have Sun Valley shows every Christmas for the next 55 years.

The four-day Thanksgiving weekend was an opportunity to hang onto Dave McCoy's two rope tows at Mammoth, 350 miles north of Los Angeles. This was currently the closest snow to Los Angeles, and I talked Dave into skiing for my camera. I was now committed to producing my second feature-length ski film.

I got some funny photos on Thanksgiving Day, as Dave sponsored the turkey toss race. Everyone who wanted to try for a free turkey lined up across the hill halfway up the rope tow, and Dave threw a frozen turkey down the hill. Everyone ran, slid, or fell down going after it. The turkey toss turned out to be a comedy highlight of the next film, called "California Skis and the Harriman Cup."

I was back working for Dick Meine, who understood that if it snowed, I would not work on Friday or Monday so I could have three days of skiing and filming somewhere. He was finally paying me $2.25 an hour. I was living pretty much expense-free except for my truck payments. I'd spend an occasional night at Berendo Street, when I needed to do my laundry and take a real bath. As I was shooting, I was also writing the narration for my next movie, featuring Mammoth Mountain, Green Valley Lake, Snow Valley, and Yosemite.

During the week, I spent every evening writing letters to friends up and down the West Coast and to those who had been my pupils at either Sun Valley or Squaw. I was soliciting shows at almost any price—$50 or $75. Any time I could get four or more people together to watch my first movie, it would be shown. One of these showings was at the house of Norma Shearer, a famous early Hollywood star, and her husband, Marty Arrouge, a former Sun Valley instructor and one-half owner of the Squaw Valley real estate. I arrived at the appointed time and was surprised that an elaborate dinner party was already in progress. A maid showed me where I was to set up and said, "The guests will be in as soon as dessert is finished." I waited 45 minutes. It was time to accept the fact that I was unpaid entertainment, but this gave me more practice, and practice in front of Hollywood motion-picture people was invaluable. I stopped on the way home after the show for my usual 15-cent hamburger, fries, and chocolate shake.

Finally, in January, snow came to the San Bernardino Mountains, 75 miles east of Los Angeles. I figured I could sleep in the parking lot of Snow Valley as easily as I did in the parking lot at Mammoth or Sun Valley or Alta. There I met Johnny Elvrum, who for years held the North American ski-jumping record. He also owned Snow Valley, which he had bought for only $845 from Sverre Engen. He had just sold some stock and installed his first chairlift to go with the sling lift and half a dozen rope tows. His big moneymaker, however, was from renting toboggans. Some of the biggest laughs I got in 55 years came from those toboggan- and sled-riding shots at Snow Valley.

That first morning I met Johnny Elvrum, he wanted to know why I wasn't out on the hill filming. I told him that I was out of money to buy film. Then he asked how much a roll of film cost, so I told him $11 with tax. Johnny said the drugstore up in Big Bear had the right kind of film, gave me $70 to buy six rolls, and told me to get right back on the hill. He was the first ski resort owner to recognize what my camera could do for a resort.

Dave McCoy wanted to see the film, so I made arrangements to show it in the upstairs of the McGee Creek Day Lodge, where he used to have a rope tow. About 15 people were sleeping on the floor that night, and during the show, my 1,000-watt projector bulb kept overloading his small generator. About every 10 minutes or so, Dave had to go downstairs and start it up again.

After the fifth intermission caused by the overload, I was introduced to a tall and very attractive lady. Just like the other 14 of us, she was sleeping on the floor that night. The next day, I thought, wait a minute: This lady works as a model for Bullock's Pasadena, the prestigious, innovative department store. It was worth holding the wet rope tow off the snow for her. She was a good skier, too, and shared her brown bag lunch with me: a peanut butter and jam sandwich, a fig bar, and an apple. Because of her, I've loved fig bars ever since.

I was so impressed with her that the following Wednesday night it was tweed-suit-and-bow-tie time, when I picked up this lady named Jean at her apartment in Pasadena. I know we had dinner somewhere, but I don't remember where, and then it was a long, conversational drive to her parents' house in Redondo Beach, where she was staying.

A lot of what happened in the first few months of our dating is just a blur. I do know I had finally fallen in true love for the first time in my life. I was almost 27 years old, and I didn't know how to handle the feelings.

BY MARCH, I HAD ASKED JEAN TO MARRY ME. SHE AGREED, AND WE SET the date for early July. In the meantime, I wanted to film in Yosemite at Badger Pass, and so I took Jean on her first filming/skiing/showing-the-film road trip. Lester Jay and his wife joined us in the red truck. Lester was the man who had kick-started my film idea back at Squaw Valley the winter before. Figuring the Jays would be good chaperones, I arranged free lift tickets and room and board for Jean and the Jays in exchange for showing "Deep and Light." We had about 100 people at the show.

Unfortunately, the weather was terrible for filming, so I persuaded the Yosemite Park and Curry Company that ran Badger Pass to let me have some ski footage from one of Luggi Foeger's old ski movies at Ostrander Lake. It worked for both of us; Luggi got verbal credit while that part of the movie was being shown the next fall and winter.

Sun Valley was my last big film shoot that winter, and I combined it with a trip to show the film in San Francisco; the Squaw Valley Ski Club sponsored it for my usual fee. The Harriman Cup at Sun Valley was the biggest race in North America, drawing almost the entire 1948 Olympic Ski Team, and it would be held down a new ski run called Olympic. Near the bottom, it was more of an obstacle course than a ski race, with half a dozen huge bumps—each one the size of a small yellow school bus.

I'd asked Pappy Rogers for a lift ticket and a parking pass for my red Chevy truck in a far-off corner of the Challenger Inn parking lot. My Coleman stove served double-duty: It heated my meals and melted the ice off the walls and ceiling of my truck-bedroom on cold mornings.

I had arrived the Sunday before the race and was able to convince Hannes Schneider to ski for my camera and my new movie. He had started the ski school in St. Anton, Austria, prior to World War l. Hannes apologized for not being in top shape, but he told me great, old-time ski stories, as well as something I have never forgotten. After World War l, when he had finished training the Austrian ski troops, Hannes said, "If everyone skied, there would be no wars."

I shot scenery all around Sun Valley, and of the beautiful snow sculptures in front of the Opera House. A tame antelope lived nearby, eating discarded cigarette butts, of which there were plenty. Late one afternoon, someone frightened him, and he came running in the direction of my truck, slipped on the ice, and hit my bumper, injuring his shoulder with a very large tear to his flesh. It took two of us to tie his legs together with long thongs so he could be carried up to the hospital, which at that time was on the third floor of the Sun Valley Lodge. They refused to operate on an antelope, of course. As I was leaving, I got tired of waiting for the freight elevator, so I walked down the hall with the antelope still bleeding and rang for the regular elevator. When we reached the crowded lobby, it was cocktail hour, and the band was playing in the Duchin Room. Women and children screamed as I walked through, covered in blood while holding a wounded antelope in my arms.

Back at my truck, a ski patrol friend had risen to the occasion, arriving with a curved needle and surgical thread. We laid the antelope down in the icy parking lot and put 15 stitches in his shoulder. Then we drove down to Dollar Lake and untied him. He stood up on wobbly legs, shook his head, and then headed out for a much-needed rest among the small trees at the edge of the lake. Four days later, he was back eating cigarette butts in front of the Opera House.

Once back in Los Angeles, Jean and I had a casual dinner, and we started to make wedding plans. It would be a small one.

CHAPTER TWENTY-NINE

1951–1953

Marriage to Jean; Family, and Illness

ON A CLEAR JUNE AFTERNOON IN 1951, JEAN AND I WERE MARRIED AT sunset while standing on a cliff in Palos Verdes. Beautiful places such as this have always been my church of choice, instead of sitting in a man-made building at a specific time of the day or week.

We had a very small wedding reception in our apartment in Glendale, where I was pounding nails at the time. It was an easy commute for Jean to her modeling career at Bullock's Pasadena. Our apartment was over a garage at the almost-unheard-of-price of $50 a month. We bought a refrigerator on credit from Sears, and we started going to the grocery store together.

Somehow I had managed to save $170 so we could take a week off and go on a honeymoon. We traveled, slept, and cooked in the red truck for the week and got as far as Fisherman's Wharf in San Francisco. We spent a few wonderful days in Yosemite before heading over Tioga Pass to Highway 395. A side trip to Reno where we gambled and lost $5 in nickels ended our honeymoon, so we headed back to start our new life as a married couple.

By August, Jean was pregnant with our son Scott. Time passed rapidly. I learned how to get by without sleep, while continuing to pound nails during the day and editing the next film at night.

In the 1950s, large amounts of smog were beginning to appear in the Los Angeles sky, and there was not much carpentry work in Glendale for me. We both realized we should move toward the beach, maybe Santa Monica. We had paid the first and last month's rent, so we gave our notice just in time and then found an apartment between Westwood and Santa Monica, near a place that was then called Sawtelle. Sawtelle was a hospital that was still caring for injured World War I and World War II veterans.

Jean transferred to Bullock's Westwood, and I got a carpenter's job as soon as we moved into our new ground-floor, one-bedroom apartment with a good view of a row of garages. I edited and mentally wrote the script for "California Skis and the Harriman Cup." Then a pregnant Jean and I headed north for our first Seattle-Vancouver-Eugene shows together.

To add to our schedule, I was able to get Howard Hermanson, who lived in Portland and became a friend for life, to organize a group of Cascade Ski Club members to look at my newest film. He helped me show it in a basement of one of his friend's homes. It was good enough to get the ski club to sponsor my films every year for the next 50 years.

There was plenty of room in the red truck for my pregnant wife and me. We still cooked our meals in the back and tried to stay with friends as often as possible. I had married an understanding lady who was betting on our future together, a life supported by my filmmaking and her modeling.

In addition to our West Coast showings, I managed to get an invitation from Pappy Rogers, the general manager of Sun Valley, to come up over Christmas vacation week as his guests and show the film. While Jean could not go skiing, she had a good time meeting my old friends while I filmed.

In January, I got a phone call from Chadwick School in Palos Verdes. It was a very upscale, private school, and someone who worked there had bought a World War II wooden-hulled sub-chaser. He was going to take 25 or more students from Chadwick on a trip to Cabo San Lucas in Mexico, and wondered if I could produce a documentary film of the trip. I called him back and asked for $35 a day plus film and living expenses; this was just about twice what I could earn as a carpenter, using my camera instead of my hammer and saw.

It had been seven years since I had a sub-chaser sink under me in a typhoon in the South Pacific during World War II. The school's ship was tied up in San Pedro, and I met the skipper. He seemed to know what he was doing, and he appreciated the fact that I had some previous experience. I could relieve him from time to time while under way, but I did not want the responsibility for the lives of 25 high school kids with wealthy parents.

Jean and I slept outside on the flying bridge, while the kids bunked below decks. The weather was sunny and calm the entire two-week trip. Scammon's Lagoon was really exciting because it was whale-breeding time. I got some great shots of whales cruising by just a few feet from our ship while we were stopped in the water.

When we returned home, I glued the film together at the same rate of $35 a day, but I refused to deliver it until I got paid for the exposed film and the work done to date. The wealthy young man who was footing all of the bills had booked the Pasadena Civic Auditorium for a show in hopes of generating more customers for his charter cruise business. He'd even opened an office, a storefront in downtown Pasadena, where he thought he'd get most of his customers. I thought it was a bad idea, and the storefront soon closed.

OUR FIRST-BORN SON APPEARED IN ST. JOHN'S HOSPITAL IN SANTA Monica on April 26, 1952. Although we had no health insurance, Dr. Wilson, who delivered Scott, helped us out on his bill and the hospital bills with an all-inclusive price of $200. Jean and I had no idea our lives would change so quickly and so dramatically. Scott was less than a month old when our rent went up $25 a month because of the extra person occupying the apartment. We could not handle the increase, so while I was pounding nails daily, Jean and her mother found a very nice two-bedroom place in an area that was going through redevelopment.

We were beginning to pack up to move when there was a loud knock on the apartment door. It was the sheriff, and he had what is called a "claim and delivery notice" for the film I had produced in Mexico. Anyone can file a claim like that, and the recipient (me) has to somehow prove that he owns the product. Jean got so upset she could no longer breast-feed Scott and had to start bottle-feeding him. I handed over the original footage, and that was the end of my involvement with the charter boat owners' problems (and another example of my nonexistent business skills).

Within a month, we were in our new apartment, working hard at becoming knowledgeable and loving parents, and producing another movie. This one would be called "Wandering Skis."

The entire next year would prove to be a fantasy for everyone in the family. Scott, Jean, and I traveled together on the L.A. to Seattle and Vancouver circuit with a few more restaurant meals than in the past. I had built a special hanging crib for Scott to play in when we were driving. I showed the film to a new ski club—Plummer Park in West Hollywood—to put on my Southern California shows. An hour before the show, there were already nine people there handing out ski brochures in front of the lecture hall. This gave me the idea to sell advertising in a giveaway program at all of my shows for the following year.

The program started out as an 8½-by-11-inch, single-fold, giveaway and eventually became a 64-page, four-color program, which in turn expanded into an award-winning 200-page magazine called *SnoWorld.*

In the next few years, if someone already had brochures, I would place them on theater seats for the cost of postage or 3 cents a seat. A single brochure in a thousand seats earned me another $30 a night, which added to the bottom line.

By the first of November, Jean, Scott, and I had driven north for the show in Seattle that was being taken over by Scott Osborn, partner with Olav Ulland in the Osborn and Ulland Sporting Goods Store. Back in the fall of 1948, Scott Osborn had become the largest retailer of my nylon parachute ski bootlaces. There were and still are, more skiers per capita in the Seattle area than the rest of the nation; this was very good for me back when I was in the ski bootlace business. He sold several thousand pairs.

He had married my friend from Squaw Valley, Dodie Post's sister, Lois Post, and they welcomed Jean, Scott, and me to park in their driveway and sleep in their guest room. The show was in the Metropolitan Theater once again, and the tickets were still $1 including tax. Sales were not quite as good as the year before, and I chalked it up to the fact that Scott was too busy running his ski shop to sell tickets to my movie.

Meanwhile, Jean began to have a backache, and so we visited a good chiropractor I had been using. After a few visits, she seemed to feel better, and we were looking forward to the Christmas show in Sun Valley for the second year in a row.

In November, when I was showing "Wandering Skis" in Denver, I met Merrill Hastings and Dick Wilson, who had just started a publication called *Skiing News Magazine* and were going head-to-head in marketing with *SKI* magazine. *SKI* was already helping John Jay, and Merrill proposed a partnership: He'd back my film business with editorial coverage and other support, and I'd run a commercial in the next film for his magazine. On that handshake deal, Merrill Hastings gave me enough publicity to jump-start our fledgling ski film business.

The first thing Merrill did was get Scandinavian Airlines to send Jean and me to Europe to include Swiss and Austrian ski resorts in my next movie. Jean and I both firmly agreed that filmmaking was our future.

However, this plan was not to be.

By the first week of December, Jean was suffering severe back pains and was unable to travel. After a long discussion, she insisted that I go to Sun Valley alone, show the movie, earn some more money, and get started on our next movie. I didn't want to leave Jean alone with a backache and a young son to take care of. She and her mother persuaded me that I had to work on the next movie because our future depended on it. We had a successful Sun Valley show, and I got some great, back-lit action shots of the ski instructors on Baldy in packed powder and bumps.

Jean and I were lonely apart, and three days after Christmas, I woke up with a start and felt as though I was gagging, with my mouth filled with ashes. Two hours later, I got a phone call from Jean's mother, Esther, who simply said, "Warren, it is very important that you get home as soon as possible!"

Within an hour, the red truck was on the road. I finally had to grab some sleep in Las Vegas for a couple of hours, and when I talked to Jean's mother, she gave me the phone number of Dr. Wilson. I went to his office as soon as I arrived in town. "Sit down, Warren," he said. "Your wife's backache was getting so bad we had to do some surgery on it. I had hoped I would not have to tell you this. She has malignant cancer of the spine. It is vicious and rapid-growing, and there is not a doctor in the world who can save her life. When the pain begins to increase again, we will have to cut the sensory nerves in her back to try to preserve the motor nerves. That way she will still be able to walk until she dies."

I stared in abject terror at the doctor, unable to speak.

"Isn't there some chance, another doctor somewhere?"

He shook his head slowly and said, "Maybe one chance in 10 million, but right now, there is no known cure, except sometimes an X-ray in heavy doses will slow down its growth."

I thanked him for his expertise, and several days later, I brought Jean home from the hospital, lying down in the bed in the back of the red truck. What do I do next? We still had shows to do in Whittier, Santa Barbara, and Santa Ana. After a few days at home together, with Jean's mother helping, we started to talk collectively about what was next. Her mother, father, and I agreed that we would keep the news from Jean because of that slim chance of recovery. I debated whether to abandon the film business and become a building contractor instead, but they would not hear of it. "You have to think of Scott's future and yours." Jean was adamant: "We have a good business plan, and I will back it to the best of my ability when I get over my backache." Two weeks later, by the middle of January, her backache had returned.

All looked bleak, but her upbeat spirit remained strong, even from the hospital bed I had rented and set up in our home. She insisted we continue the film business as usual. Arguing with anyone has never been my strong point, and Jean started to plan our European trip as though we were both going to work on next year's film together. A round-trip ticket for two to fly to New York and return was too expensive, so we planned on driving. We'd stop in Aspen on the way, show the movie again, pass the hat, and buy more unexposed film for the next movie.

Jean was incredibly unselfish and courageous under the circumstances. I had a long talk with her most generous and supportive parents. They lived in Redondo Beach at the time, and her father, Harold, suggested the following: "Jean's sister Pat has gotten a divorce, and she can help you take care of Jean and Scott in your absence. There are new tract houses being built in Torrance that are selling for $4,995 with only $500 down and about $50-a-month payments. Why don't Esther and I put up the down payment, you can make the monthly payments, and her sister Pat can move in with you and take care of Jean and Scott?"

So the decision was made, but until the new house was built, Pat and her young son moved into our Sawtelle apartment, and I headed east for

New York and Europe alone, with my skis and camera and Jean's love. En route, I was able to show the film in Aspen. Afterward, someone wanted me to show it to their sons' private school just north of Chicago in Wilmette. This put me over the top financially, and I was able to buy another 20 rolls of Kodachrome to expose in Europe and have more than $50 extra for expenses. My room, board, and travel were to be paid for by SAS and the Swiss and Austrian tourist bureaus. Merrill Hastings had delivered big time.

Once I got to New York, I hid my truck in the SAS employee parking lot and slept 15 hours straight. I got some help from the local manager with my overweight luggage: A suitcase with 40 rolls of film in it, and my camera, tape recorder, skis, boots, and poles in a never-seen-before shipping bag. There was also a suitcase full of ski clothes, a wash-and-wear dress shirt, extra sets of underwear, and an itinerary typed up in precise order by SAS and the Austrian and Swiss tourism offices. My knowledge of any other language except English was nonexistent. I could say "please" and "thank you" in German and point to what I wanted.

I plopped down, exhausted, into my window seat and watched the men with the fire extinguishers standing ready. The propeller-driven plane moved slowly on its way to take off with one wide-eyed 29-year-old (though still mostly a 14-year-old kid) from Southern California. I was sound asleep within minutes after the plane took off. The four-engine DC-6 could not fly across the Atlantic without refueling, so we set down in Iceland for more fuel. In the men's room, I had my first experience with European toilet paper. It was as soft and porous as the wax paper that I used to wrap my peanut butter sandwiches. In future years, I always traveled to Europe with my own private supply of toilet paper.

After reaching Zurich, my next leg was on a train headed for Davos and the world-famous Parsennbahn cable railroad. In Davos, there were more than a dozen porters at the railroad station, each with the name of his hotel on the front of his hat. Checking my itinerary, I picked the right porter, who loaded my stuff on his wooden sled. I followed and soon checked into my first ski resort hotel: The Hotel Fluela was right across the street from the longest lift line I had ever seen—up to two hours.

My hotel, along with most of the other big hotels in town, had been a tuberculosis sanitarium, built in the late 1800s and early 1900s. Winter in the clean, pure high-mountain air was the only known cure for tuberculosis 100 years ago. The room was very big, and the bathtubs and toilets were only a short walk down the hall.

In those days there were no ski lifts or skiing on north slopes. In 1953, if you wanted to ski in powder snow on a north slope in Davos, you could ski from the summit of the cable railway down to the village of Klosters, and then take a train or a taxi back up to Davos and stand in line for another hour or two. At the summit of the Parsennbahn, Hans Thorner was working on his own feature-length ski film for exhibition in the U.S., just like John Jay was doing and I was starting to do. I filmed local color, which included everything, and ran into several of my Southern California friends who skied for the camera. In my narration, I gave the best skiers complicated European names and the comedy shots American names.

The Davos Hotel was deluxe, and I had to wear my tweed suit and bow tie to eat in the dining room for lunch and dinner. The stay lasted four days, and then it was a short train ride to Arosa, where there was a small chairlift and a slow T-bar on a small hill.

I also filmed in Zermatt in Switzerland and then Kitzbuehel, Bad Gastein, and Zurs in Austria. I returned to Zurs every year that I filmed in Europe because it had T-bars on both south- and north-facing slopes, with powder snow everywhere, and it's the home of my favorite hotel in all my travels, the Hotel Lorunser.

It was three weeks into the trip when I got a message through the Austrian tourism office to return home as soon as possible. The filming got cut short, and two days later I was in my red-panel truck driving from New York City to Redondo Beach. I couldn't sleep, and yet I couldn't drive 24 hours nonstop. I managed to drive about 18 hours a day and somehow stay on the road. Sleep escaped me as soon as I lay down exhausted in the back of the truck, with my mind turning over and over about Jean's pain and health.

I arrived home to a phone call from Dr. Wilson. "I will try to sever only the sensory nerves in Jean's back," he told me. "However, the cancer may have spread too far, and eventually I will have to sever the motor nerves as well. When the pain returns, I will have to do that. She will never walk again and will have to wear a catheter."

Everyone has to play the cards they are dealt, and Jean got dealt the bad hand. The pain was again getting worse in her back while we were in the process of moving to the Torrance house. Jean's sister Pat, and Pat's 8-year-old son, Jimmy, helped out and then moved in with us.

I took Jean to the hospital for one more radiation dose when Dr. Wilson said, "I think it's time to do the second surgery." Three days later, Jean was a paraplegic, though I didn't know the meaning of the word back then. I rented a hospital bed and moved it into the back bedroom of the Torrance house. Then I went back to the hospital and carried Jean out to the bed in the red truck and drove her home to our new rented house.

We soon settled into a routine of my getting up at 5:30 A.M. to pack my peanut butter sandwich lunch, chatting with Jean for a while, and then waking up Scott, Pat, and Jimmy, who were sleeping in the living room. I spent my days framing houses and my evenings in the room with Jean, chatting and planning our future life together, as though our world was all OK.

When I received the developed film back from Europe, I shared it with Jean. I had brochures from everywhere I had been so I could talk with enthusiasm about going back there together the following season. It was hard for me to perpetrate such a blatant lie, but we needed to stay positive. It was not an easy thing to do.

CHAPTER THIRTY

1953

The Turkey Dinner and Death

THE RED TRUCK WAS PARKED IN THE DRIVEWAY, AND SOMETIMES THE bedroom light was on all night long as I talked with Jean about our future, the past, and life in general. I had a very small desk against the wall and my air mattress under her bed. When I was typing up yet another solicitation for a ski club to book our new film, I could glance at a photograph over my desk of John Jay, America's leading ski filmmaker in 1953. It was from an ad he had placed in *Ski Illustrated Magazine*, and underneath was my hand-lettered sign: "What does he do that I can't find a way to do better?"

To fill the dark hours, I worked on a scale model of a clipper ship that I still have today. My nail-pounding wages were stretched beyond the breaking point, but Jean's mother would occasionally bring groceries on her daily visits to be with her now terminally ill, paraplegic, fashion-model-beautiful daughter.

OTHER THAN HER MOTHER, JEAN AND I HAD ALMOST NO VISITORS OVER the entire summer; neither my parents nor my sisters came by. My mother said she stopped by once but parked in front of the house and never got out of the car. People back then were afraid of cancer, as if it were contagious.

The only other visitors were old friends of mine, Margaret and Erwin Lenkeit. I had worked for Erwin the summer before I taught at Squaw Valley, testing air mattresses for leaks. We had become good friends while surfing together at San Onofre. Margaret was a special-duty, registered nurse, which meant she could stay with a patient for 24 hours straight. When I told Erwin about Jean, Margaret was at the Torrance house within the hour.

Jean's sister Pat, who lived with us every week from Sunday night until Friday afternoon, took care of Jean during the day, feeding and bathing her and dressing the X-ray burn. She and her son would go to her mother's on the weekend, and it was up to me to wash the dirty clothes, including Scott's diapers, and hang them out on the line to dry. I made up my mind then that someday I would buy a dryer.

Before I knew it, it was early September, and Jean's spirit was still intact, upbeat, and unafraid. Either all of us were damned good liars, or she went along with what we were telling her about our being together in Europe for the winter. One Saturday in September, Margaret and Erwin invited us up for a turkey dinner and to watch the sunset. The sunset was glorious, and we all sat together in front of the Lenkeits' house at the top of Rolling Hills, looking at Catalina across the channel. By 11, Jean said, "I'm getting tired. Would you please take me home now?"

Erwin and Margaret lived at the top of Rolling Hills, and I parked for a few minutes so Jean could take in the lights of Los Angeles, stretching below her from Laguna to Malibu, the entire Los Angeles basin in the distance. Scott slept the entire way, and I put him to bed when we got home. Then I carried Jean into her bed and hooked up the catheter drain bottle sitting under the bed. About one or two in the morning, I was in the kitchen heating up water for a pot of tea when Jean spoke from the nearby bedroom, "Would you crank my bed up, please?"

I did so and was no sooner back in the kitchen when she called to me to lower her bed because she was having trouble getting air to breathe. I lowered the bed, and almost as soon as it was flat, she said, "No, raise me back up." I did, and suddenly the almost year-long nightmare ended. We did not get to share that cup of tea. I was alone in the world now, with our 18-month-old son.

Because of the hour, I saw no need to wake her parents. There was nothing they could do, and I knew that they needed as much sleep as possible for what lay ahead. This was a major mistake on my part. They really wanted to be there to help in any way possible. Instead, I called Dr. Wilson, who came right over and took care of everything that was necessary. He called the right people, and they came and took my wife, and Scott's mother, away forever.

Margaret and Erwin were there within a half an hour. I thought I had to go to work, and after a day of pouring concrete, I went to the cemetery to make arrangements for Jean's burial. I had always hoped Jean would not die, and I had seen no need to buy a burial plot in advance. The man in charge in his gray-and-black suit with the perfect gray mustache and matching gray hair asked me, "Is this purchase for immediate need or for an investment?"

"What's the difference?"

"The prices are different." He meant "immediate need" was twice as expensive.

The next few days were a complete blur. A lot of our friends came to the funeral, who, I felt, had been afraid to visit while Jean was ill. They didn't know how to handle someone with terminal cancer, someone who might even die while they were in the same room. It was a different time with different behavior. None of my family—mother, father, or sisters—attended the funeral.

I accepted the Lenkeits' offer of letting me stay with them and having them take care of Scott while I was working. Esther and Harold, Jean's parents, were wonderful grandparents to Scott, but I felt that it would be better to have Scott living in a younger household with the two Lenkeit boys, ages 7 and 9. Plus, Margaret had been helping so much with Jean's nursing care that it seemed natural. Over the years I've been tempted to second-guess this decision, but that's a lesson in futility.

So Scott and I went to live with the Lenkeits. I took a hard look at the calendar and realized that I had only five weeks to edit and script the film, create the musical score, and drive to my first show. Before I did anything, I went by the job site where I had been pouring concrete and pounding nails and explained why I had missed work. The contractor understood, wished me well, and said, "You have a job whenever you get back."

I got busy cutting the original film according to my written notes, and had it done in two weeks, ready for a release print so I could organize live rehearsals. I also made the poster for "Ski Fantasy," which was a subconscious tribute to Jean: I put the border in black. I didn't even think about it at the time.

Next I selected the music. I've always loved music, and I knew that the $1 discount, 33⅓ phonograph records I bought had to work in the film because I couldn't afford the royalties for modern music. The classical music performances worked well for that era, for the pacing of the skiers' action, and for the beauty of the mountains. Some customers started asking for more current music, but classical music was the mood of the mountains, of skiing, and what the blend of the two meant to me.

One night, I had found a roll of unexposed Kodachrome and went for a solitary drive in nearby Palos Verdes Hills. I shot the entire roll of film of just headlights in the dark. These shots wound up as the introduction to "Ski Fantasy," with background music from a popular TV show of the time, "Dragnet." Because I played the theme song live at the shows and never recorded it to the film, I was able to avoid a licensing payment.

Within those five weeks, I lost much of my hair from the stress. I fattened up from 185 to 220 pounds by living on hamburgers, chocolate shakes, and fries, three or four times a day. Most of this weight I foolishly carried around for the next 50 years.

One day, as I slowly drove back toward my new home with the Lenkeits, I wondered—as I had occasionally before—if all of the bouncing around in the red truck caused Jean's cancer of the spine. I parked the truck and ripped out all of the cabinets I had lived with for 125,000 miles. Within two hours, I had traded it for a Chevy station wagon with a softer ride. I could still sleep in the back, but I couldn't cook my dinner like I could in the truck. My overhead for traveling and showing my movie took a serious increase when I had to do three restaurant meals a day.

But now, with 35 more pounds on my body and 45,000 fewer hairs on my head, I was ready for my next film tour.

CHAPTER THIRTY-ONE

1953–1954

"Ski Fantasy"; Up Early and Late, Too

IN THE FALL OF 1953, I EMBARKED ON AN ALMOST-ENDLESS, SOLITARY trip to connect the many cities in which I showed and personally narrated the movie—as well as shoot footage for the next film. By this time, there were more and more ski resorts in America at which I could point my camera. But I was still a one-man crew and could only get to so many places. After filming Sun Valley during Christmas week, I could take my skis with me on the show circuit, often filming during the day before showing the film at night. Things were coming together in my one-man-does-it-all manner. I would continue to do all of the creative work myself until 1964: filming, editing, scripting, musical scoring, and each show's narration.

My days and nights on the road across America ran together like a postman on his daily rounds. Many sponsors had three years of experience promoting the movies, and they were the people who were fueling whatever success there was at the box office. After finishing a personal appearance and narrating the show live, I would go with the sponsors for a celebratory after-show dessert and sign the contract for the "same time, same theater, same date" the next year. With luck, I would get back to my hotel by midnight or start driving to the next town. I'd try to get there as quickly as possible in case of bad weather, airplane-engine failure, ice-covered roads, or any other of the thousands of things that can go wrong when you are traveling.

If everything worked right, I would be in the next city by noon and, if I wasn't filming that day, get a nap—but only after washing out my nylon wash-and-wear shirt and hanging it up to drip dry. Then I'd hang up my suit in the bathroom and turn on the shower to steam out the wrinkles for that night's show. The motel phone would ring and wake me at 4 in the afternoon, when it was time to get ready so I could be at the theater two hours before showtime.

With a sometimes seven-day-a-week show schedule, there was little time to do anything else. Partying did not interest me because I never drank alcohol—that was the only positive influence my father had on me. Not drinking made a huge difference in my health in my later years, and I wish I knew how to share this information with kids today. There was no time whatsoever to get involved with any ladies or to have any social life, other than an occasional late lunch with a sponsor and his wife. I was pretty sure no one would want to get involved with me: a 30-year-old widower with a young son. Plus, I was very self-conscious about all the hair I'd lost.

In Seattle that year, we moved from the Olympic Theater to the Eagle Auditorium and sold out two nights, with Scott Osborn doing the promotion. Sandy Martin in Vancouver also expanded to two nights, and everything was working smoothly with "Ski Fantasy." My Los Angeles sponsor, the Ski Club Alpine, moved the show to the very prestigious Wilshire Ebell, the best theater in Southern California for travel-film producers to show their films.

This was also the first year I took one of my films to the East Coast, and I already had showings in a lot of Eastern cities, such as Fitchburg, Pittsfield, Wooster, and North Andover in Massachusetts, to mention just a few. When the film opened with the familiar "Dragnet" theme music, the East Coast audiences went nuts. However, after that, things didn't go as well. Jokes that made viewers laugh in Wenatchee or San Diego were met with silence in Hartford or Boston. The East was just different from what I was used to.

Businesswise, I remained an amateur. I didn't keep very good records of who did or did not pay me. One day I was looking for something in my wallet, and I found a dozen $200 checks from one of my swings through small towns in the East. I got an envelope from the hotel front desk, bought 3-cent stamps, and mailed them to Erwin Lenkeit so he could open a bank account for me.

Credit cards as we know them didn't exist in that era, but in my naïveté, I wouldn't have even thought of applying for one. I paid in cash for the $5-a-night hotels and motels I was staying in.

That season, I also hired my first employee: my mother. Merrill Hastings and his *Skiing News Magazine* had given me a front-page review of the film, and as the calendar of shows filled up, it got so busy that I hired my mother part-time to type my letters. I would record the letters on the same Wollensak reel-to-reel tape recorder I used during my shows and mail her the recorded tapes. She would then type them and send them out for me. When she was busy for more than one day a week, I was able to increase her pay to $15 a day. (McDonald's was already paying as much as $4 a day.) It worked for her because the ozone business was fading away.

I didn't give it much thought at the time, but my camera and my annual film had become my constant mistress. They were very demanding of my time—and expensive, too. If the film was shown in 50 different cities with a $200 guarantee at each, the gross would be a minimum of $10,000 for a year's work. That seemed to be an amazing goal. Business for me was booming, and I did not even know it.

CHAPTER THIRTY-TWO

1954

"Symphony on Skis": A Financial and Emotional Breakthrough

As my American film tour came to a close, it was time for my second European tour. This time, the drive from Los Angeles to New York went quicker in the station wagon than in my truck. So I took a side trip up to Vermont. I slept near Stowe, in a rented room in a farmhouse. During the night, it rained a lot, and then the temperature dropped to 10 below. I filmed what I thought was an artistic take of farm equipment half-buried in a foot of crystal-clear ice. My narration over the shot was, "It was so icy you could read a newspaper through 10 inches of it. That was the good news. The bad news was it was last night's newspaper." Funny or not, Stowe's general manager Sepp Ruschp was so mad he wouldn't let me park my car in his parking lot for the next decade. I guess I was too dumb to kowtow to the resort owners; instead I tried to make the films as entertaining as possible.

In New York, I hid my car in the same SAS employee parking lot and again boarded the flight with a lot of overweight luggage. It was a nail-biter. Halfway between Gander, Newfoundland, and Copenhagen, a bright light out the window woke me, and I saw only one propeller working on my side of the airplane. The captain came on the intercom and told us not to worry, because the plane could maintain altitude on only two engines. Half an hour later, when an engine on the other side of the plane coughed to a stop, we were going to find out whether we would keep flying or not. We did.

We finally landed a few hours later in Denmark with fire engines and ambulances alongside the runway, just in case. Two hours later, I was on the last leg of my way to Zurich for the second year in a row. On this tour, I went back to many of the same resorts.

An Austrian ski maker, Franz Kneissl, made a lot of skis back then. He had borrowed Marshall Plan money from the U.S. government at 2 percent so he could buy hickory from Tennessee and ship it to Kufstein, Austria, to build better skis. The American importer wanted me to film the manufacturing process and include it in my next movie. So I caught the train to Kufstein, where it took four days to film the factory, without anyone available who could speak a word of English. I understood almost no German. We somehow accomplished the filming. I left Kufstein with a bonus of a special pair of skis that had been picked out by Franz Kneissl himself. They were too stiff to turn, so I sold them in Zermatt four days later for $30, still unable to kick the 24/7 insecurity of growing up hungry.

SAS wanted me to include a Scandinavian ski resort in the movie, so on the way home, they sent me to Geilo, Norway. This was supposed to be an up-and-coming ski resort north of Oslo. I traveled for five hours on a train and arrived after dark. Nice hotel, nice red carpet, but when they took me out to the ski hill, the cable for the new ski lift was still lying in the snow. They had scheduled me to film the resort one year too soon. With virtually no backup help in the business, I didn't think to confirm things like this in advance.

Once I was back in New York City, I loaded up the station wagon, changed a flat tire, and got ready for the 3,000-plus-mile trip back to Los Angeles. While I was in an office at a meeting, someone broke into the station wagon and stole my movie projector but nothing else. I was lucky, because there was a rucksack and a suitcase full of exposed European Kodachrome in plain sight in the back of the wagon.

When I got back to Los Angeles, I was excited to see Scott and take him to San Onofre to go surfing. While there, I bought a well-used Airstream house trailer for $900 from a schoolteacher friend named Bob

Grabage. I had already cleared this purchase with Erwin and Margaret so I could be with Scott as much as possible and still have an office and a bedroom on their property.

I had no more than unpacked my stuff in the new trailer and was starting to edit rolls of film when Merrill Hastings called about marketing plans. He had promoted a trip to South America for me in July that was being funded by Panagra Airlines and included Portillo, Farellones, and La Parva in Chile.

I spent three weeks there in July, away from Scott and surfing. I skied a lot and filmed my former boss, world ski champion Émile Allais. While there, I entered the Émile Allais Cup, and I have the first-place trophy in my house to this day. It was staged for Northern Hemisphere racers who had come down to train, including Roger Brown, who went on to become world-famous a decade and a half later when he, together with Barry Corbet, made the classic ski film "Moebius Flip."

When I got back from the month in Chile, I had to play catch-up. In my trailer, I made an office out of the living room, painted everything inside green, and started full-time editing on the several miles of film shot in North and South America and Europe.

I had been more relaxed in Europe this time and used more classical music, so I decided to call the film "Symphony on Skis." I had filmed Stein Eriksen during his only winter teaching at Sun Valley, but it was on a day when he was trying to teach Christian Pravda and Jack Reddish how to do a forward somersault on skis. It would be more than a decade before the somersault became a ritual of grandstanding on skis, and eventually the cornerstone of the freestyle ski movement. Today, any self-respecting young skier or snowboarder has multiple back and forward flips and spins in his bag of tricks while his parents are still paying for his lift tickets, room and board, tuition, and health insurance.

The "Symphony on Skis" poster included the following locations: Austria; Switzerland; Norway; Stowe; Franconia, New Hampshire; Sun Valley; Stevens Pass and Mt. Baker in Washington; and Portillo and Farellones/La Parva in South America.

I had learned how to get along on very little sleep when Jean was sick, and I began to do the same thing again while working on this film. And I was back on the hamburger menu, too. When I was not writing scripts and press releases or designing posters, I wrote letters to schedule more shows—or at least dictated the letters on my tape recorder for my mother to type and mail.

However, with "Symphony on Skis," I made a breakthrough both financially and emotionally. I paid Margaret and Erwin rent for my trailer space and food by the month, the film grossed enough money to get me through the summer without banging nails, and life got better as I began work on the next year's film.

CHAPTER THIRTY-THREE

1955–1956

European Travels; a Visit to the Neighborhood Church

I FINALLY HAD SOME CLOUT IN SELLING ADVERTISING AND PRODUCED THE small giveaway program that was shipped free to all of the show sponsors—the quantities based on how many seats they had in their theaters. The program attracted attention among potential advertisers, and we collected names and addresses from cards that were filled out for a door-prize drawing. Everyone who filled out a card received a one-year subscription to *Skiing News Magazine.* I shipped the name cards home and had my mother type up labels that we sent back to the ski club when they signed on for the next year's film presentation. Then I supplied the ski clubs with free postcards to mail out when promoting the show the next fall. Their only costs would be postage and spit to glue on the stamps. My marketing ability was growing.

In the 1955 program, I had a little space left over after I wrote about living in the Sun Valley parking lot, so I inserted this line: "These are excerpts from my forthcoming book, *Wine, Women, Warren, & Skis.* To reserve your copy at the pre-publication discount price of $2, send me a postcard and I will send it to you C.O.D. when I publish it." Instead of waiting to have the book arrive C.O.D., nearly a thousand people sent me $2 checks!

Also, I used my introductory speeches to promote my first-annual, personally conducted ski tour to Europe. Merrill Hastings had talked SAS into two free tickets for the ski tour as a grand prize. After hustling the trip from the stage all winter, there were 14 customers who climbed on the plane with me one "fateful" February afternoon in 1956. When we got to Europe, the tour operator in Norway had thought no one would sign up for such an expensive ($645) three-week trip, and so the tour company didn't bother to make reservations in Kitzbuehel, Davos, Zurs, St. Anton, and St. Moritz at the height of the ski season. I really had to scramble to find rooms for everyone. By the time the smoke cleared, the man in charge in Copenhagen was fired, and I talked SAS into refunding everyone's money for the land portion of their trip. Through all of the chaos, enough film was shot to complete the European segment, and I got back to New York very tired.

Just before the Fourth of July, I flew to Seattle and drove to Mt. Baker for the annual Slush Cup, a ski race that ends in a glacial pond full of floating ice. While there, I met a very attractive young lady named Joan Gambel from Portland, who needed a ride back to Seattle when the race was over. We stopped at Scott Osborn's and stayed up all night sitting by the swimming pool, just talking about life. Something was happening to me that I didn't understand.

It was as if Jean were watching and saying, "It's OK to get on with your life, Warren." Joan and I became very good friends; however, my mixed-up life of being a widower and living in Southern California in a house trailer kept coming up in my mind. When learning that her father owned a TV station in Portland as well as the local Pepsi-Cola bottling company, I knew that I could never provide her with the standard of living to which she had been accustomed.

Later that summer, my son Scott and I drove to San Onofre for a few days of surfing and getting reacquainted before I had to get deep into the film workload. I had met a couple of interesting ladies at San Onofre and was quite surprised when one of them called to borrow my key to the gate to get into San Onofre. It was a private surfing club in those days. I told her she would have to stop by my trailer to get the key. My house trailer was about 10 minutes up a winding road from the Pacific Coast Highway. When she arrived, we sat around Erwin and Margaret's new swimming pool and watched Scott jump in and try to swim. I was surprised at how much interest she took in Scott, so we had our first dinner date when she brought my key back.

Something must have impressed Dorothy Roberts, because that one date led to another. One day, in midsummer on the beach at Malibu, she said, "Warren, you can keep talking about Jean and revisiting the ordeal like chapters in a book, or you can start with a blank piece of paper and start writing new chapters."

I had never thought of life that way before. Later, I paddled out and rode some more waves and thought about what she had said. Her analogy made sense. My memories of Jean were still uppermost in my mind, but I was starting to put them into a cubbyhole instead of letting them dominate my thoughts.

One day in August, Dorothy, or "Dottie" as she preferred to be called, announced that she was not going back to teach school in September; instead, she was going to become a United Airlines stewardess. This seemed strange, but I felt that to be happy, people have to do what they want to do.

Dottie climbed on a plane to go to stewardess school, and I went back to editing film and preparing for the tour with my usual 60-hour work week. We wrote a lot of letters, and before I knew it, she was a certified stewardess, and I was on the road showing the movie once again. I don't remember when I asked her to marry me, but I think it was sometime in the fall when I was in Los Angeles for the shows.

I had a week off before Christmas. We could get married then and go to Sun Valley for a honeymoon over Christmas. Margaret and Erwin would take care of Scott for us, and when I went on the road in January and part of February, Dottie could live in the trailer, and she and Scott could spend time together. When I led my tour to Europe, she could go with me, and we would rent a house when we got back. This sounded as if it could really work for everybody. However, I was still surprised when she said "yes" to my proposal and gave her 30-day notice to United Airlines, only one month after she had become a stewardess.

By now, the show was booked seven nights a week from early October until just before Christmas, and Dottie had to handle the wedding plans without me. Dottie was a Catholic, and her mother said she would not come to the wedding unless I became a Catholic, or at least signed away the religious birthright of any children her daughter might have. I did not feel that it was my right to make that decision, so I refused to sign up my children with her church. Dottie accepted that, but we missed her mother at the wedding.

We were married in a nondenominational church called "The Neighborhood Church" on a cliff in Palos Verdes. It was a classic wedding and a classic foggy night, with many guests unable to find their way in Palos Verdes when they could only see 50 yards ahead. A traditional white gown for Dottie and a traditional navy-blue suit for me—then it was off to the Lenkeits' house, where they staged a wonderful reception for us. We disappeared together in the fog in my '56 Chevy business coupe and reappeared two days later, moving into the house/trailer/office behind the Lenkeits' garage.

Timing worked both for and against us. There was a new subdivision being built in the adjacent city of Rolling Hills, featuring homes selling for $20,000 with four bedrooms and a double-car garage. For an extra $1,000, you could be on the side of the street that had a view of the entire Los Angeles basin, from Malibu to Laguna Beach, as well as the San Gabriel Mountains east of Los Angeles. This was the same view I had shared with Jean the night she died.

I opted for the better view and opened escrow with that amount. I was grossing a minimum of $1,400 a week, so I felt I could afford it. I signed the papers when I got home, the week before we went to Europe together. We were real homeowners for the first time in our lives, not counting my unfinished log cabin in Sun Valley, of course. While I was on the road, I hoped that Dottie and Scott had bonded while living together at the Lenkeits', but I found out later, sadly, that had not happened.

The European tour went off as advertised. Seventeen people, my new wife, and I were on the road together. A lady on the tour broke her leg in Kitzbuehel the first day, and a guy broke his in Bad Gastein four days later. In Langen, one of the guys on the tour had too many French 75s after skiing in Zurs and walked out from behind the tour bus. He was hit by a VW Bug going 50 mph and thrown up on top of our bus, but he only had a broken thumb and left leg. In this case, it was good he was drunk, or he would have been killed. We had to leave him in a hospital in Liechtenstein, and I had to keep on chaperoning the remaining members of the tour.

In order to get more spectacular footage while we were in St. Anton with the tour customers, I checked the train schedule and figured I could ski and film all day in St. Anton and take the night train to Kulm and film ski-flying all the next day, where the mythical, 400-foot flight record had been broken. The hill was roughly twice the size of any Nordic jump hill I had ever seen. The longer-distance jumping style was changing, and some of the jumpers were already holding their arms at their sides and using their hands like the ailerons on airplane wings.

The side trip worked, but on the train I made up my mind that I would never lead another tour. It was too much responsibility to take care of all of the people and all of their problems while trying to make a new movie at the same time.

When the tour was over, Dottie and I flew back to Los Angeles and rented an apartment while we waited for our new house to be finished. My house trailer was still my office, and about the third day at work, the phone rang from Dottie, who was with Scott—a phone call I will never forget. She said "Warren, if you married me to get a babysitter for this kid of yours, you made a big mistake. Get down here and pick him up right away." This ultimatum came from my wife of only two-and-a-half months.

I should have put my arms around Scott and walked away right then, but my history with women was already one of failure. I'd had my Sun Valley mistake, and now I was still blaming myself for contributing to Jean's death from cancer, which I thought may have been caused by riding in the truck while pregnant. Back then, I didn't have the strength nor the experience to see things clearly. It would come back to haunt me.

CHAPTER THIRTY-FOUR

1956

"Have Skis, Will Travel"; New Wife, New House, and a Growing Family

DOTTIE WAS NO LONGER WILLING TO WATCH SCOTT, SO I ENROLLED HIM in a day-care center in Rolling Hills. This gave me four hours of uninterrupted work time before I had to go back and pick him up.

Whenever I stopped by our new house that was still under construction, I was pleased with the decision we had made: a master bedroom for Dottie and me, a bedroom for Scott, another bedroom for the future child that Dottie had recently informed me we would have, and a fourth bedroom that would make the perfect office for me.

We moved in during June. Despite ragtag furniture and no carpets, it was a great feeling. I planted a lawn, while Dottie did kitchen and household things. People now call it nesting, and it's a wonderful time in a new family's life. The bedroom/office I worked out of suited me just fine, and I got a lot done with all of the space. My editing bench was in the sliding-door closet, and my collection of mismatched Army and Navy surplus olive-drab filing cabinets, a desk, and a squeaky wooden chair fit nicely in the rest of the room. We still managed the occasional trip to San Onofre with Scott, and I won a third-place trophy in a San Onofre surfing club contest that summer. I still have it in a closet somewhere.

Before I knew it, showtime was on top of me, and I started the routine of previews once again. The previews were an invaluable tool, as my friends could tell me what they liked, and more importantly, what they did not like.

I still was not writing a script, creating it instead on the spot from the folds of my memory bank of what I was thinking when I shot the pictures. During the intermission of a preview, I'd ask the audience to tell me what they liked and didn't like. The same thing happened at the end of the movie. The next day I would make many of the suggested changes.

That fall, Dottie and Scott went with me on the early show trip to Seattle, Vancouver, Bellingham, Portland, and Eugene. That trip lasted about two full weeks with a show almost every night. When we got back to our new Rolling Hills house, I geared up for that year's first Los Angeles show at the Wilshire Ebell again. This time, the Ski Club Alpine members had outdone themselves and sold out the theater four nights in a row, more than 4,000 tickets.

Scott came to one of the shows, and when we were finished looking around backstage together, I showed him my dressing room. It had a big star on the door. When Scott saw the toilet inside the star's dressing room, his comment was "Daddy, is this where the stars tinkle?"

Once again it was time to head east and show the movie seven nights a week for over a month straight. There was even a personal-appearance show on Thanksgiving night somewhere in Canada, because the Canadian Thanksgiving Day is in early October. It meant a lot more driving, but it made no sense for me to just sit around a hotel room for a night. With so many responsibilities, I couldn't afford to waste any time.

Merrill Hastings had lost the Scandinavian Airlines account but quickly shifted to TWA and included my endorsement in exchange for a pair of round-trip tickets to Europe for Dottie, me, and my camera gear.

To get around in Europe, I'd buy a new Volkswagen Bug for about $900 and pay for it with a 90-day note from my bank in Los Angeles. When I was done traveling and filming, I would ship the VW to Southern California, put a "For Sale" sign in the window, and sell it for about $100 more than I paid for it, including freight from Hamburg, Germany. Then I would pay off my 90-day loan. The car would only have a couple of thousand miles on it, and in Los Angeles, Volkswagens were selling for $1,300 new. I managed to make $100 or break even on transportation six years in a row.

After a very good season as a newlywed, I decided to buy a VW van instead of the small Bug. Bumper stickers were part of my ski movie promotion package that year, and the first thing I did when I got the new van was to put the name of next year's film title on it. "Have Skis, Will Travel" stickers were pasted on the front and back, something I did as long as I bought new European cars each winter. At almost every ski resort where I parked in Europe, I would come back from filming, and there would be notes from skiers who had seen my movies. They gave me their local addresses and said, "I would like to ski in your new movie." All I needed was to buy them a ski lift ticket. "Stop by such and such restaurant." Bob Smith, who later invented Smith goggles, left a note in Val d'Isère back in 1957, and we remained good friends for decades.

While I was showing "Have Skis, Will Travel," I was also producing the next film, which I called "Anyone for Skiing?" It featured Sun Valley; Alta; Mammoth; Aspen; Lake Placid; Mt. Tremblant; Chamonix; Courchevel; Val d'Isère; Alyeska, Alaska; White Pass, Washington; and Sugarloaf, Maine. Just visiting all of these ski resorts for a couple of days would be a world-class vacation and cost a fortune. I was now bringing that kind of variety to the screen, and people could see the films, all with a full musical score and in-person narration, for only $1. Somehow the cash-flow numbers came together, and I assumed that everything was working fine at home with Dottie, because she never once complained. Looking back, I realize I was on the road about half of the year, which is tough on the people you leave behind.

The Ski Club Alpine had made so much money on my shows by now that they didn't know what to do with it. I suggested they start a race camp at Mammoth in the spring, sell spaces in camp at cost, and I would film it. I made arrangements for Dean Perkins from Ogden, Utah, who was on the American ski team; Ernie McCulloch from Mt. Tremblant; and the Canadian ski team to come out for a week to coach at the camp. Dave McCoy was most cooperative and offered the use of his new Tucker snowcat to haul the racers up to steeper places on the mountain to practice downhill. I don't know if it was the first ski race training camp in America, but Dave McCoy set the standard for others to follow.

I became hooked on the French ski resorts when first filming Émile Allais at Courchevel in the late 1950s. This was after seeing the French tourist office poster featuring the Aiguille du Midi gondola in Chamonix. The upper section of this lift rises almost 3,000 vertical feet, and there is not a single tower between the top and the bottom. At one point, it is more than 1,000 feet in the air. I was now introducing audiences to a country that had no out-of-bounds skiing restrictions and where a hundred or more people every year were dying in crevasses when they skied in these awesome mountains.

Audiences got very excited watching these pictures of a ride on the teleferique to the Aiguille du Midi summit. In my opinion, this is the world's most spectacular ski lift. When you get to the summit, you can ski down a seven-mile-long glacier. Along the right-hand side of this flowing glacier are giant ice blocks, thrust up by the 1,000-foot-thick sea of ice as it moves almost imperceptibly toward the valley below. If you are skiing down it without a guide and you get hurt, you have to pay to be hauled down to the hospital in the valley below. If you have a guide and get hurt, the guide company's insurance pays for your evacuation, even if it's by helicopter.

Since the glacier has retreated substantially in the last century, the excellent restaurant Le Bonnet, is now about two-thirds of a mile below the end. On my first visit in 1956, I met two porters who hauled food and other supplies up to the restaurant. It was a several mile hike and about 2,000 vertical feet; they were paid a penny a pound for the trip. They had just hauled up over 100 pounds each and made $1 for a morning's work. They would make a second trip later in the day and earn $2 total for their efforts.

When we got back to our new four-bedroom house in Rolling Hills, it was again time to work day and night on the expanding movie business. Dottie also dropped a bomb, informing me that I had to move my film business out of the house, because she was tired of the occasional business meeting in my home office. As a not-yet-diagnosed co-alcoholic, one of my basic behaviors was to do anything to please other people, rather than to take my own position on anything, so I obeyed.

But where to move? My mother was taking on an ever-expanding responsibility with my correspondence and bookkeeping, but I didn't think she would commute an hour or more each way to a beach location, which would be preferable to me. But any office worth renting started at a minimum of $75 a month. My mother offered to rent me an upstairs office where her ozone clinic was located: "How does $25 a month sound?" Before I knew it, I had made my decision; the office was 15 minutes from the film lab in Hollywood, and what was that to a young guy like me? Before long, I was leaving the house at 4:30 A.M.—sometimes six days a week—and getting home after Scott was in his pajamas and ready for bed. I did this hour-and-a-half commute each way for two years. It was stupid and expensive.

CHAPTER THIRTY-FIVE

1956–1957

Finally, the Book Is Finished

IN THE FALL OF 1956, WITH DOTTIE SIX MONTHS PREGNANT, I ONCE again set off on the road tour by myself. I was pleasantly surprised at every market, as the shows increased in size with larger and larger auditoriums—some of them filled to standing room only. With luck, our baby would be born before I had to go on my second Eastern swing in the middle of January.

For the Eastern shows, I hauled my 10-pound, 110/12-volt converter with me so I could dictate letters from the front seat of a rental car while I was driving to the next show. There was usually a package of correspondence every four or five days that was sent to my sponsor of that day, and I shipped the reel-to-reel answers back by the next night one way or another. There was no FedEx or email, of course; the best method available in 1957 was Railway Express, and if you wanted something in a hurry, you had to take it to an airport and give it to an airline ticket checker. The airline would then send it along, "counter to counter," at whatever airport you wanted someone to pick it up.

When I got home in the middle of December from my first Eastern tour—all 35 one-night-stands of it—it was obvious that if I were going to fulfill my annual Sun Valley Christmas commitment, I would have to go there alone. Dottie was OK with that because our overhead would be going up when the baby was born, so we needed the money. The day after Christmas, I left with a friend named Bill Barner to help me drive. When we got to Sun Valley, he was so excited that he called home and quit his job. The Sun Valley magic got him. He was hired as a bellhop and stayed until the lifts shut down.

After I returned with excellent footage of my annual trip, it was time to scramble around doing the Southern California shows. Then when they were over, it was off for a show in Dallas and then 28 days straight on the road with a show every night.

Dottie gave birth the day after I left. When I got to the show in Dallas, there was a telegram that Chris Ann Miller had been born and that both she and Dottie were doing fine. It would be 29 days before I got back to see them. I had no summer income in those years, so I had to make it all between the second week of October and the first week of February. I had to keep the film on a screen every night I could—something I don't think Dottie or Chris has ever understood. That was the way it was, right or wrong.

THAT SUMMER, I FINALLY FOUND THE TIME TO WRITE *WINE, WOMEN, Warren, & Skis*, because I had long ago spent the $2 deposits that I had collected from all those people who had sent in money for the prepublication discount, and I did not want to have to dig down in my low cash reserves to refund it.

I had already written the highlights of the book as inclusions in the previous three years of programs, so all I had to do was add more anecdotes of living in the parking lot all winter, draw some cartoons, round up some of the still photos that Ward Baker and I had taken, hire a printer, and order 3,000 copies for $1 a copy. I would double my money with every copy I sold from the stage.

After telling the audience about the book and showing them a copy, I would sell books from the stage at the intermission. While making change for $5 bills, I was rewinding and changing the reel-to-reel musical score on my tape recorder. I finally got so I pre-autographed all of the copies. There were evenings when I managed to sell up to as many as 60 copies during what was a frantic, orchestrated, 20-minute intermission. I went through five or six editions of the book in the next two years and am currently selling copies of the 14th edition for $10.95. Not bad for a 1947 story written and first published in 1957. More than 100,000 copies have sold to date.

In an effort to expand the revenue from the film I was exposing, I started to offer stock footage of ski action in 8-MM format. My sales pitch was that you could now have powder snow shots of great skiers at Sun Valley, Mammoth, Aspen, and several other ski resorts to insert in your own home movies. A lot of copies sold, so I decided to expand the business into underwater and waterskiing photos, too. To do this, I filmed the man whom I believed was the ultimate surfer and diver, Pete Peterson. He could do almost anything on top of or under the water. I took a day at Long Beach filming Pete waterskiing, as well as riding on a round sheet of plywood. He had a 4-foot-high wooden stool that he put on the plywood called a skimboard, and he would climb up and stand on top. As if that weren't enough, he started doing 360s while standing on the unattached stool.

I was still saddled with my long, daily commute to Hollywood. I should have given up the commute and asked Dottie to help in a nearby office for four hours a day. But I didn't ask and she never offered—nor helped with any of the business, for that matter. Years later, I heard that she had taken credit for making me famous and our company a success. Of course, behind every successful man there is often a talented, helpful lady. But other than being very social, she did nothing for the growth of the company.

As I look back on that era from a skier's point of view some 60 years later, it's clear that anyone who could make a dozen turns without falling was a good enough skier to perform in front of my cameras. I never did figure out a way to pay skiers the right amount of money for their time. My belief was that it was a trade-off, because my camera was giving anonymous skiers great publicity that they could not get any other way.

One day, when in Davos, Switzerland, I was looking at all of the 30 or more ski pins on a Tyrolean hat a man was wearing. It must have weighed 4 pounds; he had a pin from everywhere he had ever skied. They were his trophies. That gave me an idea: Why not have a ski-pin trophy made of my Ski Bum caricature? My skiers could be told, "The only way you can get one of these ski-bum pins is to appear in one of my ski movies." There is one of my pins in Pepi Gramshammer's trophy case in Vail, and Stein

Eriksen's in Deer Valley. Occasionally, when I run into a decades-old friend who skied for me, they'll remind me that they still display their Warren Miller ski-bum pin proudly in a frame in their office or den.

In the fall of 1957, with Chris less than a year old and Scott nearly 6, we decided that it would be too much to try to keep such a large group together on the film tour. Consequently, I would take my small luggage trailer on the road with a lot of stuff: projector, screen, tape recorder, PA system, and hundreds of copies of *Wine, Women, Warren, & Skis* to sell at the shows. The only problem during the fall tour was finding a place to park my trailer within hauling distance to the stage door if, in fact, there was a stage door.

I was looking forward to my show at the Berkshire Museum in Pittsfield, Massachusetts, where I had shown the November before. I had it all figured out—there was an easy train ride from Boston to Pittsfield, about a hundred or so miles. The supposed four-hour train ride got me into Pittsfield four hours late. I had phoned ahead and told the sponsors what train I would be on, so not to worry about potential snowstorms or bad weather. I soon found out how you can be four hours late on a four-hour train ride. All you have to do is buy a train ticket. The train was so late I had to use paper towels and a bar of soap to shave and spruce up in the men's room.

The next night's show was in Hanover, New Hampshire. This was not a problem because there was a complex bus connection from Pittsfield to Albany, New York, to Hanover. The shower at a friend's house in Hanover, home of Dartmouth College, cleaned me up, and he delivered me to the theater. After the show, he drove me the seven miles to White River Junction, Vermont. There was a midnight train for New York City that stopped at every farm on the way to pick up that day's milk. No sense in my renting a bed on the train because every time it stopped or started, the slack in the couplings between the cars would rattle loudly from one end of the train to the other and wake me up. I would arrive in New York City three or four hours late, hurry to the airport, and grab a flight to my next show. In some cases, it was Duluth, Minnesota.

The temperature was always below zero by the time I got there in mid-December. One year at the high school auditorium, a member of the motion picture projectionist union was picketing outside. The union projectionist in San Diego early in my season had gotten a copy of my program and written to every one of my towns, alerting the union of my show dates to make sure the show had a union projectionist. It was now the 15th of December, 5 below zero with a 10-mile-an-hour wind blowing. I offered the union picketer $50 if he would go away so all of the Duluth skiers could see the show. He had never run a 16-MM projector in his life, and he told me what to do with the $50. So instead, I offered to let him sit in the projection room with the high school kid who was going to run the film; he would still get paid his union scale for a show and make his share of the payment to the union for the night. No dice. About half of the people who came to the show turned around, got back in their cars, and went home to watch Wednesday night wrestling on their black-and-white televisions. Duluth was a very strict union town.

WHEN YOU SPEND 125 NIGHTS A YEAR ON THE ROAD ON A FILM TOUR, the stories mount. One of my earliest ski club sponsors was David Graebel of Wausau, Wisconsin. David has become a close skiing friend during the past 25 years, and he tells the story of how his ski club always debated whether to rent the sound version for $150 or splurge to have me personally narrate for an extra $50. One year, they could not make up their minds, and when they did, it was too late to schedule. They lost their place in line, and from then on it was the rental film only for them.

David was working in a ski shop and bought a $500 pickup truck to haul gear back and forth from the warehouse. One weekend, a friend asked him to help move a refrigerator and gave him $10. That job led to Graebel Van Lines, and today David owns 1,700 semitrucks and trailers with his name on the side and ships worldwide. He built the largest, privately owned moving company in the world.

At a showing in Lake Forest, Illinois, in December 1957, I first learned about man-made snow. Walt Stopa in Wilmot, Wisconsin, had cobbled together galvanized iron pipe, rented an air compressor, and pressurized a jet of compressed air, blasting it into small droplets. When the water spray went out into the freezing cold air, it fell to the ground as artificial or man-made snow.

One of the ski club members who worked in a nearby camera store said he could round up a 16-MM camera and a six-pack of 100-foot rolls of Kodachrome. We met early the next morning at Wilmot, a 200-foot-high hill covered with green grass. Under the ski lift there was a big patch of white snow that blended into the green grass around the edges. I got a great shot of someone making turns in the snow and completing his turns out into the green grass without missing a beat. That type of footage made the movie, and eventually snowmaking would have a game-changing impact on the sport.

I filmed Vail in 1962 when it opened, with the help of cofounder Pete Seibert and Morrie Shepard, the ski school director, both of whom appeared in the film when they could find a free moment. The beloved late Christie Hill, the Grand Dame of Vail (she went by "Blanche" in the early years), and the late Dick Hauserman also made a lot of deep-snow turns for my camera in Vail. When I took that film on the road, my narration was: "Get out here and buy some of this real estate, because they aren't going to make any more of it."

When I showed the film in Grand Rapids, Michigan, I stayed with the sponsor, Ted Kindel, and his family. We talked into the wee hours of the morning, and within two weeks, he took my advice. The Kindels sold their furniture business, moved to Vail, bought a big chunk of land, and built a sizeable condominium complex, a theater, retail stores, and office space (it was called Crossroads then, and is now the site of Solaris). Ted would end up serving a few terms as the mayor of Vail.

When I showed the film in Colorado Springs, the commander of the North American Aerospace Defense Command came to the show. This was the year of the Cuban missile crisis, and the commander had a red-alert telephone in the chair next to him while he watched my ski film.

CHAPTER THIRTY-SIX

1957–1958

The Jantzen International Sports Club

IN OCTOBER 1956 IN PORTLAND, OREGON, HOMER GROENING HAD LEFT a note at the front desk of my hotel. He wanted to have lunch the next day. That casual lunch was a real career changer for me. Homer was a one-man advertising and public relations agency for Jantzen—at the time, the world's leading swimsuit company and one of the leading makers of men's casual clothes. Homer had recently created the Jantzen International Sports Club, and he asked me if I would be interested in being a member. The others were Frank Gifford, who was playing pro football for the New York Giants; Bob Cousy, who had just retired from the Boston Celtics; and Ken Venturi, the professional golfer who in 1964 would win the U.S. Open. We would wear Jantzen sweaters and take a nice trip every summer to pose for national ads. The offer seemed like a good idea, and besides that, I got a dozen sweaters thrown into the deal. The next thing I knew, I was posing with Frank Gifford in his football uniform and appearing in full-page ads in national magazines such as *Life* and *Esquire*.

The first get-together of the Jantzen International Sports Club would be held in Jamaica at the end of July 1957. Groening had hired Tom Kelley, a world-famous photographer who had jumped into the famous category by taking published photos of Marilyn Monroe naked.

I was awestruck to be in the company of these all-American athletes and all-around-great men and their wives. I had never paid much attention to golf, but I got to watch Ken Venturi one afternoon on the driving range. I decided to wait until I was too old to ski and then take up golf. Unfortunately, there was no basketball court or football field, so I couldn't watch Gifford and Cousy perform their magical athletic abilities.

The next January we all got together at Pebble Beach for another photo shoot. Pebble Beach was chosen as the location because Ken Venturi was going to play in the Bing Crosby Pro-Am. I had a couple of shows in nearby Cupertino and Palo Alto, and Bud Palmer, former NBA basketball player and an American Sportsman master of ceremonies, had joined our group. We spent a couple of days having group and individual photos taken of us wearing a variety of the latest Jantzen sweaters. At the big dinner to wrap up the photo shoot, we were told to save the last week of June for a photo shoot in Hawaii. We would be staying at the Royal Hawaiian Hotel.

In June, Dottie and I met up with Homer Groening and the rest of the Jantzen group in the lobby of the Royal Hawaiian. It was time for drinks all around while our schedule was reviewed, and then we were all given the keys to new Triumph sports cars to drive while we were there. Mine was fire-engine red. I got several funny movie shots of all of the members playing "Dodge 'em" in the sports cars we had been loaned. I took the footage from the third-floor balcony of a nearby hotel and doubled the speed of the cars by motion-picture trickery. I filmed it with my camera upside down, so the cars were going backward at high speed and barely missing each other. The footage got a lot of laughs.

One of the photo shoots was on the other side of the island at Makapuu, and everyone was standing around barefooted in the strong, tropical sun. I warned everyone to at least wear socks so that the tops of their feet would not get sunburned. Ken Venturi's, of course, were really white from wearing golf shoes all of the time. He did not pay any attention to my advice, and he missed dinner that night because the tops of his feet were so sunburned that they swelled to the size of footballs.

Those sunburned, swollen feet slowed up Ken Venturi's winning golf career for a while. He was edged out in the Masters twice by a rising young player named Arnold Palmer. Ken went on to have a very long career as an announcer for worldwide golf tournaments on television.

Unfortunately, the trip to Hawaii also was the end of my working with Jantzen. I had shot a fair amount of surfing footage on my time away from the group, and Homer Groening wrongly assumed that he owned the footage, even though I had purchased the film myself and dragged my camera and tripod along almost as an afterthought. Another bad business decision was not getting that sorted out in the beginning. I think I'm beginning to understand, at age 90, that it's a wise idea to use attorneys to work out agreements ahead instead of having to spend hundreds of thousands of dollars to clean up the mess afterward.

Otherwise, the trip was fabulous from any point of view. In particular, I got to watch photographer Tom Kelley and memorize his composition of sports stars and identifiable backgrounds. I know Jantzen got everything they had hoped for from the photo shoot and used the photos in advertising the entire next year.

I spent a lot of the time with Cousy, listening to someone whom I really admired for what he did with a round ball and a small ring 10 feet above the floor. I was able to see the respect these outstanding people received as spokesmen for the sports they had devoted their lives to, making a very good living along the way. It would be interesting to check in with all of them and see where they are in life, almost 50 years later.

One thing I know for sure is that Homer Groening's son has been phenomenally successful by creating the animated, but in my mind, of rather poor taste, cartoon series, "The Simpsons." Bud Palmer was retired but was still the highlight of every gathering either in his home area in Florida or visiting back in Vail where he lived for many, many years. Unfortunately, we lost Bud in the spring of 2013.

CHAPTER THIRTY-SEVEN

1959

The Trip Sounded Like an Adventure, So I Signed On

MORE THAN 20,000 PEOPLE EACH YEAR FLOAT THE RAPIDS AND CANYONS of the Colorado River through the Grand Canyon. It's considered the "granddaddy of rafting trips," and I highly recommend you make the time in your busy schedule to do it.

I was asked to make the trip in 1959. This was not your normal float-down-it-in-rubber-rafts type of trip. Bill Cooper was going to lead an expedition of two powerboats *up* the Colorado River. He hoped to go from Lake Mead to Lees Ferry. This was before the Glen Canyon Dam that formed Lake Powell was built. The deal we shook hands on was simple. I would supply my camera and edit a movie of the trip. He would buy the raw stock, and we would own the finished film as partners.

Dottie was pregnant again at the time, but I saw no danger in going for a boat ride for a week or so. What I didn't know was that the wives of Bill Cooper and another crew member, Chuck Fester, were also pregnant and expecting about the same time as Dottie.

The trip sounded like an adventure, so I signed on. In the 1950s, the biggest motor that Mercury made was 75 horsepower, and so with two of those engines on the back of two homemade plywood boats, we crossed

Lake Mead and headed up the muddy, brown waters of the Colorado. A trip like this had never been attempted. Along with Bill Cooper and me, the group included the driver of the second boat, Jimmy Pflueger, an automobile dealer from Honolulu; a dentist named Jim Beardmore, also from Honolulu; and Chuck Fester, a salesman from Los Angeles.

The boats had plenty of horsepower for their light weight. But the water in the Colorado River was so muddy that when you stuck your fingers into it up to the palm of your hand, you couldn't see your fingernails—so we couldn't see rocks or anything under water unless white foam indicated they were there. Fortunately, Bill had brought along almost a dozen extra props and four complete lower units for the motors. We would need all of them.

About four days up the river, we reached Lava Falls—reputed to be the worst rapids on the entire river. Bill and Chuck's boat got thrown from the left-hand side of the riverbank by a violent back eddy just below the biggest tail wave on the entire river. As they tried to climb up and over the wave, they just sat there for a minute with the props cavitating. The props finally caught, and Bill and Chuck lurched over the top of the wave into the air and buried the bow of the boat in the next wave halfway to the stern.

I captured all of this disaster on film, but I missed the aftermath of Bill and Chuck swimming in the rapids. So a couple of days later—with my camera in the homemade waterproof box that I used to take my surfing movies—Chuck, Bill, and I held hands and waded out into other big rapids. We let the current sweep them off of their feet, and I held on and filmed them as though they were swimming for their lives. The audience never knew the difference, because my camera would go under the water in a wave, and then as it emerged, you would see Bill or Chuck swimming hard for the riverbank. The sequence turned out to be the highlight of the finished film of an unfinished expedition—we didn't succeed in getting to Lees Ferry.

After the accident that damaged both engines, we took one of the good engines off the boat that hadn't sunk, salvaged what we could, and with one good engine on each boat, motored back down the river to Lake Mead. I glued the film together and eventually sold some of the stock footage to a TV series called "Man and the Challenge."

Bill Cooper bought my raw film, and we co-owned the movie that I produced of the expedition. Did we make any money with it? Probably not, but my bookkeeping, as you already know, was anything but accurate in those days. The entire trip was a real blast for me, while Bill managed a big write-up in *LIFE* magazine about the expedition. With all of that press and a dollar or so, back then you could still buy lunch.

CHAPTER THIRTY-EIGHT

1959

Hollywood Office; My Indecisions Are Final

DURING THE FOURTH SUMMER OF MY COMMUTING TO MY NEW OFFICE in an old building in Hollywood, someone from the City of Los Angeles appeared in my mother's ozone clinic downstairs and shut her down. They said she was creating too much pollution. She'd been turned in for offering a service that the local medical community didn't sanction. She now depended on me for her income, so it was necessary to raise her salary accordingly. It was now up to $65 a week, the going rate for a good stenographer in 1959, which was what she was doing for me. Minimum wage was still 25 cents an hour.

About the same time, my sister BJ appeared because she was in the middle of a divorce and she, too, needed a job. So I created a job for her as the receptionist and accountant. Why I did that I don't know, other than feeling sorry for her. No receptionist was necessary, because no one ever came to my office unless they wanted to sell me something. The occasional phone call could have been easily answered by my not-very-busy mother.

Now my overhead for employees was $130 a week, plus $25 a month rent. I worried about things that I knew nothing about, simple things such as business management. But somehow I managed to struggle through, keeping both of them reasonably busy and beating them both to work every morning despite my hour-plus commute.

Even though I didn't finished college, never once did I lose a client or a contract to produce a movie because I didn't have a college degree. My survival skills learned from adversity taught me enough about business to scrape by. I never took any business courses because I thought I'd never own a business, and I never took any accounting courses because I knew I'd never have enough money to need to account for it. As a result, in those two very important disciplines, I was way beyond bankruptcy several times during my career, but too naïve to know it.

When the ozone business shut down, I moved my office downstairs where there was a lot more space, even though I didn't need it. One day while working on the narration for the "Up the Raging Colorado" film with Bill Cooper, he asked me, "Why is your office clear up in Hollywood when you live down here near the beach?" I replied, "Well, it is where the film business is, so I should be there." Then he asked, "How often do you do business in Hollywood, and who do you do it with? I thought your customers were throughout the U.S. and Canada."

"Well, I go to the film labs occasionally."

That is when I finally realized how much of my life was wasted commuting. Before I went on the road that fall, I found an office in Palos Verdes Plaza that rented for $75 a month. This was a six-minute drive instead of sometimes 90 minutes. Also, the owner would put in the partitions for free. For $50 a month more rent, I could eliminate 15 hours of commuting time each week. Sounded good to me.

I rented the space in September, and just before leaving on the road that fall, I told my mother and sister that the company was going to move, and if they wanted to keep their jobs, they could commute instead of me. The move would be in the spring. Neither one of them had the skills to compete for jobs in the open market.

So the ground rules were established for the following spring. In the meantime, we would stay in Hollywood for that year's tour season. That meant creating all of the copies of the press releases, collating them, and mailing the press packets to all of my personal-appearance sponsors. By this time, the fee had gone up to $300 for personal appearances. I was traveling to 100 cities, so I was guaranteed a minimum of $30,000, minus the cost of producing the movie and travel expenses. That was huge money for my family.

My mother and sister also had to pack and ship all of the posters to the sponsors and fill their orders for free postcards. There were also the press pictures and a 12-page outline of how to promote the show, using my shoot-from-the-hip marketing approach. When you have no money to hire a marketing or advertising firm, or to even buy advertising, you utilize everything that is free, such as interviews, even in high school papers, and use inserts and posters in any way possible.

The production and the marketing must have worked, because when I sold the company after 50 years, we were still using the same formula. During the first 14 years, I was doing 100 percent of the creativity, and all of it was fun. I enjoyed every minute of it, except the commuting to Hollywood and substituting for the janitor on the nights when he didn't show up.

CHAPTER THIRTY-NINE

1959

My Voice on Film; My Second Son Is Born

BY NOW I WAS ADDING MY VOICE AND MUSIC TO THE LATEST FEATURE films, so I didn't have to narrate every showing. That gave me the opportunity to reach dozens of cities I could not get into my personal-appearance schedule. I still was not writing a script, so when we recorded the sound track, I just sat in the recording studio watching the movie and narrated it as though it was a standard, 1,000-seat-theater performance.

There was now a program for high school assemblies. Most high schools had auditoriums that could provide seating for half of the student body. As a result, the high school assembly show business was simple. The sponsor would pay $75 for the first assembly and $50 for the second show. We could handle one school in the morning for a pair of shows and another school in the afternoon for another pair of shows. That added up to a $250 show day, so I hired someone to guard the film, introduce it, sit down, and repeat this three or four times. Keith Wegeman of the 1952 Olympic ski-jumping team in Oslo carried the film around and kept half of the money for his efforts—a good day's work for both of us. It was now up to me to get on the phone and book a lot of shows, which was easy to do. We showed the film at about 25 to 35 Los Angeles schools a year and exposed a lot of kids to skiing in the process.

In 1958, a man had appeared in my office to appraise my ability to produce the official 1960 Squaw Valley Winter Olympic film. I think he took one look at my very shabby office and wrote me off immediately. However, he invited me to join the movie-cameramen pool, and anyone who joined it could use everyone else's footage. I paid the fee and received all of the official accreditations, but when the Olympics finally started, I decided not to be part of the group.

In January 1959, I took Dottie, Scott, and Chris with me to Squaw Valley for the tryouts of the Olympic venues. I shot a lot of film, and the races were almost over when Dottie, who was pregnant, thought she had a miscarriage. All of the doctors who had volunteered their time as official Olympic doctors were there practicing what to do in an emergency, but were restricted from taking care of anyone who was not a competitor or an official. I thought this was a big emergency, but they had been given strict orders.

I was angry enough that I was ready to force someone into our room to examine Dottie. That was when Dr. Bud Little stepped up, helped me get her into the van, and drove her to the nearby Truckee hospital. Fortunately, she was OK, because miscarriages are common when women get above 6,000 feet in altitude in their first couple of months of pregnancy. The hospital said it was almost a daily occurrence with people driving over the 9,000-foot-high Donner Summit on their way to or from Reno. (Bud became a friend for life and, just a few years ago, I got to know his grandson, Dave Morin of Facebook fame. Small world. Bud passed away a short time ago after giving a great deal to the world.)

When Dottie was well enough to travel, I loaded the family into the VW van, and drove to our home in Rolling Hills. Neither of us had planned this pregnancy, and I had to leave in four or five days to conduct a seminar in Florida for a group of White Stag clothing company dealers, after which Dottie and I were supposed to fly on to Europe. When you allow yourself to get locked into schedules such as I had, how do you not show up when you are the paid speaker? In retrospect, I realized there was no negative reaction from my wife when I once again left on the road without her. I should have figured out what was going on, but I didn't for a long time.

THE PORTUGUESE TOURIST OFFICE HAD CONTACTED ME MANY MONTHS before to film its new ski resort for my next film. I was still a one-man band and way too busy, so I neglected to have someone check things out for me. I took them at their word that all would be ready.

I flew to the seminar in Florida with my skis, boots, and many pounds of overweight camera gear, spoke at their seminar, and then boarded a plane for Portugal. Prior to Dottie's pregnancy, it had made economic sense for White Stag to fly us to Florida and then on to Portugal. I went alone and was met by the tourist official with maps. My VW of the year had been delivered to a hotel in Lisbon. I left early the next day for Portuguese skiing at its finest.

At the end of the road to the new hotel, while looking around for the ski lift, I remembered the time I went to Geilo in Norway. The new ski lift cable was still lying on the ground, and no workmen were anywhere in sight. It is a long drive from Lisbon to skiing in central Europe, but I hurried to make up for the lost Portuguese footage.

In Courchevel a couple of days later, Émile Allais had a surprise for me. It had snowed enough to cause small avalanches, but he had a special slope for me to film the ski patrol skiing in and around the small avalanches while they were sliding. Each of them had a large, red weather balloon filled with helium on a 10-foot string tied to his waist, and it was fantastic footage. My narration was, "They had the balloons tied to their waists so if they got buried, you could follow the strings from the balloons down to their bodies and dig them out before they died." The film and narration really worked together for the audience.

A few days later I was in Planica, Yugoslavia, for a ski-flying tournament. The jumpers broke the hill records at 430 feet (the record is now more than 800 feet), but the scary part of the day for me was different. I had heard that Marshal Josip Broz Tito, the communist dictator at the time, was going to be watching from the judge's tower. He had to walk up a narrow path through a lot of small trees to get there, so I hid in the trees to get a good shot of him as he walked. While I waited patiently for him to show up, there was a sharp jab in my back and the metallic click of a rifle being cocked. I quickly lifted my camera and my other hand over my head, and turned around very slowly. In those days, Yugoslavia was still a communist nation, and the soldiers meant business. I don't usually carry my passport, but for some reason it was on me that day, and the only word in English the soldier could speak was "Passport?" They let me point at my rucksack, and he found it, scrutinized it, and motioned me to pack up and get out of the trees and into plain sight on the jump hill. Later, I was able to show many shots of Tito, and the best shot of a crash in my entire filming career. A talented jumper was reaching for the 430-foot mark when a gust of wind hit him hard. He tipped upside down in mid-flight and did a 300-foot egg-beater down the hill after landing on his back. He was OK, and my audiences loved it.

I made it home to Rolling Hills as Dottie was getting close to having the baby. One evening, I frantically drove her to the hospital. My car was, as usual, low on gas, so I had to stop and buy some, even though Dottie was already in labor. As usual, I found a discount gas station.

She was back home with baby Kurt several days later.

CHAPTER FORTY

1960

The Olympics and the Porsche

AT THE LAST MINUTE BEFORE THE 1960 OLYMPICS AT SQUAW VALLEY, Dottie and I snagged a room with bunk beds from Howard Head so we could attend. We drove up from Los Angeles in my now high-mileage 1956 Chevy in time to get squared away for the opening ceremonies. I'd made the decision not to be part of the filming pool so I could keep all of my film for my own use.

I was riding on a pair of red Hart skis, in direct competition with Head. It was awkward to put the skis in Howard Head's garage, along with several hundred pairs of his shiny, black skis that he was generously giving to anyone of any importance. We had argued a lot about fiberglass versus aluminum in skis and had long ago reached a truce, because neither one of us would give up our positions. (Two very stubborn and bald heads colliding.)

It was good to renew friendships, and because I knew all the lift operators personally from my winter there, it didn't matter that I didn't have the credentials to get up to the top of the mountain.

This would be the first Winter Olympics to be televised live, and I was skeptical that the camera crews could pull it off—until seeing what unlimited budgets could create in the form of gigantic camera scaffolds.

Every inch of every event would have a camera whose range would overlap the cameras on each side of it, thus providing a seamless documentary of any event and of the downhill in particular.

During the opening ceremonies, I was able to walk right out on the ice rink, mingling with and filming the various celebrities up close and personal. It was snowing right up to the grand finale, when the clouds parted and the officials released a hundred white pigeons that were already half frozen. The cold would finish the job before the sun came up the following day. People reported finding frozen white pigeons over a 50-mile radius during the next month or so.

The Alpine events were all that interested me. When the giant slalom gates were installed, they were made of thick-walled, 3- or 4-inch-diameter aluminum poles. During the first day of training, Linda Meyers, who had been coached by Dave McCoy and was now with the U.S. Ski Team, hit one of them and broke her shoulder. The games were over for her before they started.

By today's standards, the downhill was a real nothing: just one long, straight, steep run down from the summit, a long turn or two, and it was over. While the races were going on, I was filming Stein Eriksen carving his usual spectacular turns, set against the thousands of people milling around in the valley below.

Every night, we attended a party, and one night Dottie and I invited an interesting group to dinner: Stein Eriksen; Willy Bogner, Sr., and his wife, Maria; and their daughter, Rosemarie, who brought her new fiancé from Fresno, California, Jim Tobin. I had introduced Rosemarie and Jim a couple of years earlier.

Willy Bogner, Jr., was on the German Olympic Team and had the fastest first run in the slalom. Unfortunately, he fell in his second run. He went on to run the Bogner ski-clothing company and produce truly innovative, colorful ski movies for 35-MM theatrical release.

While spending time with Willy Bogner, Sr., I made arrangements for him to buy me a Porsche in Munich for my European tour as soon as the Olympics were over. We were still driving a VW van and my 1956 blue Chevy business coupe.

Once the Olympics began to wind down, and I had bootlegged enough footage for my next year's movie, we began our long drive back to our home in Rolling Hills, about 230 miles to the south. Shortly after we got home, I'd be leaving for Europe.

There was very little time to get ready for the trip, but all that was needed was my ski equipment, my camera gear, and 50 rolls of 16-MM Kodachrome. With our passports out for inspection and a welcome from an Air France station manager, we were able to sneak on an extra 60 pounds of baggage. My company started promoting Air France at that time, and I was also working for Jantzen to try to spot fashion trends in the resorts we would visit. This meant I would take a lot of still photos, in addition to my movie footage.

I had never ridden in a Porsche, much less driven one, and the car had a couple of surprises. The first was that there was almost no room whatsoever for luggage, much less my camera gear. Second, the Porsche Willy bought for me was a convertible hardtop that was able in four seconds to accelerate from zero to 120 miles per hour, or as they say in Europe, "200k."

We stored a few suitcases at the Bogners' after I tried and retried to pack the Porsche with all of the stuff necessary for filming every day. I decided I'd have to do laundry every night before going to dinner with the local mayor or tourist director of the resort we were filming.

I can't remember for sure, but this may have been the trip when I hired a guide to rappel me into a crevasse on the Eiger Glacier in Switzerland. I wanted to get shots from an ice ledge at least 30 feet down in a crevasse. When I got all set to film him rappelling down to me, my shaky voice echoed off the ice, "What makes you think this crevasse won't close up and crush us while we are down here?" He replied, "What makes you think it will?" He was hired because he knew what he was doing. I sure didn't, but I had laid my life and my camera on the line with him. As it turned out, the images were worth the risk.

I also remember the train that leaves from Wengen and makes a 360-degree turn inside a tunnel as it climbs its way to the summit. Most of the trip is inside the tunnel, but there is one spot where the train stops, and you can get scared just looking down out of the window at the 9,000-vertical-foot, granite North Face of the Eiger. It is sobering to stand there looking at that wall and realize how many men and women have died trying to climb it. One of the best mountaineering books of all time is *The White Spider*, the history of the triumphs and deaths on that wall. The year I rappelled down into that crevasse was the first year anyone had made an ascent of the Eiger in the winter. It took the team over a week to do it. In 2011, a man soloed or free-climbed that same granite face in one hour and 43 minutes. He did it without any ropes, pitons, or anyone for support, all alone with an ice axe and crampons.

WHEN I GOT BACK TO CALIFORNIA, SELLING THE PORSCHE WAS ENTIRELY different than the Volkswagens that I had previously offloaded. About two weeks or so after I got it out of customs, I was driving home on a rainy night in Palos Verdes when the car spun out 360 degrees. When I got home, I painted a "For Sale" sign (I wanted $3,500). However, at that time it was almost impossible to sell such an expensive car, because very few people had ever even seen a Porsche.

The closest Porsche dealer in Los Angeles back then was in Pasadena, and finally someone said, "Go there and talk to a guy by the name of Vasek Polak. He might be able to help you." When I went to see him, he was under a Mercedes on a creeper. He wheeled out from under it, and we talked. "I will try and sell it for you. Keep it insured until I do, and we will stay in touch." He managed to sell it five weeks later, and I broke even on the $3,500 Porsche deal. Vasek Polak later became one of the largest Porsche, Mercedes-Benz, and BMW dealers in L.A., as well as a famous race-car mechanic team chief. Years later, I received a phone call from someone who had bought the Porsche at auction for $72,000.

I MOVED INTO MY NEW $75 A MONTH OFFICE IN THE UPSCALE PALOS Verdes Plaza. There were plenty of parking spaces in the vacant lot across the street from my office, and the post office was close for easily shipping out my films.

In the middle of the summer, I hired Roger Brown and helped him look for a low-priced apartment. He set up a second editing bench in the office and also filmed me driving a miniature Model T Ford as a transitional device to segue from one ski resort to the next. As September rolled around, I snagged a filming job for him: He would set up his 16-MM camera in the bleachers of a high school football stadium and photograph every play. Then he would deliver the film to Hollywood Film Enterprises for development. I think his pay was $25 a game.

Near the end of September, Roger came to me with a proposal to show my latest feature film in ski resorts all winter and give me all of the money he took in. At the same time, while he was at the resort, he would run his own camera and produce his own feature-length ski film for the following winter. This sounded like the perfect deal for him and a bad deal for me. I let him go his own way, and he produced many outstanding commercial films for clients, from ski companies to FedEx.

The highlight for me that fall on the film tour was when Otto Hollaus, who ran the ski department for Dayton's/Schuneman's department store in Minneapolis, rented the St. Paul ice hockey stadium to put on the show. The managers put down a wooden floor on top of the ice, and more than 7,000 people watched the movie.

Otto had me introduce a couple who had been married that afternoon. I urged them to stand up and be recognized, because they had postponed their honeymoon until after they could watch my ski movie that night.

CHAPTER FORTY-ONE

1961

The Missing $160,000; Mine Was a Strange Family

IN THE LATE 1950S, I MET THE MAN WHO RAN THE SPORTS DEPARTMENT and discount basement of Raymond's Department store in Boston. He was a superb marketing man, and after a show one night in a Boston suburb, we arranged to have lunch the next day.

He had a simple question, "Can you cut a couple of your feature-length films into a dozen 10-minute shorts? I can buy the downtime between the broadcast of an East Coast NFL game and when the West Coast game starts." I knew there would be some trouble with some of the small ski shops who had already supported my shows in a big way and would see this as competition. The phone started to ring when Raymond's started broadcasting my TV shows. There were not a lot of color television sets in homes in those days, so I told the ski shops to rent a big color TV every Sunday, serve hot cider, and invite their customers in to relax, watch the show, and talk about skiing while they spilled hot cider on the new ski clothes. The second year, I wrote and filmed an intro and a close for each show. It worked well for both Raymond's and myself for the next five or so years.

The marketing guru from Raymond's also had a pipeline to Detroit, and in 1961, I met with Ford and worked out a deal with them so that they annually delivered a new, top-of-the-line station wagon for me to use. So each year's model was mine to use for the next seven or eight years. They also provided a top-of-the-line Ford van, and my side of the deal was to give the vehicles good exposure in the films, which was easy to do.

The Ford Motor Company also had a fleet of deluxe cars in all of the major airports in America. When I flew into Boston or San Francisco or anywhere, all I had to do was go to the United Airlines ticket counter, and there would be the keys to a new car. This cut the cost of rental cars to almost nothing.

ONE DAY I WAS PLANNING TO GET FOOTAGE AT STOWE, BUT IT WOULD not stop snowing, so I gave up and skied my brains out instead, while figuring out what time I should quit to get to the next town for a show that night. Just before leaving for the high school auditorium to do the show, there was time to call my wife, and the news was terrible. She had tried to cash a $25 check, and it had bounced. Instead of about $75,000 in the bank, my balance was only $5 and there was nothing in Dottie's household account. I had been paid handsomely by Raymond's for the weekly television series and had done over 70 personal appearances that were, by then, averaging $400 a night.

In the spring of 1958, my sister had talked me into getting my first credit card. Until then, I was cashing a $25 check once a week to buy gasoline and the occasional lunch when not brown bagging it. The Diners Club credit card was another major mistake. My sister secretly got one for herself. She was my bookkeeper by then and, foolishly, I never examined my books. If you cannot trust your immediate family members, your sister and mother, who can you trust? I never saw my sister again. I only saw my mother once and that was in the back row of a show in Glendale a year later. They had been siphoning nearly every last dime out of my bank accounts.

In retrospect, I wonder why I ever hired my mother in the first place after she walked off in 1948 with all of my bootlace money. Back then, she got away with more than $8,000. At the time, I rationalized that she had kept the family together when I was growing up.

I couldn't come home because of the show schedule, so I phoned for a first-hand report on what was going on. The report was my worst nightmare. All of my books and records were gone, so nothing could be done until I finished the last shows of the tour. The problem was reported to the Palos Verdes police, and I started mailing my guarantee checks home instead of to the office, while worrying about all of the unfilled shows that were not happening and how to act on the sponsors' well-deserved nasty letters.

There were only 11 days to fix this between getting home and going to Europe for three weeks, My first day back, I met with the IRS because I knew that my income tax statement would be a mess. I should have been able to deduct all of the stolen money, but the investigator took the position, after meeting with my sister, that, "A woman as beautiful and innocent as she is could not have possibly stolen the money as you claim." The photo-stats of the bank statements revealed that when Dottie and I were in Hawaii working for Jantzen the summer before, my sister had written a weekly paycheck to herself every day that we were gone.

After getting back from filming in Europe, I hired a local accountant to straighten out the mess. He got melodramatic and insisted that we get out of town for a week or so until everything settled down. He pulled a revolver out of his desk drawer and suggested that it might get real messy, but not to worry because he had handled embezzlements like this before.

The most disturbing part of the entire mess was when my wife blew up and said, "You had me on a tight monthly budget all of that time, and your sister and mother were able to get all of that money. From now on, I'm going to get my share of it." And she did.

TO GET OUT OF TOWN, WE DROVE TO TIMBERLINE LODGE NEAR PORTLAND, Oregon, for a week of skiing, filming, and family fun. Dick Kohnstamm, the owner, had just built a swimming pool, and so I got some good shots of "want-to-be-in-a-ski-movie?" skiers flying off a 10-foot-high snowbank into the pool against the backdrop of Mt. Hood and its steep glaciers. While there, Dick and I had yet another discussion about why he should build a chairlift on the high-up glacier so he could offer summer and year-round skiing.

Dick was convinced that because the glacier moved down the hill slowly but perpetually, he could not build a lift. I showed him the outcrop of rocks where he could build towers, and the rest is history.

The too-short vacation with the family was enjoyable for them, but I dreaded getting back into the mess I had created by my inattention to detail, lack of business skills, and zero controls over the cash. At the bottom of the problem was my co-alcoholic behavior—always avoiding confrontation with anyone.

I had to pay $26,000 in income tax on the missing $156,000 that my sister and mother stole, money I never even saw. My sister's theft does not include her credit card charges, which disappeared when she and my mother walked out with all of the books and records, which they later burned.

My sister, within a month, had a fake robbery in her apartment where she claimed her full-length mink coat was stolen. It later appeared in my mother's closet. My mother conned the IRS agent into believing that this beautiful, sweet lady would never steal anything. BJ later married the insurance agent who substantiated the fake robbery. If I wrote a script about this for a TV show, no one would produce it because the entire episode is too bizarre to be real.

Many years ago, I received a phone call from my other sister, Mary Helen, who had cut short her ski vacation at Mammoth. We talked about her four children, the snow, and our general family gossip. As the conversation began to wind down, there was a pause, and she then said, "Oh, by the way, our mother died two weeks ago."

With that statement, my entire life with this nutty family came into focus. I was the third, completely accidental and unwanted, child in a family that just did not have any emotional or financial support for me. It explained all of those years of sleeping in hallways and closets on a small mattress and being ignored. I think the saying is "Neglect and silence are the worst form of child abuse." However, the roof never leaked, and there was usually enough peanut butter available for sandwiches.

BJ passed away while living with her son in 2004. Mary Helen is gone, now, also. I am not the least bit proud to say that I don't know where either my mother or father is buried, nor can I tell you the dates of their deaths. I do know that my mother died of cancer, and my father's alcoholism turned into diabetes, and he had to have a leg amputated. The doctors told him to stop drinking, or they would have to amputate the other leg.

He kept on drinking, and they did, and then he died. Their lives went on without me as soon as I was able to deliver newspapers, buy my own clothes, and pay my own way 100 percent. And that was at about the age of 13 or 14. Am I bitter about it? Sometimes. I've never had much time to be bitter, but I still haven't forgotten it.

A lot of people have had it a lot worse, but this was the way I had it. Mine was a strange family.

CHAPTER FORTY-TWO

1960s and Beyond

Many Very Nonroutine Flights

LONG BEFORE COMMERCIAL AIRLINES HAD JET AIRPLANES, I HAD LOGGED about a million miles sitting midway between four propellers that got me from Point A to Point B through, rather than above, storms. Often the ride was rough, and on some flights the stewardesses would run out of those paper bags stored in the seat pocket in front of you. Aside from some pretty bumpy rides, there were some pretty scary ones as well.

In the 1960s, I was lucky enough to take a $10 ride with Hermann Geiger, flying over the Gornergrat Glacier in Zermatt, when he was experimenting with landing and taking off. With my eye stuck to the viewfinder while filming out of the windshield, we flew off a massive cliff. Way down below, suddenly, was the village of Zermatt instead of a snow-covered glacier. While flying with Hermann, I managed to expose four minutes of never-before-seen footage that stunned my audience.

Sadly, a few weeks later I learned that Hermann had made a mistake and suffered a midair collision with a glider. He and the glider pilot were both killed. Hermann was a real pioneer in pushing the boundaries of what you can do in the mountains with a small airplane.

One day en route to Hartford, Connecticut, in a small commuter plane, the pilot did a 180-degree turn and headed back to JFK airport. When the plane settled on its new course, the stewardess came through the cabin and talked quietly with each passenger: "Take any sharp objects out of your shirt pockets. When we tell you to, lean forward and grab your elbows with your forearms under your legs. We will be landing on a foamed runway, so there is no need to worry about fire when we land."

A landing gear light had malfunctioned, and as it turned out there was no real danger. It was exciting, though, as the plane slowed down to 70 mph, to see a string of fire engines racing alongside. The mechanics put in a new lightbulb, and we were on our way an hour and a half later to Hartford, with half of the passengers taking a bus instead. Somehow, I made it to my show date in Hartford that night.

In 1962, Dottie and I were on our way to Japan on a Pan Am plane for the filming of "Around the World on Skis." We ran into violent, clear air turbulence and were slammed down 10,000 vertical feet. Half of the passengers did not have their seat belts on and were instantly pinned against the ceiling. I had time to tell my wife, while we were falling, "I hope someone raises our kids right." (We did not fly together on the same airplane ever again. Instead, I would catch an earlier one and rent the car and be ready when she got there.)

The 10,000-foot instant drop caused enough trouble to the airplane and passengers that we landed in Kwajalein and had a three-hour airframe inspection. The mechanics even took the access hatch off the vertical and horizontal stabilizer parts of the tail and crawled up into the tail with flashlights looking for aluminum stress fractures.

In 1994, when my eventual wife Laurie and I lived in Vail, we spent a lot of time skiing with Frank Wells. He was the copresident of the Walt Disney Company at the time. Laurie and I had packed up for our spring migration to the Northwest when Frank called and invited me to heli-ski with him at Elko, Nevada, the next weekend. I told him that I already had a commitment and couldn't make it. We joked around a bit, and then he called me again on Wednesday and said, "C'mon, Miller. Change your plans. This weekend is on me: food, housing, and helicopter rides." I apologized and said, "I just can't do it this time." There was one final call from him on Thursday, and though Laurie said she could drive the car and trailer home, I just did not want to change my plans.

While spending the two days driving from Vail to Orcas Island, I kept thinking about what I was missing with Frank Wells, Clint Eastwood, and half a dozen or so of Frank's good friends skiing fresh powder snow in the Ruby Mountains.

On Tuesday afternoon, the phone rang on Orcas Island, and it was Frank Wells' son. He said, "My mother would like you to speak at my father's funeral." On the last helicopter ride out on the weekend, the helicopter engine had flamed out, and the pilot hit a big tree at over a 100 miles per hour. The pilot and Frank, who was sitting directly behind him, died instantly, along with another passenger. The guide and Mike Hoover somehow survived because they were sitting on the other side of the helicopter. I miss Frank and know that I would still be skiing with him today if his helicopter had not hit that tree outside of Elko, Nevada.

Many years later, my friend Jim Salestrom, who toured with John Denver and Dolly Parton for decades, was performing at one of the annual dinner fundraisers for the Warren Miller Freedom Foundation at the Yellowstone Club. Jim was playing the guitar and between songs he announced that on the flight to Bozeman it occurred to him that no one had ever written a song about Warren Miller. He went on to say he wrote one on the flight up, but the only paper he could find to write it on was the air-sickness bag in the seat-back in front of him. Laurie framed the barf bag with the original lyrics, and it hangs in our Montana home, where we often have Jim's CD playing in our Sonos system.

CHAPTER FORTY-THREE

1950s–1970s

Grease, Gravel, Atom Bombs, and Other Tales from the Road

EARLY IN MY TRAVELS, I HAD BECOME GOOD FRIENDS WITH HERBERT Jochum, the owner and proprietor, as was his father before him, of the Hotel Lorunser in Zurs, Austria. He had gone to England to learn to speak proper English and then came to Aspen to learn proper American—and to find out what Americans wanted in a ski resort hotel. He worked as a ski instructor in Aspen for a year, spent a winter teaching at Sun Valley, and also was the U.S. Women's Olympic Ski Team coach. Over the many years I filmed in Europe, I returned to Zurs almost every year, and included Herbert in 15 or 20 films. He was a great powder snow skier, and I could always depend on a powder snow sequence in Europe by simply staying in Zurs for a few days and filming Herbert.

Herbert would always take good care of me, no matter the circumstances. There was a span of time in the 1970s and 1980s when I didn't get to ski with him. When I walked into the lobby in the winter of 1985, after such a long absence, the desk clerk was there along with the night manager, who was working on his computer with his back to me. I asked the desk clerk, "Is Mr. Jochum on the property tonight?" Without even turning around, the night manager said, "Yes, he is, Mr. Miller; I will call him." Then he turned around and welcomed me back after a 10- or 15-year absence.

During the 1950s, my interest in filming at Mammoth grew as my friendship with Dave McCoy grew. Dave, who started Mammoth with a lot of 18-hour days, very little money, and lots of energy, was bigger than life: He was strong and smart enough to make Mammoth grow from its one rope tow to a couple of gondolas and 31 chairlifts, when he finally sold it 60 years later. He helped me by building those chairlifts: it was easier to get good pictures in less time.

In the 1960s, when I read about Walt Schoenknecht at Mt. Snow, Vermont, building a radical new kind of chairlift, I stopped by to film it and his newly designed lodge. He was very creative, and instead of having chairs hung on a cable like every other chairlift, he welded together steel I-beams that formed a track similar to the ones in a manufacturing plant that would be used as a conveyer to bring component parts to the assembly line. With wheels running on this steel I-beam, the chairs would hang from the wheels and be pulled up the hill by being linked to the chair in front. It was a bumpy ride as the wheels went over the welded joints in the I-beams, and Walt had to apply a lot of grease to keep the wheels turning.

Walt soon learned that grease is subject to gravity, and it will fall from the rolling wheels to the chairs below. Walt had to quickly weld a roof on every one of the chairs. The roof had to be at least 7 feet, 6 inches long to cover the length of a pair of skis. It was innovative, different, and did not work very well. He also had a large dry-cleaning bill to pay to everyone who rode the chairlift before he added the roofs.

Walt was so innovative he once applied to the Atomic Energy Commission to set off a few atom bombs at the bottom of his mountain to make a big crater so he would have more vertical feet on his ski runs.

His base lodge had a gravel floor. That way it was classified as a picnic area and his property tax bill was lower. Very clever. He also built it without a foundation so that he could move it somewhere else when he got enough money to build a bigger one. The lodge was cold, so he had several aquariums installed with tropical fish in them. He would point to them whenever anyone complained about the cold to show that his tropical fish were doing just fine.

Another tall tale from Mt. Snow was how the ski industry came up with the number of skiers in America, which could be used to attract more investment. Two ad agency guys were at the top, and one said, "Look down there. There must be a million skiers!" The other guy said, "It looks like several million to me." That number might have been the basis for getting more people into the ski business. I never did know how many skiers there were the entire time I made movies, but my films made them dream about places to ski beyond their local mountain. We have to always remember that the local areas are the kindergartens for Sun Valley, Mammoth, Big Sky, Vail, and all of the destination resorts.

From a Detroit newspaper in 1959:

> "The mushrooming popularity of skiing is vividly illustrated by the recent history of the new Ford Auditorium in Detroit. The 3,000-seat theatre has been full only three times since it opened three years ago. The first time was on opening day with a first-run Hollywood epic on the screen. The Detroit Symphony with Jack Benny as the featured soloist filled the place the second time. The third standing-room-only attraction was Warren Miller's 'Let's Go Skiing,' which was there this fall. Apparently everybody in Detroit is going skiing."

For many years, the Detroit show was on the night before Thanksgiving. It was exciting to walk out on the stage that evening and talk to 3,000 people in a theater with red velvet seats, but there was always more to my evening. My car was always parked close to the stage entrance. I could have my tape rewound by the time the projectionist came down with my film. I'd grab it, jump into the rental car, and try to make an 11:15 flight to Los Angeles to spend Thanksgiving with my wife and children. I usually made it.

I showed in that same auditorium to capacity crowds until selling half my company many years later. That was when my partners changed the date and theater of the show. So many people had been making it a night-before-Thanksgiving ritual to go to my movies that about 800 of them showed up at the Ford Auditorium anyway, though the show would not be in Detroit until three days later.

A lot had changed since my first movie was shown, back when there were fewer than 15 chairlifts in North America. The first one ever built in the world was moved from Sun Valley to Michigan's Boyne Mountain and installed on a hill too steep to grow potatoes. Everett Kircher had bought the land for $1 and the lift for $4,800. As the legend goes, Everett had his sign painter increase the vertical listed on the ski area's billboard every year by 5 or 10 feet. Today, Boyne Mountain must be 100 feet higher on the sign than the year it opened!

PART FOUR

Lurching Forward

Averaging 175 days a year on the road, narrating and filming.

CHAPTER FORTY-FOUR

1960s

Raising Kids on the Beach in the Surf-Skate-Board Culture

IN THE EARLY 1960S, WE DECIDED WE WANTED TO MOVE TO THE BEACH. Our house in Rolling Hills had increased in value—I had put my carpentry skills to work and remodeled it with a bedroom for Kurt between the house and the garage—so we knew we could get a good price for it.

Dottie started searching for just the right house: We needed four bedrooms, plus space to park a couple of cars, and we wanted to be right on the beach. After looking at dozens of properties, we found the perfect place in Hermosa, eight miles northwest of Rolling Hills. The lots in Hermosa are all 30-feet wide, and this house had been built on a lot and a half. With a lot of juggling, we could make the move if we did not do any remodeling for the first year.

It was a real thrill for me the first morning to go surfing right in front of my own house, something that I would do whenever there was any surf for the next few years. But trying to raise three children on the beach in Hermosa in the 1960s was not an easy task. It was an era of drugs, when wannabe surfers would bring their surfboards back from Baja hollowed out and filled with contraband. This was before drug-detecting dogs and the surveillance we see today.

Other trends had started there, too. A surfing friend, Don Guild, whose father owned the local drugstore, told me, "This guy keeps trying to sell me some bun boards to sell in my store. They are painted red, and one-half of a pair of metal roller skates are screwed on the bottom." The bun boards had been used in a local bakery but were worn out from spending too much time in a hot oven. Don finally bought a half a dozen of them and sold them for $9.95 each. The six boards sold quickly and more would follow, as surfers started riding what were the first skateboards in the South Bay in about 1957.

My family spent many years living in Hermosa and dodging the ever-more-efficient skateboarders. Many of the best skateboarders were in the surfboard shops working for surfboard-marketing gurus Dale Velzy, Hap Jacobs, Bing Copeland, Dewey Weber, and Greg Noll. Noll had a batch of innovative surfboard-manufacturing ideas. He would make several hundred surfboards every week in a bunch of garages right alongside a half-dozen almost-50-year-old oil wells that had been slant drilled under Hermosa. Noll was also busy producing a new feature-length surfing movie every year. When I had my office in Palos Verdes, Greg hired me to help him edit a couple of his films. I charged him twice what I could earn as a carpenter, or $4.50 an hour. I helped him primarily with his narration, in the comedy sequences, and in smoothing out the flow of his films.

Two Hermosa brothers, Bob and Bill Meistrell, founded a company to improve and manufacture the wet suit. When it hit the market, hard-core surfers appeared wherever there were waves, as far north as Alaska, the Pacific Northwest, New England, and even many beaches in England full of freezing cold water but big surf. The sport grew enormously, just because surfers could stay warm.

Another one of our favorite ocean pastimes was sailing our Pacific Catamaran, a beauty that Carter Pyle had designed and started selling commercially in 1960. It was 20 feet long, with 350 square feet of sail and a 500-square-foot spinnaker. It had enough power in the sail so that when the wind blew in the 15- to 20-mile-per-hour range, we were fast enough to tow a water-skier. My son Scott, at the age of 10, started crewing for me, and in three seasons we managed to work our way up from the back of the fleet to second in the National Championships in the class. There were almost 50 P-Cats in those championship races.

I took my Pacific Catamaran to San Onofre one weekend to try to ride the waves, just as I had done for years on my surfboard. It worked perfectly when the waves were shoulder-high and the wind was blowing at just the right speed and from the right direction. Soon, my friends were lined up on the beach for rides.

One of my passengers that day was surfboard builder Hobie Alter. To the best of my knowledge, it was his first ride in a small cat and his first ride in one on a wave. He soon bought a used Pacific Cat so he could sail off the beach in front of his home in San Juan Capistrano. However, it was too heavy to push across the beach all by himself. With his experience with fiberglass, the rest is history: a super lightweight catamaran with asymmetrical hulls and no centerboards. An asymmetrical hull has one side straight and the other side curved. He initially made each hull in a slightly different shape, and as he reached back and forth in front of his house, one of the hulls, either port or starboard, performed more efficiently through the water, so he kept the fastest hull and made another different-shaped hull to replace the slower one. I don't know how many different hulls he made, but when the smoke settled, he had created the Hobie 14. It was a great single-handed boat that was followed by the Hobie 16, because a lot of people wanted to sail with their girlfriends or wives, and the 14 could only handle one person effectively. Today, there are more than 250,000 sailboats around the world with my eventual next-door-neighbor's name on the sail. Hobie changed the landscape of sailing forever when he invented the Hobie Cat. You could buy a 14-foot Hobie Cat for less than $1,000, and an entire generation of sailors grew up on them. We lived next door to Hobie on Orcas Island, Washington, for more than 20 years before he passed away recently, and still enjoy being next door to his wife, Susan.

The Hobie Cat was created more than 50 years ago, and it has taken that long for the rest of the sailing world to wake up to how great catamarans are. The America's Cup was finally raced in 72-foot catamarans in 2013. They are capable of speeds as high as 54 mph.

One catamaran highlight for Scott and me occurred at Dana Point before they built the breakwater. Scott was 14 by then, and we rode waves that were tall enough to hide the numbers on the sails hung on a 25-foot mast.

The catamaran was also good for the occasional trip to Catalina with my son Kurt, or often just on my own. I would put my sleeping bag into a plastic garbage bag—adding my Primus stove, some backpacking food, and a gallon of water—and setting out for a few days alone, roaming the island looking for buffalo and goats to photograph—and having the time entirely to myself. Sailing the 22 miles across the channel alone and getting back safely was a real adventure for me.

I was completely and totally free.

CHAPTER FORTY-FIVE

1962–1965

Hiring Key Staff and Finding Our Pier Avenue HQ

WHEN I GOT HOME FROM FILMING IN FRANCE IN THE SPRING OF 1962, I was still in the office in Palos Verdes. This would all change that summer when the second floor of a building became available in Redondo Beach. It was the same building I had worked on as a novice ditchdigger/carpenter for a $1 an hour more than 10 years before.

We suddenly had a lot more room to spread out and get work done. I had the space to hire a couple of ladies who could do almost anything connected with the business. We needed several more electric typewriters and a dictating machine, and we used them relentlessly.

Our new salesman, Art Lawson, and cameraman Don Brolin made a big difference in the company's success. I had met Art Lawson on a Sugar Bowl film shoot; he was doing the resort's PR, plus tending bar in his spare time. He had been a suit salesman in Dayton's Department Store in Detroit and was more interested in partying than skiing, but he could really sell, so I offered him a job as my first salesman. When the season was over, he moved to Redondo Beach with his wife and a guaranteed salary of $500 a month, plus a 10-percent commission on any orders for my films he was able to sign up. It was one of the smartest moves I ever made. Within two years, Art was taking home more money every month than I was. That meant the company was also making more money. The film business was growing like crazy when he suggested that I hire a friend of his from Sugar Bowl, Don Brolin.

Don had a good eye for compositions for still photos, and because he was currently doing the PR work for Sugar Bowl, he knew how the system worked. There was, however, one major problem: He did not even know how to thread up a 16-MM camera, much less use it. Art suggested that I send Don a camera and half a dozen rolls of film and see what he could do with it. I asked him to shoot a movie on Junior Bounous' ski-instruction techniques.

Don did a great job with camera angles and creativity, except for one thing—his exposures were so far off I had to make a full aperture print of his film and then make a full aperture print of the print in order to see it. I gave him a job regardless. Don started at $400 a month and showed up at work in a suit and vest, driving a sports car that had not seen a car wash in months. He was smart enough to park it down the street until he settled in and washed it.

The first time Don ran a camera alongside of me, I had picked him up at Art's house at 4:30 A.M. to go film a sequence at San Gorgonio. It was almost a three-hour drive to get to where we parked the car. Then it was a one-hour climb to the bottom of the ski hill that we had to climb for every shot. By the end of the day, Don was tired, and by the time we got back to my car, he got his boots off and fell into the backseat. He was asleep before I started the car to make the three-hour drive back to Redondo Beach. He was in the office at 8 the next morning, bright and shiny and very sunburned, and we got under way on a 35-year-long ski adventure.

Don traveled all over the world for most of those years, getting the great shots for which I received all of the credit. As we started to hire other cameramen, Don and I trained them with one rule: If you are not the first person in the lift line in the morning, with your camera gear and your skiers, someone else will get to cut up the untracked powder snow first.

Meanwhile, Art was so busy he needed his own secretary. As his 10-percent commission on all of his sales began to approach what I was taking out of the company as a salary (as much as $1,000 each month), I did not quite know how to handle it—until I realized that if he made that many sales, the company could buy more and better equipment to make more and better movies. Sometimes I wondered if I had a brain big enough to keep making the whole thing work.

In 1965, I finally hired a full-time bookkeeper/office manager. Juanita McVey was an awesome lady who kept the books (and me) on the straight and narrow for 15 years.

ONE DAY—WHEN THE COMPANY HAD BEEN WORKING OUT OF THE second story of the building in the Hollywood Riviera, Redondo Beach, for two or three years—a neighborhood friend who sold real estate called me about a good deal on a piece of property on Pier Avenue, the main road into Hermosa from the Pacific Coast Highway.

The property had two storefronts, with large plate-glass windows and room to expand into an alley in the back. It was also zoned for a second story and had parking for four cars. Juanita told me we could probably handle the purchase, because the company had been under her strict financial controls and was back on its feet after the embezzlement.

The building had been the headquarters for the South Bay Real Estate Association and was only half a block from the post office. It had a lot of glass looking out on the street, and I was a little worried my male employees would be distracted by the bikini-clad young ladies on their way to the beach for a day of sun, fun, and the start of some incidental melanoma.

To half of the building, we added a second story that was more than a bit larger than the law allowed. We also built a cinder-block fireproof film vault that took four years to fill up with original film from the feature and many contract films we would make, all protected in a climate-controlled environment.

That second summer, Don Brolin had gone to Australia and New Zealand to spend three or four weeks gathering "down-under" footage. He had switched from a Bell & Howell camera to composing his shots through the lens of a Bolex. Neither one of us realized that a Bolex had a different distance from lens to film than a Bell & Howell. Almost all of Don's entire trip was out of focus and wasted.

CHAPTER FORTY-SIX

1962

"Around the World on Skis" Is a Very Long Trip

WHILE PRODUCING "AROUND THE WORLD ON SKIS" IN 1962, I FINALLY realized I had to take that 24,901 mile trip around the world myself. It is a long, long trip, particularly when you are riding in a minimum-space coach seat.

We had to find a babysitter for our three kids for the month, but first there was the need to secure a couple of airplane tickets for the trip. My amazing friend, Stan Washburn, supplied the two tickets for Dottie and me on Pam Am. Stan was a certified marketing genius. He received half of his salary from Pan American and the other half from J. Walter Thompson, Pan American's advertising agency.

For our first stop in Japan, my plan was to document Shiga Heights. It's one of the country's premier resorts within a short train ride of Tokyo, with some 20 ski resorts (including Nagano, which would host the 1998 Olympics). It was easy to get a lot of fun stuff for the comedy portion of the new film, especially the chairlifts with miniature seats for all of the small people. There were no backs to the chairs because almost everyone wore a rucksack with their lunch in it, which usually consisted of a large rice ball wrapped in seaweed with a center of some sort of seafood, either raw or barely cooked.

In Shiga Heights, I showed my film with the help of a Japanese interpreter. I backed up the time for my normal narration, so she could translate it in her head and deliver the Japanese narration at almost exactly the right time and get the same laugh the film got in Buffalo or any other American city. There were about 200 people sitting on tatami mats watching the film. When it was over, while I was rewinding the film, none of the people left but just tipped over and started to fall asleep. By the time I finished packing up everything, half of the 200 people had gone to sleep right where they had been sitting and laughing at my movie. It was a bit weird: my first experience with a Bed, Breakfast, and Movie joint.

OUR NEXT STOP WAS HONG KONG. WE WANDERED AROUND FOR THREE days with my movie camera in hand, taking very few pictures. It was so hypnotizing to watch the organized chaos that I just plain forgot why I was there. For example: watching, but not filming, Chinese workers with baskets of about 75 pounds of wet concrete balanced on their heads climbing up steps on a bamboo scaffold to the 23rd floor, dumping their heavy load of concrete into the forms for the high-rise building, getting their chit in exchange for their load, and then walking back down to the ground for another 75-pound load. The entire 24-story scaffold was made out of bamboo that was lashed together with some raffia.

We later sat in the same miniature airplane seats while traveling from Hong Kong to Munich. It seemed as though this part of the journey took at least 953 hours to complete. We were both exhausted, but we picked up our next VW Bug and drove from Munich to Grindelwald, Switzerland, with its unbelievable scenery. There, exhaustion and a Hong Kong superbug knocked me out and forced me to spend four days in bed, getting help from the hotel doctor when he finished his day shift at the local hospital.

Words cannot describe the stunning beauty of Grindelwald, the two nearby resorts of Wengen and Murren, and the treacherous North Face of the Eiger rising almost 9,000 vertical feet above the town, almost as vertical as a kitchen wall. When I was finally able to get out of my sickbed and onto my skis, I met Art Furrer for the first time. He was a freestyle pioneer with his never-before-seen acrobatic turns and stunts. Art appeared in many of my movies during the next decade or more.

I was able to purchase a bit of the culture that made this part of

Switzerland so famous. In a gift shop in Kleine Scheidigg, there were a couple of wood carvings that I suddenly coveted, but I didn't want to tip my hand and watch the price go up. I wandered around in the store aimlessly and kept my eye on the door to the shop. When a man who looked like the owner left for lunch, I asked the young lady attending the store if one of the wood carvings was for sale. The carving was very dusty, and she had to get a stepladder to get it down from its long-forgotten shelf. It was delicately carved from walnut, and the costume of the skier placed it right around 1900.

The carving was 24 inches high, and the skier was doing a perfect telemark turn while wearing Bilstein leather bindings, soft leather boots, pistol-barrel pants with wraparound leggings, and a turtleneck sweater with a button-down shawl collar. The wood carving is so accurate that the skier's little finger is cocked at just the right angle to make him look relaxed and in control. As I looked at the walnut carving, the young lady said, "There is also a statue of a lady behind the man. Would you be interested in her as well?" The lady skier/statue was in a full-length dress, with very long skis over her shoulder and a small rucksack on her back. She was also carrying a long, heavy pole that was very strong and designed with a cone-shaped piece of wood on the end, so you could put it between your legs as it dragged in the snow behind you, and you could sit down on it and slow down your speed.

I had long admired the delicate craftsmanship of the early Swiss carvers. I was afraid to ask the price, thinking it would be at least $500. That is what it would have been worth to me back then.

The clerk finally turned the statue upside down, and there was the price written in chalk: $26, American. I said, "The tip of one of the skis is broken off. I will pay you $23 right now." I closed the deal when she said, "What about the lady?" Based on the price of the larger statue, I bought the statue of the lady for $4.

Back at the hotel, I had the concierge hire a carpenter to build strong wooden boxes to ship my new treasures home. They sat on my office desk for many years, and almost everyone who visited me wanted to buy them. They were not for sale at any price. Years later a client said, "Why don't you find a foundry and have a lost-wax casting made of them, and I will buy a set of them."

I didn't do it then, but later we did a find a foundry to make copies. Over the years, we have shared sets of these statues with others who appreciated their authenticity and beauty, in a limited number of bronze castings of 50 each.

CHAPTER FORTY-SEVEN

1964–1966

"Buy Low, Sell High," or Vice Versa

BILL JANSS, THE MAN WHO GAVE ME MY FIRST SKI LESSON AT YOSEMITE'S Badger Pass, and his brother Ed bought Sun Valley in 1964 from the Union Pacific Railroad for a reported $4.5 million. That included 4,000 acres of the land, the ski lifts, all of the buildings, and the rolling stock. It was great to see him again and, of course, I reminded him that he had taught me how to do a proper snowplow turn. Our friendship resumed just as though we were back at Badger Pass 20 years earlier.

That Christmas, I drove the 900 miles to Sun Valley from Hermosa Beach. I would once again show my most recent film and document the latest happenings at Sun Valley for the next year's film. By now, we had to show the film for three nights to handle the demand. After some soft selling, I persuaded Bill Janss that he needed a four-season film to truly sell the sizzle of the place.

In 1965, he installed the first Warm Springs lift, but it would not be until early summer of 1970 that I took off from the Santa Monica airport with Bill in his small plane to start the Four Seasons movie, designed to promote the year-round appeal of the resort. Sun Valley is one of the most beautiful summer resorts in the world, and my camera, along with Don

Brolin's later in the summer, showed it at its best. When the editing, scripting, and musical score were finished, I was proud of the work and flew up to show it to Bill. Almost no changes were necessary, except for a few words in the script.

The first time Bill showed the film to the Johns Manville Corporation, he sold all the land that became Elkhorn for $4.5 million, the amount he originally paid for all of Sun Valley. The film expanded my resume beyond ski movies into marketing films.

In 1966, Bill announced his purchase of the Snowmass ranch and his plan to develop it into a ski resort right next door to Aspen Highlands and Aspen. My camera and I spent a couple of days skiing and filming it in a snowcat, and the opinion of everyone in the group was that it was too flat for fun. How wrong they were, but this was the opinion of a testosterone-laden group of good skiers with enough money behind them to spend the winter in Aspen. They all wanted to become famous in front of the 16-MM hand-wound camera that I was operating.

Snowmass was just the right degree of difficulty for the majority of skiers, and it would eventually host more skiers than the other three Aspen areas combined. The original, ski-in, ski-out condominiums that were built there sold out very quickly. Bill told me one day that he had all of the ski lifts built and ready to go, but he had decided not to run them for another year because he wanted more infrastructure first: restaurants, ski shops, and places to just hang out. Was he right in sacrificing a whole year of lift ticket sales because there were not enough places to eat? Works fine if you have very deep pockets.

YOU DON'T ENTER THE SKI FILMMAKING BUSINESS TO MAKE MONEY, AT least not with me running the show. I am now fortunate to be financially well off, mostly because of a few smart real estate investments. My one big real estate blunder was back in the late 1960s, when I bought prime property on the soon-to-boom access road to Mammoth Mountain. The land turned out to be on an earthquake fault and worthless.

In the late 1970s, I asked Bill if he had a bastard piece of land at Sun Valley that he could sell to me at a good price so I could build a small house on it for my retirement years. I had no real ties to any place on the planet at the time and still had good memories of Sun Valley.

The next thing I knew, we were walking over 11 acres on the Ketchum side of Dollar Mountain. I thought it would be an ideal place to put down roots and was able to structure a deal with Bill that I could afford. It was during the high-interest-rate days of Jimmy Carter, and the property had a couple of obstacles. I would have to build a bridge over an irrigation ditch and put in the street, curbs, underground utilities—water, electricity, telephone, cable TV, and sewers. Not a cheap undertaking, and I made up my mind I would not do any development unless I could pay cash for it.

The bridge was the first obstacle after the survey, and by today's numbers, it was cheap at $25,000. It was three or four years before I had enough cash to pay for the development of the property sufficiently to offer a lot for sale. I had 11 of them to sell, and that was a lot of money that could go back into my bank account as the project progressed. Since I had generated $4.5 million in real estate sales for Bill with my film, he was generous with this odd piece of property that ran very steeply up the back, or Ketchum side, of Dollar.

After I had financed and built the bridge over the irrigation ditch, the nearby neighbors decided they did not want all of that extra traffic going down their street to get to my subdivision. They were somehow able to get my 11 vacant lots declared an avalanche zone, so it would require massive amounts of money to build avalanche-diversion fences above each vacant lot. I took this position: If an avalanche is diverted and damages a nearby house, then the planning commission and the neighbors will be liable because they required the diversion fence to be built. It was at this point that the neighbors realized their liability and decided that a little traffic was a lot better than a massive lawsuit (and no avalanche had been recorded through all the record-keeping back to 1936, or from the knowledge of any old-timers who had lived there for over 60 years).

I quickly sold my first two lots, which more than paid for the land and the infrastructure. From then on, the value mounted on the property until the final lot sold for many times what I had paid for the entire 11 acres and the development investment, too.

With this success, I thought about switching careers from moviemaking to real estate development, but my desire to share what I was seeing all over the world greatly overshadowed my urge to make a lot of money.

In those days, my motto was (and still is), "Buy low and sell high!" But business for me in reality was more of a "buy high, sell low" proposition. I certainly made more money in real estate than I ever did making ski movies, but making the movies was so much more fun.

CHAPTER FORTY-EIGHT

1960s

Network TV Hires a Small Hermosa Beach Film Company

A LOT WAS HAPPENING ON A DAILY AND SOMETIMES HOURLY BASIS. THE film business was booming, as Don Brolin got better coverage of ski resorts with each one he filmed. I was still on the road a lot, running a camera or doing a close-up and personal sales job. Despite all the travel I did, Dottie didn't complain. I know I missed the kids and life on the beach, but the overhead was always about equal to the income, and I could not sit around. Dottie had her teacher's credentials but never taught after we got married, a situation that is rare today, when most wives help with the family income and most husbands take a greater role with raising children, a much healthier approach.

I had hired a very reliable East Coast cameraman, Rod Allin, and we stayed a team for many years. Rod filmed one of the best comedy sequences ever, of Rudi Wyrsch falling off a chairlift, stumbling up a rope tow, and being run over by a snowcat. Rudi would later do a European film tour with my latest film, narrating it in German.

Rod spent his non-ski time in the summer working for a wild animal TV show. One winter when he showed up, his wooden tripod was all scratched and beaten up. He explained, "Those are where the polar bear got his teeth into the movie, but I did get some good close-ups before we opened up with our pepper spray." Rod eventually moved his wife and family to Jackson Hole, where he would visit occasionally between his many days of location shooting. Rod was one of a half-dozen great photographers who had an addiction to Kodachrome and what can be done to put images down on it.

In another great comedy sequence years later, David Butterfield filmed Buddy Levy as "Magneto Man" in Sun Valley, dressed in a tinfoil suit. Buddy did a great job pretending to be magnetized and therefore attracted to metal—or it to him. He was hilarious when he skied into the chairlift towers and his ski poles flew up to stick to them. He was also very good when he skied into the river in Sun Valley, under the Warm Springs lift. Many years later Don Brolin put them all together in a short film, "Men of Steel, Wings of Wood."

In the spring of 1964, my company was able to invite several world-class skiers to the annual Silver Belt Giant Slalom the last weekend of April at the Sugar Bowl on Donner Summit, California. The 1964 Olympics at Innsbruck had come and gone, and commercialism of ski racing was loosening up. Quite a few racers were getting equipment and money under the table, but if caught they would no longer be "amateurs." It was at the Innsbruck Olympics when Edward Scott unveiled his lightweight ski poles at the same time as Peter Kennedy. However, Scotty showed up in advance of the start of the alpine events with a trunk full of his new poles. Some of the medal winners used Scott poles at no cost as advertising—and because the poles were so good, it would have been foolish not to use them. Today, some Olympic skiers get high-six-figure dollars to use a certain piece of equipment.

Scott was the last of the true independent individuals in ski equipment manufacturing. I knew him well from my Sun Valley parking lot days, when he was a ski repairman for Pete Lane. He was good at it, and while he was looking for a permanent place to live after leaving the sanctuary of Union Pacific Railroad employment at Sun Valley, I rented him space for his sleeping bag on my $5-a-month garage floor in Ketchum: no running water, very little heat, and he had to furnish his own slop bucket and dispose of its contents every morning at least six blocks away from the garage—my rules, because I only charged him 50 cents a night's rent. His next move was to rent a small storefront and open a ski shop; he was really good at splicing broken skis back together. Scotty went on to make a lot of money on his lightweight ski poles, and then he lost a lot of it trying to market ski boots that were so lightweight they kept breaking.

Bud Palmer had a great TV show going with a variety of sporting events, including a hot-air balloon race across the Alps. He agreed to use the Silver Belt race film for a show if I did all of the production. For the first time, I was able to open up network TV's wallet and watch some of the moths fly away in the sunshine. We invited the hot Austrians to the race, such as Christian Pravda and Karl Schranz, and America's best, Jimmie Heuga and Billy Kidd, as well as Buddy Werner. We would pay all of their expenses, and all they had to do was show up and race to win. "We" of course, meant Bud Palmer's production budget and definitely not mine.

Two weeks before the race, Buddy Werner, the first American to win the famous Hahnenkamm downhill in Kitzbuehel, Austria, was killed in an avalanche while skiing in a movie in St. Moritz, Switzerland, for Willy Bogner. This tragic accident altered the entire mood of the Silver Belt race, and we decided to change the name that year to the Buddy Werner Memorial Race.

While we were getting ready for the race, Bob Beattie, the coach of the U.S. Olympic Ski Team, had flown to Switzerland to accompany Buddy Werner's body back to Steamboat Springs, Colorado, where he was born and raised. When Bob finally got to the Sugar Bowl, he set some time aside for an interview. Before we got through with it, we both choked up and cried.

In filmmaking, anything can go wrong, and it always does at the worst time. A soundman I had used dozens of times before taped the interview. This time he sent the wrong voltage to the recorder from his battery belt, and we had to scrap the entire interview.

Also during our race-prep time, Don Brolin showed what he was capable of when he organized the First Annual Gelandesprung and Falling Contest. Our company put up a generous, for us, $50 first prize for the best crash and another $50 for the most ridiculous jump. It was hard to believe what some of these people were doing just to try to win $50 and at the same time tell all of their friends that they might appear in one of my movies.

When race time came, we hired four extra cameramen, and everyone's footage worked well. When the shoot was over, we all returned to Southern California and started editing the Bud Palmer TV special. Bud flew to Los Angeles, we put a small crew together, and then we went up to a snow patch in the nearby San Bernardino Mountains to do more interviews and segues with Bud standing in the snow.

To get ahead of the labor curve, we edited the film before Bud came back to Hermosa to narrate the show two weeks later, using my normal feature-film format. That was a major mistake. Bud did not like our editing job, so we had to reconstruct the entire show in the format he wanted. We had Bud for an extra week as a guest, sunbathing in the sand and swimming in front of our beach house while I supervised the editing of his show in exactly the format he wanted. He would come by the office whenever we had a sequence done for his approval. The company's hard work and long hours at the film-editing bench led to Bud hiring our company to produce another one-hour TV special.

This one would be a car race, the Pikes Peak Hill Climb, an exciting race from Colorado Springs to the end of the narrow road near the summit of Pikes Peak. It started at 4,712 feet and ended at 14,000 feet, with 156 curves over a distance of 12 miles. Some of those curves are 360-degree turns, and all of them are at an average grade of 7 percent. Some places in the road were covered with asphalt and others with gravel. This is a dangerous road, where a mistake can mean a flight through space on the downhill side of the road. We could not tolerate a mistake of any kind, because there was no chance for a second take. Adding to the challenge, we were covering the entire race with our hand-wind Bell & Howell cameras without zoom lenses.

Unfortunately, this was the first time in my 40 years of life I had ever felt the dizziness of oxygen deprivation. I was leaning against a small tree when I blacked out and almost fell down. Regardless, we were able to get the footage we needed. In fact, this Bud Palmer TV show worked even better because we had learned from the first experience about what he wanted. Filmmaking is indeed a lifelong work in progress if you have a passion to make each film better than the one before it.

Another roundabout development in our television breakthrough started in 1963—the second year Vail was in operation. I was following a man down to the double chairlift at the bottom of the Back Bowls when he fell into a big tree well. He put out both of his hands, they slipped off the tree trunk, and he hit his forehead as he fell against the tree. "Are you hurt?" someone asked. He said, "No, I just have a small cut on my forehead from my glasses."

While helping him up, I saw no obvious cuts or blood. He did, however, have a small twig about an inch long and about half the diameter of a pencil sticking out of his forehead—there was no blood, but there was a clear liquid that was slowly oozing out around the small wound. Instinctively I knew that this was a serious situation, and the closest ski patrolman was at the top of the ski lift.

The man with the twig sticking out of his forehead got on the lift with me. No one dared put a bandage on his head, not knowing how long the twig was. As we got on the lift, he and I put our four ski poles across both of our laps in case he passed out on the way up. I had never seen a wound like this before. The ski patrol met us at the top, and he was eventually ambulanced to Denver, where surgeons removed the small tree branch from his forehead. It had apparently slipped through the center of his brain between the folds. The only permanent damage was his loss of taste and smell.

The man and I became telephone friends, and it was then that I learned he was DeWalt "Pick" Ankeny, the chairman of the board of the Hamm's Brewing Company. He graciously offered me a five-year supply of free beer for my help on the chairlift ride. Kind of him, but I don't drink beer, unless it's root beer.

A year or so later, he filed a lawsuit against Vail, claiming they should have cut down that almost 4-foot-diameter tree. I was subpoenaed and questioned in three different cities by three different attorneys while traveling with my film the next winter. Each time I was questioned under oath, I told the same story: That it was a skiing accident, and Vail had nothing to do with it. He wasn't trying to get rich off Vail; he was simply angry that he never received a phone call or a get-well card from anyone in Vail management and assumed that they didn't care. Sadly, that kind of gracious consideration is all but gone in the world today because we've become so litigious and people think that it would represent fault. But it would go a long way to easing certain situations.

Within two years, Hamm's was the main sponsor of our weekly television show. Our show was broadcast in 47 different markets in one season, and all of those shows required their own 16-MM color print.

As a result, Art Lawson, Don Brolin, and I had come up with what we thought was a good idea. Why not offer our films to TV markets in trade for two of the commercial spots? There are seven one-minute commercial spots in a half-hour show, or at least that was the way it was in the 1960s and 1970s. They could have five of the seven spots to sell, and Art Lawson would sell the other two spots to add to our income stream. The formula was a good deal for everyone. We were making the shows out of outtakes that did not fit in the annual feature-length film, and would have otherwise gone to waste. In his sales pitch, Art simply used the fact that if it worked for a top brand such as Hamm's, it should be good enough for the company he was hustling at the time.

CHAPTER FORTY-NINE

1960s

Thinking I Could Compete with Hollywood Was Another Big Mistake

DURING THE MID-1960S, ANOTHER DOCUMENTARY FILMMAKER, BRUCE Brown, roared onto the silver screen with a blockbuster surfing movie called "The Endless Summer." Bruce traveled around the world with a couple of surfers, Mike Hynson and Robert August, looking for the perfect wave. He had great success showing his documentary to surfing audiences stretched along the East and West coasts of the U.S. With no shows in the middle of winter, a friend of his, Paul Allen, took the film to Wichita. In the middle of a snowy, windswept January, Paul rented a theater and showed the film. On opening night, it was reported that one person showed up to see the giant surf of Makaha, Hawaii, but the word got around and by the end of the week it was standing room only. In the spring, Paul and Bruce rented a small theater in New York City called Kips Bay to show the film.

They had the promotional help of Bud Palmer, who had done a one-hour TV show using some of Bruce's surfing footage. At the time, Bud was the official greeter for New York City, representing the mayor. Bud invited some of his inside friends to the movie, and the rest is history. *TIME* magazine and every other publicity outlet saw the movie because of Bud. The reporters wrote great stories about the film, and it ran continuously in Kips Bay for a year to turn-away crowds. Bruce had good off-the-wall, laid-back narration and made enough money on that one film to retire for life. He eventually made a second film about motorcycle racing with Steve McQueen. "On Any Sunday" was also a great success, not only because it was very good, but it was up close and personal.

Based on Bruce Brown's success with "The Endless Summer" in the off-season, a New York film distributor got the idea that he could do the same thing with my film by having a world premiere on a hot July night at the World's Fair in Montreal in 1967. The distributor started hounding me in the winter of 1966. I believed his sales pitch and was happy with the large amount of upfront money he was willing to pay me to enlarge the film into 35-MM, create an original musical score, and also get some shots of Jean-Claude Killy racing at Jackson Hole, Wyoming, in the spring. The promoter insisted that the premiere would be at the World's Fair in Montreal in early July, and then he would open the ski film in New York City near the end of July while it was still above 90 degrees.

Ever since being denied entry into the glee club in the third grade, I've accepted that I have no ear for music, though I love classical music. The original music the promoter contracted for the theatrical version of my 16-MM movie was, in a word, terrible. I was sold a bill of goods that theatergoers, as opposed to high school auditorium crowds, had different tastes, and the music would work very well. The Montreal show was a success because the promoter had invited the Canadian Ski Team members and all of their friends at no charge.

After the show, the promoter told me I had to cut the film by 10 minutes, the exact length I had added to squeeze in Killy's last-minute appearance. Dottie had traveled to Montreal with me, and the next day we all flew down to New York City for the premiere. Now I had a gut feeling that I had made a major mistake. We were greeted at LaGuardia by the standard black-suited guy holding up a card with the promoter's name on it. An hour later, the guy returned with the information that there were so many limousines in the parking lot that he could not find his. The promoter, Dottie, and I all wedged into the same cab, along with our luggage, and started to get set for the American premiere of the film that I had shown all over America the previous fall and winter before to a full house, but back then, with different music, my choice of music. The promoter rejected my suggestion of booking a smaller theater, nor would he have anything to do with Bud, a major mistake.

I appeared on two talk shows, including Johnny Carson's. The promoter offered free admission to anyone who came to the opening matinee in their ski clothes, which attracted one senior citizen and his two grandchildren, wearing Tyrolean hats and lederhosen. They got to watch the movie all by themselves. It picked up a little bit for the evening show, with a couple of ski writers in attendance. (Of course, they came for free.)

Speaking with both of them after the show, they told me how much they had enjoyed the movie. However, in their newspaper columns the next day, they blasted the film, and they had every right to do so. It was not a Hollywood-type production. The films had been made for a select audience, who owned skis and used them every chance they got. Everything about the theatrical experience was a total disaster—financially as well as creatively. Dottie was so distraught with the bad publicity that doctors were able to trace her sudden partial blindness to the stress of realizing that her husband was not the wonderful filmmaker she thought he was. She was diagnosed by the doctors at the Jules Stein Eye Institute at UCLA with a traumatic stress disorder that affected one of her eyes.

Thinking I could compete with Hollywood was another one of the biggest mistakes I made in the business. I had started to believe what the newspapers were saying about my work. In the back of my brain was the naïve thought that if Bruce Brown could walk away with $7 million of profit from his one film, I should be able to walk away with at least $1 million. I was totally wrong. Not only did I not walk away with any money, the promoter refused to pay me the second half of the upfront money. The contract I foolishly signed contained a clause that I could not show another ski film while he was exhibiting his. It was another terrible time for me financially, not to mention emotionally.

The only way I could produce and show the next year's film was to forget the second half of his payment, which was in the high five figures. I was flat broke once again. I still had my film company overhead with rent and seven full-time employees, a wife, three kids, and a beach house to pay for every day.

We were barely surviving on the 15-minute film rental business, and I was still sending the films for free to entertain the troops fighting in Vietnam—it was the least we could do for them. A letter arrived one day from PFC Michael Golaveri of Cape Cod, with his photo enclosed. After watching one of my ski movies in Vietnam and consuming a few too many beers, he had my ski-bum company logo tattooed on his upper right arm. In a letter to me, he wrote that he would never be able to earn the right to wear the pin by skiing in one of my movies, but he could wear it on his body the rest of his life.

CHAPTER FIFTY

1960s

The Kennedys Come to Sun Valley, and to My Camera

WHILE MY KIDS WERE YOUNG IN THE MID-1960S, WE WERE STILL GOING to Sun Valley for every Christmas holiday. Jackie Kennedy, Bobby, Ted, and all of their untold collective number of children also came for a long Christmas ski vacation.

Jackie wore a pair of the brand-new, over-the-boot ski pants. Within a week, those pants drew enough worldwide press to make every pair of in-the-boot stretch pants in every ski shop in the world obsolete. Ski boots were getting so big then that they looked bulky and ugly, and over-the-boot pants eliminated that.

During this same vacation, Bobby also made his own fashion statement. The lodge dining room during that era required coats and neckties for the male guests. A tieless Bobby was refused entrance one evening, and he asked the maître d', "Do you know who I am?" The maître d' replied, "Yes, I do, Mr. Kennedy, and I make the rules in my dining room. No necktie, no dinner."

Bobby left, and when he came back to eat at the head of a very large dinner table, he did have on a necktie, but he came into the dining room barefoot. I've never appreciated people who thumbed their noses at established, socially acceptable behaviors.

Every year Sun Valley had a giant slalom on the Roundhouse hill. I was the only cameraman they let on the course. One day I was hauling John-John up between my legs on the T-bar when the lift suddenly stopped, and there was a security guy in a trench coat with a rifle. He thought I was going to harm John-John, but we quickly cleared up the confusion.

The Kennedy name had enormous power. The following winter, when the bus drivers in Sun Valley went on strike, the Kennedys didn't dare cross the picket lines. So they all got on their private plane and flew to Aspen, where management somehow found beds two days after Christmas.

CHAPTER FIFTY-ONE

1960s

"Is That a Firm Offer?"

DURING THE MID-1960S, I HAD BEEN DRIVING BY AN EMPTY OFFICE building overlooking the ocean in downtown Hermosa Beach and wondering why no one ever occupied it. In the late spring of 1966, I was at a wake when a real estate agent told me the building was for sale. "It's a bargain at $250,000," she said. "It has 42 small, 300-square-foot suites, all with ocean views." I was halfway through my second root beer and acting like a big shot when I said, "It's only worth $100,000."

She replied, "Is that a firm offer?" Still acting like a big shot, I said, "Yes, it is a firm offer until 10 o'clock tomorrow morning."

The real estate agent showed up in my office at 9 the next morning and asked me, "Will you go as high as $125,000?" We walked down to the building and had to break a window to get in and examine it. It was four years old, and only two of the 42 suites had ever been occupied. It had never-been-used carpets and drapes, and was wired for hi-fi speakers throughout.

Downtown Hermosa stores were about 60 percent vacant at the time. J.C. Penney had moved out, the Guild Drug store was leaving after 30 years, and only one clothing store remained. A couple of restaurants had survived yet another long winter—but bars were still abundant. In short, downtown Hermosa was really in the dumpster. My thinking was that if I could find a master tenant to fill up the building, there might be enough bodies to buy lunches in the restaurants and clothes in the men's store, and the new employees just might turn downtown around.

I gambled. An escrow was opened for 90 days with $1,000, and I started to look for a master tenant for the building. Fate was on my side, because just before I made the offer, there was a small earthquake that had slightly damaged the headquarters for the South Bay Union High School District's administration. Once I signed them up, they would be a State of California, government tenant, and the building would go off the tax rolls. Plus, they had their own maintenance crew. It was just a matter of giving them a deal they could not refuse.

My monthly payments would be $1,000, and if I rented them the building for 10 cents a square foot, I would be clearing a couple of hundred dollars a month. That would take care of any expenses above the low-interest loan I negotiated with the savings-and-loan company that had repossessed it from two different previous bankrupt owners.

While our company would happily remain in our Pier Avenue offices, I called on my team to help out with this side project. My ace salesman Art Lawson was a great bartender in his former life, so he set up a generous party for all of the high school employees on the third floor of the building with its fabulous ocean view. The party started an hour and a half before sunset, so we could walk around with the most important employees and show them where they could position their desks to see the ocean. Don Brolin and I handled this, while Art made sure that our guests' cocktail glasses remained potent and always full. At sunset, the administrator and I shook hands on a deal. The next morning, my attorney drew up the lease. I had no idea at the time where I would get the other $4,000 to get the building out of escrow and take ownership.

Within a month, the new tenants wanted to install their telephone switchboard, and I could not let them do it because I didn't yet own the building and was scrambling to find the money to close escrow. I finally filled my real estate agent in on the problem, and she said, "Look, I want to get my commission on the sale so I will loan you the other $4,000 to close escrow. You get your building, you sign a note to me for $4,000, I get my commission on selling a $125,000 building, I'll give you two years to pay me my $4,000 back, and everybody is happy."

The tenants stayed five years before they completed their own shiny, new headquarters for $4 million of local taxpayers' money. Over the years, the building was nearly always full because I set the rent 10 percent below any other office space in that part of the world. Each suite was only 300 square feet with an outside door, a perfect design for people just starting a business.

I should call this time in my life the real estate era. I was able to exercise some good deals in local real estate, but at the same time, the next ski film had to be filmed, edited, scripted, put to music, and booked in a 100 different markets that I would, once again, visit personally. The number of cities that would book the voice-recorded show went way over the 200 mark. We were also renting the film for the season to a dozen resorts, including Aspen, Vail, and Sun Valley, for $1,000 each. They were given permission to show it as often as they wanted.

Don Brolin had become good enough with his camera and storytelling eye that I decided to send him to Europe instead of my going there and taking another month out of my already overbooked life and away from my three children. Europe had a very bad snow year, so I sent him off with the thought, "If he comes back with good film images, he has a job as long as he wants it." It lasted for 35 years.

CHAPTER FIFTY-TWO

1963

The Governor and the Dangling Easter Eggs

It was 1963, my second season of skiing and filming Le Oueff at La Flegere in Chamonix. I had named the gondola cars the "Dangling Easter Eggs" in my ski film, which had just been shown in theaters across the U.S. Each brightly colored gondola carried three passengers and was shaped just like an egg. The lift went up the south-facing side of the valley to one of the world's most spectacular mountain views: the massive icefalls of 15,000-foot Mt. Blanc's North Face.

I had returned to rendezvous and ski with my new friend, the president of the resort. We met at Le Chapeau restaurant for a standard two-hour French lunch: pommes frites, steak, salad, and introductions all around the table while everyone but me sipped high-budget champagne.

"Warren, I'd like you to meet the Governor."

"Hello, Governor," I replied.

Lots of people in the world are called "governor," so I thought it was no big deal. He was tall, dark-haired, handsome, and had a very beautiful wife. Unfortunately, neither could speak a single word of English, and my French was still limited to being able to say hello and thank you, and of course, to order an omelet.

It was late spring, and because of its southern exposure, the lower section of La Flegere was completely without snow. So I rode down on the gondola with the governor, his wife, and the president of the resort. As we neared the bottom, the president said, "The Governor would like you to come to dinner at his home while you are here in Chamonix."

"Sure, why not?" I replied.

"How about Wednesday night?"

Three days later, after a long day of filming good skiers in corn snow, I took a shower and slathered my face and the top of my bald head with moisturizer to ease the sunburn pain, and then started the very long drive on a very narrow and very winding road down through Megeve to Annecy.

Two hours later, in a wind-driven rainstorm, I arrived on the outskirts of Annecy. There, I located a petrol station that was still open, and with the Governor's address clutched in my wet hand, I used expert sign language to talk to the mechanic. Ten minutes of arm waving later, I was given directions with what appeared to be a certain amount of reverence.

Soon, in my dim headlights through the slanting rain, loomed a big iron gate, probably 40 feet wide and 10 feet high. To the right was a sentry box resembling a phone booth with a peaked roof and no windows. It was painted with 6-inch-wide, slanting, red-and-white candy stripes. Standing out of the rain was a soldier wearing a gold-buttoned coat with epaulettes and holding a heavy rifle with a fixed bayonet. Professionals were guarding this house!

I knew I was in trouble because I was driving a Volkswagen with German plates, and I couldn't speak but a few words of junior-high French.

"S'il vous plait? Le mansion Msr. Governor?"

"Oui."

"Msr. Miller. Le Guest."

"Oui. Oui!"

Marching stiffly to the far side of the gate, he leaned heavily against it and it swung slowly open. The headlights illuminated 600 feet of wide driveway, flanked on either side by immaculately trimmed shrubbery. The brightly lit house, off in the distance, resembled a 47-room luxury hotel I had once stayed in at Geneva.

As I coasted my rent-a-wreck to a stop behind a long line of limousines (nine Citroens, three Mercedes, one Rolls-Royce), I knew I was in trouble. Maybe this guy really is the Governor, and I might be underdressed.

Let's see: I'm wearing a red-and-yellow ski parka over a brown-and-beige tweed suit, a red polka-dot tie, and a nylon wash-and-wear shirt that is sort of pressed. I guess I shouldn't have worn my $2 Army-surplus, sheepskin-lined flight boots, because the sheepskin lining was going to get awfully sweaty at dinner.

I knocked on the massive wood, wrought-iron, and cut-glass front door. When it swung open, I could see a highly polished, marble-floored foyer with a pair of gently curving stairs that were 12 feet wide, one going up each side of the foyer.

The butler, clad in tails and white gloves, was visibly shaken by my appearance. He started talking rapidly in hushed tones of what sounded to me like Norwegian with an Italian accent. He probably thought I had gotten lost and belonged in the youth hostel down by the lake. I couldn't understand a word he was saying. All I knew was he wanted me out of there, and quickly.

"Meester Miller!" a voice shouted from the top of the stairs. It was the Governor, and with him was my friend, the president of the ski lift company. I think they would have both slid down the banister to greet me, if they hadn't been wearing tails.

The ski resort president spoke his junior-high English, and it was then that I learned the formal dinner party was in my honor. It was a payback for all the American skiers I sent to Chamonix to ride the dangling Easter eggs.

"Yes, your host really is the Governor of the Haute-Savoie Province."

"Yes, this is the Governor's mansion."

"Yes, everyone except you is wearing a tux or tails."

"Don't worry, Warren. You are a motion-picture producer from Hollywood, so the other guests expect you to be a little weird,"

"Your clothes are no problem. The Governor has an idea."

I followed the two of them into a large library off the reception area, where the Governor lifted the lid of a walnut and silver chest resting on a beautiful antique table. Inside the chest were half a dozen sashes similar to the one that the Governor was already wearing. They were all different colors: red, green, blue, and white. Alongside the neatly folded sashes were at least two-dozen assorted medals.

The Governor picked out a red sash to go with my red bow tie and ceremoniously draped it over my head so it rested on one shoulder. Then he rummaged around among his many medals, picked out four or five, and, one by one, pinned them on my red sash, starting with the most important medal at the top.

Together we began climbing the winding marble stairway to the Grand Ballroom. On the first landing, I glanced at myself in a full-length mirror and, as I did, I tripped in my Army-surplus, after-ski boots and fell flat on my chest full of medals.

"Yes, I am from California. No, I haven't been drinking."

In a few moments, I would be dining with 12 formally dressed men and 12 elegantly gowned women. I began to walk very carefully in my tall, sheepskin-lined after-ski boots, holding my sunburned head high, and wearing my tweed suit with dignity. My hand-tied red bow tie rested about 12 degrees off the horizontal, and I was proudly wearing my sash of the Order of Napoleon and other medals signifying my many accomplishments: the Legion of Merit; the French Balance of Payments Booster; the Academy of Arts and Crafts Award; and the one with six stars for perfect attendance in soccer camp all through grade school. An incredible gastronomic seven-course dinner was served and enjoyed by all, during which I assumed that most of the laughter was at my expense.

The rain turned to snow as I climbed in altitude during my drive back to Chamonix on a long winding, snow-covered road, and I didn't get to my hotel until about 3 A.M. By previous arrangement, I had to meet three skiers at the "Dangling Easter Egg" lift at 8 A.M. The rainstorm in Annecy also hit Mt. Blanc, and left good powder snow skiing that morning in La Flegere.

The Governor and his wife missed that morning of untracked powder snow, but I found out at lunch that they and their guests had spent another hour and a half together after I left. They were drinking champagne and laughing at the crazy American from Hollywood with his weird tweed suit and polka-dot bow tie.

CHAPTER FIFTY-THREE

1968

Going off a Cliff with the Olympic Triple-Gold Medalist

WITH NO CHANCE OF MAKING A NEW FEATURE FILM IN THE WINTER OF 1967–68 because of my 35-MM, thinking-I-could-compete-with-Hollywood debacle, I was scratching for business. At the New York ski trade show, just after Jean-Claude Killy had won his three gold medals in Grenoble, I was approached by an employee of Mark McCormack's, whose company had just signed on to represent the Frenchman and also contracted with Chevrolet to produce a 13-week television series featuring Killy skiing around the world.

Unfortunately, I was the low bidder, and I got the contract to produce and direct these 13 shows. During the negotiation process, I was invited to Cleveland to meet with Mark. With all of the world-famous athletes the company represented worldwide, including Arnold Palmer and Jack Nicklaus, they were interested in creating an in-house production company to do all of the films. I spent a couple of days in Cleveland and walked out of their offices giddy with excitement when they made an offer to buy my company and have me make all of their sports-celebrity films. Their offer was too high for me to even imagine. I should have thought it out more. I believed people too easily, and nothing was ever put in writing.

The guy I was working with is now dead, and that's what happened to the offer as well.

Time was already too short to get organized to produce the first proposed episode of the series in Portillo, Chile. When the snow did not show up on time, we had to switch to Australia and New Zealand. When I said that it would cost more to go there, I was told, "Don't worry about it. When the series is over, we will make sure that all of the overbudget items are taken care of." I should have worried more and done something about it right away.

Operating under the premise that they were going to buy my company, we pulled out all of the stops to make the films as good as time and snow conditions allowed. We left for New Zealand with a crew of 12, including a soundman, a gaffer (lights), a production manager, two people to haul stuff around, and my son Scott, who was 14 years old and already quite good with a still camera.

We arrived on New Zealand's North Island at Mt. Ruapehu full of enthusiasm and talent, but were met by endless rainy days. You've read about our New Zealand volcano experiences in the opening of this book. When we finished in New Zealand, we flew to Australia, where we were going to make up for lost time, but again the weather did not cooperate. Instead of sunshine and skiing in powder snow, amongst the eucalyptus trees with kangaroos we'd rented bouncing down in the bumps ahead of Jean-Claude and Leo Lacroix, there was lots of rain, set against the backdrop of a muddy village.

While we were filming in Australia, our production manager Larry Morrison had hired an editor to help him edit the New Zealand shows. When we finally got back to Hermosa, I had to quickly write the narration, as well as call Cleveland to get them to make the production payments larger and sooner.

When it came time to preview the first show for McCormack's people and Chevrolet, it was clear that we were producing the movie I had agreed to produce. I would narrate it the same way that I did my feature films. However, they had completely changed their minds, without telling me or negotiating. They wanted Killy's voice instead of mine to narrate. Then the network and Chevrolet suits refused to believe what we had filmed on the active volcano and refused to let us show it without a complete re-edit.

Mark McCormack's rep decided that I was incapable of directing a TV show, so he hired someone I had never met to direct the remaining 11 shows. Never mind that neither McCormack's rep nor the new director had ever been on a pair of skis. I thought I had been hired for a track record of filling 3,000-seat auditoriums with screaming, laughing people, but I was wrong.

Now began the longest marathon of travel and filmmaking in my more than 55-year career. Keeping the cameras running to produce the dozen half-hour shows for the Killy TV Series was an exhausting, expensive, and monumental task.

I gathered my cinematic troops together for a long meeting and assumed the role of director of the second unit, meaning that I was responsible for all of the scenery, travel, ambiance, and ski action for the next 12 ski resorts, stretching from Mammoth in California to St. Moritz in Switzerland. I still had to pay all of the bills, both mine and those of the director they insisted on hiring.

I had hired Paul Ryan, Rod Allin, and Bob Walker to run cameras, with Don Brolin filming and myself directing the ski action. There were highlights: Killy and Lacroix were our houseguests for a couple of days. When the sister of a friend of ours living in San Francisco heard Killy was in town, she immediately flew to Los Angeles, took a taxi to Hermosa Beach, and stood outside our dining-room window watching Killy eat dinner. He had charisma.

The costs were soaring out of sight with the director and the extras. I was also staging parties wherever we went so that we could film the Frenchmen, while the resort VIPs could have their moment to meet and greet. We at least got the crew free lift tickets and a discount on our accommodations.

By now, the word was out that we were doing the TV series, and resort owners were courting me to film at their resorts. We moved on to Vail, and the powder in the Back Bowls was really deep. Resort management kept the runs closed so the slopes would be perfect for our cameras.

I was feeling a little more comfortable getting the shows done in five or six days, but the overhead was still way over budget. I kept getting reassured from Mark McCormack's guy not to worry about the extras: They would make it right when we were done. I was getting dumber with each passing day.

The day after Christmas, I left for Europe with the director in order to show him all of the resorts before the crew arrived a week later. We spent a day at each resort, so he could see the culture and scenic beauty of Grindelwald, Chamonix, Courchevel, St. Moritz, Zermatt, Val d'Isère, and Wengen. Trains ran all night, and we rode a lot of late trains.

Before I'd left for Europe, I made the decision to start up the feature film tour for an October 1969 premier; it needed to happen if I wanted the company to survive. After a long talk with Don and my bookkeeper Juanita, we made the decision that I would have to buy back the theatrical release film that was my previous disaster. I did it by giving up the second payment, a lot of money at the time. Don would not go to Europe with the crew. Instead, he would go on a nonstop trip, filming resorts in the U.S., including Alaska.

I have been asked many times, "Why didn't you just walk away from the project?" One, I had signed a legal contract to produce the shows for a fixed price; two, I was constantly reassured by McCormack's man that I would be reimbursed; three, I trusted the wrong man, who has since passed away; four, I also felt that if I defaulted on a Mark McCormack and Chevrolet contract, I would be sued for everything I owned and then some.

I never watched a single one of the Killy shows after they were completed. By the time we finished, I was so far in debt and so bummed out over the entire process that I just wanted to get on with my life. McCormack's company never did follow up on the verbal offer to buy my film company or make me whole for all the extra expenses I'd incurred. I was beyond bankrupt, but too blind or dumb to know it, probably both.

I still gave the project my full commitment. In St. Moritz, we staged one of the most difficult shots I ever created. There was a T-bar that went over a bridge that went over a road that was wide enough to drive the latest model fire-engine-red Chevrolet Corvette through. The car had been air-freighted to Europe for that purpose.

I had Killy and Lacroix ride up together on the T-bar, and as it crossed over the bridge, the Corvette would pass by underneath. To make it even more complicated and interesting, we rounded up a Swiss ski instructor who could do a backflip on skis as the car passed under the Frenchmen riding up on the T-bar. We chose the right camera angle, so that he would fly over the car and in front of Killy and Lacroix. He would only charge me $500 for each time he did his flip.

I clued everybody in, and as the two rode over the bridge on the T-bar, the Corvette drove under the bridge at exactly the right moment. As my rare good luck would have it, I hollered for the instructor doing the flip, and he did it right over the Corvette and in front of the Frenchmen. There was no need for $500 take number two, and I was able to relax.

The next morning, with the filming complete, I quietly caught the train out of St. Moritz. I feel bad because I never said good-bye to the two Frenchmen and haven't seen much of Killy since then. I'm sorry now that we've not stayed in contact.

When Juanita showed me the total financial chaos, I started selling my filmmaking and business equipment to make the payroll for everyone but me. Three weeks later, the staff of 47 was reduced to only seven people. I left it up to Larry Morrison, my production manager, to start cutting expenses radically while I went to Alaska with Don Brolin to film the Junior National Alpine Championships. By the time we returned, we'd figured out we had enough footage in the can for the next feature film.

While Larry Morrison and Don Brolin were in the editing bays working on that next film, I was scrambling to keep the remnants of the company together to fight, film, and show another day and night.

This was about the time when the Cleveland rep said, in a simple sentence, "If you want your money, sue us." I devised a desperate personal and corporate financial salvation plan. Adding up all of the bills, including the substitute director, I calculated the individual bills to a percentage of the $160,000 Cleveland had stuck me with (this was in 1969 dollars, well more than $1 million today).

I pleaded my case with each creditor personally. "If you want your money immediately, it will force me into bankruptcy, and you might get 15 cents on the dollar. However, until all of these bills are paid, I will only take out of the company for my personal needs the monthly cost of my house mortgage, $500 for gas and any emergency such as the occasional bar of surfboard wax, and food for my wife and children. Whatever money that comes in, I will give you your percentage until every one of you is paid every last cent."

About $50,000 was owed to one vendor, and he made me take out a life insurance policy. It had to be outside the framework of my company, with him as the beneficiary. I was a little nervous, but I had no option.

The total fixed overhead for the company was about $8,000 a month. I had to raise it somehow every 30 days, except February when there were only 28 days to come up with the money.

The only practical solution was to start the annual ski film business all over again after this one-year absence. To do that, a brochure was mailed out to all our venues, ski shops, and ski clubs, saying simply: "Bald head shining, Warren Miller has been busy all winter making a brand new film just for you. Call collect before all of the best dates for your area are taken." Within three weeks, more than 50 percent of my former sponsors were back and ready to show the new film.

My financial solution worked, and a friend of mine who was a young lawyer took my lawsuit against McCormack on a contingency-fee basis. While the lawsuit was moving slowly through the courts, my company was whittling away at the debt.

When we finally went to court almost five years later, the Cleveland rep met me on the courthouse steps. There he reached out, squeezed my forearm very hard, and said very quietly and very slowly with a menacing look in his eyes, "Mr. Miller, I don't think that you should pursue this matter any further. Do you understand me?" I nodded, and then he said he was prepared to settle with a $25,000 payment, a long way from the $160,000 they owed me. I took the deal.

CHAPTER FIFTY-FOUR

1960s

Our Home Theater, and the French Animal House

OUR OFFICE AT 505 PIER AVENUE IN HERMOSA BEACH HAD A 20-FOOT alley on the southwestern side, where the afternoon winds blew in. We soon found out that kids from the junior-high school up the street gathered there to smoke a joint before they went home to do their homework and mow the lawn. My staff alerted me to the fact that the marijuana had started to give them a proximity-high. A little later, the decision was made to buy the alley, put a roof over it, and eventually create a theater. The mortgage company that owned half of the alley and two storefronts to the west said, "Why don't you buy our building and get the other half of the alley that way?"

They arranged the financing for me, and suddenly four storefronts and an alley were mine. About the time this deal was closed, three more adjacent storefronts came up for sale. One of them had a dentist of long standing as a tenant, another had a restaurant, and the third one housed a dog-grooming business—all good tenants, who were afraid that I would immediately raise their rent. What I did instead was tie their rent to the inflationary index, and it became a regularly increasing income that helped pay off the mortgages.

Warren with his daughter, Chris. He traded four $2 tickets to his ski movie for the hat in Montreal in 1960.

WHITE STAG PR PHOTO

Warren's son Scott was already addicted to motion picture production at age 3.

WARREN MILLER PHOTO

Warren with Kurt, Chris, and Scott in 1964 at their beachfront home in Hermosa Beach, California. They were dressed for a wedding.

It was not quite a sold-out house, but 7,200 skiers showed up at the St. Paul arena to see Warren's film, including a newlywed couple who postponed their honeymoon just to see the show.

While narrating 100 shows in 100 nights in 100 different cities (well, almost), Warren uses his downtime to work the phones.

Warren's life-art classes paid off. His hand-painted lithographs of 1947 skiers, clockwise from top left: Jack Reddish, Barney McLean, Toni Matt, and Leon Goodman, with Warren, in the middle.

Warren directing Jean-Claude Killy and Leo Lacroix for the ill-fated TV series, filming in 13 different ski resorts in 13 weeks, from New Zealand to Zermatt. DON BROLIN PHOTO

Warren mailed out this notice to his sponsors that he was returning to the annual film-tour business after the disastrous 35-mm Hollywood tour and the Killy TV series. The response was overwhelmingly positive.

Warren would occasionally cross paths with his ace cameraman Don Brolin (in dark hat), here working on a White Stag promotional film titled "Stein, Stork and the Chick," featuring Stein Eriksen and Warren's daughter, Chris, in Deer Valley.

Warren lured Don away from the Sugar Bowl in 1964, when Don didn't even know how to thread film into a movie camera. They worked together for 35 years, with Warren getting credit for much of the footage Don shot.

WARREN MILLER PHOTO

Warren at the longtime company headquarters, two blocks from the surf in Hermosa Beach, California, where his hundreds of films were stored in a vault.

Warren was always looking for a new angle, whether from in front, alongside, or above.

SUN VALLEY PR PHOTOS

Getting around with a rucksack full of cameras has never been a problem for Warren.

Warren bought this 1931 Model A from Ned Bell of Sun Valley, the original owner, and it played a feature role in the 1977 film "In Search of Skiing." EARL RICKERS PHOTO

Warren's son Kurt drove the boat to third place in a field of 96 in the World Championships J/24 Class in Sydney, Australia, in December 1982. Warren supplied the credit card.

Warren's last surfing expedition at San Onofre in 2010, joined by his two sons, Kurt (left) and Scott. CHRIS MILLER PHOTO

It happened in Sun Valley at the top of Baldy on a windy, below-zero day, when Warren met Laurie for the second time. Warren took this photo of Laurie on his first trip to visit her in Seattle, two weeks later.

WARREN MILLER PHOTO

During one of their first summers together, Warren invited Laurie on a horseback ride: 126 miles across the Continental Divide through the Bob Marshall Wilderness north of Missoula in Montana. This photo was taken at the summit of the Divide at 11,000 feet.

SYD COOK PHOTO

At their condo on the North Shore of Maui, Laurie stayed on top of business while Warren wrote scripts in the morning and windsurfed in the afternoons. NANCY BYERS PHOTO

For a dozen winters in Vail, Warren and Laurie could coast down to the Lionshead gondola from their home.
WARREN MILLER PHOTO

Warren, Jack Kemp, and Tim Blixseth in March 1997, surveying the Yellowstone Club topo map at Rainbow Ranch in the Gallatin Valley.

The original ski bum finds his favorite drug—skiing powder snow—at the Yellowstone Club; in the early years, a crowded day meant 6 or 8 skiers on 5 quad chairlifts.

TRAVIS ANDERSEN PHOTO

Laurie found Pepper when he was 4 weeks old and the size of a baby squirrel with a big head. Buller, an Australian Dingo, was rescued from the Utah desert with his face full of porcupine quills. Buller gets first tracks in front of Jon Reveal and Warren at the Yellowstone Club.

WARREN MILLER PHOTOS

The Millers' Orcas Island dock is less than an hour flight from downtown Seattle and the Lake Union Kenmore Air Harbor. They were lucky to receive such personal service.

Exciting and scary powerboating adventures from Orcas Island included this trip on "SacaLaurie" to Chatterbox Falls in British Columbia.

In a little league game, nine kids always lose; in a skateboard park, everyone wins because there is no score. The Orcas Island skatepark at one time was ranked among the top 5 in the world.

WARREN MILLER PHOTO

Ward and Jackie Baker at home on Maui; Ward is still free diving at age 91.

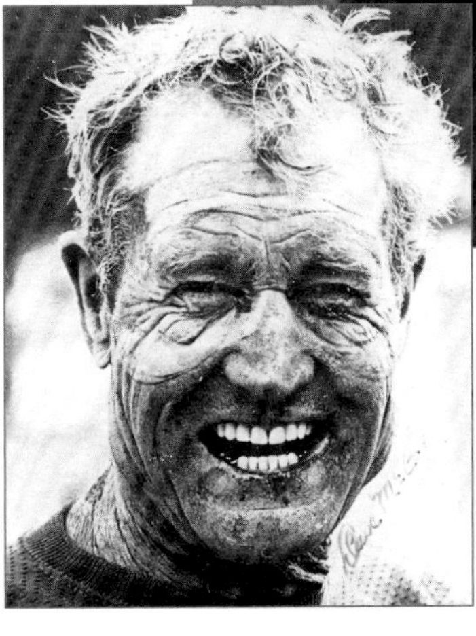

Warren always admired Dave McCoy's tenacity as a resort developer and as a gritty motocross racer who could still beat the kids. Warren and Dave are shown in Dave's motorcycle shed in 2008: Just a couple of old geezers with a combined age of 190 years, with 90 percent of that time spent on skis.

"I appreciate you spending time with me, and I hope to see you again next year, same time, same place. Thank you, and good night." CHRIS MILLER PHOTO

I immediately built a roof over the alley and then had space to build a theater inside. We did all of the interior carpentry and wainscoting ourselves; we built a sloping floor and a projection booth. Forty-eight antique theater seats from the old Portland Paramount in Oregon were installed. The staff surprised me by putting nameplates on the arms of each seat, with the titles of many of the films we had produced. It cost more to ship the theater seats to Los Angeles than it did to buy them at $2.50 each. Ten of them are now in the entry hall of our Montana winter home for guests to sit in while they take off their ski boots and parkas when they come in for afternoon tea.

This small theater enabled our company to have screenings for our short-film clients, as well as the preview for the feature-length annual ski films. We would get an entirely different reaction when they were shown in a theatrical setting, and we held our previews there for as long as I owned the film company.

THE '60S WERE REALLY ROARING FOR SKI RESORT DEVELOPMENT IN France. Every time I went to Courchevel, I hardly recognized the town. Janeau Tourneau and his brother had opened a bar called the Farm Yard Bar. Behind the bar, instead of the usual display of bottles of booze, there was a very large plate-glass window. Behind that was a barnyard scene full of live animals: a couple of cows, a mule, pigs, chickens, you name it. In true European custom during winter, they were in a closed barn, and whenever the bar was closed, it was dark and the animals slept. When the bar was open after skiing until 2 or 3 in the morning, the bright lights illuminated the farmyard. As far as the animals were concerned, this was daytime, and they did whatever farm animals do in the daytime, standing around eating and producing manure. The owners were pleased with the arrangement: The only cost for their floor show was a bale of hay a day, while the pigs lived off of leftover dinners from the restaurant next door.

In midwinter, they would bring in a pregnant cow and you could buy a lottery ticket predicting the exact time when the pregnant cow would deliver.

The bar with the farm animals was right down the street from a hotel called Bachelors Only. The owner had a simple marketing strategy. When you checked in, the attendant had you stand on a set of scales. He wrote down your weight, and then pointed to electric lights above each place where the room keys hung.

"Each bed is mounted on a set of scales, and if the weight on your bed gets over what your registered weight is, that light where your room key hangs will go on. I will know that you have a guest in your room. When the light goes on, I automatically call the police because you are cheating me by not paying the double-occupancy rate."

During the grand opening, he paid the local gendarmerie the equivalent of $25 to arrest a guest and a lady of the night for double occupancy in one of his single rooms. The story and photographs of the arrest appeared in almost 400 newspapers all over the world, giving him great free publicity.

CHAPTER FIFTY-FIVE

Late 1960s

Did I Learn from My PR Blunder? Probably Not

IN THE LATE 1960S, THE FILM COMPANY SIGNED OLD CROW WHISKEY as a client. For many years, Old Crow had a Broken Leg drink made from their whiskey. The company used a 23-minute movie of mine featuring Art Furrer to show in ski-resort bars after the lifts closed. Art would give a little talk about skiing, serve Broken Leg drinks in special mugs that most everyone kept, and then he would show my movie of him and his trick-skiing. A few years later, Old Crow Whiskey had four or five prominent skiers, including Corky Fowler, showing the movie in various parts of the country, with each of the ski celebrities doing a lot of personal appearances. They each had a 16-MM projector, a screen, and a copy of my special film for them to show. They booked their own shows and got their expenses and a fee for each one. Apparently, there is a lot of money in making and selling whiskey with my movie. I understand it—I just don't drink it. This series of Broken Leg film tours ran for almost six years, before the ski-resort bars were saturated with Old Crow Whiskey and Broken Leg mugs.

In the late 1970s, I apparently became the go-to guy on skiing, because I was regularly asked to appear on "Good Morning, America" and many other shows to talk about the sport and my latest films. The appearances required flying from Los Angeles to New York after a day's work in the office and getting as much as three hours of sleep before a limo picked me up to take me to the studio at 6 A.M. One January, it was warm with no snow anywhere in the East, except for some man-made snow here and there. When the host asked, "How is the skiing here in the East?" I said, "It's OK if you stay in the middle of the trail, but don't get over near the edges because it will be mud. If it were me, I would save my money and fly out West or wait until it snows more and then go."

The National Ski Areas Association was having its annual meeting in Vermont, and everyone saw the show. The members wrote a letter to all of the ski resorts in America asking them to never let me park my car in their parking lots, much less take movies of their resorts. Some of them actually did turn me down, forgetting how much publicity I was annually giving the sport of skiing.

That year my film had less American skiing in it, particularly Eastern skiing, but I did have a lot more from Europe. Did I learn from this public relations boo-boo? Probably not, because I always filmed for entertainment value. My recommendations were valid, because you could not pay me for them. I had to really like a place to endorse it. I always relied on ticket sales to finance the films, not product placement in the movie.

During this same time, someone snagged me a personal appearance on "The Tonight Show Starring Johnny Carson." Unfortunately, my interview followed Buddy Hackett's, and Buddy had 10 million jokes in his brain and tried to tell all of them. He got on the show through Ski Industries of America, the trade group for all the gear and apparel suppliers; he wore a red Bogner powder suit, and used up more than half of my allotted time slot.

Another time I caught an early flight for "Good Morning, America," so I could get some sleep before the show. While I was in the air, an earthquake hit San Francisco. When I got to the hotel in New York, there was a note for me from the producer, informing me that earthquake news had trumped my spot on the show. I caught a cab to JFK airport and was on my way back to Los Angeles before the sun came up. There was no pay for these appearances, but they generated publicity for my films and, usually, for the sport.

CHAPTER FIFTY-SIX

Late 1960s

The Constant Search for New Things to Film

ONE OF MY MAIN OBJECTIVES AS A FILMMAKER WAS TO FILM THE LATEST and greatest ways to get up and down the mountain, hopefully without crashing and burning. In the late 1960s, a young man named Jeff Jobe arrived in Sun Valley to fly his hang glider off the mountain. He had never gathered enough speed on skis to actually take off, but he assured me he could do it. We went to Dollar Mountain for his first try. Unfortunately, there was a tailwind coming down Dollar Bowl, and he only ascended a few feet in the air. My next suggestion was to tie a rope to the back of a car and tow him fast enough so that he could fly over the road to Ruud Mountain. Jeff did not like that idea, so we ended up on the Baldy lift the next morning, before someone could say "You can't do that!"

I told Jeff, "I want you to fly down the west ridge of the Christmas Bowl and then turn left and come over my camera, which I will set up under the Christmas Bowl chairlift. Make a right turn, and go over the trees at the bottom of the Christmas Bowl ridge and land on the catwalk. OK?"

This would be a first, and at the time Jeff was just a few years past getting his driver's license. The weather was perfect, with no wind as I filmed him assembling his strange-looking pile of aluminum and Dacron. When he was finished, I wished him luck and skied down to where I would set up my camera.

He executed my flight plan perfectly. After the flight, a man standing next to me wanted to know what I had just filmed. After explaining it to him, he said, "Thank you. I thought that was what I saw, but if I told my wife that story without a witness, she would never believe me."

Jeff Jobe went on to fly off of a lot of mountains for many TV commercials and to start a water-ski and life-jacket business. You might even own a pair of Jobe water-skis. He made thousands of them. Jeff is still a good friend and is still alive, despite all the scary things he's done. He stays with us at the Yellowstone Club in Montana and rides his snowboard with the same attention to detail that he had that first day on Baldy a long time ago. He flies a power glider, a 25-year-old Hughes helicopter, and a Malibu Turbo, often giving us rides to wherever we are going or just stopping by to visit.

FREESTYLE SKIING WOULD COME ALONG IN THE LATE 1960S AND GIVE the sport, and my films, some new and needed excitement. During the early 1970s, Hermann Goellner and Tom Leroy completed the first double flips on skis, and Barry Corbet and Roger Brown came out with their new-era ski film "The Moebius Flip." The following winter, I was able to bring the double flip to the big screen for my audiences, and they really enjoyed it. Tom Leroy had supplied the footage to me at no charge, realizing that the exposure would lead to other things.

Freestyle skiing was getting under way, with demonstrations where a skier had to ski nonstop through a field of giant moguls, do some aerial trick off of a big jump, and then perform ski ballet tricks in the flat at the bottom. The run was continuous back then, but over the years it was broken up into three separate disciplines. Wayne Wong, "Airborne" Eddie Ferguson, Scott Brooksbank, and a lot of other talented skiers tried to do all the tricks that the skis of that era would let them, and they made regular appearances in my films.

Freeskiing is today's evolution of freestyle, with skiers (and riders) doing quadruple flips with a double twist as though it were no big deal. It's hard to follow except in slow motion on film.

One of the staples of my films was to tell not just how you got down the mountain, but also how you got up it. I sent Rod Allin in the late 1960s to Blue River, British Columbia, where Mike Wiegele was pioneering helicopter skiing. That first winter, Mike had no two-way radios because he had no employees. He put everyone up in the Blue River Motel and fed them at the Bus Stop Diner. That entire winter he had only 13 customers, at $1,400 each for a week.

Mike had invited Wayne Wong, a great freestyle skier, to ski for the cameras, along with two other then-famous skiers. The audiences went nuts when we showed them this kind of skiing, and Wiegele was in my films every year as long as I owned the film company. Rod really captured the awesome remoteness of a glacier above timberline, with some of the world's best skiers performing for the first time for cameras in such a great location. For the next 30-plus years, it was a must-have segment in the movie. Sometimes my cameramen even scared themselves getting spectacular scenery for skiing. But thanks to the careful safety requirements of Wiegele and his group of guides, he has the best safety record of all the helicopter-skiing operations.

After a decade, I had enough footage to make Mike his own ski movie of the Canadian helicopter life. We called it "Seven Days in Paradise." It's also where I came up with the line that has seemed to grow in importance every year since: "If you don't do it this year, you will be one year older when you do!"

Today, Mike owns his own lodge and 11 helicopters in Blue River, and his rates, as with everything, are not what they used to be at $200 a day all-inclusive. Today the experience includes the best of food and wine, as well as massages and other activities. If I were still in the feature-film business, I would still send a crew to film Mike Wiegele skiing every year. And if I just wanted a great ski experience, I'd go ski with him for a week every winter of my life.

SOME PEOPLE CREDIT ME WITH INTRODUCING THE FIRST IMAGES OF snowboarding to the masses. In the early 1970s, we featured the Winterstick in the film. "It looks like a tongue depressor for the Jolly Green Giant," I said in my narration, "and it's ridden just like a surfboard if you had to ride one at high tide."

The first year we put them in the film, I got an earful out of the resorts that wouldn't allow snowboarders on the hill. "How dare you!" they cried. My response was that if snowboards had been invented before skis, the resorts wouldn't be letting you ride the chair with those funny things hanging from each foot, and I don't think they would have.

Unfortunately, some of the young snowboarders who weren't accustomed to resort restrictions and etiquette occasionally misbehaved in chairlift lines on the hill. There were some collisions between skiers and snowboarders. I saw the need for snowboarding and quickly got over it. We've featured a lot of great snowboarding over the years, including Jake Burton and Craig Kelly in 1989. We ended the 2003 film, "Journey," to heartfelt applause with a tribute to Craig, who we had lost in an avalanche.

CHAPTER FIFTY-SEVEN

1976

A Marriage Spinning into Chaos

WITH SEVERAL FILMS UNDER PRODUCTION AT THE SAME TIME, THINGS at home were unraveling. In retrospect, they were a lot worse than I noticed or imagined. We finally started going to a family counselor to see if we could both change the chemistry and get things back on track. I felt the worst was behind us financially, but apparently I had been away from the beach house and Dottie too much in the last few years of filming.

It all seemed unreal when Dottie got home from a trip to Europe and said, "Guess who I ran into in the lobby of my hotel in Paris?" It turned out to be a former neighbor with five daughters, and it wasn't the only time she'd "run into" him.

However, I was so in denial that I once again went out on the road with my every-day-a-new-town schedule. My kids knew something was wrong; my neighbors and friends did, too. However, when you are checking into a different hotel seven nights a week for almost two months, a lot of things are put on the back burner. There were monumental bills to pay for the production of the new movie, but a glimmer of hope lay ahead for me: our annual family vacation over Christmas and New Year's to Sun

Valley, where my son Scott had moved and was pounding nails for a contractor in Ketchum.

When we left for Sun Valley, you could cut the tension between Dottie and me with a knife. Once there, while I was shaving in the bathroom of our lodge room getting ready for the evening's show, I heard a key in the door and froze. My wife and the local tennis pro barged in, giggling and laughing; they stopped in mid-embrace when I walked out of the bathroom.

Unfortunately, I had to conduct business as usual by putting on two shows and gathering footage for the next year's film. Chris and Kurt had a good time, and Scott was working in the Ore House washing dishes when construction slowed down in order to get through the winter and ski every day. I was certainly not being a good father to my first-born child at the time. I refused to believe my marriage of many years was falling apart, and it took years to admit I should have worked harder to get Dottie to be kinder to Scott and to get along better in the earlier years.

The almost 900-mile drive home was a virtual sprint, except for gas and bathroom stops. I again ran away from marital problems in order to pay bills. The office was the only place where I had some control over my life, or so I thought, as I buried myself in catch-up work before I had to go on the January and February seven-nights-a-week show schedule once again. Two days after we got back, Dottie called me at the office and said in a very friendly voice, "How about going out to dinner tonight with me?" It sounded good to me because I was still in denial about everything that was crashing down around me.

I was surprised when she came down the stairs to the front door in a spaghetti-strap, sleek, black evening dress that I'd never seen before. We went to a small Japanese steak house in the neighborhood, and maybe this was when I noticed that her wedding ring was not the one I had given her, which she had worn for years. She had traded the ring I gave her for one she liked better—without even discussing it.

At the restaurant, there was polite conversation about the rest of the film tour and whether she was going to Europe with me to film this winter. Then she dropped the bomb.

"I want a separation!"

"What does that mean? For how long? What about the kids? Who is going to pay the bills while we are separated?" I had dozens of other questions, such as who will be taking care of the kids when I'm working and you are out on the town with whoever is your current beau? How long will this fling of yours last? When do you think you might want to get back together, and is this just a shopping-for-a-better-husband deal or what? Ten-thousand questions raced through my mind. She did not know how long the separation would be; she just needed her freedom, which to me, of course, meant that she wanted to sleep with her boyfriends in our bedroom overlooking the beach. None of the thoughts that were spinning through my mind were very good or beneficial for the future.

The next three or four days are a complete blank in my mind, as they have been ever since that dinner in what I now call the Freedom Restaurant. Scott was living in Sun Valley, Chris was a senior in high school, and Kurt was still in junior high school. As I came to find out, Dottie had not been taking care of the kids very well during my many absences. I tried to find answers, yet there were none. I knew I had a major financial and parental obligation to Chris and Kurt, and it was hard to leave town knowing that strangers to my children might be living from time to time in what used to be our house.

I rented a room in a friend's apartment, bought a chest of drawers for my clothes, and went back on the road. Surviving that tour was difficult. I had responsibilities to my children—and to all of my customers who depended on my films for their annual ski club fundraisers. That old adage "the show must go on" is absolutely true.

While I was on the road, I had my secretary round up a good real estate agent to find me an apartment for my return to Hermosa Beach before I went to Europe once again to gather footage. There is, of course, no way possible to appraise the damage something like this can cause your children. I did know, however, that I had to get on with my life. By now, it was very obvious to me that I wasn't enough for Dottie, which was very painful. The world of skiing and film production worldwide was full of single women whose husbands had wandered away, as my wife was now doing. In all of those years of marriage, I never once took advantage of being on the road alone.

In the meantime, I continued to make the mortgage payments and cover the expenses. She had her house on the beachfront and took care of two of my children, while I worked harder than ever on films that seemed to just get better. As Don Brolin used to say, "Warren was at his best and funniest with his weird sense of humor when he was in the middle of a divorce."

Before I knew it, the summer was almost over, and I was getting one last weekend of surfing at San Onofre when Dottie showed up. Before the day was over, she cornered me, asked for forgiveness, and wanted to make a go of it. It was the last thing I had on my mind—I'd had enough.

How do you split up the following: a 42-suite office building, seven storefronts on the busiest street in Hermosa Beach, a house on a lot and a half on the waterfront, my part of the 160-acre Mammoth property, and 11 acres in Sun Valley, Idaho, plus the film company as an asset?

Not easily. But by this point in my life, I knew that half of what I owned without her was better than all of it with her.

If Dottie were narrating this, her version might be a completely different story, and I'm sure I wasn't easy to live with. However, this all happened about 40 years ago, and it's the way I felt about it and saw it back then. Today Dottie is in her 80s and lives in San Clemente, California. She has a small dog and a boyfriend and still rides a bellyboard at San Onofre on occasions. I'm glad she's happy.

I had lost most of my hair when Scott's mother, my wife Jean, died of spinal cancer in 1954. Now, I was more than 50 years old, and it looked as though I would be starting all over again in the romance department. The dating game was something that went on in nightclubs and bars, without me. Potential dates weren't at yacht clubs or on the beach where I hung out in my spare time. Certainly, when I was at a ski resort, it was out of the question—I was just too busy.

CHAPTER FIFTY-EIGHT

1970s–1980s

"The Chimpanzee Was a Lousy Skier"

JIMMY CARTER ENTERED MY LIFE WITH HIS GASOLINE SHORTAGE, AND SO that my cameramen would not run out of gasoline in the desert somewhere, I quickly had an extra 20-gallon gas tank installed in the backseat of our company's Ford Pinto station wagon. We could now drive from Hermosa Beach to Alta, only stopping for the bathroom. The tank was added right when the Pinto-exploding-in-flames controversy was at its peak. Every one of my cameramen survived and never once ran out of gas.

Brian Sisselman from Pittsfield, Massachusetts, asked for a job interview one day. The film he showed me—which he'd put together as a student in the UCLA film school—was a re-edited version of one of the many ski movies that I was renting at the time. He did a very good job, and while I didn't need another cameraman right then, I hired him as a messenger to drive back and forth from Hermosa to the Hollywood film labs. That job was short-lived, as he soon moved to Vail, where he met his future wife and handled some stock-footage photography for me.

The next thing I knew, he had moved back to Hermosa, married, and was filming for me regularly. He barely survived his first assignment, but he did learn what working for me would be like. We'd received a phone call from someone who said he had a chimpanzee that could ski, and of course I wanted that in the movie. The only place we could find a motel that would accept Brian, the chimpanzee, and its owner was at Mt. Shasta in northern California. When Brian got back after 10 days, he had very little footage, maybe 200 feet. When I asked him why so little film, he had a quick answer: "The chimpanzee was a lousy skier."

Brian was a hard worker and learned from Don Brolin as he worked his way into the top tier of filmmakers. For example: He called while filming skiing in the Atlas Mountains of Morocco, complaining that all it was doing was raining. All I said was, "Let's change the story line as if the skiers had traveled clear to Morocco to ski in Atlas powder snow, and all it does is rain!" A simple narrative line made the entire sequence resonate—as well as being ridiculous, which added to the humor.

On a trip to India, Brian got out of a helicopter in the Himalayas at 18,000 feet and filmed hard all day. He skied and filmed down to a small village at the base of the mountain, where almost every kid in town skied. Their skis were 2-and-a-half-foot-long hunks of apple trees. For their bases, the kids used old pieces of large band-saw blades turned up in the front. They wore rubber galoshes, and the bindings were made out of woven vines. Every kid in town had a smile on his or her face and skied very well, considering the equipment. Another time, Brian led a filming expedition to Antarctica and camped out with his skiers on the Antarctic polar ice cap for almost a month. Closer to home, while filming in Telluride in 1989 and looking for local color, Brian discovered Zudnick, the part-husky, part-wolf canine who would become a star in the film, along with his owner Scott Kennett. Zudnick the Wonder Dog would hop on the lift and then chase Scott down the steep and deep, including a spectacular descent of Telluride's signature Plunge.

With Brian and Don Brolin in the field, there was no need for me to travel anymore except to visit the location, lay out the shooting script, and catch up with the other cameraman.

There was hardly a place with a ski lift anywhere in the world that Don or Brian or I didn't point our cameras at during the 1970s and '80s. Because my name and voice were on the film, I got most of the credit for creating the films. However, without Don Brolin, Brian Sisselman, Rod

Allin, Gary Nate, Fletcher Manley, and half a dozen other part-time cameramen, those dozens of films would have never happened.

FROM DAY ONE, TELLING STORIES WAS THE BACKBONE OF THE COMPANY, but no one ever told me that and I never actually realized it while in the process of doing it. Don Brolin spent those early two weeks with me in Sun Valley watching how it was done my way; he then went east with me and saw the hustle that was necessary to cover a small resort for a segment of the next film in one day. He definitely figured out what I was doing, though I couldn't have put the goals into words.

Apparently a lot of the hustle rubbed off on Don because he always came back with the shots we needed. One absolute was a shot of the mountain from the parking lot and the lift or lifts. Also, the cameraman had to get ski-action shots of the best skier at the resort and anything that was different and new about the place. Rope tows were always good for some funny footage, as were small mountains where we had to get a shot of the sign saying, "342 feet high," although everyone who had ever skied there knew it was not that high. It was a lifelong game of show-and-tell, with the hope that we could sell enough one dollar theater tickets to pay the overhead for a year, with enough left over to produce the next movie and raise my family at the same time.

IT TOOK A LONG TIME TO DECIDE TO SEND DON BROLIN ALL THE WAY TO an unknown ski resort in Russia to bring back the first footage of a ski trip behind the Iron Curtain. Questions arose, such as the cost of room and board for two or three weeks, where to film, and could we find people enjoying, even temporarily, freedom on skis in Russia? We wondered, too, about the quality of skiers there. The trip was not cheap, but the results were extremely good, particularly for that era. Don researched the entire trip's cost, what to film, and when permits were needed to execute the sequence we chose to film and bring it all back to Hermosa Beach for editing.

Don wisely chose the Russian National Ski Championships. The resort had at least one single chairlift. To add humor to the scene, Don got some shots of two guys riding up on the single chair together. One ski racer would be sitting in the chair, and the other one would be hanging from the chair by his hands until his strength gave out, when he would fall a long way to the ground. Since most of the racers had the same strength, they all fell to the ground at almost the same place.

I had the film editors make sure that they emphasized that all of the racers had skis for downhill, slalom, and giant slalom, but each racer only had one set of bindings. The highlight for Don was when he unpacked his rucksack and found, hidden under the foam pad at the bottom, 23 letters from Russians who hoped he'd mail them to their relatives in America to let them know they were still alive. The Iron Curtain stopped the mail in both directions in those days.

We were spreading the freedom of skiing around the globe, and doing it in my trademark seat-of-the-pants style. The husband of an American Airlines stewardess, who was also a good cameraman, could get free airplane tickets anywhere in the world. So I hired him and his free airline ticket to film a ski resort in Israel. He brought back tales of hearing artillery fire in the distance while skiers were lined up waiting for the next chair.

CHAPTER FIFTY-NINE

1976

Blacking Out while Skiing; Traversing to the Hospital

LATE ONE AFTERNOON, I WAS CARRYING ALL OF MY CAMERA GEAR AND traversing across Lookout Bowl in Sun Valley when I blacked out. I was only out for a few seconds, but I was sitting in the snow and did not remember how I got there or where I was. I somehow took the chairs from the Roundhouse to the top of the mountain, though pretty groggy, and started down Warm Springs. It took me about 20 minutes to get to the bottom of the mountain. I was completely out of breath and didn't know why. When I got back to my room and put my rucksack down, I called my daughter, Chris, who was working in Sun Valley at the time, and asked her to walk over to the hospital with me. (That was when the hospital was still out behind the Challenger Inn.)

The doctor took my vital signs, and the bells went off. Next thing I knew, I was on a gurney being wheeled down the hall with all kinds of electrodes attached. I had developed atrial fibrillation, which means that my heartbeat was very irregular. It varied from 48 to 170 beats per minute, with no pattern to the variations.

The doctors gave me a two options: They could stabilize the heartbeat with either drugs or electricity. I chose electricity for reasons that I cannot remember. Later that afternoon, a doctor stood over me with a small paddle in each hand. When the doctors put them on my chest and someone called clear and then hit the "on" switch, it was as though I had just gotten kicked by a mule. Whatever the electricity was supposed to do, it worked for me, but I was a very subdued and scared person for a couple of weeks.

A few days later, after I had driven to Bend, Oregon, to work on a volcano film, I hired someone to carry my rucksack for the first time in my professional life. When the photography was finished on Mt. Ashland, Mt. Bachelor, Timberline, and Mt. Hood Meadows, it was time to drive back to Hermosa Beach in my van.

I still have atrial fibrillation years later, and I take a regimen of drugs to keep it under control. Unfortunately, I don't have the kind of atrial fib that can use a pacemaker or a defibrillator to control the irregular beat. It is life as the cards have been dealt, and I try and play them as best I can with the good health I have left.

CHAPTER SIXTY

1960s–1970s

Movies Move Mountains

DURING THE BOOM TIME OF U.S. SKI RESORT DEVELOPMENT IN THE 1960s and '70s, it was possible to have a new resort to film almost every year: Vail, Heavenly, Sugarbush, Northstar, Alpental, Telluride, and Big Sky, to name just a few. This was before the tree huggers, the greenies, and the Sierra Club virtually shut down any new ski resorts in America.

This is despite the fact that an infinitesimal amount of publicly owned land is leased to ski resorts, and that the resorts pay proportionately much more for the use of that land than any other industry, including the timber industry. It seems to me that with the tens of millions of acres of land owned by the federal government, a few thousand acres here and there on the side of a mountain dedicated for a ski resort to provide jobs and a huge supply of tax dollars is a no-brainer. Apparently, however, a lot of environmentalists who like to restrict rather than find solutions had the spare time to write letters to their congressmen and shut down anyone's interest in building a new ski resort or even expanding an existing one. Of course, people who can pay for lift tickets are generally too busy earning a living and getting ahead, so they don't have loads of letter-writing time to balance things out.

After spending more than 50-odd years traveling the world with my skis and camera, I would see something that was being done in maybe St. Moritz or New Zealand that was not working; then several years later someone would try the same thing here, and again it would not work. I tried to share the good ideas with ski area managers in the U.S., but in many cases, my ideas were easily dismissed. In their minds, I was only a guy who made ski movies. However, many dreamers were using my movies to raise money to develop new resorts.

John Riley, who was the treasurer of the Carnation Milk Company in Los Angeles, owned a lot of acres of land adjoining Squaw Valley and wanted to raise money to build a couple of ski lifts. His group called me one day and asked if I would be interested in riding around in a helicopter for a day or so, shooting a lot of film, and putting together a dog-and-pony promotional show that he could take on the road. I flew up there a couple of weekends later and did just that. John then bought a motor home and went on the road for a couple of years, using my film to raise money to build his Alpine Meadows dream.

When I was showing my film in San Francisco the following fall, Riley planted a few stories in the San Francisco newspapers that I had not only produced the movie, but had invested heavily in his new resort, hoping other people would follow my lead. John was so wily, he had talked me into taking $5,000 of my fee for producing the movie in Alpine Meadows stock. It would be almost 15 years before the stock was worth the $5,000.

The first flight of Snowbird was a different story. Ted Johnson had been cooking hamburgers at Alta and started skiing over the ridge into what became Snowbird for his last run of the day. Its large bowls and great slopes appealed to him, and so he started investigating the land's old mining claims and buying them up from little old widows in such places as a Torrance, California, trailer park. Ted ran a cotton-picking machine in the scorching-hot fields of Bakersfield during the summer and would chase down the claim holders on weekends. Several years later, he had most of them, and he hired Dick Barrymore, who was just starting on his own filmmaking career, to shoot footage of Ted on his late-afternoon ski runs. The footage was outstanding, but Dick was too busy to edit it, so Ted called me. (He said, "If I want to get something done, I call a busy man.") And I was really busy. I spent three weekends gluing it together and making a narrative sales pitch about how close Snowbird was to Salt Lake City, how good the powder was, and all that sort of stuff. Then Ted left for Minneapolis with his wife, my sales-pitch film, and his dream keeping him awake for the long drive. The show in Minneapolis did not go too well, but someone said, "My friend Dick Bass down in Texas might be interested in the project. He has enough money to back it and is an avid skier with a home on Mill Creek Circle in Vail. Here is his phone number."

Ted and his wife drove around the clock from Minneapolis to Dallas to meet with Dick Bass. After Dick watched the movie a couple of times, he said, "You are sure you can build a gondola and a base lodge for $4 million? If you can do that, you can count me in."

Snowbird now had the energy to start flying. Ten years ago, it was estimated that Bass had invested more than $100 million in Snowbird. It all started with Dick Barrymore's very good film footage, my editing and sales pitch, and Ted Johnson's dream of more skiing in the Little Cottonwood Canyon. Corky Fowler was also the draw for 11 years as Snowbird's director of skiing; people came to watch him ski and learned to love the place at the same time.

Alpental also started on less than a shoestring. Bob Mickelson and Jim Griffin found an isolated section of private property, as opposed to Forest Service land, on Snoqualmie Summit, almost exactly 50 miles from downtown Seattle. It was private because of some old mining claims had been forgotten many years ago, mostly because the claims were for iron instead of for gold. For a bit of history, Jim and his brother Ted were the first ones to capture an Orca whale for an aquarium. They named the whale Namu, after the British Columbia First Nation's fishing village.

Bob was a get-it-done kind of guy, who was making and selling $9 Edelweiss stretch ski pants when Bogner's were $36 a pair. Bob called me one day excited because he had hired one of the Whittaker twins (famous mountain climbers from the Northwest) to ski for the camera, along with a couple of other local hotshots. He wanted me to make a film to sell his real estate at Alpental. I think we spent three or four days flying around in a small, three-place Bell helicopter, getting enough footage for a 23-minute sales film.

After getting all of the data from Bob and Jim, I took my camera and tripod and flew home to the editing bench. All I had to do was show the terrain, how steep it was, and how close it was to I-90 (back then, called Highway 10) and the metropolitan area around Puget Sound. Once the film was finished, it was up to Bob and Jim to sell the real estate in order to raise the money to build the initial three ski lifts, the roads, the base lodge, and infrastructure.

They had 72 lots and condos for sale, and after presentations in Tacoma and Seattle, they sold everything for full price and had a backup order for every one in case someone could not come up with the money.

In producing these kinds of films, I took a vacant lot or a condo as part of my fee, and also used the footage for a sequence in my annual film, providing more marketing for the new resort. In the case of Alpental, I made a good profit when I sold the lot about 10 years later.

Alpental opened to rave reviews in 1967, when Northwest skiers found steep and deep skiing only 50 miles from their homes in Seattle. It changed the outlook of skiing on Snoqualmie Summit forever.

In the East, Sugarbush became the favorite of discerning New York City skiers. Marketer Damon Gadd had an eye for the luxurious with a five-star restaurant at the base, and Sugarbush soon became known as Mascara Mountain because it was getting so much magazine coverage with fashion-model spreads. Damon hired Stein Eriksen as his ski school director and had the perfect model to ski in all of the press coverage. After I had filmed Stein for Gadd and Sugarbush co-owner Jack Murphy for a few years, Damon announced he was going to develop a new condominium complex and asked me to make a sales film.

It was another no-brainer, because I had so much footage already of Stein and the rest of Sugarbush. I mentally reviewed the footage that had been shot in the last several years and set a few days aside to shoot establishing shots, along with old barns and other New England–looking architecture.

Damon was most generous when my price was an acre of land on the far edge of the new condo complex with a stream running through it. Again, I got my normal salary for shooting, my expenses, and the acre of land. The good thing for Damon is that the film sold a lot of the condos, but not enough to build clear out to my acre of land. The road was never developed, and there was a time when I tried to give the land away, and no one wanted it—including the Boy Scouts to whom I offered it—so I just paid minimal taxes on it for about 20 years. Not too many years ago, the phone rang: Some good things were happening at Sugarbush. I had long ago virtually forgotten about owning the lot, except when the annual tax bill came. The voice on the other end of the line asked me if I would take $15,000 for it. I think that was the total price of the original film 25 or 30 years earlier, and of course, the answer was yes and the deal was done.

My old friend, Bob Maynard, was the president of a new ski resort called Keystone just west of Loveland Pass in Colorado. He needed a five-minute film for his PR man Jerry Jones to take on the road right away. The hotel was not finished yet, and the windows were covered from the inside with Visqueen, so it was necessary to wait until the windows quit flapping in the wind. But I was able to finish the film, and the rest is history.

There is a town in Colorado off the beaten path and up a narrow canyon that the ski world had passed by. It became famous when Butch Cassidy robbed his first bank there in 1889. Telluride had been sitting there waiting for someone to build a ski lift and move it into the group of world-class ski resorts.

Several famous skiers, including Willy Schaeffler, said it was an impossible place for a ski resort. Émile Allais, the famous French world champion, breathed some life into the dream when he said it could be done. However, it took someone with vision and a thick wallet to chance it.

That man, Joe Zoline, appeared in my office one day, and we talked for a long time. Every minute that Joe was in my office, I was under the watchful eye of his personal bodyguard, who stood by my office door.

Joe had bought a sizeable chunk of land in downtown Telluride and needed one of my movies to kick-start skiers going there. Being really busy at the time, I gave him my very busy price, which is a lot higher than the not-so-busy price. We shook hands, and he then expected me to leave on the next airplane to Montrose, Colorado.

Three days later, I was on that plane, along with a good cameraman and his wife. Telluride was a sleepy town, with a sheriff who thought everyone he didn't know was a drug dealer. When my cameraman and his blonde wife and I came out of the combination gas station, grocery, liquor, and sporting goods store, there was the sheriff demanding that we put our hands against the wall while he patted us down. Welcome to Telluride!

We had arranged to meet Bill Mahoney, who worked in the mines before they were shut down more than 50 years earlier; he was the only miner who stayed. He was living in the biggest house in town, which he reportedly bought for $25. I had heard he was a great skier, and he was.

Joe Zoline had insisted on building the first lift from town up a run they called the Plunge to the flat meadows near the top of the hill. The meadow was the perfect replication of what had happened in France many years before. Build a road to these high meadows, and the lifts will follow. We took all of our ski-action pictures in that meadow and above it and traveled by snowcat to the locations. It took the people of Telluride many years to recognize that they should develop from the meadow up to the spectacular skiing above it, and they finally did, with a big gondola and a road to the Mountain Village, which includes Oprah Winfrey among its celebrity homeowners.

CHAPTER SIXTY-ONE

1976–1979

The Model A; Meeting and Marrying Bobbie

OVER THANKSGIVING WEEKEND IN 1976, I HAD A SHOW IN SUN VALLEY, where I ran into Ned Bell, who owned two Model A Fords that I had coveted since I first saw them in 1947. One was a 1931, four-door, cabriolet convertible, and the other was a 1931 pickup truck. Ned was working on the roof of his house, and we chatted for a while before he told me that he might sell the pickup truck to for $1,976 to celebrate the bicentennial. I told him he would never get that much, and he should sell it for $1,776. He said, "Sounds like a good idea. I might just do that." I wrote him a check on the spot.

When my three children and I returned to Sun Valley for yet another Christmas vacation, there was almost no snow. One day, the four of us hiked up to the Roundhouse on dirt and had a nice picnic. I still had to get my one-owner Model A pickup truck from the Sun Valley garage where I had stored it since Thanksgiving to a garage in Hermosa Beach, where I had arranged for a complete restoration with a good friend of mine who owned a body repair shop.

After I towed the Model A back to Hermosa, I ran into a lady named Bobbie MacFayden, who had been married to a neighbor when I lived on the beach with Dottie. She had two boys and lived in a house in Redondo that was so full of termites it was about to fall down. Almost before I knew it, I was walking from my apartment to her house and taking her out to dinner.

Within a year or so of dating her, I did something I should never have done: I married her and moved out of my apartment into a three-bedroom, three-bath house in Palos Verdes with an unbelievable view of the ocean. At the time, I didn't realize that I was way too busy to ever sit down and look at the view.

The time seemed to just fly by, working on my movie for the following season and getting comfortable taking Bobbie to Catalina on the Tornado. She seemed to enjoy it, but another life-changing thing was about to happen for me.

Bobbie had started a small ski-clothing company called Pumpkin Designs that made kids' ski clothes. As I said when I featured some of her clothes in the movie that year, the clothes made kids look like kids, not miniature adults.

I followed the same routine of showing my movies all over America and Canada, but I knew something was not right as soon as I married Bobbie. After one bad divorce, I made sure I had a very precise and itemized prenuptial agreement that we both signed prior to the wedding. Her reluctance to sign it should have been a tip-off for me, but I was such a co-alcoholic I was guilty of trying to please everyone by never confronting things directly.

Before I knew it, she was hiring carpenters to remodel the house I had bought when we married. The master bedroom became the dining room. Bobbie's two boys had bedrooms of their own, and Kurt had a place he could live in when he was not traveling to sailboat races all over North America.

CHAPTER SIXTY-TWO

1980–1981

Co-Alcoholism and Sailboat Racing

ABOUT TWO MONTHS BEFORE I MARRIED BOBBIE, I WAS INTRODUCED TO an alcoholic/co-alcoholic clinic in San Pedro. I turned out to be one of the worst co-alcoholics in the history of the clinic. I started with three visits to the clinic each week. Sometimes on a Saturday, I would be so tired from the Friday-night session all I wanted to do was sleep all day.

Each counseling/treatment session lasted three hours. The first hour was spent with a counselor and eight or 10 co-alcoholics. The second hour we would listen to noted specialists and hear former alcoholics say things such as, "Don't offer me a drink, because a drink for me is a hotel for the weekend and a case of scotch." A Vietnam vet who is now a counselor said, "I would never fly my helicopter without at least a fifth of scotch in me." He had been an alcoholic since high school, when he would drink half a pint of scotch in the bathroom every day before geometry class. The third hour would be spent with a group of co-alcoholics and their alcoholic significant others.

One evening I was on a rant in the co-alcoholic session about what a chronic alcoholic my father was and how I had spent the first 18 years of my life living with him and trying to change him and never could. While waving my hand and pointing at my imaginary alcoholic father, I paused in midsentence and said, "Wait a minute." I bent my finger back, pointed it at myself, and said, "This is the guy I have to change."

And I had to work hard to change myself. It took me two six-month periods, three nights a week, to finally decide that I could break my bond with hanging around with alcoholics. In this sick relationship, the co-alcoholic (me) will do anything to please the alcoholic and anyone else as well, while not understanding that they are as sick as the alcoholic. I know for a fact that if I had started my counseling in San Pedro six months earlier, I never would have rebounded into that marriage, nor bought a house, especially with this particular person. Never. I had been programmed as a child to react to my father's degree of intoxication at the time, and I spent most of my life reacting to other people and doing almost anything to make them like me. I never realized that I did have a few likeable attributes and did not have to curry favor to be accepted.

My only regret is that I did not discover this treatment many years earlier, although my understanding is that the treatment wasn't discovered until 1976 or 1977. Apparently, I did get into one of the first classes held at the San Pedro Hospital. When Betty Ford was able to quit her drug and alcohol problem, it was Dr. Zuska from the Long Beach Naval Station who performed his magic for her, and they went on together to help open the Betty Ford Clinic in Palm Springs, California. Almost no one can cure himself or herself of either one of these problems. If you even remotely think you are a co-dependent, which is anyone who is in a relationship with anyone who abuses alcohol or drugs, I strongly suggest you find an Al-Anon meeting place in your own town and get with the program. My counselor, Donna Griggs, has been a very good friend ever since those sessions. She was able to change my life forever.

My kids refused to go with me, which is understandable. I knew they had grown up in the drug culture of the beach and surfing, but the sessions had done so much good for me, I knew it would change them for the better as well. The second year, my daughter Chris finally said, "I'll go with you just this one time." That very night she turned herself in as an alcoholic and was in for 21 days. The change was miraculous, except when I called her mother and told her what was going on. I was vilified and sworn at in language you seldom even hear from the toughest guy in the neighborhood.

I was really proud of Chris for sticking with the program in defiance of her mother, who had apparently supported her habit for many years. The only night that Dottie showed up for a counseling session, she was in one of her full-length, spaghetti-strap cocktail dresses, and she really attracted a lot of attention. Everyone else in our small class, like me, had just enough time to drive to San Pedro from work somewhere, and it was not a place for a fashion show. Dottie never did acknowledge her part in our daughter Chris' addictions, which Chris and I each learned a lot about during those sessions.

While I was in treatment, someone invested $25,000 in my then-wife Bobbie's Pumpkin Designs children's ski-clothing company. The first thing she did with the money was to buy GM's new small Cadillac. As the family appeaser, I didn't dare tell her otherwise.

Naturally, it had to have all of the bells and whistles, which added up to about $12,000 of the $25,000. It sat in the garage alongside my Model A, while my green van was parked out on the street in front of the house. The Cadillac did nothing to stimulate the sales of her children's ski clothes, and when the investor heard what she had done with his investment, that was the end of their relationship.

Bobbie's parents lived in the San Joaquin Valley in the foothills of the Sierras, and the second summer of our marriage, she went up there for a couple of days with her boys. When I tried to reach her on the telephone, her mother said that she had gone to a neighbor's house for dinner. When she hadn't called me back by 10 o'clock, I called her parents again, and she was still over at the neighbor's house. I was really worried, but I gave up calling at 2 in the morning when she was still at the neighbor's.

That fall, in 1981, while I was on the road with the film, the same thing happened, only at our house. I tried for three days to reach her and finally sent a good friend over to the house to see what was wrong.

Her report was a little out of the ordinary. "Your wife was not at home, and by the way, there is nothing else left in your house except one bed, a bookcase, and the carpet strips in your living room. The cooking utensils, bedding, knives and forks, dishes, dining room table, chairs, couches—everything is gone."

This all happened about three months after I signed away half of the house to her in my typical, co-alcoholic behavior, breaking down from my stand with the prenuptial agreement. As I remember it, she said to do it or else she'd take me to court for a divorce. I was stupid in relationships, because of my need to avoid confrontation.

Enter more attorneys in my life, all due to the problems caused by my co-alcoholic behavior. Rumor had it that she had a romance with a turkey farmer in the San Joaquin Valley near where her parents lived. It doesn't really matter now what went wrong, but it ended. Like Dottie, she later wanted to get back together, and I wisely said "no."

After I had my day in court, I was living in another Redondo Beach apartment with an ocean view. My table saw, drill press, skill saw, jointer, and all my hand tools had a great view from the second bedroom of this new apartment.

After I had put him through the L.A. Art Center, Scott was blossoming into a big-budget TV-commercial director, so I helped him buy his first house in Redondo Beach to remodel. It had a guest house in the back that he could rent.

In the mid-1980s, my daughter Chris followed in Scott's footprints by going to the Art Center College of Design in Pasadena and studying TV production. Kurt went on to Orange Coast College, with a major in sales and marketing and a minor in sailing; he was an All-American three years in a row.

Kurt was campaigning the J/24 aggressively. He had a sailmaker friend, and so the three of us competed in the North American Championships in San Francisco Bay. We finished far enough up in the fleet of almost 75 boats to qualify for the World Championships in Sydney, Australia, the following January. My part of crewing for my son was to run the spinnaker and bring the credit card. He and his two friends in the King Harbor Yacht Club handled everything else.

I missed Sun Valley for Christmas for the first year since 1947. Kurt and a couple of crew members had already left for Australia, and I followed them. We had chartered a local J/24, rented a car, and found a place to rent. The three of them worked for two weeks sanding and rigging the boat with every secret for speed that they had learned in their 10 years each of active racing.

The races were exciting, with my son driving the boat and my handling the spinnaker. After six races against 96 others, we were in a three-way tie for first and one of the only boats in the first 10 without a sailmaker on board. We finished third in the last race. I figure third place in a world championship is not too bad at the age of 58.

CHAPTER SIXTY-THREE

1979 and Beyond

Stein Eriksen, Robert Redford, Jack Kemp, among Other Skiers on Film

IN 1979, WHEN WE WERE PRODUCING A FILM FOR WHITE STAG CALLED "Stein, Stork and the Chick," we went down to Sundance from Park City because our client thought he could get Robert Redford to do a cameo in the film. Knowing better, we still had to ride down and find out in person it would not work, while the daily rate meter was running on my film crew.

At the time, Redford was working on "Jeremiah Johnson," and when we found him up a narrow road, he was in the middle of being filmed trying to start a fire to cook dinner. He was hunkered down under a small, transplanted tree and was the only actor on the set. However, this was a big-deal Hollywood movie, and they seem to film by the numbers. There were 32 people on location to get this particular shot: the director, the assistant director, the director of photography, the prop man, the cameraman, the assistant cameraman, the boom operator, the makeup people, a person in charge of costumes, a couple of guys to lay the tracks for the dolly shots, the gaffers or electricians, the two people in charge of the dressing-room trailers and their furnaces, the soundman, and about eight or 10 truck drivers with their various trucks. Since this was a location shoot, they needed hot coffee and hot lunches, as in steaks—and people wonder why Hollywood movies cost so much. Some of the people I just described had a backup person for each of their jobs. My crew was gigantic by my standards: I was directing Don Brolin, and we had a soundman and three actors. In those days, I'd produce a half-hour movie for as low as $20,000, and with luck it usually sold for a whole lot more.

During my 50 years in the film business, I conducted virtually zero business with Hollywood studios. With three cameramen on the payroll at one time, I was busier than I wanted to be, but I managed to get through the work overload, often with overtime for everyone and without union hassles. Plus, most of the union guys could not ski. The company never did lose a film-production contract because we were a non-union filmmaker. When it occasionally came up that I went to USC for three and a half years, people would immediately want to know if I had taken any filmmaking courses. I hadn't, of course. What I should have taken was accounting, business management, marketing, and sales classes to be able to sell my ideas more effectively at a competitive price.

A few years later, my friend Bob Maynard, who was now the general manager of Sundance, Redford's ski resort, arranged for me to ski and film with Redford as the celebrity-of-the-year in my movie. He was a very good skier and a great steward of the land. Sundance is a good, quiet resort off the beaten path, and Redford wants it to stay that way. I had fun trying to keep up with him for the cameras on an almost deserted mountain. My soundman recorded our conversations, resulting in a very interesting, off-the-record one-hour tape that has never been edited or used in a movie.

With Redford opening the door as a celebrity skier in the annual movie, it was wide-open for others, such as Martina Navratilova. I was pleasantly surprised at how good Martina had become in only a few years of turning right and left. Her world-class tennis ability helped, for sure, and so did instruction from her then-partner, champion ski-racer Cindy Nelson.

There is only one reason anyone who spent the day skiing for my cameras survives the editing and that is that they had some kind of unique ability worth pointing a camera at. Occasionally, in a comedy role that they did not anticipate, I would make a joke about a famous skier while he was doing something unbelievable, such as skiing down a nearly vertical wall of ice. In one instance, one person invited all of his friends and relatives to see him perform in my movie, and when he heard my off-the-wall humorous narration, he became angry. After the fifth phone call from him about hiring an attorney and suing me for defamation of character, I told him that it would cost him $500 an hour for setting up a screening to look at my movie with his attorney. He lost interest and went back to his job of adjusting bindings in the local ski rental shop.

LATER, WHEN LAURIE, MY LAST AND FINAL WIFE, AND I WERE LIVING IN Vail, I was on the chairlift with Jack Kemp, who was telling me a story about Washington, D.C. When I responded, the guy sitting on the other side of Jack interrupted me and said, "You sure sound like Warren Miller." So that I could continue to listen to Jack Kemp's story, I replied, "I'm told that quite often." "Yeah, but you even look like him. I think you really are him. Wait till I tell the guys in my Scranton ski club I rode up with a Warren Miller look-and-sound-alike."

In Vail, Dick Hauserman put together a ski and lunch group one day at Beaver Creek. It included Kemp and astronauts Alan Shepard and Scott Carpenter. Riding on the lift with them, I knew I was in the presence of a rare, honest politician and two ultimate astronaut heroes. On our second ride on the same lift, the operator at the top shut the lift down after we got off and hollered down at us, "Are you really Warren Miller?" When I answered, "Yes, I am," he ran down the ramp and said to Kemp, Carpenter, and Shepard, "Will one of you guys take a picture of Warren and me? My mother will never believe I have a photo of Warren and me together!"

About 30 years later, I got a phone call from a lady at the Johnson Space Center in Texas who said, "Captain John Phillips would like to speak with you." So I said, "Put him on the line." She replied, "I would like to, but he is up in the International Space Station going around the world 24 hours every day at about 17,500 miles an hour. He has been up there for six months, and he's getting a bit bored. He has watched some of your DVD ski movies at least a dozen times each. He grew up in Vermont watching your movies and would just like to talk with you." So we made arrangements to place a telephone call from a secure phone in Seattle when the capsule would be flying directly overhead.

On the line with Capt. Phillips was his Russian space partner, Sergei Krikalev. They explained how they'd come back to Earth in a Russian re-entry vehicle, landing somewhere in the Gobi desert. Helicopters would fly in, the hatches would be opened, and John would have a welcome-back telephone conversation with his wife, Laura.

I invited John and Sergei and their families to come to Montana to ski with us, which the Phillips family did the following winter. He had taken photos of the Big Sky area from the space station and enlarged one for me, so now I have a photo of our home, next to the ski run in Montana, from 220 miles above Earth.

CHAPTER SIXTY-FOUR

1980s

Guerrilla Marketing at Its Best

In the early 1980s, my son Kurt was working for me full-time, and he wanted to expand the traditional handout and print a larger program to give away at all of the Southern California shows my company produced. I told him, "Why don't you just distribute the local ski shop and ski resort brochures?" With almost 25,000 seats to fill in Southern California, that is a lot of brochures. He sold the idea to 16 shops and ski areas, and now he had a real distribution problem. My suggestion was to go to the largest ski shop in town and get plastic bags with their advertising on the sides to put the brochures in. Stuffing that many brochures is very labor intensive, so I suggested he go to a local church and get the members to do it as a fundraiser. He'd pay minimum wages, and that money would go directly to the church as a tithe from the people doing the labor. It turned into a real moneymaker, it was a bargain for the ski businesses, and it was part of the learning for Kurt, who would have ample opportunity to use his sales skills in the future.

Guerrilla marketing is something you learn when you don't have the financial clout to hire an expensive public relations or advertising firm: Hunger drives innovation. Each year I was in business, some new way to drive free marketing emerged, and my son Kurt was on the front lines. He learned his lessons the hard way by actually being out there and wrestling with the big companies, though he never had to do it out of hunger.

My best job of guerrilla marketing was in Corvallis, Oregon, back in the early 1950s. A member of the ski club sponsoring the show was also a good mountain climber. From the top floor of the tallest hotel in town, he tied a mountain climbing rope next to his hotel room window. He then called the local television station and told them that someone was going to jump off of the roof of the hotel and commit suicide. As soon as the TV crew showed up and had their cameras unpacked, he called the police. He watched from his top-floor room as the crowd grew and the sirens came screeching to the front of the building.

He then opened the hotel window (it was a very old hotel) and started rappelling down from the fifth floor. When he got a signal from another club member in the crowd that the TV cameras were rolling, he pulled a cord in his rucksack, and a 25-foot-long banner fell out, announcing the movie that night at the local high school. In Southern Oregon this was called a prank, and it hit TV screens all over the Northwest, at no cost to anyone except a 50-cent roll of white shelf paper for the banner.

I was relieved they didn't put us in jail for causing such a disturbance. I closed the window of my fifth-floor hotel room before I went to bed that night, just an hour after drawing one of our first standing-room-only crowds.

CHAPTER SIXTY-FIVE

1980

Never Believe What the Press Says about You

I HAVE WRITTEN AND SAID THIS NUMEROUS TIMES: "IF YOU BELIEVE WHAT they write about you in the press, it can divert you from your goals of making your product better. With all of your press clippings and a quarter, you can make a phone call (if you can find a pay phone). Without the quarter, you can't make the phone call—clearly showing the value of PR, other than to advertise your product."

This became crystal-clear when a feature writer for the *Los Angeles Times* interviewed me in October 1980. Charles Schreger sat in my office for a while and then watched a couple of short films, while he asked a lot of questions and made notes. Here is what he wrote:

> "Dateline October 29, 1980
>
> There are two ways to describe how Warren Miller makes his living:
>
> Version No. 1: Miller is a middle-aged businessman who turns out a few dozen commercial/industrial films every year for his moderately successful production company. His job is to enhance the image of clients like Coors Beer, Continental Airlines, and the State of Colorado. He runs a nice little

> family business with revenues of about a million dollars a year.
>
> Version No. 2: Miller is ski bum Numero Uno. To the millions of ski fanatics in this country and around the world, he is a combination of Jean-Claude Killy/Robert Redford/Ingmar Bergman/Woody Allen. That's a modest appraisal.
>
> Besides his annual, 90-minute ski films shown around the world, and the short films he turns out for Coors and Continental, Miller makes surfing and sailing films and short films sponsored by ski equipment manufacturers. They are viewed in bars in Aspen, Taos, Vail, and Zermatt, Switzerland, and the patrons swear that is why beer tastes so good in ski towns."

Two years earlier, I'd received a call from Ishpeming, Michigan, home of the U.S. Ski Hall of Fame, informing me of my selection to the Hall. I was 54 years old and 28 years into my career, and I was both surprised and excited. I made arrangements to go to New York City, do some business, and then stop in Detroit on the way back, rent a car, and drive to Ishpeming. I didn't realize that Ishpeming, which is in the Upper Peninsula, was about a seven-and-a-half-day drive from Detroit; I think I ended up going through Chicago to get there for the induction ceremony. I also managed to get up to Copper Peak to film the ski-flying tournament for the next year's film.

About 10 years later, I received the prestigious AT&T Skiing Award for contributions to the sport, joining a distinguished club that included Billy Kidd, Bob Beattie, Serge Lang, Jimmie Heuga, Willy Schaeffler, Stein Eriksen, Andrea Mead Lawrence, and Franz Klammer. I was also inducted into the Colorado Ski Hall of Fame. Marty Head received the honor on my behalf, because I was too busy making personal appearances on the film tour.

If I really believed what the newspapers or the award committees said about my work, I would have traded in my Econoline van for a deluxe car, gone to nicer restaurants, and stayed in better motels. The films never made enough money to support that type of lifestyle, even if I wanted to live that way. All I wanted to do was share what I was privileged to see and film with as many people as I could.

This can be looked at as eccentric, but I prefer to remember how it all started in the trailer years ago, with a $79.95 8-MM, single-lens Bell & Howell camera and respect for what every skier had to go through in those days. In our home in Montana, I had the mantle carved with the image of my old Buick pulling the teardrop trailer, with the legend, "Remember where it all began!" It's a good reminder. We may live in a skier's paradise and luxury at the Yellowstone Club, but I think it's wise to remember what it took to get there.

CHAPTER SIXTY-SIX

1980s

New Sailing Challenges; Renting a Rattlesnake

JIMMY CARTER'S GAS CRUNCH STRUCK AGAIN, FORCING MANY POWERBOAT manufacturers to start building sailboats to keep their factory doors open. Bayliner did it, and Dave Slikkers in Wisconsin did, too.

Fortunately for me, the Slikkers were skiers and had seen my films in Aspen and then later in Vail. I was surprised when the phone call came that they were interested in me filming their new line of sailboats for showing to the powerboat public at yacht clubs. Though I had a fair amount of knowledge about sailboats, I knew very little about powerboats. I did realize I'd probably need one to use as a camera boat for all the boating/sailing filming I was selling.

After a few telephone conversations, I flew to Wisconsin, where I was very impressed with the construction of both their sailboats and powerboats. After spending two days in their factory and finalizing plans for the production of their movie, I decided I would need to buy one of their powerboats to get the best shots. Don Brolin was busy on another film in some part of the world, so I decided I could teach Gary Nate how to film sailboats in the Caribbean. Gary could bring along one of his young lady friends from Salt Lake City as a model.

The film worked well for the client, and the 20-foot Pursuit powerboat worked well for the next 10 years as a camera boat. The small cuddy cabin was big enough for Don Brolin to go inside to change film, while Bill Amberg drove it for not only the SlickCraft movie but also for a half-dozen other boating films later on.

IN THAT SAME TIME FRAME, AFTER TAKING A NISSAN (DATSUN BACK then) executive to lunch occasionally for six or seven years, I finally persuaded him to have me produce one of his off-road-vehicle TV shows.

Every December, when the desert temperatures in and around Las Vegas are at a minimum, the off-road aficionados have a major race. To be competitive in a pickup truck, you need to turn it over to an off-road modifier and leave a blank check that can easily run over $150,000 to get it ready, probably more these days. One simple item is shock absorbers that have a 16-inch throw. Even some Volkswagen dune buggies are modified with a Porsche engine and are usually financed and raced by a successful doctor or professional person of some sort.

The first year's film was "Vegas to Reno the Hard Way." The race follows dirt roads across the desert the entire way, and with a 9 A.M. start, the fastest vehicles got there by 2 or 3 the following morning. The production logistics were challenging. We had to position eight cameramen along the first part of the course in the most exciting places, and then, as the field passed them, land a small plane nearby, scoop them up with their gear, and fly them ahead of the racing field that at times was going almost as fast as the small plane could fly.

I had hired a director to scout the course and lay out the camera and drop-off/pickup locations. There were probably 150 off-road vehicles in the race, with two people in each car and a shovel in case they got stuck in the sand—and a lot of them did. There were also a lot of guys on motorcycles, which takes a certain IQ to do!

It was exciting to follow the race with my radio in a motor home with my client Nissan. My director had already gotten the complicated shots of a rattlesnake by renting one for a few hours in Pahrump, Nevada. All told, the eight cameramen exposed close to 15,000 feet of film for this hour-long TV special. It had taken me seven years to get the job with Nissan, but the success of our production made sense for them and our company, too, and we would film the race for the next half-dozen years.

In that era, in my Redondo Beach apartment, I had a bed, a cabinet for the TV set, kitchen stuff, and of course my power tools. It was easy to stay at the office and work for 20 hours. The feature film was working well, and in the grand scheme of things, my life was finally pretty good.

CHAPTER SIXTY-SEVEN

1980s

The Hobie 33 Fell a Dozen Feet through the Air

ABOUT THIS TIME, I WAS GETTING REALLY INTERESTED IN WINDSURFING. Just like my first pair of skis, the windsurfer had a mind of its own and went wherever it wanted to go, regardless of what I tried to tell it. Several of my former surfing friends had taken up the sport at the same time, and once in a while, we would all wind up at Cabrillo Beach on the same day. Three of my very colorful, good friends from the past—Matt Kivlin, Art Newman, Porter Vaughn—and I would sit on the beach and talk about the old, old days at Malibu—1940–1965 roughly—and how windsurfing had almost the same feeling of the early years of surfing.

There were lots of adventures available if you were as inept as I. For example, there is a one- or two-knot current southbound on the ocean side of the breakwater at Cabrillo Beach. I was still unable to do a water start, and so one afternoon I was carried south of the shorter breakwater as the wind was dying and the sun was setting. I could not get back to the beach, with the main entrance to the harbor half a mile from me. Instead of trying to get to the beach, I finally took the rigging of the sail and boom apart, rolled up the sail, and started paddling in so I would be at the harbor entrance when the current would carry me in. The sun had gone down about the time I was trying to paddle through the entrance, when I saw a boat heading my way. Someone had seen me and called the Coast Guard, and they were a welcome sight to my tired eyes and hungry, hurting body. I had already decided that climbing up on the inside of the breakwater and spending the night there in my full wet suit (though it meant sleeping on piles of pelican poop) was preferable to wearing myself out by trying to paddle back to the beach. No one knew I had gone windsurfing, so no one would miss me. Mind you, I was about 59 when this happened, no spring chick, or spring rooster, or whatever it's called when you're a guy.

As the calendar rapidly moved right along, I began to slow down on the 16- and 18-hour days and tried not to paint myself into more deadline messes. Business was really booming with half-hour movies about winemaking, horse racing, French tourism, and even remote Micronesia. I was having a lot of fun pouring my energy into these movies, and before I could deliver one, other clients wanted me to do another film for them.

Hobie Alter, together with Phil Edwards and John Wake, had designed a nice little 16-foot runabout. Their theory was that Hobie could get many of his hundreds of catamaran dealers to also sell the small runabout. Unfortunately, they would learn later that the catamaran-sailing dealers couldn't care less about trying to sell a boat with a motor. As a promo, we photographed them at Lake Havasu, the site of the relocated London Bridge. Don and I spent a week there running film through cameras, and I came home with a bad case of walking pneumonia. Apparently, there is no instant cure for it, and the doctor said, "Just take a month or six weeks off work, and you'll gradually get well." Of course, I could not take that much time off. Up until this point in my life, I figured it had been one long vacation, and I wasn't going to stop vacationing now.

WHILE WE WERE FILMING THE SMALL RUNABOUT FROM OUR PURSUIT camera boat, Hobie himself showed up at Lake Havasu with his Hobie 33—a breakthrough design of a lightweight, downwind sailboat/flyer. He wanted to see how strong the hull was, so we hoisted it off the trailer, as far above the water as the hoist could lift it. The plan was to film it falling the 12 feet to the water to see if anything broke. Don Brolin filmed the crash at 1,000 frames per second. When we projected the film, it took 42 seconds to watch the one-second, 12-foot fall—and nothing on the boat broke when it crashed.

When the film was delivered and used as a sales tool about the strength of the new Hobie 33, I was approached by a Hobie executive who wanted to sell me one. My J/24 was still being used a lot, and I had no urge to own a larger sailboat, so he offered it to me at half price. By the third phone call, he was down to a 60-percent discount. I finally realized the boat could broad-reach to Catalina in a lot less time than my J/24. The Hobie was a better boat for me, and I was tired of charging around the buoys every weekend anyway, so I finally bought it, figuring the price was so low that I could make some money if I didn't like it and wanted to sell.

A friend of mine put a crew together after I said that I would loan him the 33 for the Marina del Rey to San Diego race if I could go along for the ride. There were more than 175 boats in the race, including some famous 75-foot ocean racers. As the sun came up after racing all night, a lot of boats over 50 feet were becalmed just outside the entrance to San Diego Harbor. I knew that the Point Loma cliff faced almost due east and should generate a morning thermal from the rising sun. There was an incoming tide, so we were able to glide over to the sunny, warm cliff on a whisper of wind and sail around that couple of dozen boats. We were the third boat to finish the race.

A month later, with the same crew, we finished second in the Santa Barbara to King Harbor race. However, at this point in my life, I was enjoying cruising to Catalina more than simply going through the starting line, putting up the spinnaker after getting to the weather mark, and going through the finish line.

Don and I sailed the 33 and filmed it for the next year's annual film. (I always tried to include water sports to vary the pace and interest: waterskiing and surfing in the early years, and then windsurfing and sailing later.) Sailing along for the camera, the Hobie 33's mast broke, and we later discovered that there was a weakness in the spreader that caused the mast, loaded with wind-weight of the full spinnaker and main, to topple down on deck. Pretty spectacular footage for the film, but I was never sure how Hobie felt about it.

CHAPTER SIXTY-EIGHT

1960s–1970s and Beyond

My Incredibly Talented Film Editors

IN THE ENTIRE CREATION OF A FILM, NO ONE IS MORE IMPORTANT THAN a film editor. Here is my favorite description of what an editor does:

> "Editing is the process that transforms a miscellaneous collection of badly focused, poorly exposed, and horribly framed shots containing reversed screen direction, unmatched action, disappearing props, light flares, and hair in the aperture, but no close-ups, cut-ins, or cutaways, into a smooth, coherent, and effective visual statement of the original script, for which the director takes all of the credit."

By the mid-1960s, the film company had six editing bays to keep six editors busy, and there was even enough money to buy a used Moviola so our very best editor, the fantastic Ray Laurent, could more easily cut the action to match the music. Ray took all of our footage and sometimes matched the visual images with his choice of music so well that it was unnecessary to even narrate the segment.

Ray was openly gay at a time when it wasn't easy, and his partner was black. He commuted each day from Hollywood in a flashy convertible with the "Hollywood" vanity license plate, which he'd won the rights to when the state of California ran a lottery. While spending almost his entire career working for me, Ray smoked a pack or more of cigarettes a day. When the company could afford to buy a flatbed editing table, a prism sent the image of the film onto the screen so the editor could perform his magic. At least once a week, Ray had to shut down and clean the nicotine and coal tar off the machine's prism.

When Ray died from HIV, we lost an incredibly creative editor. He led the way for three or four other editors who eventually became full-time staff editors when they were not out filming, too.

IN 1977, I WAS SHOWING AND NARRATING THE LATEST SKI FILM IN Cupertino, California, which was a three-night stand in an auditorium of only 1,500 seats. After the show, a young man approached me on stage and said, "I have an 8-MM movie I have just finished, and I would like to show it to you, if possible." I made a date for him to show me his movie the next afternoon at my motel at 2:15.

At the agreed-upon time, there was a knock on my motel door, and I saw Kim Schneider standing there with his 8-MM projector, screen, tape recorder, extension cords, and film. He was fully prepared, on time, and able to quickly set up the show. He screened a well-edited 8-MM ski movie that was cut to music. Editing 8-MM film to music is extremely difficult. I was impressed when he said he wanted to come to work for my company as a film editor. He had the talent but not the experience of handling 16-MM editing equipment. Because we were always facing impossible deadlines, I told him, "You should go to film school for a year and learn how to edit at a commercial rate of speed. With the talent you have, my company would be able to use you, but we don't have the time to teach you how to do it."

Kim Schneider went to a film school and spent a year learning how to run a Moviola and flatbed editing bench. A year later, he showed up in Hermosa Beach, and based on his sample reel, I hired him.

A couple of years later, Kim bought a motor home and lived in it behind the film-company office whenever he was working for us. In later years, when he got married and raised two boys, he actually lived in a house, but as soon as the kids were grown, he was back in the motor home, though his main house was later in Sun Valley. He had his own flatbed editing bench in the living room of the motor home. A flatbed occupies a space about 4 feet wide and 6 feet long. Kim was as dedicated to the art of film as anyone who ever worked for me.

When the film was finished, he would ski every day all winter, and then return to the editing bench in the late spring. It was not unusual for Kim to work 40 hours straight without noticing the clock, maybe stopping for a quick hike and a couple of salads. He started to work for the film company more than 35 years ago, and as of this writing, he's still there. His sons Travis and Kyle, who grew up with Warren Miller films embedded in their lives, now contribute to the feature film. Travis handles the music with his dad, and Kyle edits occasional segments.

I was lucky to have such incredibly talented and independent artists as Ray Laurent and Kim Schneider. I credit them for helping pioneer the quick editing that you have seen so much on TV and film in the past 30 years.

CHAPTER SIXTY-NINE

1983–1984

A Rock 'n' Roll Business Partner Comes into My Life

MY PERSONAL LIFE AND WORK LIFE BECAME ONE AND THE SAME AS A bachelor. I did not like the dating game even a little bit. I had made a couple of bad mistakes, so I played my cards the way they were dealt, and every moment of every day became an adventure. By 1983, I loved what I did: conceiving the next year's film, evaluating the footage, writing the script, and seeing the film finished. However, I was getting tired of the annual schedule of personal appearances necessary to keep the company running.

In the fall of 1983, I was preparing to entertain a third sold-out crowd at the Santa Monica Civic Auditorium, with a show scheduled in Modesto, almost 300 miles north the next night. At a preshow get-together, I was introduced to Terry Bassett. He was in partnership with two other men, Bob Geddes and Tom Miserendino, and they owned a concert-production company that put on shows across the country. They were big players in the entertainment business. At its peak, their company was the largest concert producer in the world, staging more than 700 shows annually, including the Rolling Stones, Elvis, Frank Sinatra, the Eagles, Led Zeppelin, Jimi Hendrix, John Denver, Elton John, and many more.

Terry was telling me how he was going to set up his son and create a surf film company. I said, "That is a very small market and very competitive. Why don't you just buy part of my company and give him a job making surf movies, and I could mentor him while he is making them?"

I was tiring of my role as an absentee manager and father wearing a thousand different hats, plus being the only one who took responsibility for things at the office such as cleaning the bathrooms. Terry had never seen one of my shows but had heard about them and knew of my following. The next day, after he'd seen the show and the audiences' reactions, we rode up to Modesto together and talked nonstop about the opportunity for both of us. Before I knew it, the merger was beginning to happen, and before the end of the year, we had worked out what seemed to be a good partnership.

The first thing they did was hire a manager, Paul Gongaware. He had a lot of experience in the concert-promotion and staging business, but I thought he was very abrasive, which I suppose that form of entertainment requires. Just like most of the people who work in the motion-picture business, he wanted to be working on the creative side of the film itself.

However, under their partnership and guidance, the company was suddenly making more money than ever. My son Kurt was working full-time and learning as much as possible from the new partners. To reward him for his hard work, when we had our annual corporate meeting and split up the profit for the year, I gave Kurt 10 percent of my bonus.

Terry took over the films' music selection, and it became very contemporary. I was still old-fashioned. I believed that when someone was floating in powder, that some form of symphonic music was more appropriate, with perhaps a solo instrument out front in rhythm.

BEFORE THE HOLIDAYS IN 1984, SCOTT HAD A TV COMMERCIAL TO produce, and my daughter Chris was spending Christmas with her mother and then joining me. Kurt was meeting me at Sun Valley so I drove up there alone, and we had a gigantic condo at the lodge. Except for the year I went to the race in Sydney, I had not missed showing the movie at Sun Valley over Christmas since 1950.

Kurt helped with the marketing, so anyone within 20 miles of the opera house could not miss reading about the movie. However, this

Christmas at Sun Valley would be a lot different. It would be a life-changing moment with yet another unanticipated consequence, this time from drawing some cartoons.

"It Happened in Sun Valley," as the song says, but more specifically, in my case, at the top of Mt. Baldy, in the Warming Hut at Sun Valley.

PART FIVE

Settling Down

At his fifth and final wedding, with Laurie, in 1988. MIGGS DURRANCE PHOTO

CHAPTER SEVENTY

1984–1985

On the Top of a Mountain, My Life Was Changed Forever

I HAD NO IDEA THAT DECEMBER 27, 1984, WOULD CHANGE MY LIFE FOR the better, forever. The snow was hard, the wind was howling, and the visibility nonexistent, so I opted for an early-afternoon break for a warm-up cup of hot cocoa in the Warming Hut at the top of Baldy. My good friend and Academy Award–winning motion-picture animator Bill Littlejohn and I started drawing cartoons for the kids, who had been blown off the hill by the bad weather. Bill was skilled at drawing the Peanuts cartoons and particularly the Snoopy dog. Before we knew it, there was a line of four or five kids waiting for their cartoons.

I looked up to see a beautiful lady, and she said, "I'm sorry my son is intruding on your family time."

"That's no problem," I said. "And by the way, I've met you before. Correct me if I'm wrong, but I met you and, your, I hope, ex-husband seven or eight years ago. It was in the Edgewater Hotel in Seattle, and after the breakfast meeting you gave me a business card with blue ink on it. I don't remember what it said, but it had blue ink on it. Is that true?"

She said, "Yes."

We were talking with the table between us, but I asked, "Can I ski down with you?"

She was nice enough to wait for me at the bottom. Then I invited her to my movie that night, making sure that she brought all the young people with her. That turned out to be 10 children she was chaperoning until their parents arrived after their Christmas cleanup in Seattle. I made sure they got to the opera house early so they had good seats in the back, and Laurie would be with them. I sat her there because I knew if she were sitting down front, I would be watching her instead of looking for cues in the film to deliver my narration.

I had turned 60 just two and a half months earlier, and I realized this lady, who lived in Seattle while I lived in L.A., was 20 years younger. I found there was no sense in all of this. However, I sure felt different from the moment I met her on the top of Baldy—and still do feel different almost all of the time, 30-plus years later as of this writing.

The next morning, I had to work until 10:30 on a project. She had given me that business card for the ski shop she owned, which once again had the blue ink on it, but the phone number she had written on the back was her Seattle home phone number. Knowing she was a good skier and was probably skiing on the Warm Springs side of the mountain, I headed there. I slid into line for the lift and saw her standing in the single's line, after getting all 10 kids on the lift. I joined her on the chair and she skied with me, but really she was just waiting for me at the end of every run. After a couple of runs, I invited her to lunch, if you could call it that. I didn't believe in long lunches in a sit-down restaurant on a day when you can ski, so I always had some trail mix in a parka pocket. A couple of lift rides later, I brought out a handful of trail mix from my 10-year-old White Stag vest, and she had to wait until all of the stray feathers had been picked out of it before we shared it. The weather was much better than the day before, and we got in a couple of extra runs in the bright sunshine, on a day when I was really at peace with the world for a reason I did not yet know.

For me, New Year's Eve—with all of the funny hats, alcohol, and noisemakers—is no fun at all. I have always considered it amateur hour, and I had to be back in L.A. to get ready for business in the New Year. Before leaving, I managed to have a few more ski days with Laurie, meet some of her friends, and enjoy dinner with them. I also was very proud to introduce her to some of my friends at a Sun Valley party.

I left her in a ski shop parking lot, acting like a junior high school kid when I drew a heart in the palm of her hand with a red Sharpie pen and wrote our initials in it. I kissed her good-bye and started the 900-mile drive back to the reality of editing and scripting the off-road film for Nissan, as well as starting my next annual ski film.

On New Year's Eve, about 10 minutes before midnight, the phone rang in my apartment and woke me up. It was Laurie wishing me a Happy New Year. She told me later she was surprised to find me at home asleep on New Year's Eve. We did talk for a while, until the background noise of the party at the Duchin Room got the best of the telephone company and we were forced to hang up.

Within a week, the first bouquet of flowers I had ever received arrived in my office, and they were from Laurie. After I'd told her about a few bad days in the office, she had sent the flowers to commiserate. Hey, I was this 60-year-old bachelor and could not understand why someone as young and beautiful as she was paying any attention to me, much less sending me flowers!

The bouquet of flowers prompted an almost-immediate short "thank you" phone call to Laurie that wasn't short at all. This was followed by another call a day later and a question, "I can take Monday off—is it OK to fly up to Seattle? I can rent a car and take you out to dinner, which I would enjoy and hope that you would, too."

She said, "I have an old 1909 Craftsman house with four bedrooms, and you would be welcome to stay here with my son, Colin, Julie, and me." Since she was 16, Julie Raney had been helping Laurie in the soccer camp, in her ski school, and in the ski shop for, by then, six years. Julie now lived with Laurie and Colin while she was also going to Seattle University to get her business degree.

Who could refuse an offer like this? I made arrangements for the flight and the rental car and was pleasantly surprised when she said, "Since the store will be closed when you get here, why don't I just pick you up at the airport?"

Before I knew it, I was riding toward West Seattle with Laurie on a very foggy night in January. She lived 42 steps up from the street, overlooking Puget Sound, a couple of miles south of Alki Point. It was a climb of about 14,000 vertical feet up to her house—or so it seemed with my heavy suitcase. Just in case, I had brought a white shirt, a dark suit and tie, shoes for a dress-up dinner date, and some comfortable shoes for walking on the beach. What I forgot on this first trip to Seattle was a couple of extra sweaters and galoshes for walking in the rain. We rode a ferryboat to somewhere and drove the long way around the Sound back to her house on the hill above the beach. We danced together at the Olympic Hotel, and just as with skiing, she could dance a lot better than I. I stayed an extra day and visited her ski shop in Seattle and met some of her many employees.

It was surprising to meet someone as busy as I. Here was a beautiful lady, 20 years younger, who owned and managed a ski shop a thousand miles from where my company headquartered. She had a 13-year-old son and also a ski school that she ran every weekend at Snoqualmie Pass with 105 instructors. She also owned this great 1909 Craftsman home with a fantastic view.

Southern California was full of single, 40-year-old ladies who would not require me to fly 1,000 miles to visit. Something was going on in me that had been dormant for a lot of years, since Jean had died, and I was a little bit on edge the entire, enjoyable time with Laurie.

Spending a lot of time with Laurie on the phone for the next couple of weeks kept me going until it was time to make my second trip to Seattle. In spite of my bad record with women, whatever was happening between Laurie and me was beginning to feel very comfortable and right.

The last week of January, Laurie went helicopter skiing at Mike Wiegele's in Blue River, British Columbia. She had known Mike and his wife, Bonnie, through her ex-husband, an old friend of Mike's. Small world. Meanwhile, I spent a lot of office time getting caught up, which seemed to be the way I'd run the company from day one in 1949, always taking on too much of a workload because I thought I had to.

For many of those years, I was running away from bad marriages. I did have a lot of friends tell me that same thing. "Slow down, relax, and smell the roses." What those people never realized is that I enjoy doing almost all the things other people consider work. But meeting Laurie caused me to look at things differently... maybe it was time to put things into perspective.

Later in March, during the ski industry trade show in Las Vegas, Laurie arranged to come visit me for the first time. I did something that was out of character: To show her my part of the world and the whole of the South Bay, I chartered a small plane. We flew from Torrance north to the edge of the airspace at LAX and then across the water to Catalina Island for lunch. I had told her about a few buffalo on the island that had been left over from a movie filmed there years ago, but she, of course, did not believe it. After arriving on Catalina, I was able to prove that I didn't *always* exaggerate.

We took a short walk over a ridge, and there were four buffalo in a small gully nearby. In the café on Catalina, Laurie had her first genuine buffalo burger, which she seemed to enjoy. The Catalina trip was followed by a drive to my nearly favorite place in the world, in San Onofre, to show her where I had spent a lot of my early years surfing. Then we cruised through the Terminal Island Navy-surplus yard in San Pedro, another one of my favorite "scenic" spots. It is full of anchor windlasses from battleships and all sorts of other nifty Navy stuff that had been taken off ships as they were decommissioned after World War II. In short, it was a World War ll junkyard of keen but useless stuff. Right in the middle of it, a lady was living in a broken-down trailer with some chickens and a couple of goats. It was a very impressive place to me, but Laurie, for some strange reason, did not share my enthusiasm.

I still did a lot of personal appearances with the feature film, but I was finally settling into letting other people make decisions that I had been making since day one of my film career. I quickly began to slow down on the sometimes 60-hours-a-week schedule, as my new partners learned how the business worked. Some of it changed immediately, and some of the changes were almost dogfights, right up until one of us gave up (usually me).

While the romance was progressing, I received an invitation to a celebrity ski race in Vail. I had not skied there in almost five years, so I asked Laurie to go with me. I had a good time with Laurie, sharing many of my old friends in Vail, and making new ones with her, some of whom became lifelong friends: Howard and Marty Head, and then later Dr. John Feagin, Dr. Jack and Kathleen Eck, David and Linda Graebel, Art and Elaine Kelton, and Dr. Richard and Gay Steadman.

After our fourth or fifth long-range commute to get together, I had taken Laurie to look at a house I was considering buying in Manhattan Beach. It was definitely not a fixer-upper—I'd done several tours of duty with those. This one was a slam-dunk move-in. It had a workbench in the garage and car-dealer-type linoleum on the garage floor. There was even a hot tub in the backyard between the house and the garage.

The view from the second-story porch stretched all the way to Malibu. Laurie helped me move in and worked on making it a home. I used one of the bedrooms as an office, and in the other I installed a pull-down bed. The double garage was a good spot to park my restored 1931 Model A Ford pickup truck.

The house was only three blocks from the beach and the bicycle path that went all the way to the Santa Monica Pier to the north and to Palos Verdes to the south. If I got up early, I could find a parking place at the beach below my house and surf for an hour or two before going to work three miles away in Hermosa; leaving early for Cabrillo Beach in San Pedro gave me lots of afternoons to go windsurfing.

With Terry Bassett as a working partner, I was finding more time to spend in the production department supervising the editors, and we were delivering a lot of finished films before deadline and under budget. I was reenergized to get back to what I enjoyed the most: making movies with my own concentrated input on them and not just a brief overview of the finished product, without the time to make all the needed changes.

In the summer of 1985, I worked hard on what would be the last feature-length ski film over which I had complete control. Terry Bassett had taken over the selection of the background music, as well as handling some of the bookings for the show, which he did very well. The audiences were getting bigger, as Terry changed some venues to larger theaters and raised ticket prices, while I continued my own habit of looking for cheap motels when I traveled. Some habits die hard.

By the middle of summer, it was time to work long hours in Hermosa and spend long weekends with Laurie, sailing to Catalina on the Hobie 33. When she could get away from Seattle and the ski shop for a few days to visit me in Southern California, I was so proud of her that there was always someone I wanted to invite to dinner so I could introduce her to them. Toward the end of that summer, I made one big mistake: Colin's soccer team was going to Canada for a tournament, and Laurie had asked me to come along. She was so disappointed and mad because I wouldn't go that she threw a pillow at me. In my usual way, I wanted to do what I wanted to do, which wasn't watching kids play soccer. I packed up and drove back to Southern California. Laurie still remembers how she nearly called off our relationship right then.

I'd had a roughly 10-year period of the bachelor life, during which it was easy to get selfish and spoiled, doing only what I wanted to do: either work, ski, or windsurf—on my own. Laurie reminded me that she came with a package too: a son, her parents, her friends, her business, and her home.

CHAPTER SEVENTY-ONE

1986–1987

Vail Seemed Like a Good Place to Settle Down

THE 50TH ANNIVERSARY OF SUN VALLEY IN 1986 WAS ALSO THE 40TH anniversary of my living in the parking lot with Ward Baker. I had received a lot of press recently, and I thought it would be a good idea to get another parka for a different look. Laurie called Doug Campbell, the president of the Roffe ski apparel company, and he stopped at the warehouse on the way home, drove the parka to Sea-Tac airport, and overnighted it to Sun Valley. As I put on the brand-new red parka, personally selected by the president of the company, I noticed the Roffe label was upside down. Out of the 5,000 Equipe models made that year, Doug grabbed the only one with the upside-down label. My story was that I bought it secondhand at a discount, which fit my MO. This attracted so much publicity that Roffe supplied me with upside-down-logoed apparel from then on.

The snow was almost nonexistent for that holiday season in Sun Valley, so when the shows were over we decided to go to Vail, where we were welcomed by a friend, Craig Altschul, who was the public relations director at the time. The first time we skied together, although haltingly because I had a bad back, we got to know George Gillett and his wife, Rose. The Gilletts owned the entire place. The first thing George did was invite us to his annual holiday dinner party at Beano's, the cabin restaurant at Beaver Creek. When we were getting in the snowcat-driven sleds for the ride up, the man in front of me was wearing shoes that lit up with each step. I made some comment about them, and he turned around and said, "You sound a lot like Warren Miller." I said, "I get told that a lot." He was Frank Wells, who became copresident of Walt Disney Company. We became good friends and went skiing together every time he came to Vail.

It was nice to be in a place where no one knew us from the time when we'd each been married to someone else. A dinner invitation to Beano's, along with Craig Altschul's contacts, opened up almost every door in Vail. Frank Wells' wife, Luanne, while hosting us at their Christmas dinner party in Minturn, told me, "Our first date together at Stanford was to one of your ski movies."

At Beano's, Laurie and I had been seated next to Jack and Joanne Kemp. I was not familiar with Jack's pro-football career or his Super Bowl MVP award, but I knew of his career as a congressman from Buffalo. They were very nice people. We later wound up as best friends in that part of the world, and I would watch Jack run for president and then later for vice president with Bob Dole. He was appointed Secretary of Housing and Urban Development under President Bush #1. We had a lot of great ski days with Jack and Joanne. Jack had grown up in the era when everyone was trying to ski like Stein Eriksen, with one knee locked behind the other. This technique, of course, led to the occasional big-time crash when he caught an outside edge. Until the Kemps bought their first condominium in Vail, they would store their ski equipment and clothes in our basement between trips back and forth to D.C. Later, through them, we became good friends with Judi and Pete Dawkins as well and enjoyed the same great relationship with them.

Frank Wells, along with Dick Bass, was attempting to climb the highest peaks on all seven continents. They made all of them except Everest, although Dick tried again later and succeeded. Frank was such a fitness nut that he would have someone take his skis up the lift, and then jog up and meet us at the top for a day of nonstop skiing. He always went right to the gym for an hour workout after a day of top-to-bottom, nonstop, no-lunch skiing.

We were riding on an old double chairlift, Number Nine, when I said to Laurie, "I've been living in Holiday Inns since they were invented, using towels with a green stripe down them. Maybe it is time to build a house and settle down. Maybe Vail would be a good place to do it." We had become good friends with Don and Nancy Byers. They were building a ski-in, ski-out duplex only a 200-yard ski down the hill to the Lionshead Gondola. Laurie and I looked at the plans and then wandered around the neighborhood. The location was perfect: nestled in the trees at the end of a cul-de-sac, with no traffic and access to a private pond full of giant "trouts" for which, if we lived there in the summer, we would have fishing privileges.

WITH TWO OR THREE MORE YEARS ON MY CONTRACT WITH TERRY AS A partner, the obligations that went with a commitment to the annual film, having a home in Manhattan Beach, and falling in love with Laurie, who lived almost 1,000 miles away in Seattle, I needed a second home in Vail like I needed a brain transplant. Well, maybe I really did need that brain transplant, but it would require too long a recovery time.

When the lifts closed that afternoon, we took another look at the subfloor of the smaller half of the duplex and realized this was not going to be a typical mountain chalet. Maybe the snowflakes, like the stars, were aligned for me to make the decision. I realized later that Laurie left the decision entirely up to me, not wanting to push me into something if we didn't stay together. In our almost third year, while windsurfing in Maui and staying with the Byers in their Sugar Cove townhouse, I had asked Laurie to marry me. She made me ask her seven times before she said, "Yes." I should have taken her to a jewelry store and bought her an engagement ring right then. It took me three or four days to even tell our hosts, Don and Nancy, that we were now officially engaged. A shrink might tell me I was afraid of failure in this newfound life, but I thought there would be less chance of a failure if no one but Laurie and I knew what was happening.

Her main reason for not wanting to be a part of the decision about the Vail house was that although I'd asked her to marry me, I hadn't done anything about it, so she didn't know whether she could trust my proposal. I was a bit gun-shy after my previous marital experiences.

After viewing the house property, we stopped by the Byers' condominium, and over a cup of tea for Laurie and me and beer for Don and Nancy, I said, "We're interested in buying the other half of your property. Now, how much was it that you wanted for it?" When he threw out the number, it sounded OK to me, but before I could reply, Laurie was asking him details on the price. Two cups of tea later, she had a $50,000 discount, and as soon as he got the papers drawn up, I would be the proud owner of some Vail dirt.

CHAPTER SEVENTY-TWO

1987–1988

Yours, Mine, and Eventually Ours

WE MOVED IN ON DECEMBER 20, 1987, THREE YEARS AFTER WE HAD MET, and the house worked great for us. After many discussions about the time we had spent in Maui, we also decided to buy a townhouse in Sugar Cove near several friends. That was a lot of real estate to buy in one year, but we did it with Laurie managing everything.

We had a small but beautiful wedding on March 9, 1988, in our living room in Vail. My son Kurt, my daughter Chris, Laurie's son Colin, her parents, and about a dozen close friends were there with us. Laurie looked like $10 million in her beautiful, pale-pink coatdress. At the last minute, she suggested I wear my tuxedo, and that seemed like a good idea (it would put off my having to die to fully amortize the cost of it, after all). After a quiet ceremony, Don Byers hired a horse-drawn carriage that took us around Vail, while we sipped champagne and said hello to our friends in the middle of a beautiful snowy afternoon. Laurie was wearing the mink coat I had given her on our first trip to Sun Valley together, and I had on my gray overcoat. She had been so thrilled at the coat, she crawled into bed in it the first 37 nights she had it! (Well, maybe only the first night.) She had bought me a wedding band that I have worn with pride ever since that day—and that includes my numerous stays in the hospital for assorted emergencies and creeping old age.

Don and Nancy had prepared a big dinner party and hired a great piano player from the Sonnenalp Hotel, and the whole afternoon was a fantastic success. Laurie had a couple of chinook salmon sent out from Seattle. She donned a large, black garbage bag over her wedding dress and filleted the fish, getting them ready for Don to barbecue for the dinner party.

Colin came to live with us later that next year and started going to school at the private Vail Mountain School in East Vail, where his soccer and ski racing ability was of value, and he learned a lot at the same time.

In the Vail house, Laurie and I shared an office in the loft, Colin had a downstairs bedroom, and we still had a guest room. It was a real thrill for Laurie and me to walk a short way down the street from our house, slip into our skis, and coast down to the Lionshead gondola. Every morning when I got up, it felt like I had died and gone to heaven, but I was still very much alive. I was living the dream that I created when I was living in the Sun Valley parking lot in the 8-foot teardrop trailer and walking to get on the nearby bus to Baldy.

My camera was a people magnet that had opened the doors to people all over the world, and after settling down in Vail, it worked its magic in a more confined space. We were welcomed to a lot of dinner parties and never needed to look for anyone to ski with. Laurie gradually took over the responsibility of managing all of my real estate, as well as her own real estate business. She had leveraged her house and bought 18 employee-housing-type condos in Vail. After buying, selling, and trading a bunch of them, she was able to finance our first big boat. I still owned the 42-suite office building in Hermosa Beach and seven storefronts on Pier Avenue; plus I had eight vacant lots left in my 11-lot subdivision in Sun Valley, Idaho.

CHAPTER SEVENTY-THREE

1988 and Beyond

The Sale of My Company and the Aftermath

TERRY BASSETT HAD PUT A THIRD PERSON IN CHARGE OF RUNNING THE company during the fifth year of our partnership, and things were working well—or so I thought. At the end of the preview season and the voice recording, we sat down for a discussion of the renewal of their 50-percent, five-year ownership contract. It was due for renewal at the end of December. During the meeting, the new manager of the film company said, "Warren, we want you to save the first week of September, because we have a surprise for you."

"I don't do surprises. Tell me what it is," I replied.

"We have reserved two hotel rooms in Carmel for a week, and we have hired the best voice coach in the state of California to work with you and your voice for the week!"

"Let me think about that, and I will get back to you." I guess my partners just didn't get why my voice and timing was important to the many film scripts.

So I took one of my lonely walks on the beach and thought about it. I knew that the narration was one of the big reasons for the longtime success of my films. People liked whatever I did that was unique. Changing my voice might make me sound like the 10 o'clock newscaster in some small town trying to get into the big time.

When I told my son Kurt what had happened, he said he had a financial partner who wanted to put up the money to buy the film company with him. This sounded like a good time for the two of them to raise the money and buy it. Why not?

Terry and his partners were surprised when asked if they wanted to sell their half to Kurt and his friend Peter Speek. Everyone except me left the meeting stunned, but within a week, everyone had calmed down, and their position, of course, was, "Why would you sell out to two young guys who had never made a movie or run a company?" Actually, they had more graphic comments, which turned out to be partly correct, but at the time, I felt the film company would be safe with the new, young owners. So my answer was simply, "Because one of them is my son."

Within a month, everything had changed, including Terry Bassett's long partnership with Bob Geddes and Tom Miserendino, when Tom retired.

I made a few mistakes in my new contract with Kurt and Peter that would come up and bite me later, but because Kurt was my son, I didn't listen enough to my attorney Harry Hathaway. It later became an expensive mistake.

When I first sold my half of the company to Kurt and Peter, they hired an Australian man to run it. They spent money in ways that I never would have. When the next payment was due, they couldn't make it, so I had to give them another year to find the money. I was also entitled to other benefits under our agreement, but I didn't take them, instead allowing them to have more cash to run the business. Soon after that, they decided to move the company to Boulder, and because they owned it, they could move it anywhere they wanted.

In the first couple of weeks of the new ownership, Peter Speek, Kurt's partner, invited me into his office for a sit-down discussion. This was a guy about 30 years old, who had never produced a movie of any kind in his entire life. Neither had Kurt, for that matter. Peter came from an advertising agency, I think, in Chicago or Milwaukee.

"Shut the door, and sit down," he said, no please included.

Peter went on to relate that Kurt and he had bought my company; that they owned it and would run it any way they wanted. He made it clear that while I'd still be scripting and narrating the film, as well as doing personal appearances, they did not want any advice from me in any way, shape, or form. He obviously wasn't remembering that he still owed me a great deal of money. I wish I'd pointed that out, but true to my nature, I didn't want a confrontation.

I replied, "Yes," and got up and left the office with no respect for or appreciation of Peter Speek. As each year of my association with Peter and Kurt continued, I looked at them with even less respect as they tried to be the producers, directors, and musical gurus; in short, they controlled everything without understanding the magic that had built the company.

For example, after I had spent four months writing a script for the finished film, I would fly to Boulder for a rehearsal, basically a preview with a focus group. The next morning, we would have a "preview review" with Peter, Kurt, film editor Kim Schneider, director of photography Don Brolin, and a guy who Kurt and Peter hired but whom I didn't have any confidence in, Max Bervy. Except for Kim and Don, the other three were afraid comedy or jokes of almost any kind might offend a potential advertiser. They were forgetting that comedy was what gave my films the culture and made them different and more popular than any of the other ski films out at that time.

During the Sunday morning review, they would systematically rip the guts out of my scripts. "You can't say that because that ski resort paid $50,000 to have us include them in the film." After a few years of this, there was one particularly bad preview review where they deleted 17 different comments that had produced genuine belly laughs in the audience the night before. The discussions became unbearable, with Kurt, Peter, and Max totally disregarding what Don, Kim, and I had done for so many years to make the film company successful.

Peter and Kurt were changing the formula more and more each year. I was presumed to be the old man whom no one could relate to anymore. One of the three of them took exception to every joke or humorous comment in the movie, until I almost quit trying. I continued to travel and introduce the film in person in select markets, but my heart was no longer in it.

With each passing year, I was becoming more of a dinosaur among Kurt and Peter Speek's 35-year-old age group—or so they thought. At opening night in Portland during that time, after Kurt had introduced me, I introduced the film with the following statement, "This is the start of my first-annual farewell tour." I tried to explain the situation that was in my heart without offending anyone, and still Kurt and Peter made no move to find a replacement strategy, so I could retire to a life of skiing and boating. I did this until I introduced the film and myself on my third-annual farewell tour. I really wanted to get away from my old film company as it was then being run.

About 10 years after they bought the film company from me, Kurt had the opportunity to sell it to Time Inc., the largest magazine publisher in the world at the time. Time Inc. had recently acquired Mountain Sports Media, which owned *SKI Magazine, Skiing Magazine, TransWorld Snowboarding,* and other assorted publications. Even though I didn't agree with how Kurt and Peter sold advertising into the movie, they were eventually very successful at making money, which is the primary goal in the business world. They sold the company for more than five times what they had paid me for it in 1989. It is hard to do business with family. Awhile after I quit working for Kurt, our personal friendship started to rebuild.

Mountain Sports Media, which had moved from Manhattan to Boulder, could expand and diversify its offerings with the film-company purchase, but it had never produced a movie of any kind. However, they did have a very competent person named Andy Bigford, who was the editor-in-chief of *SKI* and a vice president with the company. Andy had recruited me to publish my columns in *SKI,* and we were both pleased to see that, according to *SKI*'s reader surveys, it was the most popular column in the magazine. My column was soon appearing on *SKI*'s high-profile back page. It got a lot of good comments, and it would remain there for about 10 years.

I had given up my role as a writer and narrator for the film; I couldn't take it anymore. After that, Andy, along with his boss Andy Clurman, who had engineered the purchase of the film company, didn't like what they were hearing in the film. They were concerned about buying a film company that had relied on my voice for 40 years but no longer had it, and they weren't sold on the replacement options, including having Kurt take over the narration. Andy Bigford brought me back to help with the script and narrate the movie.

Andy then moved over to manage the Warren Miller company for the next few years. We got along well, and it was refreshing to work with him. I continued to write the scripts and narrate for the next couple of years, but disaster was always right around the corner. It came in the spring of 2004, when Andy was let go by Time Inc. —a mistake, because he understood the culture of the film and why it was popular, and was also a good leader. I never did understand that move.

Time Inc. named Perkins Miller to take over, and he flew to Orcas Island (where I was living at the time) to meet me—and leave me with a decision. He wanted me to continue writing and narrating the film and do about 20 personal appearances to introduce the film—with a 75 percent pay cut. He actually thought I would seriously consider such an offer.

In 2007, with the film company still going downhill while struggling with the broader challenges in the entertainment and media world, Time Inc. sold it (along with all of Mountain Sports Media) to a privately owned, Swedish publishing consortium named Bonnier. Bonnier never even bothered to call me to say hello. After watching Bonnier at work, my impression was that the film company did business completely differently, compared to my 40 years of owning it. They would go back into all of the hundreds of hours of sound tracks of my narration for the many films I'd made over the years and choose sentences here and there that might fit into whatever sequence they had. By doing this, they tried to convince the already-shrinking audience that I was still involved with the films. This, of course, worked for some customers for a few years, but the deception was obvious to most of my former annual show goers, and sadly, many had quit coming.

Around 2005, I sold my creative endeavors and the intellectual property rights to my name to Laurie's son Colin. For a decade, he worked to sell the branding of my name to commercial endeavors that would pay me a royalty on my reputation. During that time, with Colin's involvement, I'd done interviews for several of the newer, younger film companies, one of which my old company sued. As Colin had paid for and owned all the rights to my name—other than the ski films' usage, which the film company owned—Colin stepped in to protect that filmmaker as well as my name. It cost him a lot of money, but his effort was successful. We arbitrated to our satisfaction the retention of the rights to my name, which were being usurped.

I WAS ENCOURAGED IN 2013 WHEN ACTIVE INTEREST MEDIA, A MEDIA group led by Andy Clurman, acquired Warren Miller Entertainment, along with the *SKI* and *Skiing* magazine titles, from Bonnier. Andy Bigford went back to serve as the GM of the film company and publisher of the magazines for a couple of years before moving along (and helping me with this book). The company is working to bring back storytelling and humor as foundations for the movie. Kim Schneider, who I hired in 1978, is still editing away in those crazy nonstop 20-hour stretches. Tom Day—who first appeared in *front* of my camera, straight-running the headwall at Squaw—is now a talented cameraman with a dozen-plus years' experience. Chris Patterson, when he's not leading his own successful commercial shoots, goes a hundred miles a minute with ideas as the director of cinematography and as a cameraman. Multitalented producer Josh Haskins somehow manages to keep all the ideas, travel schedules, athletes, egos, and sponsors lurching forward together. Chris Anthony made a career out of appearing as an athlete in off-the-wall segments for the feature film, and he's been in virtually every one since 1990. He's still an emcee for shows in Colorado and elsewhere; I remember seeing him on-stage in Denver wearing red patent-leather shoes.

The 65th annual film in 2014 opened with a monologue from narrator Jonny Moseley that revisited why I started the film company to begin with, and why we all share that basic need to go skiing and riding. They still use footage I created, especially comedy, and you'll hear my voice at times. I wish them all the best and look forward to seeing the next film.

CHAPTER SEVENTY-FOUR

1990s

Stupid Trick Number 3,437

IN THE EARLY 1990S, I WAS STILL RUNNING A CAMERA. FOR A PRO SKI RACE in Aspen at the time, I was also directing four other cameramen. After changing into my ski clothes in the parking lot, I grabbed my skis and camera gear and jumped on the lift. As I started skiing down right under the lift, I went into a wide snowplow to slow down, and I stepped out of both bindings. Someone had borrowed my skis out of our garage, changed the bindings, and put them back without telling me. I fell over my ski tips and slid down on my stomach with my rucksack banging me in the back of the head. My hands were out in front of me, and my right hand jammed in the snow. Instantly there was a sharp pain in my right shoulder. When I finally stopped sliding, it was hard to get up and really painful to put the shoulder strap of my rucksack over my right shoulder. I didn't know it at the time, but my right rotator cuff was badly torn.

I didn't pay too much attention to it, but when we got to Maui for windsurfing, my right shoulder really hurt, and it was not fun. By the end of our stay, sleep was difficult, so we decided to stop back in Vail to see what was wrong with it before going on a scheduled boat trip.

Dr. Richard Hawkins of the Steadman-Hawkins Clinic took one look at my shoulder and said it was time for surgery; it took him 30 minutes just to bust up the calcification that had developed in my shoulder socket. It was almost six weeks before I could do much except take a walk on Vail Mountain with my right arm in a sling. I have had my share of injuries but none that have been so painful and long lasting. David Honda, a great physical therapist in Vail, kept me on the recovery path, and I learned a valuable lesson from him, as well: When the doctors tell you to do only 10 reps of an exercise, do what they say, not more. I overdid the reps and set myself back. As with all of my injuries and ailments, Laurie was right there, nursing and caring for me.

Three years later, I performed stupid trick number 3,437. I was working in my office on Orcas in September and thought it would be a good idea to do some push-ups to start getting into shape to go skiing for yet another winter in Vail. When I was younger, I could easily do 100 or more push-ups, so I thought I would start with 10. I felt good when I finished. When it came time to do 10 more the next day, I could not do a single one. I didn't know it at the time, but I had torn the rotator cuff in my other shoulder doing that first set of 10 the day before. This meant another hospital visit and six more weeks of recovery; I could be skiing by the middle of January. Maybe. My heroes—the Richard Brothers, Dr. Steadman and Dr. Hawkins—did their magic once again.

CHAPTER SEVENTY-FIVE

1990s–2000s

Finding and Building a Foundation on Orcas Island

BACK IN MAY OF 1985, MY LIFE HAD ONCE AGAIN CHANGED FOREVER. I flew to Seattle with my bicycle and drove to Anacortes with Laurie to take a ferry and then a bicycle ride from Friday Harbor on San Juan Island to Roche Harbor with a group of her friends. As the ferry moved out into the Channel, I was standing outside on the starboard side, and there was snow-covered Mt. Baker rising up into a fantastically clear blue sky; in the foreground was a sailboat broad-reaching along in front of Mt. Baker. This sight was burned into my brain, and as I sit here writing about it in our winter home on the side of a snow-covered Montana mountain, every detail of that scene is still safely in my memory bank.

On the hour-and-a-half ferryboat ride to Friday Harbor, I stood by that rail soaking up sights that I still remember. Laurie kept asking me, "Why are you so quiet? Are you sick? Can I do anything for you?" I was just stunned by the beauty of the water, the islands, and the occasional snow-covered mountain views. Having grown up there, she didn't understand the impact this trip was having on me. By the time we got to Friday Harbor, my mind was made up that I would never make any movies of this part of the world as I had made movies of the ski world for the past 50-plus years. I selfishly wanted to keep it the way I saw it that first day.

When I was recovering from my first shoulder surgery, Laurie and I realized that although we had been cruising in the San Juan Islands by boat for several years, and Laurie grew up near there, I had never driven around the islands. When my shoulder was strong enough, we drove to Seattle and bought a very small Boston Whaler from Laurie's old friends Jim and Judy Sweeney. We could launch it from each of the islands, and soon we were off on another lurching adventure. About a week or so in, we were staying in a condo in Eastsound on Orcas when I got an assignment to write a short script. Meanwhile, Laurie started looking at real estate offerings. A few days later, while still on Orcas, we visited with my old surfing/sailing friend Hobie Alter and his wife, Susan. The day before we were going to leave, Susan said, "There is a property with an old, burned-out foundation down the street that you might want to take a look at."

We walked over and looked down into the foundation—what was left was overgrown with 25 years of vegetation. Below us, tucked into what had grown in the basement of the old house, was a doe with her fawn. She just looked up at us and sauntered through the undergrowth and debris and out the door of the basement. From there, we wandered down and sat on the point for about 20 minutes, looking in both directions at the rock-covered beach with a perfect southern exposure.

Then we walked up and looked into a dirty window of the garage that was freestanding from the old house; it hadn't burned down with the house in 1954 (we found out later that the house had been built in 1936). I turned to Laurie and said, "We are going to buy this place."

The property had 350 feet of waterfront and a long driveway that made a U-turn in the east end, as though it had been designed for a horse-and-buggy estate. It was full of the small holes that are dug for perc holes, as though people had been looking for the right place to drill a well or place a drain field. There were red flags on a lot of different trees. I was afraid it had just been sold. Laurie said, "Why don't we go over to the courthouse in Friday Harbor and find out who owns it?"

We went the next day and were able to get the phone number of the owner. We went to visit them, and I asked, "How much do you want for it?" It turned out that there was no chance of drilling for water on the property because it was all solid lava with only a few inches of topsoil covering the rock, and there was also no chance for a septic tank/drain field because the topsoil was so shallow. We wanted to buy it with these two contingencies to be resolved, but the owners would have none of that. So Laurie offered them $50,000 less under the circumstances, and they took it. She had a rental property she was selling, so the timing worked out well.

I knew that people had been living in dry areas for centuries with cisterns that depended on rainwater collected off their roofs. This part of Washington is supposed to get 24 inches of annual rainfall. The garage had 900 square feet of roof. Each cubic foot of roof could bring in 8 and a half gallons of rainwater, so we could collect 17,000 gallons of water every year. All we needed to do was to build a couple of cisterns and store the water for our use. My research indicated that two people, if they are careful, use 75 gallons of water a day. That is for two showers, a dishwasher load, six toilet flushes, and one load of laundry. That meant that with two cisterns to store the rainwater, we could live there for 170 days a year. We could also buy water from Eastsound that would be delivered in a tanker truck if we ran out, and we could also get the septic tank pumped out when necessary. After we solved those problems, we got the building permit to remodel the garage into a cabin. With no boat to go north, and instead of going to Maui to windsurf, we tackled the remodeling project. We were upgrading from our Vail/Maui winter-summer lifestyle to Orcas Island and a private ski club in Montana, but more on that later.

The carpentry skills I developed when I was financing the film company with my day job in 1950 paid off big-time. We contracted out the plumbing, wiring, and drywall, but there was still three-months' labor for me and a 14-year-old kid from Eastsound. One day at the start of the project, Laurie and I were both up to our ears sweeping up dirt and dust, when I stopped and told her how much I loved her. She could have been in Maui on the beach or in Vail at a big-name concert in a meadow with all the beautiful people. But she was working right beside me, dirty and dusty, fingernails broken, as she tried to keep things clean and organized.

We got the garage remodeled into a cabin in time for the fall rainstorms, and we hunkered down in front of the woodstove. We were very much at peace with the world before I had to pack up for trips to the cities in which I was still doing live appearances for the film. Before I knew it, it was time to winterize the cabin and close the front door until spring, when we would return from Vail.

For some reason, I thought that once we got a dock and a boat bigger than the 29-footer we had sold, we could spend the rest of our lives going between this wonderful waterfront cottage, our Maui home, and a winter home in Vail. But never underestimate the power of a wife who really wants something. In 1999, when my leg was healing from a bad fracture, Laurie started collecting pictures of what she thought would be the perfect home for us. She had taken a tour of the Greene and Greene brothers' homes. These amazing brothers designed and built houses in Pasadena and other places, and before I knew it, she asked a friend and neighbor of ours in Maui, architect Barry Rand, to design what she had in mind. By now we had sold our Vail home, she had sold her 1909 Craftsman home in Seattle, and everything we owned was in storage units. She wanted to live among her many family antiques, not just pay rent to store them.

We moved into the new Orcas Greene and Greene–wannabe home in December of 2001, after three years and more than a few confrontations between the two of us. Some of the things in the plans that Laurie and Barry had worked out made no sense to me whatsoever based on my knowledge from three-and-a-half years' experience building houses, but that was in the 1950s. Laurie and I got into a stupid fight over something such as the size of the top plate for the walls that were laminated 6-by-12s. In my mind, it was nothing she knew anything about, but she believed the engineer and the builder when they said they were necessary. One evening, she got so upset with me about some construction detail I thought was unnecessary that she went up to the small bathhouse/bedroom that I'd built for our guests and went to bed. She had started out with one design-quality level, and she refused to compromise that quality, no matter how long it took or how much extra it cost.

Later I walked up to the bathhouse and said to her, "Women are instinctively nester-gatherers, and men are hunters. You continue to build the nest, and I'll go out to do the hunting to take care of us. From this moment on, I will have nothing to do with construction and design." I never did, and to this day, I realize it is a wonderful home for both of us.

The house turned out so well that when it came time to design our Montana house, we used exactly the same set of plans, including the wood finishes. However, in the Montana house, we have a full lower level that can sleep a football team, including coaches, a trainer, and three cheerleaders. We saved $150,000 in architectural fees by using the earlier plans, and when I told Laurie about that she said, “Yes, and in the middle of the night, you won’t tinkle in the closet while you’re trying to find the bathroom!”

THERE ARE A LOT OF VERY INTERESTING PEOPLE ON ORCAS ISLAND, AND a lot of stories about the old days. We have a neighbor whose great-uncle once rowed a neighbor the 25 or 30 miles from Orcas to Victoria, British Columbia. He was going to charge him $14 for the trip. The man had gotten tired of the rain and the hard life, so halfway there he said, “I’m never going to go back to Orcas Island, so that 200 acres I own is useless to me. I’m going to need that $14 a lot more than I’ll need the property, so why don’t I just give you the property instead?” Part of the land is still owned by our good neighbor, the great-nephew of the rower, and our section was a part of it, as well.

Burton Burton’s mother apparently stuttered when she filled out his birth certificate. He was a good friend who built a two-mile long, standard-gauge railroad on his property here on Orcas. He also built a full-sized railway station along the way. Out in the trees, he had an animated automobile accident at the railroad crossing, complete with realistic dummies. Burton Burton also collected old iceboxes, washing machines, and anything to do with the 1930s, from burlesque posters to uncirculated American banknotes and bills. He also had his first still camera, a 4-by-5 Speed Graphic, and a 16-MM Bolex movie camera. He was a man who made a lot of money and enjoyed spending it.

Burton had a great sense of humor in acquiring his antiques. Laurie and I went to visit him many times, and he showed us the silo that he had rebuilt and was going to fit out with a model train and tracks winding all the way up the inside walls to the top. He had a set of silver and dinnerware from the pre–World War II Orient Express, including the linen napkins, tablecloths, and all of the glassware and teacups. He had a platform for the dining table that was on a forklift mechanism, and it would rise at the same speed that the model railroad wound slowly up around the inside of the silo to the top. I have no idea the value, but it must have been huge, though he was great at buying things on eBay.

Before we built our main home on Orcas, Laurie had started two big rose beds. She loves her flowers and is talented at growing them. One morning when I went outside, a deer had chewed through the cheapskate plastic fence I'd put around them and eaten her roses right down to the ground, stems, thorns, and all. She was, of course, very upset, and I took a lot of the blame because I had built that plastic fence instead of something sturdier. Four days later, the deer ate through the fence around the upper garden, and now she had no more roses. I stayed out of the way for a while. Everyone who knows Laurie knows that she is very slow to ignite but when she does, no one is safe from the steam coming out of her ears.

Then I said, "Why don't we just have a fence built all the way around the property, and then the deer can't get in." We had the fence built horizontally along the edge of the bank above the water, so the deer couldn't climb up from the beach and it wouldn't interfere with our great waterfront view.

There was an unexpected consequence: Laurie prepared many more beds with flowers. That made it very beautiful, but our rainwater supply almost ran out, and we had to start buying it by the tankful from 12 miles away in Eastsound at $300 for 3,000 gallons. It was delivered in a 10,000-gallon tank truck, except the owner had bought a cheap one without baffles inside of it. Without baffles, he could only fill it up a third of the way but would still charge for a full load.

There had to be a better way to grow her garden, and there was. I spent a lot of time in the Navy, and we had a reverse-osmosis machine on the ship I served on. It converted salt water into fresh water, using extremely high pressure and very fine filters. A dozen phone calls later, I had all of the information to spend a lot of money for unlimited fresh water. The guy who sold us the equipment refused to install it, because he did not want to be responsible if it did not work. We had to find someone else to do it.

About $15,000 later, we had fresh water pouring into our cisterns again, at the rate of 2 and a half gallons a minute.

When we built the bigger house, we upgraded the reverse-osmosis system, and now we make fresh water out of salt water at the rate of 6 and a half gallons a minute, with a custom-built water-maker. Expensive—but it's made the property useable and beautiful, and we're grateful for it.

In 1994, about the middle of October, my older sister Mary Helen came and visited us for a few days, and our neighbor Hobie took all of us out in his 60-foot power catamaran for an afternoon cruise and lunch. On the way back, he drove right by his house, nosed his boat up to our beach, and honked his horn. About 160 people emerged from behind trees and out of the foundation of the old burned-down house, all dressed in matching white T-shirts and singing "Happy Birthday, Warren." It was my 70th birthday. It was a total surprise to me as they emerged from the hiding places. They looked like the Mormon Tabernacle Choir, but they didn't sound like them.

Laurie had reserved the dining room at Camp Four Winds and the kitchen crew to cook and serve dinner. Bob Valentine surprised me and everyone else with a special edition of my latest book, *On Film, In Print.* After dinner it was roast Warren time, and everyone did a good job of it. John Sununu, chief of staff for President Bush, senior, said, "I have been on three airplanes, a rented car, and a ferryboat today, and frankly, I don't have the slightest idea where I am."

To which Slim Somerville added, "Lewis and Clark would not have found the Northwest without Sacajawea, so it goes to reason that Warren would not have found the Northwest without SacaLaurie."

It brought down the house, and our friend Ruth Colby suggested we name subsequent boats we owned "SacaLaurie." And we did.

CHAPTER SEVENTY-SIX

1990s–2000s

9,000 Miles on the Road with a Broken Leg

BACK WHILE I WAS IN VAIL, HANGING AROUND HEALING FROM MY shoulder surgery, the publisher of the *Vail Daily* rode his mountain bike by me as I hiked up the mountain. He stopped, and we talked for quite a while about nothing in particular. Finally he said, "Why don't you write a weekly column for my paper. It should be around 1,000 words about nothing in particular except your lifetime of experiences. By the way, how much will you charge me to do this?" I like to write and draw anyway, and to get paid to do something I really like to do seems almost illegal, so I said, "How about $10 a week?" At its peak, the column was in 20 newspapers, and my price grew over the years.

I was on the verge of turning 70 when I decided to recycle the columns by self-publishing them in a book and selling the book from the stage at my personal appearances. I had spent my entire professional life working with film, and now was moving into telling my stories in print, so the logical title for the book was *On Film, In Print.* An old friend of Laurie's, Bob Valentine, owned a large printing company south of Seattle. I talked to him for about an hour, and I knew I was in the right office with the right person to do the job.

The film-tour sales plan was overwhelmingly successful, even though I was recovering from a broken leg. Laurie collected the cash as people stood in line, and we sold more than 100 copies at that first, extended 20-minute intermission. By the time the four Portland shows were over, we had sold over 500 copies. At Laurie's insistence, we always gave a percentage of our take to a charity or a cause that we both believed in.

We drove out of Portland eager to do a lot of personal appearances. I hadn't changed any since my 20s, when I was selling ski bootlaces. By the end of the tour, we had already ordered a second edition on top of our first 10,000 copies. It would be four years before we needed to publish a second book with more of my newspaper columns. This one was rightly called *Lurching From One Near Disaster to the Next*, which pretty much describes my life.

Lurching came out in paperback for $15 and hard cover for $25, and I was pre-autographing them to save time, so I could just shake the customers' hands and hand them the books. Occasionally, someone would tell me, "I don't have any money, but will you sign my program?" I never turned anyone down, and sometimes gave them a free book, too. One evening, in the very nice 5th Avenue Theater in Seattle, two girls were standing in line, and when they got up to me, the first one said, "We can't afford a book, but will you sign these?" With that, she pulled her tight T-shirt up around her neck and stuck her ample bare chest in my face. It drew a gasp from the people in the first few rows, and this still-blushing senior citizen declined and then hurried off to introduce reel two of the movie.

IN 2002, *SKI*, WHICH BY NOW OWNED THE FILM COMPANY, APPROACHED me to publish another collection of already published columns—and why not? *Warren's World*, including recycled columns, previously unpublished cartoons, and photographs, was easy to sell, especially with the aid of *SKI*.

PART SIX

Finding Home

Discovering a ski bum's sanctuary in Montana.

CHAPTER SEVENTY-SEVEN

1990s–2000s

The Fortune Cookie and the Yellowstone Club

FOR A SURF AND SKI BUM WHO LIVED IN A VAN ON THE BEACH AND IN the teardrop trailer in the Sun Valley parking lot, my lifestyle had undergone a major upgrade over the years. I next found a pretty good place to ski out my remaining years. Like everything else in my life, it wasn't easy.

On a lift ride at Vail one morning, Jack Kemp turned to me and said, "I have someone I want you to meet. I will buy dinner for all of us tonight, and I want you to sit next to him." I already knew two things: First, whoever that person was, he would probably be hustling me for something, and second, we would have an inexpensive Chinese dinner if Jack were going to buy it. Much like me, Jack was so used to everyone buying him dinner, the only credit card in his wallet was for Chinese food.

We met at the May Palace—the only Chinese restaurant in Vail at the time—and this dinner turned out to be another life-changing event. I sat next to this fellow, Tim Blixseth, who had a couple of dozen color enlargements of land he owned in Big Sky, Montana, as a result of a timber trade. His initial vision was to build a small cabin for his family, plus a couple of others for friends, along with private ski lifts and trails. The photos of the mountain showed a lot of variety. The upper half was steeper than the cornice at Mammoth, and the lower half resembled the rolling, glaciated terrain of Snowmass. During the chop suey, egg foo yong, and the fortune cookies, he invited me to visit there with Jack. His grand plan now was to develop it into a private ski resort with fewer than 1,000 lots; unless you were a member or guest, you wouldn't be able to ski there. This had never been tried before on such a large scale.

When I opened my fortune cookie, it said, "There will be a major change in your life, but beware."

I told him it might be fun to see it, but Montana was a long way from Vail. He said, "No problem. I can just pick you all up at the Vail Airport in my plane. You can ski the mountain for a day, and I'll have you back home for dinner." Laurie was, by now, fed up with so many people hustling me that she chose to stay home.

I never have turned down a free ride in a private jet. By the time the appointed day arrived, I was able to invite Jon Reveal, who had been mountain manager at Aspen, among many other ski resorts, and who could truly evaluate a mountain.

We flew to Bozeman and stayed at the Rainbow Ranch Lodge on the Gallatin River. Tim Blixseth had already had a large, expensive contour map made of his development plan to unveil for the press he had invited to dinner. I thought it was a little early to bring in the press, but that was not the way he did things. He was taking advantage of us. Jon Reveal and I stayed in the background and rolled our eyes.

Blixseth owned about 23,000 acres, with about 13,000 acres of good ski terrain. Most of it had been clear-cut, so it did not have a lot of timber value. He later sold off about 9,000 acres to the people who developed the Spanish Peaks Mountain Club, and that's another long, sad story, though with an eventual happy ending.

The road into the center of his land stopped in the meadow near the beginning of the trail to Ousel Falls in Big Sky, a small ski town at the bottom of the valley, next to the ski area of the same name. There was a rough, one-lane, pot-hole-infested dirt road into the mountain that lowered the speed limit to about 2 miles per hour.

Waiting for us at the end of the asphalt road was a helicopter, and soon we were cruising over this mountain and its acreage. Blixseth had signed Jack onto his board of directors, and he wanted me as his Director of Skiing.

Jon Reveal was impressed with the variety of the terrain and the development potential. On the way home, I found a copy of the *Robb Report* magazine, with an article about the world's most expensive wristwatches. One jeweler in Switzerland had made only nine of them because he didn't want to glut the market, and they sold out in a month for $995,000 each. I thought, "If there are that many extremely rich people in the world, there should be enough to buy expensive land at a private ski resort." I give Tim credit for having the vision.

AWHILE BEFORE ALL THIS, I WAS INVITED TO SKI WITH ANDY DALY, THEN the president of Vail, and Vail's mountain manager Chris Ryman. Andy told me, "We want to pick your brain." We met and skied, and I answered a gazillion questions, based on my life of skiing at almost every resort in Europe and North America during the previous 50 years.

By lunchtime, I was getting tired of being peppered with requests for free advice about making Vail a better year-round, destination resort. So I interrupted Andy Daly's questioning and said, "I understand that you, Vail, recently offered World Cup champ Alberto Tomba $75,000 and all expenses to spend two weeks a year here in Vail and ski with your VIP guests. Plus, you gave him a cowboy hat. I'll tell you what I think you should do instead. I live here and ski almost every day all winter. I can put Vail in my movie every year and guarantee 50,000 more skiers' fannies on your ski lift seats per winter." At that time, I was contractually free to align myself to any resort I wanted, so it made sense to me.

Andy surprised me with his answer. "Warren, we have had several meetings about just such a deal, and the consensus of opinion is that you are too old now, and skiers can no longer relate to you!" That was back when I was still writing and narrating the annual ski film, and doing about 40 personal appearances with the feature film nationwide and across Canada. I could have shared with my audiences all I loved about Vail. But Vail wasn't in our future.

The next summer, in 1998, Blixseth asked me to come over and check out the Club's progress. We drove all over the mountain and looked at his water system and where he was going to build lifts and lodges, and he wanted my opinion.

I said, "Do you want to hear what you would like me to say, or do you want to hear the truth?" I had nothing to lose, so I told him that he had built a nice private golf course in Palm Springs and that he was good at running a bulldozer, but quite frankly, I didn't think he knew a single thing about how to design and build a ski resort.

"What do you think I should I do?" he asked.

"If I were you, I would hire Jon Reveal. He has worked at ski resorts and managed mountains all over the West for the past 40 years. He supervised the replacement of all of the ski lifts at Arapahoe Basin and also tore down the lodge and rebuilt it there. He replaced many of the ski lifts at Keystone, Breckenridge, Aspen, Aspen Highlands, Buttermilk, and Snowmass. He is currently working at a small resort in eastern Canada and would like to come back to the West. I think he would be the man for a job as big and complex as this."

He asked about cost. "I don't know. That's your problem. He will be working for you, not me. I will bring his phone number at dinner tonight."

He called Jon the next day, Jon flew out within a week, and he was hired on the spot. Jon realigned two of the lifts and started cutting timber to build the trails. Then he supervised the bulldozing of some of the great ski runs, such as Quarterback Sneak, named after Jack Kemp.

To sell our Vail house, we set a high price for two reasons. The first, of course, was that it was only a 100-foot walk to where we could put our skis on and ski down to the Lionshead gondola. The second reason was that Laurie thought we might be able to sell the house on the fact that I had owned it. After the experience with Andy Daly, I tended to wonder what value my living there for a dozen winters had been.

It sold for our asking price within a month.

AT THE YELLOWSTONE CLUB, MY JOB WAS TO SKI AND SCHMOOZE WITH anyone who came for a visit, in exchange for a lot and a new home that Laurie had negotiated from Tim. During the first few years, there would be days when only two or three people would be skiing, and I got to spend all of those days in untracked powder snow with them. For two years, while they were supposed to be building our home, Laurie and I would spend our nights in a condo eight or nine miles down the road in the Big Sky Meadow. Then for two more years, still waiting for our home, we lived in a triple-wide for a year and then another year in log cabin. We finally bought the Kemp cabin property and finished out the winter, living there and waiting for the house to finally be completed.

Part of my job was to eat dinner with the guests who were staying in the small log cabins above the Rainbow restaurant. In the morning, after spending the day and evening with the prospective members, I'd call the owners and tell them if I would want to have the people to dinner in my own home. If so, they would pursue them for a membership.

One day when I got to the lift, Jon Reveal said, "Mary MacDonald (her family is member No. 6) is the only person on the property, and as a member she is entitled to ski here whenever she feels like it, so we'll turn on the lifts and the two of you can go skiing." For the next three days, Mary and I were the only people on the entire mountain. When a lift operator saw Mary and I approaching near the bottom of the hill, he would turn it on for us and then turn it off when we got off at the top. Between skiers, the lift operators would read paperback books, about one every other day.

The founders were fond of celebrities and had a lot of 8-by-10 photos to prove they were good friends with them. One morning, they showed up with former Vice President Dan Quayle. During the three days I spent skiing with Dan and his wife, Marilyn, the owners gave him a free vacant lot and an honorary membership.

One snowy day when Dan and I broke for lunch, I stopped him at the door to the Timberline Cafe and said, "Dan, those are over-the-boot ski pants that you are wearing, not in-the-boot pants. I would suggest you pull them out of your ski boots before you go in there to lunch, so you don't look like a dufus." He had to unbuckle his boots to get the pants out, but he did it. He now looked like a standard male skier, but he certainly looked very young in spite of the hard work of having been the Vice President of the United States. The media treated him poorly, but he is a smart, honest man whom we were lucky to have serve our country.

A year later, the owners showed up with Benjamin Netanyahu and his wife. "Bibi," as everyone called him, graduated from MIT with a degree in architecture and spoke English with absolutely no accent of any kind—not even a Boston accent from his college days. He had four bodyguards, and so Jack Kemp and I got to ski with all of them. These bodyguards had spent four years in the Israeli army, plus another four years of tough mental and physical training, and were the best of Israel's elite soldiers. However, they were not very good skiers, and we were always waiting for them.

One of Bibi's bodyguards was going way too fast in a very wide snowplow position, desperately trying to slow down. His eventual yard sale stretched up the hill, displaying, not necessarily in this order, his goggles, gloves, ski poles, skis, helmet, and all of the hardware a bodyguard would normally carry, including his Glock revolver and magazines full of ammunition. No one dared make a comment, but Bibi sure laughed.

The following morning, about 11:30, Bibi said, "My back is really killing me, and I am going to have to stop skiing." On the way up on the chairlift, I explained my history of back problems and the successful rehab I had from David Honda, the physical therapist at the Vail Athletic Club.

"Bibi, I think your back is hurting you because you have the entire weight of Israel on your shoulders. Would you like to try this rehab? All we have to do is push a couple of tables together in the Timberline Cafe, and I can do the magic procedure on you." Laurie was hysterically trying to get me to stop. All she could envision was my paralyzing the Prime Minister of Israel. I didn't pay any attention to her, as usual!

I soon had the Prime Minister on the dining room table, with Jack Kemp, Laurie, and the rest of the group watching and the four Israeli bodyguards hovering within an inch and a half of me at all times. Dr. Miller's method of muscle manipulation worked, and we went back out and skied the rest of that day and all of the next two days.

THE COMMITMENT BLIXSETH HAD MADE TO US BEFORE WE JOINED HIS efforts in growing the Y.C. was to deed over a vacant lot of our choice and build us a home on it, with specifics for the home's costs set in advance. But for the first frustrating five years, we shuttled from a condo to a double-wide trailer to the log cabin. I think Blixseth was way over his head financially, and so our home took him an extra three years to plat the land and build. During those three extra years, the cost of building jumped from $200 a square foot (the proposed amount that was budgeted for the

8,000 square feet) to nearly $500 a square foot. I understand that the construction virtually bankrupted the contractor, who had to finally quit his efforts on our behalf. Because the owners were three years late on our project, it cost us a great deal of money, and we ended up having to sell more of our other real estate to get through the building of the house.

While the resort was struggling through the first few years, they had hired Tom Weiskopf to build a golf course on the side of a mountain. To do that, Tom had to move more than half a million cubic yards of dirt. The course is one of the most dramatic and memorable ever created in the Rocky Mountain chain. The first three holes have a 900-foot vertical drop.

During four arduous years of construction, many of the golf course subs were not paid in a timely fashion. Many left the job all together. Tom told me several times it was the most difficult site he had worked on out of 50-plus courses. The owners knew they needed Tom's golf course expertise, and I was told they finally honored the contract and paid.

I started to play there one day with a potential member, and by the time I got to the third hole, the guest said, "This place is so fantastic, why am I playing golf? Let's go look at real estate." Later that afternoon, he bought a lot and a club membership.

Despite all the problems, I wasn't tough enough or smart enough to confront the owner and tell him I was going to leave. Laurie tried to, but they were tough on her. There are lots of stories around this subject—some funny, some that hurt, others that were just plain sad. But Laurie doesn't sit quietly by when I'm being abused: Steam comes out of her ears, and she quickly moves into action.

One night up at Rainbow, with the dining room full and the staff all working so hard, Laurie stood up to give a toast to all the wonderful people who worked at the Club, thanking them, and finishing with a joke that they had all volunteered to work on their days off to help us finish our home, something that the founders were supposed to be doing, although she didn't add that. You should have seen the looks on their faces.

Soon thereafter, the owners said we had to have a meeting. This sounded ominous. The next day I appeared in the triple-wide-trailer offices and faced Blixseth and his four executives. The first words out of his mouth were, "You are no longer the Director of Skiing at the club."

No reason was given, but I simply answered, "Well, 20 Citicorp private-banking executive clients and their wives from all over the world will be here next week, and Citicorp executives have asked me to ski with them, have dinner, and in general mix with them while they are here. What do you want me to tell them?"

There was a long silence, and finally he said, "Well, you can be the Honorary Director of Skiing."

The last winter before the house was finished, we stayed in the cabin they had built for Joanne and Jack Kemp. Before the winter ended, we wound up selling my 42-office-suite building in Hermosa Beach and buying the cabin and the four acres of land that went with it. Our agreement had stated our home would be finished to certain requirements by December 2002, but we weren't able to move in until early 2005. In exchange, they had total access to me for four months of every winter, which I gave willingly. I have devoted all my energy to the club since 1999, and most of the experience has been great because the member families are awesome.

In about 2005 or 2006, the owners borrowed $350,000,000 (that's millions) from Credit Suisse, and to do that, they had to have the club appraised. As I understand it, the Club was appraised at $1.8 billion at build-out. These numbers seemed fantastic to me. Early members Greg LeMond and Jorge Jasson had bought 1 percent of the Yellowstone Club corporation in addition to their membership. They wisely figured that 1 percent of the corporation was worth, by appraisal, $18 million—not $1 million and a vacant lot, which is what the owners offered them when they tried to buy back their 1 percent of the club. They filed a lawsuit for the amount they thought was fair.

It is my understanding that the owners pulled out most of the money they had borrowed to finance Yellowstone Club World, a private club with proposed vacation properties all over the globe, but which failed to sell even a dozen memberships. It was just not a viable idea. At the same time, Tim Blixseth and his wife Edra decided to get a divorce, which got ugly, even though they at first pretended it would be totally amicable. As I understood it, the Yellowstone Club was billed for and repaid Credit Suisse a great deal of the borrowed millions of dollars.

Laurie and I are convinced that if Greg LeMond and Jorge Jasson hadn't put up a fight with the owners, the issues wouldn't have come to a head, which led to the elimination of the owners and a hugely positive change in how the club was managed and operated.

BY THIS TIME, THERE WERE A LOT OF INCREDIBLY SMART AND SUCCESSFUL business people in the Club who got together and formed a group, the Ad Hoc Committee. Their strong and honest business ethics allowed them to earn enough money to build a home at the Club and also enabled them to pull together and stay on top of the mess and monitor what was going on legally. During the several years of the Yellowstone Club bankruptcy hearings, Laurie and I kept out of the complex financial maneuvering. Then one day, it was all solved for the best in a Montana courtroom. The more than 200 current property owners breathed a heavy sigh of relief and went back to jumping off cornices with a little more abandon. Sadly, the new owners weren't done dealing with all the false accusations that the founders continued to sling at them, but they were smart and knew how to handle it all.

Laurie and I felt terrible that so many people had believed in me and followed me to Montana to join. We're grateful that it's all cleaned up now, and the experience helped shape us into a tight community.

Back in the early years at the Yellowstone Club, when the new lodge was about one-third completed, it was announced at dinner in the Rainbow Cafe (to my total surprise) that it would be called the Warren Miller Lodge.

Now with the highly ethical, new owner in place, and good management, the Warren Miller Lodge has been cleaned up, restored, and gets constant use. Sam Byrne of CrossHarbor Capital Partners in Boston, whom we really care for and admire, bought the assets and liabilities of the Club. We are forever grateful that he straightened out the mess for all the members. The Ad Hoc committee also made a tremendous difference in keeping the membership informed and in saving the club so that Sam could buy it and make it grow. In 2015, it is still the world's largest and most successful private ski and golf club.

There are nearly 500 member families, who come there "to see rather than be seen," and more than 600 employees. On popular holidays, there might be 2,000 skiers and riders on the mountain's 15 lifts, rather than just Mary, Laurie, and me. The ski school roster includes several hundred instructors. Membership sales are brisk, property values are appreciating, and the house we built has been a great investment both financially and for all the friendships we've made, even with all the early headaches.

When finished, the base lodge was 140,000 square feet and cost, according to gossip, $100 million. It turned out to be arguably the largest base lodge of any ski resort in America and definitely the most expensive one. Despite the founders' "build it from the back of a napkin" design approach, the new owners fixed all of the problems beautifully, and the lodge includes about 20 condominiums. In this laid-back environment, members and guests leave their skis and boards overnight, or even for the season, in the ski racks in front of the Warren Miller Lodge.

The first time we went skiing out the front door of our home at the Yellowstone Club, we turned left and walked fewer than 50 feet, put on our skis, and skied down to the bottom of the ski lift. I felt as though there was nothing left that I needed in the world. I had the perfect home on the side of a perfect ski hill, a great home on an island, all of my bills paid—and Laurie was still by my side after all the years of our married life.

CHAPTER SEVENTY-EIGHT

1990s–2000s

Our Constant Companions

IF YOU DON'T HAVE PETS OR DON'T LIKE ANIMALS, YOU CAN SKIP THIS chapter—and you have my condolences for the friendship you are missing.

In 1991, at a boatyard in Anacortes, Laurie walked up to me with a little black dog that was about the size of a tiny squirrel but without the long tail. She had it tucked into the palm of her hand. With a smile I could not refuse, she said, "His mother's milk has dried up, and so the whole litter has been abandoned. Can we keep him?"

I never before had a dog, and he was so helpless-looking and cute at the same time. All I said was, "Sure, if you can get him back to Vail. Why not?"

So she stopped at a drugstore, bought some infant Pampers, made a nest in her overcoat pocket and just walked on the airplane that way. She had made up a carry-on bag with water and a large diaper, and as soon as she boarded, she took him out of her pocket and put him in the bag, under the seat.

Pepper was my constant companion for the next 14 years. He went everywhere we did, including to Alaska on our boat; he sat under my desk in Vail during snowstorms and followed either Laurie or me everywhere except when we were in Maui, when Laurie's folks cared for him. When sitting by the desk in Laurie's office at the top of the stairs in Vail, Pepper would nudge a tennis ball off the top stair and as soon as it started down the stairs, he'd jump up and run down after it. Then, with it in his mouth, he would climb back up and repeat his own tennis ball throw until he got too tired to walk back up the stairs.

When Pepper was a little over 14 years old, he started to get crabby with Laurie and bite her, as she was the one who had to do all the bad stuff to care for him, and he was becoming incontinent. One time when we were on our boat in Roche Harbor after his last potty walk at night, nearly blind, he walked right off of the dock, and I thought he had drowned because he was nowhere to be found. He had scrambled under the dock and out the other side. We finally found him after he had swum around to the other side of our boat.

He was shivering and shaking after 15 minutes in the cold water. Laurie and I talked about all of his mishaps the last six months. We both believe in ending a pet's life before they are in too much pain and can't tell you where they hurt. Laurie took him for his last trip to the vet, and he is buried in a beautiful spot on our property, overlooking the Sound, watching all of the seals, seabirds, and boats go by, just as he used to when all three of us were sitting together on the terrace doing the same thing. I know that someday I will be there at the same nice spot with a good view of the Sound, and I can sit there beside Pepper and talk about the old days.

HEADING HOME DURING THE WINTER OF 1999, AFTER DOING A PERSONAL appearance in Telluride on the broken-leg book tour, we stopped in Green River, Utah, for breakfast and parked next to a truck with a couple of dogs in it. I was hungry and headed for the restaurant, but Laurie stayed to talk to the couple. One of the dogs was a Rottweiler, and she loves them.

The couple had found another dog about 20 miles from the closest farmhouse in the Moab area, scared to death and almost dead from starvation. As I was walking away, the dog was licking Laurie's hand, and when she walked into the restaurant with the couple, I knew we had another dog to go with our little black Pepper. I was anxious to get on home and was grumbling, but after spending a few minutes with our new dog, I knew Laurie had done the right thing in adopting him. He was an Australian Dingo we named Buller, and he became our second constant companion for the next 12 years.

Later, when the Yellowstone Club would shoot the dynamite for the avalanches, Buller would cower and go hide in a closet until either Laurie or I would go and coax him back out after the explosions were over. It quickly became obvious to us that he must have been shot at when he was abandoned in the Utah desert. He was so strong and had such a good sense of smell he could run up the hill above our house in shoulder-deep powder snow and find a tennis ball I had thrown into the snowbank. After a dozen tennis ball retrievals, plowing in the deep snow, he would quit and lie down by me with the ball in his mouth and just go to sleep.

We named him Buller after the dog Beryl Markham wrote about in her book *West with the Night.* One of my best memories of him was after it had snowed about 20 inches, Jon Reveal and I jumped on the lift, without thinking about Buller. My dogs usually hung around the Buffalo Bar and Grill while I was up skiing, back then when dogs weren't a problem in the base area.

Later, when we had skied about halfway down the hill, Buller had already plowed halfway up in that shoulder-deep powder snow. He was one tough dog and in great shape. We let him rest for a bit, before we started to make turns. Buller was quickly out in front of us getting first tracks, on Al's Big Push. One of my most prized photos is of him doing just that, and it is in a frame above my desk and computer screen. No one ever saw him misbehave, and he could chase a tennis ball for as long as anyone had the energy to throw it. My only regret is that we neutered him: He was such a great dog, and I'd love to have had his offspring. He would have sired some great dogs for a lot of enjoyment for other people; everyone who met him wanted to take him home.

CHAPTER SEVENTY-NINE

2001 and Beyond

"You Have Prostate Cancer"

MY AFTERNOON NAPS DID NOT BECOME A NECESSITY UNTIL ONE MORNING in 2001 when the doctor said, "You have prostate cancer."

Less than 24 hours later, I walked into the lobby of the Seattle Cancer Care Alliance. I knew they were on the leading edge of cancer treatment, and there I met Dr. Ken Russell; within a few minutes, he had my confidence. With my age (68), there were two options: radiation or surgery. He introduced me to another doctor, who cured prostate cancer with surgery. After considerable back and forth, and considering I'd had earlier prostrate treatments in 1991, I decided on the radiation treatment.

The Cancer Institute and the University of Washington had two radiation machines, and I got to use the less expensive one. It cost only $6 million to buy and install. The lengthy treatments turned out very well for me because our friends, Ruth and Dwain Colby, had a nearby house they had fixed up to sell, and we got to live there for the nine weeks—much nicer than staying in a hotel.

It was tiring but simple and painless. I embarked on another scary journey down a never-before-traveled path in my life.

After figuring out exactly where my prostate was, the radiation nurses made a plaster cast of my lower body and legs, and then cut it in half. Every morning at 9 A.M., I would walk into the radiation room in my green, bare-bottom smock and lie down in the half of the cast that was left with my name on it. I did this so they could use the X-ray machine and shoot radiation exactly where my prostate was located. Once they got all of those measurements, they gave me a daily dose of radiation by rotating the machine in a complete circle at right angles to my spine. The entire procedure took less than half an hour, including getting into and out of that bare-bottom green robe every morning. It was completely painless: no scalpels, no anything, except conversation with a lot of helpful people.

I have lost several friends who have taken the alternative-medicine method and relied on things such as ground-up walnut shells in a hospital in Mexico. People have to make their own decisions, and Laurie was behind me 100 percent.

I would get the last appointment scheduled on Friday morning and the last one on Monday afternoon, so that Laurie and I could make the roughly four-hour trip up to our home on the island over the weekend and not have to be back until late afternoon on the following Monday.

Our friend Barbara Clever recommended a Chinese herbalist she had used to help her through health challenges. We had nothing to lose. After the appointment, we stopped at the store the Chinese herbalist recommended, where you can buy all of these herbs. Laurie walked out with almost a dozen little bags: herbs, mushrooms, and roots of all different kinds, but unfortunately the directions were written in Chinese, which we did not understand. Barbara explained how we had to boil things down into a syrup, and I was to eat steamed rice, steamed oranges, steamed everything, along with the mushroom-root syrup on everything. I have been told by many people that a good state of mind can help you along the road to recovery. With Barbara's help, my state of mind stayed upbeat through this entire treatment, and Laurie and her attitude really helped me get better and stay that way.

MAINTAINING A GOOD ATTITUDE WOULD COME INTO PLAY AGAIN IN 2006, when my eyesight dropped from 20/20 to 20/400. I had wet macular degeneration in my right eye and dry in my left eye. I caution everyone reading this to get a 6-inch-square piece of quarter-inch graph paper, put a dot in the center, and look at it regularly. I had been looking at my chart for some time, but no one told me to look at it with only one eye at a time (or maybe I wasn't paying attention?). By using both eyes, they were each compensating for the other. With one eye you will find the dot moved either right or left. The thing you have to be aware of when you stare at this graph paper is that when the lines get wavy, you must get to an eye doctor immediately.

When my macular degeneration was discovered, I couldn't read the big E at the top of the chart. We're so lucky to have a great eye doctor on Orcas Island, Dr. Chris White. The next day, he sent me to Dr. Steve Kim, a Seattle ophthalmologist specializing in retina care, who gave me the first of many hypodermic shots in each eye. Kim has continued to care for me every two months since. I'm fortunate that a treatment for slowing down the progress of macular degeneration had been discovered only six months before I was diagnosed.

Since it is not very pleasant experience, my wife always buys me the largest Baskin-Robbins pineapple milkshake after the eyeball-injection ordeal. Knowing I'll have this reward, I can manage the fear of the pain of a hypodermic needle in each of my eyes.

CHAPTER EIGHTY

1986 and Beyond

Amazing, Exciting, and Scary Boat Adventures

IF YOU ARE CHARTING THE EVOLUTION OF MY MARINE LIFE, IT GOES LIKE this: body surfing at Topanga Canyon; surfing on paddleboards made in junior high shop class before acquiring more expensive gear; surviving a typhoon in World War II on Sub-Chaser 521; sailing a P-Cat before eventually moving up to the Hobie 33; and then tossing myself into windsurfing. The next step was powerboating, which all started with that camera boat that I had bought to make Dave Slikkers' sailing film, though I had not really used it for anything but film shoots. My knowledge of a gasoline engine was limited. You put gasoline in the tank, and it runs. If it doesn't, you get out your Rolodex, look up the outboard-motor fixer, and call him for an expensive appointment.

Back in June 1986, Laurie flew to Los Angeles, and we hooked up the 20-foot camera boat and drove north. We also took along my windsurfer because I knew we would be going by the Columbia River, which still has the reputation for the best wind in the Lower 48. Laurie's son, Colin, came down on the train to join us, and we spent a few days at The Gorge, camping out in my van and sailing most of the day.

We then went up to Anacortes to launch the small powerboat. It had a single 175-horsepower outboard and a manual to troubleshoot any problems that might come up. What else did we need for a boat trip? We had a small cuddy cabin to sleep in, a Coleman gas stove to cook on, a port-a-potty to do whatever you do in them, and Colin's Gatorade jug for the water. We also had a couple of sleeping bags, a Coleman lantern for reading at night, charts of the San Juan Islands, a crab trap, and salmon-fishing gear.

We had amazing, scary, naïve, and exciting adventures on that first three-week trip into places I'd never dreamed even existed. Laurie taught me how to find and cook the clams and oysters that were on rocks. We tied up to the dock of Becky and Bruce Barr, old friends of Laurie's on San Juan Island, who taught us how to catch the wily salmon in their lair for dinner. We didn't even have a radio in case we got in trouble, and somehow we managed not to get into any serious trouble.

Those three weeks on the 20-foot boat changed my love of sailing to a new love for the thousands of islands that stretch north from Seattle to the wilds of Alaska. We did not know it at the time, but there are fuel docks and village stores about every 25 or 30 miles from Anacortes north to the lower mainland of southeast Alaska. Neither one of us knew that we should be uncomfortable living on a 20-foot runabout. We were discovering an entirely new way of life together, another way of life that fit so nicely with our love of salt water, as well as of the mountains.

We soon started developing 3-foot fever, except it grew to 9-foot fever. We put our 20-foot cruiser up for sale and located a 29-foot Regal Sunbridge that gave us a big cabin to sleep in, a nice galley, and a good shower/head. The port-a-potty finally went away. We had twin engines to cruise farther and faster north.

Mistakes?

We made a lot of them, but we collected enough memories for a lifetime. I cannot write the word "adventure" in large enough letters to tell you what the Pacific Northwest has meant to me since that first trip. How about anchoring our small boat 20 feet offshore and then backing up to a 3,000-vertical-foot granite cliff and tying the transom to small trees growing out of a crack in the rock, with the swim step close to the cliff? After taking a nap while the tide went out, we could stand on the swim step, and with a screwdriver, pry off as many oysters as we needed for dinner. Then Laurie would put them on a barbecue, and when they popped open, they were ready to eat.

Imagine the Yosemite Valley that Ansel Adams made famous with his black-and-white still photos of granite walls, 5,000 vertical feet high. Now imagine there is 500 feet of water in the valley floor that you can cruise in right up against that granite wall. This is in Princess Louisa Inlet or Pendrell Sound or lots of places in British Columbia, as well as the countless other bays and inlets of the waters along the inside passage to Alaska. And how cold is the water? Roughly 47 to 54 degrees. But deep into these inlets, in this huge expanse of islands and waterways, there is a large area called Desolation Sound (named by Captain Vancouver, as it seemed so desolate to him). The tide in this area moves north and south, never emptying the middle. As a result, the water can often be a perfect swimming temperature of 72 degrees.

On one of our earliest trips, heading down Guemes Channel to Anacortes, the wind had been blowing hard for three days, and as we eased out into the big wind waves, we could not see over the waves when we were in the troughs, so we just rode the big wind-chop waves one after the other, just as if we were surfing. I enjoyed it, but later learned that it was a white-knuckle ride for Laurie.

A few years later, we had a similar situation in our 29-foot Regal, coming around from Blackfish Sound and into Alert Bay. In my inexperience, I had no idea how dangerous it was until I got to the dock and was roundly chewed out by a Canadian Coast Guardsman for even being out in a small boat in such high winds and rough seas. But I had fun riding big waves in a small boat.

A year or two later, we learned of an Indian burial ground on a small island of about 20 acres, where we would have to land with our inflatable if we wanted to visit. The topsoil in that part of the world is, in many places, only 2 or 3 inches deep, so for many of the burials they would place the bones of the deceased in a cedar bentwood box and tie it up in a tree, away from wild animals. We anchored a mile or so from the designated spot on the chart, launched our dinghy to get to the island, and found the almost-invisible path. At the highest point on the very small island, we came upon several skeletons and skulls lying on the ground, just where the boxes had fallen from the trees and broken apart. I had a very strange feeling as I was taking pictures, and I avoided touching them. Now many years later when I look through photos, I have a wonderful feeling of peace and acceptance of death.

As our cruising time wound down in our last trip in the Regal, we headed south, and what we thought might be the final day turned into another life-changing moment. We were near the Agamemnon Channel, a rather remote nine-mile, narrow passage in British Columbia, with no easy anchorage nearby in the heavy wind we were experiencing. The current was running toward the north, and the wind was blowing south. With the heavy wind blowing, the waves were 5 or 6 feet high, and the current was stacking the waves up into nearly vertical walls of water. Even with almost no speed, our bow was coming completely out of the water, as it crested every wave and slammed down hard in the next trough. This went on for what seemed like hours, and by the time we got to Pender Harbour, we were soaking wet from head to foot.

We tied up in Pender Harbour just as it turned dark, and someone helped us out of the boat and across the dock. He nicely invited us in for a hot cup of cocoa. We stood in their cabin, with water pouring out of every piece of our clothing. His wife was sitting on the couch, toasty warm from their onboard furnace, with candlelight flickering on a side table. It was as if they were at home on a rainy Sunday afternoon.

We invited them to dinner at the Vancouver Yacht Club outstation. When Laurie and I were getting into dry clothes, I told her, "This is going to be a very expensive afternoon." She didn't understand my meaning. "Because we are going to buy a larger boat." And we did.

After the experience in Pender Harbour, we put our boat on the market, sold it, and ordered a 44-foot, custom-made sport-fisherman Pacemaker. With this move, I made one of the biggest boating mistakes ever, and with as many as I've made, that says a lot. The company went bankrupt right after receiving most of our money, and it took us a couple of years and more money to get the bank to release the hull. Finishing the boat in Anacortes and getting it into the water is another one of my very expensive experiences.

As we gained confidence in the Pacemaker, I spent some time teaching Laurie how to dock it. I wanted her to be able to come back and retrieve me if I ever went overboard. (Since she learned, she won't tell me whether she will or not.) She still does all the docking and handles most of the boat's systems.

We finally got rid of the Pacemaker in 2003. We had really enjoyed going north up the Straits and poking around all the islands and waterways of the B.C. Inside Passage and on to Alaska, so we set out on a search for the perfect boat. We wound up with a low-hour, 47-foot Bayliner at a good price, thanks to John Ripley at BananaBelt Boats in Anacortes. He probably knows more about Bayliners at resale than anyone, and he's helped us every year and every time we have problems.

Orin Edson started the Bayliner boat company along with Slim Sommerville, also our friend, and they went on to build 1,250 of the 47-foot model, so we knew that it was well designed for our purposes. Once we became comfortable, we started to prepare for a trip that would take us about 1,000 miles north to Glacier Bay in Alaska. We had made several trips there in the Pacemaker, but for a shorter duration. This trip was about six weeks, but that was still not enough time.

Throughout the entire Inside Passage to Alaska from our island, there are only two passages of about 40 miles each where you are exposed to the Japanese rolling westerlies and the wind, waves, and weather from everywhere in the northern Pacific. If you watch the weather and leave early in the morning, you can put these 40-mile stretches behind you by the time the afternoon wind comes up.

Our Glacier Bay experience was on the 200th anniversary of the year that Lewis and Clark first saw the Pacific Ocean. They had Sacajawea to help them find the Northwest, and I had SacaLaurie, the name we gave our Bayliner, to get us there.

At the mouth of one of the largest glaciers in Glacier Bay, we put the dinghy over the side and took pictures in front of the glaciers. I was driving the dinghy around in a sea of floating ice that had broken off from the face of the glacier. Meanwhile, Laurie and our two friends, Bruce Barr and Merrily Smith, were wrestling a 50-pound chunk of ice into the deep freeze on the back of our boat.

When we got back to the ranger station, we inquired how old the ice might be. The ranger replied matter-of-factly, "It is 200 years old." I romanticized and said, "Maybe this ice is from a snowstorm the same year that Lewis and Clark camped out in the rain at the mouth of the Columbia River. We can serve mixed drinks for our friends on the boat and include some 200-year-old ice in them."

The 2,000-mile trip was much too short. We left on Mother's Day and got back home on Father's Day. As usual, I made a couple of stupid lurching mistakes on the trip. The first one was a couple of hours north of Campbell River when I was not paying attention and hit a log. We had to turn around and limp back on one engine to a boatyard in Campbell River.

Once there, we found a scuba diver to assess the damage. He reported a bent port prop and port shaft; we had to be hauled out and have them straightened. I was disgusted with my exemplary ability to find a log and hit it. We had to stay there for four days to get it fixed.

The other dufus move was when Laurie—the Commodore, Admiral, and Navigator (I was Captain, but without any authority)—had pointed out a marker about a mile ahead. She went down into the galley to fix a cup of tea, and when she came back up to the pilot house, I was going on the wrong side of the red can on the top of the pile of rocks. She yanked the throttles back and spun the wheel into a left turn and missed running us aground by about three or four boat-lengths. I didn't realize yet that my eyesight was starting to fail. She saved us from disaster in a very remote place, as she has saved me a gazillion other times during the years in our marriage and while boating.

The Bayliner sits at our dock waiting for the next tank of fuel and completion of this book, so we can once again go north. It might be a good way to celebrate the eventual publication. Why not?

CHAPTER EIGHTY-ONE

2002

Building One of the World's Best Skateboard Parks

WE BEGAN THE ORCAS ISLAND SKATEPARK PROJECT IN 2002. I SPENT some time in the part-time role of fundraiser, because the only places kids could ride their boards were the grocery or drugstore parking lots. I donated all of the profit from some book signings, designed and sold T-shirts at the market and the hardware store, and started to spread the word. Paul Garwood, who owns the local lumberyard and hardware store, was the first one to help raise money. I had accumulated about $37,000, but that would not buy nearly enough concrete.

One day, in a casual conversation with the school superintendent, he said, "The school could donate as much as a half an acre of our property where you could build the park."

We were off and running, and fundraising. We started interviewing skatepark builders. There were not a lot of them in business in 2002, but one stood out: Mark Hubbard—known among friends as Monk. He arrived for his interview with leftover concrete on his arms from troweling another park somewhere. We talked for a while, and I asked him where he lived when he was building a park. I was concerned about a large hotel bill for three or four people for a couple of months, but he answered, "In my car, of course. After work, I go to the local YMCA, and for a dollar I can get a shower, a towel, and a swim if I want one. Then it's a Subway sandwich or a Big Mac and fries for dinner."

I could relate to this guy, so we asked him to let us know when he would be available and how much he would charge. A week or so later, Paul and I were sitting looking at the empty half an acre when Mark called and said, "I will be available in two weeks to start your park." We sat there on the park site and agreed. "If we start digging the hole for the park, the money will come."

And it did.

We started hustling for donations, and I had my first lunch with a potential donor and had exactly the right presentation!

"In any little league baseball game, nine kids always lose and their 18 parents also lose. In a skateboard park, everyone is a winner because there is no score."

He agreed and asked, "How big a check do you want me to write?"

I was embarrassed, because with all the serious fundraising we had done before, I had been the shill, and I'd always expected my wife to do the follow-up. Knowing his living standard, I asked, "How about $1,000?" He wrote the check before dessert showed up.

The day that Mark Hubbard arrived, a man living on the island with a large excavator brought it over to help us. He had bought it when he retired, because for all of the years he'd worked behind a desk for a living, he'd always wanted to own and operate his own excavator.

The hole for the park started getting bigger and bigger, and Mark's four-man crew showed up in their vans, tents, and cars, ready to sleep right alongside. During their work, they lived within a hundred feet of the park and the tennis courts, and they took their showers at the state park on the east side of the island.

Both Paul's wife and mine were busy keeping track of the donations, cooking, and rounding up big potluck dinners for the crew and volunteers two or three nights a week until the grand opening on the Fourth of July.

One means of raising money was very simple and got the entire island behind us. We staged the mother of all garage sales, raising more than

$6,000. Before the park was finished, we had collected over $250,000 from people on the island, which has only 4,000 year-round residents.

About two weeks into construction, Mark had an ever-increasing crew working for him. Paul and I started to get worried that he had too big a payroll; on some days there would be as many as 32 men and the occasional woman working on the park. But there were only four men on the payroll. All of the rest were volunteers coming in on the early-morning ferry from as far away as Bellingham to the north and Seattle, 90 miles to the south. A few of them spent their annual vacation time troweling concrete and living in Moran State Park on Orcas in a tent for $5 a night.

On July 4, 2002, we held the grand opening, with Mark putting on a show of how exciting the park could be, with plenty of space for beginners as well as challenges for the best riders.

I had commissioned a brass plaque for the entrance. It was a quote that I first read in Tom Watson's kitchen when I skied with him in Stowe many years before. Tom's father had invented a little company called IBM, and at that time, Tom was CEO.

It says, "There is no limit to the amount of good a person can do if he doesn't care who gets the credit."

Six months later, when we were fundraising for the park's endowment fund, I received a phone call from a lady in San Diego. Her son had skated in the park for a weeklong vacation. I remembered him very well because he wore a Batman costume while he was learning to skate. He was very quiet and never cried when he fell, or interacted verbally with anyone, even when other kids were helping him. It was as if he were deaf and incapable of speech.

The lady on the phone went on to say, "He was adopted, and we found that he wouldn't speak a word. On the way home after that week of skateboarding, we were driving through Sacramento, when from the backseat we heard, 'Dad, can I have a hamburger?' These were the first words, or any sound, that came out of his mouth since we adopted him nine years ago."

The Orcas Island Skatepark earned a reputation as one of the three best skateboard parks in the world at the time. Mark Hubbard has gone on to build more than 60 parks around the world, from Norway to Israel to Denmark.

EIGHT YEARS LATER, I WOULD SEE MY NAME ON A BUILDING FOR A project in which I didn't deserve credit. In July 2010, the Ophir School in Big Sky converted one its gymnasiums into a performing-arts center and asked if they could name it The Warren Miller Performing Arts Center. Fundraising would start with a goal of $1.5 million. Even though I was a relative newcomer to Montana, they said they wanted to honor my local community involvement and a "legacy that demonstrates a bridge between skiing and the arts." Fundraising, led mostly by Loren and Jill Bough, was jump-started when an anonymous donor said he would match the first $100,000 donated. The center is now busy every day, hosting local to national acts. During the school day, students learn from a faculty of drama, visual arts, and music professionals.

CHAPTER EIGHTY-TWO

1985 and Beyond

Despite My Nutso Life, the Kids Are All Right

HONEST, LOW-KEY HUSTLE BREEDS SUCCESS, AND IN RETROSPECT, I COULD be faulted for hustling too much, often at the expense of my family. When the sun was out and the skiing was spectacular, I could have been teaching my three children how to be better skiers. Instead, I would say good-bye to them in the morning while they were still in their P.Js and hustle off to run a camera. I'm fortunate that they grew up to be happy, healthy, and successful in life.

My kids' weddings are great memories. During one of our early Christmas seasons in Sun Valley together, Laurie and I flew to Napa Valley to see my oldest son, Scott, marry his sweetheart Melissa on December 21, 1985. It was a pea-soup-thick foggy evening. The ceremony was held in Scott's studio, and it was magic for them: Melissa looked beautiful, Scott handsome. He had moved to Melissa's property in the Napa Valley and could run his film business of creating high-budget TV commercials from there. Scott and Melissa's three children are now spread far and wide. Valeska, who had hoped to be a ballerina, is a successful model and was last heard from in Brazil. Kasamira is modeling in either New York, Los Angeles, or the Far East. Alexander, my first grandson, is an assistant cameraman, following in his dad's (and granddad's) footsteps.

Kurt married Ali Pitluck on July 8, 1989, on a beach several miles north of Malibu; his sister Chris decorated the site with large, colorful umbrellas and lots of beautiful flowers. To get there, you had to go down a steep path and a nearly vertical 200-foot cliff. It was daunting, especially since I was wearing a coat and tie and Laurie was wearing high heels and a dress. The ceremony was beautiful, and I enthusiastically approved of who Kurt chose to marry. We had all taken off our shoes so we could walk in the sand, and later I rolled up my pants and strolled down the beach into cool, clear ocean water.

Kurt and Ali and their first child, Jenna, moved to Boulder a little while later. They bought a great house on the edge of a small lake with a good-sized swimming pool for all of the kids' friends to enjoy. Their son Ryan's nickname is Blaze: While Ali was in labor, Kurt was paged in the hospital. Their house was on fire, and they lost almost everything except the swimming pool.

Today, Jenna has graduated from college and is following in her mother's footsteps as a schoolteacher, while Ryan is in school at the University of Colorado.

Our big house, as I call it, on Orcas Island was about a year from being completed when my daughter, Chris, decided she was going to get married. She wanted to do it here on our terrace; the date was set for August 18, 2001. We shut down construction for a couple of weeks while Laurie scrambled to organize the wedding. We didn't have the kitchen yet and only one bathroom, and she worked tirelessly to prepare food and activities for 132 guests, including about 25 kids.

Chris married David Lucero, a very smart, independent, 6-foot, 5-inch environmental biologist. His company looks for methane and other gases in properties before construction begins. He's a gentle giant, and we're lucky that he chose my daughter. They had been friends in high school, when Chris was already about 5 feet, 13 inches tall, while David was only 5-foot-7. They saw each other again many years later: David had grown into a wonderful, thoughtful person, and into a 6-foot, 5-inch body.

I picked up Chris in her wedding gown in our boat at a dock about four miles away and then drove her to our dock. I escorted the bride up the pathway to our house for the ceremony; Chris and David had their backs to the water so all of the guests could enjoy the the view of the Washington Sound at its summertime best. Chris and David have four dogs and three cats, or vice versa, and spend a lot of time on the beach without worrying about where their kids are.

Kurt, after his very successful decade of owning and running the film company, has established a foundation and is busy promoting it. Scott is filming TV commercials, and Chris is a still photographer covering the scene in the South Bay of Southern California.

YOU MIGHT BE WONDERING WHAT HAPPENED TO WARD BAKER AFTER WE lived in the teardrop trailer for two winters in ski resort parking lots across the West. He married a great lady, Jackie, who had been a United Airlines stewardess and is now an acclaimed quilter. They are retired and living on Maui where Ward, at my age, still free dives regularly after dinner. A few years ago, he said he could go as deep as 85 feet and stay underwater for three minutes. In 2014, at the age of 89, he complained that he could only go down to 65 feet and stay underwater for two and a half minutes. Thank you, Ward: You made our Sun Valley parking lot living a lot of fun.

CHAPTER EIGHTY-THREE

1979

My Cathedral of the Gods

"More spiritual than any cathedral I've visited."

THE SKY ABOVE THE VILLAGE WAS SLOWLY CHANGING FROM DARK GRAY to the pale blue of dawn. In the street below my apartment, the apprentice baker pedaled by on his bicycle, dwarfed by a huge, woven wicker basket full of delicious-smelling rolls for the hotel down the street.

I had already been up for half an hour, packing all of my camera gear in yet another rucksack, similar to the many I had worn out during the past 30-plus years. I was to rendezvous at the Zermatt helicopter pad at 7 A.M. with our guide, our four skiers from Idaho and Colorado, and my cameraman, Don Brolin. As I climbed in and buckled up, the anticipation was so thick you could almost slice it. I handed my skis and tripod to Ricky Andenmatten to attach to the outside rack. I always had my rucksack and camera gear along with me, wherever I was going.

The pilot, who only spoke French, started throwing switches, and the turbine engine began its high-pitched whine. The huge rotor blades above us began to bend upward from the center, as the rpms increased and the thup-thup-thup began, a sound I'd learned to love from my many years of heli-skiing and filming.

Since I owned the film company and was paying for everyone's ride,

I got to sit in the front seat to the left of the pilot and run my Arriflex during most of the flight. That way, I would capture all of the necessary scenes for the editor to work with when we got back to our studio.

As this magic machine climbed toward Theodul Pass, which leads from Zermatt to Italy, the sun was already etching beautiful, angular shadows across the untracked snow and the tumbling glacial ice fields that in places are more than a thousand feet deep. To our right, the Matterhorn once again assumed its rightful role as the Altar in this vast Cathedral of the Gods.

Barely 15 minutes later, on a tour that would have taken us 24 hours to climb on skis, we landed gently in deep powder snow on Monte Rosa's northeast shoulder. Now it was time for us to employ all the skill and knowledge that we had honed and refined during thousands of descents on skis with a camera in our hands. During the next six hours, Ricky, Bob Hamilton, Pat Bauman, Jim Stelling, and Jon Reveal leaped over crevasses, rappelled down ice blocks, and carved endless turns in untracked powder snow. Ricky kept us alive with his knowledge of where the ice bridges over the crevasses would be, where we could ski, and where we would die. He was quite familiar with the latter, as a member of the local search-and-rescue team, and in fact would be called out that night to retrieve a body.

About 3 P.M., Ricky said, "I have a great surprise. Follow me, but be sure to stay in my tracks." He then made three turns and disappeared down a slope that led right into a crevasse, again hollering, "Follow me, but be very careful."

We timidly followed. I have always been suspicious of surprises on high-mountain glaciers, especially when people disappear into a crevasse. So I took longer than usual to put my camera away, and then slowly sideslipped down to join them.

At the bottom of the slope that led into the crevasse, everyone stood in silent awe, except for me: I was scared to death. As my eyes slowly adjusted to the darkness, it was even more frightening. We were standing inside the beginning of a half-mile-long, 65-foot-wide, 30-foot-high tunnel of ice. At the far end, the sun was sending brilliant, beautiful slivers of fractured rainbows in every direction. Beside us, a 20-foot-wide, 3-foot-deep river of pale gray-green ice water was loudly tumbling its collection of rocks as it rushed by.

Overhead, the glacier's massive ice blocks were leaning together, forming a true "Cathedral of the Gods." The slanting ice walls were 50 to 75 feet high. The icy, swiftly flowing river had been undercutting them along their base for countless decades.

Ricky was calm and cool when he said, "We can ski along this ice ledge by the river. It's only about a meter wide, so be careful. This black ice is a lot harder to ski than you are used to. Be sure not to slip and fall into the river. If you do, you'll get sucked under the ice and drown before I can rescue you."

This seemed like an appropriate time to ask Ricky what I thought was a very logical question. "What makes you think this ice won't cave in on us while we're down here?"

He had a logical answer. "Warren, what makes you think it will?"

Ricky had been down here before, and he knew what he was doing. I figured he wasn't going to risk his life just to show off for us. I calmed down . . . a little bit.

As I inched along the narrow, black-ice ledge, I was spellbound by the hanging icicles, the dripping water, the water rushing by, and the many different colors of ice. We were all frightened by the occasional rumble and thunderous explosion coming from the crash of some distant block of ice.

About half a mile later, we emerged into the brilliant light at the end of this unforgettable Cathedral of the Gods—more beautiful and, for me, more spiritual than any of the many cathedrals I have visited in my lifetime.

When we finally began sidestepping to reach the brilliant sunshine and powder snow on top of the glacier, it was a lot later than we thought. We had spent more than an hour entering and traversing only a half mile, under ice that was at least 200 feet thick.

Now we would have to hurry so we could catch the last gondola before it left at 6 o'clock to take us down to the village of Zermatt. Ricky led us in a long, high-speed traverse for the last mile or two.

Ahead of us and slightly off to the left, in the late afternoon sun, the Matterhorn showed another of its many moods. To the left of this incredible mountain was Theodul Pass, and a little farther to the left was Monte Rosa. The late-afternoon sun illuminated our tracks—tracks that we had filmed eight hours and five or six miles ago. My skiers had left graceful turns, while Don and I had left long traverses and kick-turn tracks, as we moved a lot less skillfully from camera setup to camera setup.

Ricky, Jon, Jim, Pat, and Bob had quickly skied away from Don and me with our heavy rucksacks, loaded down with 45 pounds of cameras and tripods. I also had an extra 20 birthdays to carry around. I was lurching along last in the wet tracks of slushy snow, when a flash of light caught my eye way off in the distance near the top of Theodul Pass.

I was barely able to make out two tiny dots carving backlit figure-eights in the late-afternoon corn snow. They were headed for one of the high-mountain huts to spend the night.

It was a beautiful sight. I took off my rucksack, unhitched my tripod, set it up, got out my camera, mounted it on the quick release, hooked up the battery, spun the prism so I could see through the viewfinder, focused the lens, and then zoomed it to the maximum focal length telephoto available with a 12- to 120-MM zoom lens.

What I saw through the lens was truly unbelievable. The tracks they were leaving in the backlit corn snow were almost black.

As I was reaching for the "on" switch on my Arriflex, a thought occurred to me: I've been recording scenes like this since 1949, so I could share them with millions of people.

Instead, I just watched these two skiers make many tens of turns, while my own party of skiers traversed on ahead.

If I missed that last gondola, so be it.

For once in my life, I saved that beautiful figure-eight scene just for me. No one will ever see it, nor will anyone ever see the pictures in my mind of my almost-private Cathedral of the Gods. I never did turn on my camera, for either time or place.

AFTERWORD

2015

Did I Say That? Laughter Makes All the Difference

TODAY, 65 YEARS LATER, PEOPLE OCCASIONALLY STOP TO TELL ME HOW they grew up watching my ski films. The ski season did not start until the local ski club or ski shop rented the latest film. They will tell me how I used to walk out on the stage and introduce the film in their city, and they can remember the sound of my voice and seeing my bald head shining from the corner of the stage. I'm lucky they remembered it: They all helped support my lifestyle.

Looking back on what set my films apart, it was the emphasis on entertaining people that made all the difference, and that means making them laugh. I learned that the first time I saw John Jay showing his film in the late 1940s, and I never forgot it. Even though I flunked English, I had a unique view of the world that I could translate into words and phrases. Many of my lines over the years were borrowed (stolen?) from others and repurposed for my needs, so apologies (and thanks) to those who may have said some of them or part of them before me. Others, like "On the other hand, you have different fingers" or "In 100 years, all new people," were my own weird inventions.

On Life

Never tell a lie, because you don't have a good enough memory.

Two policemen are smarter than one crook.

Always try everything at least twice.

Life is what happens to you when you're making other plans.

No one can make you feel inferior without your permission.

For every opportunity to enjoy freedom, there is an equal and opposite government restriction.

At least once a year, go someplace and do something you have never done before.

In spite of the high cost of living, it is still very popular.

Freedom is located somewhere outside the box.

How many roads must a man travel before he admits he is lost?

Old habits can produce old results, and new habits produce new freedoms.

Not getting what you want can be a stroke of good luck.

Indecision is the key to flexibility.

My indecisions are final.

You can't tell which way the train went by looking at the track.

Happiness is merely the remission of pain.

Sometimes too much drink isn't enough.

Things are more like they are today than ever before.

Friends come and go, but enemies accumulate.

If you think there is good in everybody, you haven't met everybody.

If you can smile when things go wrong, you have someone in mind to blame.

Never eat in a restaurant with a bowling trophy on the cash register.

Don't you wish you'd had that second thought first?

I finally got it together and forgot where I put it.

When my ship came in, I was at the airport.

The only place to hide is behind the horizon.

The perfect driver always rides in the backseat.

If at first you don't succeed, failure may be your thing.

You are a unique person, just like everybody else.

On the other hand, you have different fingers.

Going to church doesn't make you a Christian any more than going to a garage makes you an automobile.

They say it's always darkest before dawn. So if you're going to steal your neighbor's newspaper ... that's the time to do it.

On Work

One-seventh of your life is spent on Monday.

If you can afford to go to college, then you don't need to.

Don't ever forget that you will work all of your life to be a success overnight.

Entertain the people who show up, and feel sorry for those who don't.

Making a living is very different from making a life.

If you don't wake up excited a few minutes before your alarm goes off in the morning, perhaps you have the wrong job, the wrong home address, or both.

If you don't have any idea where you're going, you'll probably end up there.

By the time you make ends meet, they move the ends.

All the world's a franchise, and it started with the pay toilet.

There is no substitute for genuine lack of preparation.

Freedom is when preparation meets the opportunity you have created.

On Relationships

When God created man, she was only kidding.

If your parents didn't have children, odds are you won't either.

If at first you don't succeed, why don't you do it the way your wife suggested?

She had an hourglass figure but her time had run out.

He used cue cards at his wedding.

He was a modest man, with a lot to be modest about.

You can walk through the waters of his mind and not get your feet wet.

He was an engineer in subterranean sanitation.

From the back, she looked like a yellow cab with both doors open.

A man without a woman is like a fish without a bicycle.

On Aging Gracefully

How old would you be if you didn't know when you were born?

Anyone who says "I can ski as well at 50 as I could at 25" was really lousy at 25.

I ate a lot of "natural" foods ... until one of my friends died of "natural" causes.

If you keep thinking you are getting old, you will become old sooner.

Why we age is a biological question; how we age is a philosophical one.

It's been a long, hard road, and some of the roads weren't paved.

Birthdays are good for you—the more you have the longer you live.

Growing old is mandatory; growing up is optional.

No one is ever too old to do something really dumb.

You've reached maturity when you discover the volume knob also turns to the left.

You're getting old when you no longer want to throw a snowball.

Don't take life seriously, because you won't come out of it alive.

One out of one people will die.

In a hundred years, all new people.

I used to think that I would live forever—now I realize that I already have.

Die living.

On the Mountain

The family that skis together goes broke together.

Remember your first day on skis? This looks like it is going to be another one of those days.

There was something magical about my camera that automatically lowered a skier's IQ.

Skiing's changed. You used to have to watch home movies of your friends' vacations to Mt. Stupid. Now you have to watch videos of their knee surgery.

You ski as well as your kids do for one day of your life.

Commuting one hour a day each way times 50 weeks a year is 500 hours, or 12.5 workweeks. Don't tell me you don't have enough time to ski more.

You can do four things with a pair of skis. You can turn right, turn left, go straight, or sell them.

For sale: Condominium-view condominiums.

Adventure is the invitation for common people to become uncommon.

You can't get hurt skiing unless you fall.

Streets are straight, houses are square, and our bodies are round. We don't belong inside. We belong outside, doing stuff.

The road to Alta is never closed; sometimes, however, travel is restricted.

The definition of extreme is to go past your known limits by an unknown amount.

The best thing about skiing backward is you can see where you've been.

The family that bitches together skis together.

Bumps on the mountain are like heartbeats; you only have so many of them in your knees, and when they are gone they are gone.

When I started skiing, my pants were baggy and my cheeks were tight. Now my cheeks are baggy and my pants are tight.

When the first fiberglass skis came out, you could buy them in any color as long as it was black.

I like to ski on the edge of total relaxation.

I don't want a cheaper lift ticket. I want an expensive lift ticket that costs less and keeps others from skiing so I can have the mountain to myself.

When it comes to skiing, there's a difference between what you think it's going to be like, what it's really like, and what you tell your friends it was like.

The best place in the world to ski is where you're skiing that day.

You want your skis? Go get 'em.

If you don't do it this year, you'll be one year older when you do.

See you next year, same time, same place.

Thank you, and good night.

OTHER BOOKS BY WARREN MILLER

THE NAVY GOES TO COLLEGE 1944

NICE TRY GEORGE 1946

ARE MY SKIS ON STRAIGHT? 1947

WINE, WOMEN, WARREN, AND SKIS 1957–58, First edition

IN SEARCH OF SKIING 1980

ON FILM, IN PRINT 1994

LURCHING FROM ONE NEAR DISASTER TO THE NEXT 1998

SKI & SNOW COUNTRY 2000, captions and introduction by Warren to support Ray Atkeson's photography

WARREN'S WORLD 2002

A NOSE FOR WINE 2004, with Jeannie McGill

Warren is now working on three more books:

HOW OLD WOULD YOU BE IF YOU DIDN'T KNOW WHEN YOU WERE BORN?

LIFE IS TOO SHORT TO LEARN HOW TO PLAY GOLF

AFTER THE SNOW MELTS

THE LIST OF AS MANY FILMS AS WARREN CAN REMEMBER

1949	Surfing Daze	1950	Deep and Light
1951	California Skis and the Harriman Cup	1952	Wandering Skis
1953	Ski Fantasy	1954	Symphony on Skis
1955	Invitation to Skiing	1956	Have Skis, Will Travel
1957	Anyone for Skiing?	1958	Are Your Skis on Straight?
1959	Let's Go Skiing	1960	Swinging Skis
1961	Many Moods of Skiing	1962	Around the World on Skis
1963	The Sound of Skiing	1964	The Skiers
1965	The Big Ski Show	1966	Ski on the Wild Side
1967	The Ski Scene	1968	The 13 Killy TV Shows
1969	This Is Skiing	1970	The Sound of Winter
1971	Any Snow, Any Mountain	1972	Winter People
1973	Skiing's Great	1974	The Color of Skiing
1975	There Comes a Time	1976	Skiing on My Mind
1977	In Search of Skiing	1978	Ski A la Carte
1979	Winter Fever	1980	Ski People
1981	Ski in the Sun	1982	SnoWonder
1983	Ski Time	1984	Ski Country
1985	Steep & Deep	1986	Beyond the Edge
1987	White Winter Heat	1988	Escape to Ski
1989	White Magic	1990	Extreme Winter
1991	Born to Ski	1992	Steeper and Deeper
1993	Black Diamond Rush	1994	Vertical Reality
1995	Endless Winter	1996	Snowriders
1997	Snowriders 2	1998	Freeriders
1999	Fifty (Warren not involved)	2000	Ride
2001	Cold Fusion	2002	Storm
2003	Journey	2004	Impact

MARKETING FILMS (DATES UNCERTAIN)

Let's Ski
Skylift to a Ski Lift
Race Tech
This Is Skiing
Olympic Preview
Skyway to a Ski Holiday
Helicopter to Alpine Meadows
California North and South
Ski Zermatt
Austria Skis
Powder Above 10,000'
Ski France
Western Skiing
Skiing the Hardway
Focus on Northwest Skiing
Ski Courchevel
Design for Skiing
Midwest Ski Madness
Skiing East & West
Little Skiers Race Today
Ski Fliers
Technique of Powder Skiing
Glaciers of Switzerland
Japan, Land of Falling Skiers
Modern Race Technique
American Ski Technique
Ski Tricks
Ski Racing for a Decade
France Is for Skiing
Winter Adventure
Ski Colorado
Ski the Sugar Bowl
Skiing Is for Fun
Ski Flying Yugoslavia
Mammoth Mountain Ski Championships
Ski Japan
Swiss Ski Antics
Junior Ski Olympians
Would You Believe Skiing?
Crystal and Boyne
Hawaiian Surfriders
Sun Valley Daze
Ski Mammoth
Southern California Skis
Switzerland Is for Skiing
New England Powder
Up the Raging Colorado
Ski Aspen
Chamonix Is for Skiing
Austrian Technique
Ski Innsbruck
Helicopter to St. Moritz
Ski Vermont
Aspen Powder
Ski Davos
Stratton Mountain Story
Ski Racing Thrills
Ski New York
Prestige Powder
Skis Above 12,000 Feet
Ski the Arlberg
Stein Eriksen Technique
Eastern Deep Freeze
Clown Prince of Skiing
Snowmass
Canadian Technique
The New Othmar Schneider Technique
Ski New Zealand
Park City
Ski Vail
Ski Snoqualmie Pass
Techniques of Short Skis
Barcelona, Innsbruck & Zurs
Swiss Ski Technique
Squaw Valley Ski
Donner Ski Party
Great Ski Falls
Steep and White
Fabulous French Alps
Performance Sailing Craft – Harken

Cameras in Motion
Betsy Snite
High Speed Sailing
Pikes Peak, Pikes Peak Preview
Twin Peaks
Ski the High Life
Ski a Go Go
Ski de France
Sun Valley
Wonderful World of White Stag
Havasu Promotion
Namu, The Killer Whale
Be Continental, Ski Colorado
Ski a La France
Skee Horse
Wild, Wonderful World of Skiing
Broken Leg (commercial for whiskey)
Skiing in Colorado
Ski Sled
Snowshoes, Sandals, & Systems
White Stag Skis Snowmass
Alpental Progress Report
Downhill Racers
Old Crow, commercial
Skiing at Boreal Ridge
The Competitive Edge
Mount Baldy Skiing
Factory Shoot
Sears Winter
Skiing at Squaw Valley
Ski the Wild Mountain
Colorado is Continental Ski Country
Sun Valley (re-edit)
A Place for All Seasons
Boreal Ridge, revision
Believe in Yourself
Turned On, preview
Nature of Sail
Any Boat, Any Time
The Fine Edge, plus two Fine Edge trailers
Any Snow, Any Mountain TV shorts
This Is the Place
Valley of the Snow People
The Best Kept Secret
Head Job (Head Ski Co.)
Ski High Life
White Stag
Fashion Fun in the Snow
American Ski Technique
Lake Placid
High Speed Sailing
Freshness of Skiing
Eastman Kodak at Sun Valley
Alpental
Sugarbush Valley
Salmon River
Utah, Greatest Snow on Earth
Be Continental, Ski Continental
Sun Valley, commercial
Mammoth
Land of Sky Blue Waters
Mod Magic on Skis
Mount Snow
Little Toot Xmas
Bongo Board
Schlitz Commercial
Gold Medal Sailors
Sugarbush is a Happening
The Red Boots are Coming
Ski Mammoth Mountain
Mammoth Is for Everyone
Spring into Skiing
Powder Danger
Turned On
Racing Rhythms
Raquel Welch (TV commercial)
A Day at Hollywood Park
Ski Time in the Rockies
A Way Out
Snowmass Condominium
Horse Racing Special
Clear the Tracks
Hi Speed Binding
Eagle Shoot
Hughes Test Track
Bodies in Motion, plus preview
Discover Telluride
Sugarbush, again

The Other Side of Winter
Discover Crested Butte
Sun Sport
Hi Performance Skis
Best of the Bunch
Look Binding
O'Brien Skis
Sun Valley Experience
Three Valleys of Freedom
Flaming Skier
What Is Keystone?
Vanguard – Harken Blocks
From Grapes to Glass
Mammoth Mountain Ski Lifts
Swissair, Your Ticket to the Alps
Keystone
Hexcel Skis
Hot Yachts, Cold Water
This Is the Place (TV promo)
Slide Show
Mammoth Ski Adventure
Ski and Ski Better
Alpine Meadows, TV commercial
Comin' Out Smokin', Beconta
Ski the Volcanoes
Continental Rockies Experience
Ski Like a Champion
Raichle Bloops
Copper Mountain
Winter Ride
Time in a Bottle
Fly Bonanza Airlines
Ski the Summit
Ski and Ski Better, (promo)
Ski the Summit, Ramada tag
Kawasaki Jet Ski
Winter Ride, preview
Scorpion Skis
Millennium Factor
Ski Turoa
My Hawaii
Hollywood Park
Sterling Mood piece
Jimmy Heuga - MS
Skier Look
Pyramid Comedy
Believe in Yourself, (TV show)
Six Million Skiers, plus preview
Ski Beeper
Mount Baldy
Sun Valley Summer
For Safer Skiing, plus preview
Ski the Continental Rockies, & preview
Skiing at Snowblaze
High Performance Sailing
A Feel for Snow
Your Ticket to the Alps
Let the Good Times Roll, plus preview
Stein, Stork and the Chick
Car Hiker
Free Ride
Lasers, A Boat for All Seasons
Get High on the Alps for Less
Invitation to Skiing, plus preview
Spirit of the West
Park City, TV commercial
White Stag, TV commercial
Discover Micronesia
Breath of Life
First Place
Raichle, TV commercial
Raichle, dealer tags
The Alpine Experience
Skiing LA Style, Snow Valley
Targhee
The Laser World
Spirit of the West
Colorado Colors, Bonanza Airlines
Techni-Ski
Alpine Sports Festival, Pennzoil
A Ballet of Competition
Colorado Colors, again
Sports Bloopers, l
Cameras in Motion, (second version)
Hooray for Hollywood
Save Baldy
Skiing LA Style
Mexico's Fabulous Pacific Coast

Seven Days in Paradise
Have Windsurfer, Will Travel
The Outer Reaches of Sailing
Beaver Creek, TV commercial
Winter of '83, Yamaha
Miracle on Snow
Sailing, Too, S-2 Yachts
Winter the Way It Should Be, Reno
Ski World
The Hall of Fame Regatta
Trappers Loop – Snow Basin
Jobe Water Ski
From Dawn to Dust
The Aloha Spirit
Hobie Skiff
Frontier 250
Eiki Projector demo
Vuarnet Clinic
Rock and Roll, 250
Timberline Lodge
Nissan Frontier 500, Off-Road Race
Learn to Ski Better
Sixty-Second TV vignettes
Nissan Mint 400 commercial
Up the Colorado River shoot
Frontier 500 (another one)
Road Atlanta – Nissan
Racing on the Edge
I'd Rather Be Racing
There's No Comparison, Vail
"I" Ski video
New Zealand Tourism film
Laguna Seca GT-06, GT-P Race
The Best of Comedy, Volume l
Fritzmeier Skis
Ski the Wild Mountain
Mt. Snow
Christian Brothers Wine
A Saska Freedom
Sun Valley, Summer
Snow Blaze
National Car Rental
Sailing with Warren Miller
Sports Blooper ll
Olympic Swimming Pool
KHQ TV, Half-Hour TV show
Skiing – Movement and Motion
Winter the Way It Should Be, Yamaha
Can Horses Fly?
The Frontier 500, Las Vegas
Mammoth Vacation
Sunshine Village
Lift Your Skiing to New Heights
WM video commercials
Ski Banff's Sunshine
The Hobie 33
Dolomite video
American Hawaii Cruises
Chalet Sports Center
Ski Legs
Interski '87
California Tourism
Comedy Reel, Men of Steel, Wings of Wood
Rock and Roll 250/35-MM version
Nissan Celebrity Show
California Summer Associates
Vail video
Swix video
Miller Brewing Rock Video
Steeps, Leaps and Powder
Heavenly Valley video
Quebec Tourism Film
Nissan Grudge Match, 35-MM film
Mint 400 Off-Road Race
Ski Film Festival
The Truth About Skiing
Ski Style Squaw
Sun Valley Music
Bear Valley
Sun Valley, A Place for All Seasons
Sun Valley, Winter
Three Valleys of France
Nordica

INDEX